Contemporary Sociological Theory

Titles of Related Interest from Pine Forge Press

Sociological Theory, by Bert N. Adams and R. A. Sydie

Classical Sociological Theory, by Bert N. Adams and R. A. Sydie

Sociology for a New Century, by York W. Bradshaw, Joseph F. Healey, and Rebecca Smith

Adventures in Social Research: Data Analysis Using SPSS for Windows 95/98®, by Earl Babbie, Fred Halley, and Jeanne Zaino

Taking It Big: Developing Sociological Consciousness in Postmodern Times, by Steve P. Dandaneau

Illuminating Social Life: Classical and Contemporary Theory Revisited, Second Edition, edited by Peter Kivisto

Key Ideas in Sociology, by Peter Kivisto

Multiculturalism in the United States: Current Issues, Contemporary Voices, by Peter Kivisto and Georganne Rundblad

Social Prisms: Reflections on Everyday Myths and Paradoxes, by Jodi O'Brien

The Production of Reality: Essays and Readings on Social Interaction, Third Edition, by Jodi O'Brien and Peter Kollock

The Social Worlds of Higher Education: Handbook for Teaching in a New Century, edited by Bernice Pescosolido and Ronald Aminzade

The McDonaldization of Society, New Century Edition, by George Ritzer

Worlds Apart: Social Inequalities in a New Century, by Scott Sernau

Of Crime and Criminality: The Use of Theory in Everyday Life, edited by Sally S. Simpson

Sociology for a New Century: A Pine Forge Press Series

EDITED BY CHARLES RAGIN, WENDY GRISWOLD, AND WALTER W. POWELL

An Invitation to Environmental Sociology, by Michael M. Bell

Global Inequalities, by York W. Bradshaw and Michael Wallace

Schools and Societies, by Steven Brint

Economy/Society, by Bruce Carruthers and Sarah Babb

How Societies Change, by Daniel Chirot

Ethnicity and Race: Making Identities in a Changing World, by Stephen Cornell and Doug Hartmann

The Sociology of Childhood, by William A. Corsaro

Cultures and Societies in a Changing World, by Wendy Griswold

Crime and Disrepute, by John Hagan

Gods in the Global Village: The World's Religions in Sociological Perspective, by Lester R. Kurtz

Waves of Democracy: Social Movements and Political Change, by John Markoff

Development and Social Change: A Global Perspective, Second Edition, by Philip McMichael

Aging, Social Inequality, and Public Policy, by Fred C. Pampel

Constructing Social Research, by Charles C. Ragin

Women and Men at Work, by Barbara Reskin and Irene Pakavic

Making Societies: The Historical Construction of Our World, by William G. Roy

Cities in a World Economy, Second Edition, by Saskia Sassen

Gender, Family, and Social Movements, by Suzanne Staggenborg

Law/Society: Origins, Interactions, and Change, by John R. Sutton

Contemporary Sociological Theory

Bert N. Adams

University of Wisconsin

R. A. Sydie

University of Alberta

PINE FORGE PRESS
An Imprint of Sage Publications, Inc.
Thousand Oaks, California • London • New Delhi

For information:

 Pine Forge Press
An imprint of Sage Publications, Inc.
2455 Teller Road
Thousand Oaks, California 91320
(805) 499-4224
E-mail: order@pfp.sagepub.com

Sage Publications Ltd.
6 Bonhill Street
London EC2A 4PU
United Kingdom

Sage Publications India Pvt. Ltd.
M-32 Market
Greater Kailash I
New Delhi 110 048 India

Printed in the United States of America

Library of Congress Cataloging-in-Publication Data
Adams, Bert N.
    Contemporary sociological theory / Bert N. Adams, R. A. Sydie.
      p.   cm.
  Includes index.
    ISBN 0-7619-8781-9
  1. Sociology.   I. Sydie, R. A. (Rosalind Ann), 1940–   II. Title.
    HM586 .A33 2002
    301—dc21

                                        2001007145

02   03   04   05   06   10 9 8 7 6 5 4 3 2 1

Production Management: *Scratchgravel Publishing Services*
Copy Editor: *Margaret C. Tropp*
Typesetter: *Scratchgravel Publishing Services*
Indexer: *James Minkin*
Cover Designers: *Ravi Balasuriya, Michelle Lee*

About the Authors

Bert N. Adams (Ph.D., University of North Carolina) has taught sociological theory extensively, both in East Africa and at the University of Wisconsin–Madison. He has published on consensus and coercion theories and on the importance of classical theory to a degree in sociology. He also teaches and writes on the sociology of the family. He and his co-author, R. A. Sydie, have written a paper on C. P. Gilman and Beatrice Webb, which was published in *Sociological Origins* in October 2000.

R. A. Sydie has been professor of sociology at the University of Alberta in Edmonton for the past 30 years and is the current chair of the department of sociology. Her research interests include sociological theory, art and culture, and gender studies. Professor Sydie is the author of *Natural Women, Cultured Men.* Her latest research project involves a historical examination of sociological work on love and eroticism.

About the Publisher

Pine Forge Press is an educational publisher, dedicated to publishing innovative books and software throughout the social sciences. On this and any other of our publications, we welcome your comments.

Please write to:

Pine Forge Press
An imprint of Sage Publications, Inc.
2455 Teller Road
Thousand Oaks, CA 91320-2218
(805) 499-0871
E-mail: info.pineforge@sagepub.com

Visit our World Wide Web site, your direct link to a multitude of online resources:

www.pineforge.com

To Diane and Campbell

Brief Contents

———•———

Detailed Contents

Preface

———•———

There are many sociological theory texts currently available. So why produce another? What makes this text unique? How will the student reader benefit from it?

Rediscovery

Robert K. Merton once referred to the importance of giving "credit where credit was due" (1967:26). Sociological theory has not done that. By 1950, male scholarship had either ignored or marginalized women theorists and many others, excluding them from the history of social thought. However, in recent decades, increasing numbers of theorists and theory instructors have recognized that the "dead white male" approach to the history of social thought is at least incomplete, if not insidious.

We consider Harriet Martineau in the mid-1800s to be one of the founders of sociology.[1] Throughout this book, which covers sociological theory since the 1930s, the views of women theorists and others are represented in far more than token fashion. Thus, rediscovery means hearing the voices of important women theorists such as Raya Dunayevskaya, Theda Skocpol, Arlie Hochschild, and Patricia Hill Collins. It also means becoming acquainted with Niklas Luhmann, contemporary Marxist Erik Olin Wright, evolutionist Elman Service, and Immanuel Wallerstein.

This text, then, pays attention to the questions asked and the answers given by more than the "usual suspects." Such rediscovery is intellectually exciting and challenging.

Organization

With the wealth of information covered, our aim is for readers always to be aware, chronologically and intellectually, of where they have been, where they are headed, and how the different parts of their reading "journey" relate to one another. To accomplish this goal, we have organized the book as follows.

Schools of Thought   A key organizing principle of this text is to trace the following major schools of thought as they appear and reappear from chapter to chapter:

---

[1]It is worth noting that we have also published a text, *Classical Sociological Theory* (Pine Forge Press, 2002), that focuses on the period from 1850 to 1930. For a single-volume version that covers the entire history of sociological theory, see our book *Sociological Theory* (Pine Forge Press, 2001).

1. *Functionalism*, from Parsons and Merton to Luhmann.

2. *Evolutionism*, with Elman Service.

Together these two sociological theories have generally been supportive of the capitalism and the status quo.

3. The anticapitalist *revolutionary and conflict perspective* began in the work of Karl Marx and Friedrich Engels in the nineteenth century. We trace it through the third- and fourth-generation radicals, including Antonio Gramsci, Raya Dunayevskaya, Nicos Poulantzas, and Erik Olin Wright.

4. A closely allied brand of theorizing is *critical of capitalism* but is less optimistic about curing its ills. This begins with the pre–World War II Frankfurt School, and continues with Immanuel Wallerstein and Michel Foucault.

5. The first two sections of the book (Chapters 1 through 6) are organized around functionalism, radicalism, and critical theory, with some variations, such as Anthony Giddens's structuration. The remainder of the volume covers a wide variety of challenges to the functionalism that dominated the mid-twentieth century.

6. An important theoretical perspective in this book concerns gender or *feminism*. In this book we introduce the works of Dorothy E. Smith and Patricia Hill Collins, among others.

7. The *micro*-perspectives on society theorize about the self and interaction. They include Herbert Blumer, Erving Goffman, and Arlie Hochschild.

8. Rational and exchange theories are found in the work of James Coleman and others.

While these are among the major theoretical schools introduced, other branches of the sociological "tree" also appear from time to time.

Consistent Organization Within Chapters   Readers new to sociological theory often face the "forest and trees" problem—that is, they become immersed in the details of one theory after another and are unable to compare or relate them. This problem becomes particularly difficult in texts that do not provide consistent means for making connections. We address this problem by following a consistent organizational scheme within the chapters. After covering the setting and background of a particular theorist or school of thought, each chapter follows a pattern of presentation that includes:

Central Theories and Methods

Nature of Society, Humans, and Change

Class, Gender, and Race

Other Theories and Theorists

Critique and Conclusions

Final Thoughts

The section titled "Nature of Society, Humans, and Change" examines a theorist's fundamental assumptions underpinning his or her theoretical views, often leading to a consideration of the theorist's ideology—what that individual thought was good or bad, right or wrong, better or worse about society and human nature. Each chapter includes a "Class, Gender, and Race" section, with one or more of these topics sometimes being the primary focus of a particular thinker. For example, Wright focuses on class, Smith on gender, and Collins on race and gender. We devote a section of each chapter to these topics—despite the fact that not every theorist treats them thoroughly—because the broad theme of *inequality* is an important one in this textbook.

An important section of each chapter is "Other Theories and Theorists." This section presents theoretical issues less central to the writer, but nevertheless noteworthy. For example, in the "Other Theories" section of Chapter 2, we introduce Merton's "self-fulfilling prophecy." In this section we also connect the theorist under consideration to others who are directly referred to in the theorist's work but who have not yet been discussed in that chapter. The "Critique and Conclusions" section summarizes the ideas of the theorist or theorists considered in that chapter and presents criticisms of each theorist from critics of their own day as well as critics of today. Each chapter closes with "Final Thoughts," sometimes poignant, sometimes ironic, and sometimes offering a broader view.

Important Themes in Sociological Theory That Cut Across Chapters
We also seek to help students recognize connections across social theories by noting additional key *themes* beyond those included in the chapter headings, themes that recur as theoretical topics. These consistent themes include the following:

The characteristics of modern societies

Attitudes toward capitalism

Power and inequality in society

Relationship of the individual to society

As these themes appear and reappear throughout the chapters, the terms are *italicized* so students can more easily make connections across chapters.

Additional Learning and Teaching Features

In addition to the content, organization, and thematic innovations of this book, several other learning and teaching features are worth noting. First, a *timeline* in a three-panel foldout in the back of the book places all the theorists clearly into their historical periods. This timeline includes theorists who preceded 1930 but who were important in the history of social thought. The theorist's life span, and the chapter in which she or he appears in this book, are superimposed on important world events occurring during that time. The birth and death dates of each theorist help readers relate the theorists to one another. Students can also see and remember which theorists are alive in the year 2001.

Each of the three sections of the book begins with a *section introduction* that ties the individual chapters to each other in groupings, usually focusing on a school of thought and helping the student look both backward and forward.

Key terms are **boldfaced** in the text when they are first defined and discussed, and they are also boldfaced in the index.

The *References* at the end of each chapter include both the original publication date and the republication date, if any, of the edition referred to or quoted in this volume.

An *Index* at the end of the volume makes it possible to look up topics as well as important individuals.

Brevity

A central goal of this text is to be as concise as possible while also doing justice to a wide variety of theorists. Instead of covering four to twelve theorists, we give substantial treatment to more than twenty thinkers. Our intention has been to cast the net widely enough to capture diversity both within and between theoretical viewpoints or schools of thought. Thus, given the range of ideas, historical contexts, and theorists covered, we believe this book is both brief and thorough.

Limitations of This Book

As we have just said, this text covers a large number of theories and theorists as cogently as possible. There are, however, two limitations. First, we have not introduced the important non-Western views of society. Confucius produced a philosophical and theoretical basis for understanding Chinese society. Ibn Khaldun, in the fourteenth century, explained society from a North African perspective. More recently, Kwame Gyekye (1987, 1997), a Ghanaian thinker, has written about the nature of society as viewed from within his culture. A compendium of world sociological ideas needs to be attempted, but this volume is not it. We believe it is enough to rediscover, among others, the women theorists, and to bring them into the corpus of Western sociological theory.

A second limitation is that, despite covering more than twenty major thinkers, we may have included a theorist considered by one instructor to be superfluous and left out another's favorite classical or contemporary thinker. One might question why we have included Service on evolutionary thought, Wright on contemporary Marxism, or Hochschild on symbolic interactionism. The justification for each of them is that each does an outstanding job of bringing together and contributing to the issues in his or her theoretical specialty. After expending considerable effort sorting through contemporary theorists, we decided that the ones included are the best for both creative and summary purposes. No one knows, of course, whether Luhmann, Poulantzas, or Coleman will be considered an important theorist twenty-five years from now.

If we have omitted one of your favorite theorists, you can introduce that particular thinker through supplementary materials. We optimistically think this will be necessary in only a very limited number of cases.

We hope you and your students will find the pages that follow to be as worthwhile and exciting to read as we have found them to write during these past five years. We welcome your criticisms and suggestions as well as those of your students. Please write to us in care of Pine Forge Press, or e-mail us at adams@ssc.wisc.edu.

Bert N. Adams
R. A. Sydie

References

Gyekye, Kwame. 1987. *An Essay on African Philosophical Thought: The Akan Conceptual Scheme.* Cambridge: Cambridge University Press.

———. 1997. *Tradition and Modernity: Philosophical Reflections on the African Experience.* New York: Oxford University Press.

Merton, Robert K. 1967/1996. *On Social Structure and Science* (Peter Sztompka, Ed.). Chicago: University of Chicago Press.

Acknowledgments

This book has required the efforts and dedication of many people. First and foremost was Steve Rutter, former publisher of Pine Forge Press. His enthusiasm, encouragement, and insights kept us going throughout the project. Rebecca Smith's knowledge of students and of editorial style helped make the entire manuscript more "reader friendly." Anne Draus at Scratchgravel Publishing Services competently oversaw the process of copy editing and typesetting.

At the Pine Forge office, Sherith Pankratz encouraged us at the early stages, and Ann Makarias kept track of details and deadlines in the later stages. Jillaine Tyson designed and rendered the original timeline. University of Wisconsin–Madison colleague Mary Campbell reviewed the literature and references included in some chapters. Janet Donlin and Sandy Ramer of U.W.–Madison computerized portions of the work and worked on permissions.

We are grateful to the publishers who gave us permission to use lengthy quotes from their materials. We also thank the reviewers who read and criticized portions of the book at the early stages:

Joan Alway, University of Miami
Kevin Anderson, Northern Illinois University
James J. Chriss, Kansas Newman College
Harry Dahms, Florida State University
Anne F. Eisenberg, State University of New York, Geneseo
Kate Hausbeck, University of Nevada, Las Vegas
Peter Kivisto, Augustana College
Steven Lybrand, College of St. Thomas
Neil McLaughlin, McMaster University
Chris Prendergast, Illinois Wesleyan University
Robert E. L. Roberts, California State University, San Marcos
Kathleen Slobin, North Dakota State University
Dana Vannoy, formerly of the University of Cincinnati

These reviewers were absolutely essential to the final product, although, of course, they are not responsible for any lingering errors or misinterpretations.

Finally, the authors' spouses, Diane Adams and Campbell Sydie, have both encouraged and tolerated this multiyear endeavor. Without their good humor, patience, and suggestions, this project might never have seen the light of day.

A Note to Students

—●—

You as Theorist

Are you already a social theorist? Think about the following questions: Do some people have the cards stacked in their favor, while others have them stacked against, or do we all get pretty much what we deserve? Do you act the same way at a basketball game, in a bar, in a grocery store, and at a religious service, or do you behave differently as you move from place to place? Why are people in one country always fighting, while in another they seem so peaceful? Are they peaceful because they like one another or because some keep others under control?

Are men and women actually pretty much the same, except for their roles in childbearing? As Steve says, "Well, you know how women are." As Maureen jokes, "Why is it men won't ever ask for directions?" Just what is it that women, or men, really want? And why? Why do politicians change their message "at the drop of a hat" to suit their audience? Do they really believe in anything? "The more things change, the more they stay the same"—how could that be, and what does it mean?

"What is good for General Motors (or Toyota) is good for the country"—is that true? Why does the head of General Motors make a seven-figure salary, a doctor six figures, a schoolteacher five, and a day care provider four? Does the salary correspond to how hard they work, or how long they went to school, or how smart they are? Is the world actually run by money? If so, what does it mean to "run the world"?

Whenever you make any of these comments, or ask or answer any of these questions, you are a social theorist. You theorize whenever you try to make sense of, understand, or explain your social world. This book introduces you to insightful and interesting answers that have been proposed over the years to these and other such questions. It does not tell you what to think, but helps you clarify your own thoughts, relating your various views of society to one another and to the views of others.

How can the study of sociological theory help you understand your world? An example, addressed in this text, may help answer that question. In our society many believe that success or failure is basically an individual matter, that no one should be allowed to stand in the way of your success, and that wealth is the best measure of success. However, not all societies have these as central values. In fact, in some societies the individual is expected to subordinate herself or himself to the good of the family or community. Such societies de-emphasize the unique personality and may also limit worldly gain. Theorists have explained how such societies got that way and why such societies make sense to those who live in them. The study of different sorts of societies is not intended to make an individual less committed to his or her own society and its values, but such a study may at least broaden the individual's perspective on, and comprehension of, the varieties of workable human societies.

How This Book Is Organized

Answers to the kinds of questions raised at the beginning of this Note to Students tend to be joined together into *schools of thought*. For example, those who believe people get what they deserve are apt also to believe that society exists because people like one another and like their society's rules. Such clusters or schools of thought are presented in most of the groupings of chapters in sections of this text. For example, you will find in Chapters 2 and 3 the thoughts of consensual theorists who believe that the various parts of society work together for the good of the whole and satisfy those living within it. Likewise, Chapters 4 and 5 examine the critical and coercive theories of those who believe capitalist society has many negative characteristics, is oppressive, and is run by a small number of individuals who keep the others under control. Most chapters focus on one or more individuals who represent these or other schools of thought.

Internally, chapters are organized consistently according to the following topics:

1. Central Theories and Methods
2. Nature of Humans, Society, and Change
3. Class, Gender, and Race
4. Other Theories and Theorists
5. Critique and Conclusions
6. Final Thoughts

The consistency of chapter organization makes it easier to compare, contrast, and relate the issues raised by one theorist with those raised by another. Another way we have tried to ease your way through this book is the introduction of *themes* that run through the volume. Some of the headings listed above, such as change, class, gender, and race, are also themes. Other important themes include how individual theorists have thought about the characteristics of modern society, what their attitudes are concerning capitalism, their views on power and inequality in society, and how they see individuals and society affecting each other.

You have glimpsed the great variety of issues—some of which you already have an opinion about and some of which you may never have thought about before. Putting your views of society into this larger context is an adventure in learning and understanding. So let us begin the journey together.

Chapter 1

Introduction to Contemporary Sociological Theory

Sociological theory—the attempt to explain society scientifically—began in the nineteenth century. The foundations of sociology were laid by the middle of that century, and many of the concerns and explanations of the classical theorists still inform sociological theory today.

Although our beginning point for contemporary theory, 1930, is somewhat arbitrary, perhaps the best way to look at it is to say that there have been five or more generations of sociologists, the last three generations beginning about 1930 with the functionalists Talcott Parsons and Robert Merton (see Chapter 2). Thus, our book on contemporary sociological theory concerns the writings of those whose contributions appeared from 1930 on. But first, let us take a brief look back into the changes of the past 150 years.

We live in the era of cable television, e-mail, and the Internet. It is difficult to project ourselves back two generations, much less to the period prior to 1930. If you ask your parents and grandparents, you will find that in 1950 "high-tech" families often listened to the radio in the evening, and some went to the movies. Television was available to only a few people, and personal computers did not exist. Fifty years before that, at the turn of the century, there were no airplanes or cars, no factory assembly lines, no automation (machines running machines), and no movies. In 1900, communication was not only not instantaneous, it was slow. What is now called "snail mail" was all there was, and it was considered fast. There had been no so-called "world wars." Society, then, was very different. So, what important events occurred before 1930, and what theories had been produced to explain them?

Nineteenth-Century Sociological Theory

Two aspects of nineteenth-century history that greatly influenced Western theories about society were numerous technological changes and imperialism. If you look at the timeline at the back of this book, you will find a series of

..important political events that influenced the theories of society propounded at that time. For example, in the 1800s several Latin American countries became politically independent, although they were still dominated economically by the United States and to a lesser extent by Great Britain. In 1885 the European countries agreed on how to divide Africa into colonies. India was struggling under British rule, being the single most important colonial possession in the British Empire.

The second set of important events pertains to technology. As the Timeline shows, developments in the 1800s included the railroad, steamship and steam engine, steel converter, telephone, and telegraph. The Suez Canal was completed in 1869, giving Britain and France easier access to the Far East. In addition, numerous breakthroughs in medicine were altering health and life expectancy. Not surprisingly, these technological and political realities greatly affected the theories of European and U.S. sociologists.

Dominant Theories and Ideologies

The dominant nineteenth-century theories were those of Auguste Comte, Herbert Spencer, Emile Durkheim, Max Weber, and Georg Simmel. In large part, they arose in response to the events noted above, which followed the American, French, and industrial revolutions.

The dominant theories of the time included *positivism*, with its belief in the scientific study of society for its own sake and its commitment to objectivity. These sociologists, especially Durkheim, argued that social facts are not reducible to either biology or psychology.

Another nineteenth-century theory was *functionalism*, which equated societies with organisms, with a division of labor determined by the functions performed by the organism's (society's) parts. In addition, the division of society into institutional subsystems (such as health care, education, and religion) provided the explanation for why individuals were becoming, as is still said today, "more and more expert in less and less." These nineteenth-century theories suggested that such differentiation continues to evolve.

Another societal factor shaping nineteenth-century theory was the expansion and legitimation of "rational-legal" or *bureaucratic* authority, resulting in the increasing strength of nation-states and corporations. These developments were seen as positive, or indicative of progress. Finally, some theorists focused on analyzing social *interaction* in various kinds of groups.

Although many other theoretical issues were raised, these were the dominant ones. They were mainly reactions to the rise of capitalism and the increasing industrialization of the Western world.

These theories were intermingled with ideological elements, or the values common to the time and place. For the most part, the theorists offering these explanations were optimistic about and supportive of industrial capitalism. Increased productivity had resulted in economic progress, at least in the Western world. The division of labor, especially the development of bureaucracy, made for greater efficiency in accomplishing many tasks of life. The evolutionary maxim "survival of the fittest" was considered good, even though it meant the nonsurvival of the less fit. As we noted, understanding for its own sake was seen as a sufficient goal. Even when improvements were needed, these nineteenth-century theorists believed the improvements could be made incrementally through established, legislative means. In short, industrial capitalist competition was considered a good thing, leading to a better world. The enthusiasm for this dominant ideology, especially in the United States, went hand-in-hand with the Western theories described above as explaining Western political and technological developments.

Radical Theory and Ideology

Not all nineteenth-century theorists saw the growth of industrial capitalism as positive, however. Some, such as Karl Marx, viewed capitalism from the standpoint of the industrial workers. His theoretical arguments included the exploitative, oppressive nature of capitalism; the meaninglessness of work in the industrial factory system; the importance of economic classes in world history; the expansion of capitalism into worldwide imperialism; and the expected eventual revolution of the world's working classes against the capitalist owners of the means of production. Instead of the outcome being a functioning organism, Marx theorized that the division of labor results in widespread alienation from meaningless work.

Ideologically, the first- and second-generation radical anticapitalists (or Marxists) argued that explanation (theory) and understanding must have change and emancipation as their goal. They, too, were optimists, convinced that the revolutionary overthrow of capitalism was not only needed, but inevitable. Thus, at the turn of the twentieth century much sociological theory was optimistic about the future. However, the two competing theories saw capitalism either positively or negatively and focused upon social analysis versus change.

Early-Twentieth-Century Sociological Theory

In the first thirty years of the twentieth century, a series of disruptions to the status quo—the First World War, the Russian Revolution, and worldwide economic uncertainties and fluctuations—called for new explanations of how society operates. These events were accompanied by dramatic changes in and additions to sociological theorizing.

Gender and Race

Prior to the twentieth century, the status quo included both gender and racial inequality. The dominant perspectives on gender included patriarchy and the belief that women are innately nonrational and inferior. Those on race were used to justify colonialism and slavery. But by the turn of the century, social scientists such as C. P. Gilman, Marianne Weber, and W. E. B. Du Bois were questioning the theories behind these inequities. They argued that behavior had preceded ideology. In other words, oppression needed a justification, and it came to be expressed _r the ideology of the inferiority of women and the nonwhite races, or the superiority of males and the white race. Gilman, Weber, and Du Bois theorized about the equal abilities and unique contributions of women and blacks and then argued for their equal treatment.

Criticism and Social Change

Optimism about evolutionary progress was severely shaken by World War I. Critical theorists, including the Frankfurt School (see Chapter 4) and Thorstein Veblen in the United States, questioned the nature of capitalism. They observed that economic domination had led to many abuses, both of individuals and of categories or groups of individuals. Wars were seen as useful only to capitalists while costing common people their lives. Capitalism was seen to further individualistic competition, or selfishness. This competition did *not* benefit society as a whole; it benefited only the favored few.

During the same period, Vilfredo Pareto and others argued that both capitalist and radical optimism were misguided. By the "iron law of oligarchy," Robert Michels stated, there will always be a ruling class, and capitalism's ills will not lead to its overthrow. The "final revolution" leading to equal sharing in the means of production is not only not inevitable, it is impossible.

Between them, critical theorists and ruling class theorists produced a theoretical position that denounced capitalism but saw little chance of dramatic change for the better.

Ideology, Society, and Human Nature

As you will have noted by now, theory (explanation) and ideology (justification) are intertwined. Those who theorize that capitalist society is a self-corrective organism that meets people's needs are usually status quo conservatives, or supportive of the capitalist system. Even the positivists, who claim that their goal is simply understanding, are likely to be covert conservatives, because they are willing to accept "what is" in the process of studying it.

In contrast, those who explain society as a system of exploitation and oppression are ideological radicals. They view capitalist society as evil and its revolutionary overthrow as desirable.

Ideology appears in classical explanations of human nature as well. Some see human beings as good but corrupted by society, whereas others view humans as selfish and aggressive, requiring control by civilization. Many of the contemporary theorists in this book, however, believe that humans are eminently malleable, adaptable to what the environment contains, what society expects, and what technology provides.

The Self

An important theoretical issue that emerged in the early twentieth century concerned how the self develops in society. Sigmund Freud emphasized the individual's biological drives and society's attempts to control them. C. H. Cooley and G. H. Mead focused on the influence of other people and on the importance of symbols shared by the individuals in any given society. All of these theorists made it clear that the individual who adjusts to one culture may, with the same character and personality, be maladjusted in a different culture.

Sociological Theory by the 1930s

By the 1930s, the dominant historical figures in U.S. sociology were Emile Durkheim and Max Weber, with Auguste Comte considered to be the discipline's "father." As a result, functionalism and positivism were dominant—and they became increasingly so in the mid-twentieth century. The ideas of turn-of-the-century feminists, such as C. P. Gilman, had been obliterated by the 1930s.

In Europe, however, where world war and the Russian revolution had taken place, evolutionary optimism was no longer dominant by the 1930s. Functionalism was not dead, but critical and radical Marxism had many proponents—and critical theory was to become even more important by mid-century.

You have very likely recognized that many of the classical theorists' themes, issues, and questions are still current today. And in fact you will read about contemporary functionalists in Chapter 2, which introduces Talcott Parsons and Robert Merton. You will read about contemporary critical theory in Chapter 4, including the Frankfort School and Jurgen Habermas. The contemporary Marxists discussed in Chapter 5 include several French theorists and Erik Olin Wright.

However, although the dominant theoretical perspectives of classical sociology—functionalist, critical, and radical perspectives—can still be found, sociological theory today is extremely varied. The growth of feminist theory, symbolic interactionism, rational and exchange theories, world system theory, and others is a reaction to the complexity of the world in which we find ourselves in the twenty-first century. Keep that complexity in mind as we begin our journey into contemporary theories of society.

Twentieth-Century Functionalism and Beyond

An important approach to sociological theory has been to examine the issues of order and integration in society, and to seek answers to questions such as What does it do? What needs does it meet? How does it work? In the nineteenth century this was found in the theories of Herbert Spencer and Emile Durkheim.

Chapter 2 picks up the themes of societal integration and functional analysis as they were expanded upon by Talcott Parsons and Robert K. Merton in the middle third of the twentieth century. Parsons developed various schemes—the pattern variables, AGIL—to organize his thinking on social action and on the social system. Later he turned his attention to modernization (also see Chapter 6), agreeing with those writers who were convinced that the whole world would eventually accept Western culture.

Merton was a student of Parsons, but attempted to avoid the straitjacket of order and function by introducing ideas such as latent function and dysfunction. Still alive and writing at the turn of the twenty-first century, Merton has dealt primarily with middle-range or lower-level theories, instead of the grand-scale, society-wide theories of the Parsonsian kind. Parsons and Merton dominated sociological theory at mid-century, and thus provide the baseline for this volume on contemporary sociological theory.

In Chapter 3 you will meet two theorists who may very well be the most prolific writers since Herbert Spencer. Niklas Luhmann's work on social systems outgrew his discipleship to Parsons, and he wrote at length about trust, power, risk, and reflexivity as well. Anthony Giddens, whose "structuration" theory has parallels to structure-functionalism, also wrote on the topics just listed, as well as modernization and others. Luhmann died only recently, and Giddens is still active. Both made their theoretical contributions in the last third of the twentieth century.

Chapter 2

Twentieth-Century Functionalism
Parsons and Merton

Andra Lyons can't explain how she raised four children alone on a $5-an-hour job pumping gas. She only knows it's been a numbing struggle. . . . Her hardships are familiar to neighbors on the St. Regis Mohawk reservation, where roughly half the 13,000 residents lack full-time jobs and per capita income is $14,000, two-thirds of the national average.

But with today's opening of the $30 million Akwesasne Mohawk Casino, Lyons believes the Mohawks' luck is turning.

"We've needed something like this for a long time," says Lyons, who trained for weeks to become a card dealer at the casino.

But the Mohawks do expect gambling to have the same . . . impact it did for the Oneidas, who have pulled themselves out of poverty and used their new wealth to start other businesses, buy back ancestral lands and build homes. . . . Some opposition to gambling remains on the reservation.

Still, no one expects another outbreak of the violence that roiled St. Regis almost a decade ago, when two men were killed.

Almost a dozen casinos operated illegally then, . . . run for the profit of their owners, not the tribe. (Kates, 1999)

What does it do? What and whose needs does it meet? What is its purpose? How does it work? What function does it perform? These are the questions raised by functional analysis. It is important to note that the previous quotation makes no moral judgment regarding gambling. It speaks only to the issue of what function it performs, what needs it meets and will meet, and for whom. Perhaps the legal casino will meet an economic need for the tribe, while the illegal ones were beneficial (functional) for a few owners.

The larger issue within which such questions arise concerns the integration of society by means of consensus, or agreement on how its needs will be met. Order, integration, structure, and function are issues that first arose in the work of Herbert Spencer and Emile Durkheim in the nineteenth century. Now you

...n full grown in Talcott Parsons and Robert K. Merton, central figures in ...s. sociology and sociological theory during the middle third of the twentieth century.

Talcott Parsons (1902–1979)

Charles Camic (1991) has done a great service by bringing to light the early years of Parsons's productive life, from 1923 until the publication of *The Structure of Social Action* in 1937.[1] Talcott was the youngest of five children. His father was a "social gospel" Protestant and a professor at Colorado College; his mother was a progressive and a suffragist (Camic, 1991:x). Wrongly dismissed by the college, his father took the family to New York City, where he worked for the YMCA for a year, and then became President of Marietta College in Ohio.

In New York, Parsons spent his last two years of high school at the Horace Mann School for Boys, "which was affiliated with Columbia Teachers College and renowned at the time for making available 'the very best American education had to offer to high-ability children who planned academic and professional careers'" (Camic, 1991:xi, quoting Cremin, Shannon, and Townsend,1954:104). From Horace Mann he went to Amherst College, which at the time was undergoing a transformation that would turn it into one of the leading liberal arts and intellectual environments in the United States. Parsons at the time was sympathetic with the Russian Revolution and the British Labor Party, but above all he was thinking broadly about politics and society (Camic, 1991:xiv).

When Parsons entered college, he was leaning toward the natural sciences, with secondary interests in philosophy and the social sciences. In his junior year, a course on institutional economics completed his conversion from biology to social science. When he graduated from Amherst in 1924, Parsons spoke at commencement on social and economic reform in the United States.

He spent the next year at the London School of Economics (LSE), where he became familiar with what he called the "antecedents of modern industrial society" (Parsons, 1962:888). While there, he also learned of and appreciated the British social anthropologist Bronislaw Malinowski's view of societies as systems of interconnected parts. More influential, however, was his acquaintance with the sociology of L. T. Hobhouse, whose viewpoint incorporated social philosophy and the various institutional specialties (religion, economics, politics) into a large field called sociology. To Parsons, this meant that sociology should include the institutional economics he had learned at Amherst.

Though his family might have preferred him to come home after his year at LSE, he proceeded to Heidelberg, Germany, to work on his PhD, and while there spent a summer studying in Vienna. His time in Germany brought to Parsons's attention the work of Max Weber, especially *The Protestant Ethic and the Spirit of Capitalism*. He also became acquainted with Weber's wife Marianne, an important scholar in her own right, and several young German thinkers. While

---

[1]For the complete treatment of Parsons's early work, see Camic, 1991:ix–lxix.

working on his dissertation, he went back to Amherst as an instructor, and in the summer of 1927 he returned to Heidelberg to receive his degree.

In the fall of 1927, Parsons was appointed as a nonfaculty instructor in the Economics Department at Harvard, the center of orthodox social scientific thought in the United States at the time (Camic, 1991:xxiii). For the next ten years, his project was threefold.

First, in debt to Weber, he wrote essays on capitalism and its origins. Suggesting that some social scientists had gone too far toward a progressive, genetic interpretation of society and Marx had gone too far toward a purely economic theory, Parsons showed a clear preference for Weber's unwillingness to simplify in either of these directions. A subagenda was to introduce historically based German social science to the individualistic, rationalistic, pragmatic outlook of U.S. sociologists such as G. H. Mead. Before 1930 it was already clear that Parsons believed a higher synthesis would emerge, incorporating both German and Anglo-American contributions (Camic, 1991:xxvi). Although the synthesis was not yet available, Parsons himself expected to be the one to provide it.

A second theme of Parsons's early work was a theory of action. This was not to be the individualistic/rationalistic outlook of many of his colleagues, but was to involve recognition of religious motives, of social regulation and norms, of goals and choices, and of society as a system of interrelated elements. During the early 1930s he was still struggling to bring together a synthesis of such elements.

His third early theme Camic called "The Fundaments of Analytic Sociology" (1991:liv). Parsons described these fundaments in a 1933 letter. Though no element is more fundamental than any other, "action" and "value" are essential. Next, the various aspects of society are inseparably tied together in a single, indivisible whole. Third, in the attempt to be analytically objective, one must not ignore the problem of the "subjective" (recalling Weber). These complexities—action, value, unity, objective, and subjective—were essential parts of Parsons's developing thought from the mid-1930s on (Camic, 1991:lv).

An important aspect of Parsons's background concerns his early experiences at Harvard. Though privileged to study with Joseph Schumpeter and other esteemed Harvard economists, it is noteworthy that Parsons himself spent the nine years from 1927 to 1936 "lower in rank than an untenured assistant professor" (Camic, 1991:xl). Not on the tenure track in economics, Parsons was recommended to the budding Sociology Department because of his obvious sociological interests. The result was a three-year position as a faculty instructor in sociology. However, two great barriers lay ahead. The first was a lack of enthusiasm on the part of the Sociology Department Chair, Pitirim Sorokin, himself a renowned theorist, who was not impressed by Parsons's kind of synthesis. The second resulted from the retirement of Harvard's president, and his succession by a distinguished chemist. The new president decided that appointments at the lower levels had become mediocre, and he determined to make retention and tenure more difficult to obtain. Parsons continued for six years as an instructor, with no change in rank. Having seen his father dropped from Colorado College and President Meiklejohn fired by Amherst, his anxiety and his bitterness were understandable.

Late in 1935, Parsons's materials were finally circulated to the tenured sociology faculty. These materials included his early essays and writings and most of

ͅꞇers of the book that made his early reputation, *The Structure of Social Ac-
ͅꞇ* (1937). Again Sorokin's reaction was mixed, but with the support of other
professors, Parsons finally received an advance to Assistant Professor in 1936,
though still without tenure. When Parsons received an attractive offer from another university, he was retained by Harvard with a promise of tenure in two
more years (Camic, 1991:xliv). As you can see, success did not come easily or
quickly for Talcott Parsons. But his ability and confidence kept him working and
pursuing his goals.

Parsons's Central Theories and Methods

Parsons was a "grand-scale" theorist, somewhat in the mold of Herbert Spencer.
Like Spencer, he was more than a functionalist; not all of his theoretical insights
fit comfortably within that framework. He was extremely prolific, and was a
master at collaborating with other notable scholars of his time. We will begin
with a few comments on his style.

First, as William Mitchell has commented, there is no hint of "wit, satire, or
other literary devices in the writings of Parsons. He who would like to be enter-
tained, amused, inspired, moved, or given flashing insights is well advised not to
consult Parsons" (1967:17). No anger (à la Karl Marx), passion (à la W.E.B. Du
Bois), or iconoclasm (à la Thorstein Veblen) is found in Parsons.

Second, he was a notoriously poor writer. His defense, of course, would be
that the complexity of the social world demands complex language. However,
when the needed complexity is coupled with a Germanic sentence structure, it
makes for hard going. At the end of an edited volume devoted to Parsons's
ideas, in which the murkiness of his writing was often noted, he was given the
opportunity to defend himself. His response was itself one of his most obscure
writings. Is the complexity necessary? Is his work worth the effort? Those questions will be held until the end of our discussion.

Third, after his first book, Parsons footnoted sparingly, referring mainly to
his own writings or those of his students (Mitchell, 1967:17).[2] In this he was
reminiscent of Vilfredo Pareto, though perhaps not as extreme.

At a 1961 symposium on Parsons's theories, one sociologist expressed his
fear at trying to summarize a theory still being written and revised. "Like
Birnam Wood, . . . it moves: Parsonian theory in the late 1950s differs in some
important respects from that of a decade ago" (Devereaux, 1961:2). Another
comment put a more positive spin on Parsons's changing ideas: "The zest with
which he responds to the stimulation of others' ideas and the rapidity with
which the salient features of these are incorporated into the snow-balling of his
work reveal the scientist's quest for knowledge no matter where it may lead"
(Loomis and Loomis, 1961:365). Although his ideas did change over the span of
his productive life, his goal was to cover, as completely and generally as possible, the major dimensions of social life and society.

---

[2]There are exceptions to Parsons's tendency not to footnote. For example, his 13-page
paper on "The Present Status of Structural-Functional Theory in Sociology" (1975)
concluded with three pages of footnotes.

Parsons's primary concern throughout his life was the problem of order in society. Many critics have claimed that this focus caused Parsons to virtually ignore conflict and change. Yet it is also possible to argue that since the conditions or variables affecting order were his concern, he must have at least recognized the possibility of disorder.[3] "The problem of 'order,' so fundamental for Parsons, could not even be a problem if it were not contingent on conflict," or disorder (Mitchell, 1967:37).

Some themes, such as social action and systems, run through virtually all of Parsons's writings, from the early essays until his death. Although his theoretical position changed, as already noted, the central issues that interested him were continuous for more than four decades.

Social Action   Parsons's view of social action changed or expanded during his scholarly life. Don Martindale (1960) perhaps overstated the change as one from "Social Behaviorism" to "Macrofunctionalism," but there is no question that at about the time of World War II, Parsons expanded his action framework. Let us look first at his action framework in *The Structure of Social Action* (1937) and other prewar writings.

Social action, wrote Parsons, is (1) voluntaristic, or a matter of making choices; (2) subjective, or based on internal orientations and responses; and (3) at least partially governed or limited by the norms and values of one's culture (1937:43–51). These three factors explain not only rational social action, but much irrational as well.

In developing his voluntaristic or choice-based theory, Parsons rejected, but to some extent incorporated, the insights of positivists, of classic economists, and of cultural idealists. Devereaux (1961) has explained clearly what Parsons was trying to accomplish. Positivism was unacceptable because it did not allow enough freedom of choice. Classic economics models were elegant, but did not fit the real social world. Idealism placed too much emphasis on the spirit, or ethos, and relativity of cultures, making comparison virtually impossible. In Parsons's pre–World War II work, then, social action involved an actor, with goals, choosing between alternatives, and influenced by norms and values.

The beginning of the expansion of Parsons's social action theory can be seen in a 1945 essay, in which he stated that "the structure of social systems cannot be derived directly from the actor-situation frame of reference. It requires functional analysis of the complications introduced by the interaction of a plurality of actors" (Parsons, 1945:229). Thus, social action takes place not only between actors but also within a social system.

Had Parsons changed his mind and abandoned individual actors, or simply expanded his attention to include the context within which social action occurred? Apparently it was the latter, because in 1951 he stated that action is "behavior oriented to the attainment of ends in situations, by means of the normatively regulated expenditure of energy" (Parsons and Shils, 1951:53). Modes

---

[3]Parsons has been accused of not only paying attention primarily to order, but valuing order to the exclusion of the sorts of conflict or struggle that Marx and Du Bois saw as absolutely necessary. We will say more about this in the "Critique" section.

.ion or motivation for individual actions include the cognitive, cathec-
.u evaluative (Parsons and Shils, 1951). These terms are close to the every-
.y meanings of thinking, feeling, and valuing or willing.

Parsons believed that his expanded theory of action was broad enough to include consensual and conflictive, rational and irrational action. But it would be
unwise to separate his expanded action theory from the contextual aspects
found in his systems theory.

Systems Theory   A **system**, in Parsons's theory, is a complex unit of some
kind, with boundaries, within which the parts are connected, and within which
something takes place. Parsons distinguished three systems: the cultural, the
personality, and the social (Parsons and Shils, 1951). The cultural system includes the values and norms that influence the individual's choices. The personality system involves individuals' motivations and need-dispositions that govern, along with the norms, the choices they make. The social system is based on
the interrelations between actors. These three systems are not reducible to each
other; thus, the social system is not merely an aggregate of individual personalities, nor is it determined merely by the cultural norms that govern it. It is worth
noting that of the three systems, the only one that received book-length treatment by Parsons was the social system (1951)—a reminder that society was
Parsons's primary focus of attention. Within the social system, Parsons looked at
roles, equilibrium, and pattern variables.

1. The simplest unit of a social system is a **role**. The nature of social roles is
seen most clearly in Parsons's analysis of the simplest social system—the relationship between two actors, ego and alter. Each has an orientation toward the
other, involving shared goals and values. (A problem arises, we should add, if
ego and alter have divergent goals and values.) Role reciprocities between actors result not only from the values and norms of the culture, but also from
long-term or patterned interactions between them resulting from their personalities and preferences. Such patterns become more or less stable or "institutionalized," meaning that they are governed by rules, or even by habits. So we
have "social action" taking place between actors playing roles within a "system" having boundaries that separate it (more or less) from other systems and
from its environment.

2. Once we accept the system principle, several additional issues arise. Besides roles, another system concern is **equilibrium**. Some readers of Parsons
see him as saying that in social systems equilibrium is the basic condition. Even
though it may sound that way, one of Parsons's later writings indicated that
equilibrium or order is an empirical question, or a variable. The concept of equilibrium, he wrote,

> is a fundamental reference point for analyzing the processes by which a
> system either comes to terms with the exigencies imposed by a changing
> environment, without essential change in its own structure, or fails to come
> to terms and undergoes other processes, such as structural change, dissolu-

tion as a boundary-maintaining system (analogous to biological death for the organism), or the consolidation of some impairment leading to the establishment of secondary structures of a "pathological" character. . . . Whether maintenance actually occurs or not, and in what measure, is entirely an empirical question. (Parsons, Shils, Naegele, and Pitts, 1961, 1:37)

3. Besides roles and equilibrium, another systemic issue for Parsons was what he called the **pattern variables**. Looking at individual choices from a macro-cultural perspective, Parsons and Shils (1951) noted that different cultures guide individuals toward one or the other of a set of dichotomous choices. Though he did not use Durkheim's or Weber's terms, Parsons noted that one set of choices is dominant in the mechanically solidary or traditional society, while the other usually occurs in the organically solidary or bureaucratic (modern) society. These choices or variables are listed in Exhibit 2.1.

Exhibit 2.1 Dichotomous Choices

Traditional Society	Modern Society
Affectivity	Affective neutrality
Collectivity (Selfless)	Self (Selfish)
Particularistic	Universalistic
Quality (Ascription)	Performance (Achievement)
Specificity	Diffuseness

Source: Parsons and Shils, 1951:172–183.

Let us examine these dichotomies one at a time.

Affectivity/Affective Neutrality. Are the actors emotionally involved or not? Are they immediately gratified or disciplined—that is, under control? This reminds one of Sigmund Freud's distinction between an individual's id gratification and ego control. Modern or "civilized" society, according to Freud, generally demands the latter.

Collectivity/Self. Do the actors choose in favor of group or community interests, or are they oriented by what is "best for number one." Here we have the assumption that modern industrial societies are characterized by greater individualism.

Particularistic/Universalistic. Do the actors orient to different "alters" according to particular characteristics, or do they treat everyone alike? In traditional society, according to Parsons, alter is treated differently depending on whether she or he is a relative or royalty or has some other favored status, is an acquaintance or a stranger (à la Georg Simmel). In modern society one is expected to treat customers or clients or job applicants alike, or in terms of universalistic criteria.

Performance. Does the actor interact with other people according to ⌐ they are in relation to the actor, or according to what they have accomplished? The modern bureaucratic actor, in Parsons's view, is concerned with what people have accomplished, not who they are, or who their parents were.

Specificity/Diffuseness. Is the actor's obligation to others diffuse, or general, or is it restricted to the specific function they perform? As Weber noted, the bureaucrat is obliged to be an expert only in a specific role, whether teaching a course or bagging groceries or making quilts, and the relationship to "alter" is restricted to that role and function.

Several issues arise immediately regarding these dichotomous choices. First, is this an exhaustive list of culturally determined potential choices? It seems that, at least at the beginning, Parsons and Shils would have answered yes. Second, are these choices really dichotomous? Although Parsons called them pattern variables, he treated them as if they were opposing choices. This might hold for the macro-perspective, meaning that a specific culture or society is dominated by one choice or the other. From the standpoint of the individual, however, it would seem that variation in intensity of commitment would make it possible to choose one side under certain conditions and the other side under other circumstances, or to feel more or less strongly about one's choice. Third, are the five dichotomies equally important? Parsons himself seemed to indicate that two choices are most important in distinguishing modern from traditional societies: universalism/particularism and achievement/ascription (Mitchell, 1967:71, 107). One set of choices, we might say, is "functional for," or more appropriate to, one type of society, and the other set for the other type of society. Using the language of functionalism leads us to a fourth major issue under Parsonsian system theory: the functional problems that a society or social system must solve.

4. The **functional problems** or dimensions of system structure and process are an aspect of Parsons's thought that changed over the years. One of his latest and clearest expositions of these problems is in his 1961 essay, "General Theory in Sociology." All social systems, he asserted, "are organized, in the sense that they are structurally differentiated, about two major axes" (1961:5). One axis is the internal/external—the relationships among the subparts of the system, and the relationships between the system and the environment or other systems. There are parts of a social system whose function is to solve internal problems, and other parts intended to solve external problems. The other axis is instrumental/consummatory—Parsons's way of saying means/ends. Some structures function in terms of a society's means or processes, and others according to its ends or outcomes. Parsons admitted that he has had some "difficulty in stabilizing both conceptualization and terminology in this field" but went on to present "the best formulation I have been able to attain to date" (see Exhibit 2.2; Parsons, 1961:6, 7).

Exhibit 2.2   AGIL Scheme of Social Systems

	Instrumental	*Consummatory*
External	A (Adaptive Function)	G (Goal-Attainment Function)
Internal	L (P)* (Pattern-Maintenance and Tension-Management Function)	I (Integrative Function)

Source: Parsons, 1961.

*Parsons usually discussed Pattern maintenance (P) as "Latent" Pattern maintenance (L). Why this is latent, rather than recognized and intended, Parsons did not make clear.

In relation to the external world, the means are aimed toward adaptation, and the ends are the attainment of the system's goals. In relation to the system itself, the means involve pattern maintenance and the management of tensions (conflicts), and the internal end is integration, or smooth functioning. Since these are problems that a system must solve, it is obvious that Parsons recognized the possibilities of lack of adaptation, non–goal attainment, tension and conflict, and nonintegration. However, as we have said, his focus was on order or equilibrium, not disorder.

Parsons himself wrote, in a lengthy footnote, about the relation between this AGIL(P) scheme and the pattern variables presented earlier:

> Readers familiar with the "pattern-variable" scheme but not with the present scheme of four functional problems and two axes by means of which they are classified may wonder about the relation between the two schemes. In the present analysis I do not use pattern-variable terms because I think the new scheme is a more generalized one from which the scheme of pattern variables can be derived. . . . What the newer scheme does is to consolidate, except for the self-collectivity variable, the other four pattern variables into a set of four rather than eight categories. The self-collectivity variable I interpret to be a special case of the external-internal axis. The categorization for the instrumental-consummatory axis is new. (1961:7)

This note illustrates Parsons at both his self-declared clearest and at his murkiest. He leaves it for the reader to connect the four pattern variables with the cells in the 2 × 2 AGIL table. And he leaves us to explicate what he means by self-collectivity as a special case. Self, presumably, means an internal orientation not to the system but to the individual him- or herself; collectivity, then, must mean an orientation that is external to the self and focuses on the system or community. This is a good example either of lack of clarity in Parsons's thinking or of his inability to communicate to the reader what was perfectly clear to him.

What makes the four problems an exercise in functional analysis is that they are intended to explain what a system must *do* to attain and maintain equilibrium—or, if you will, to operate or function.

~ciety, Humans, and Change

~ood sources on Parsons's view of the nature of the social world and on his ~ology are Black's (1961) edited volume and Mitchell's (1967) look at Parsons from a political science perspective. We have already seen Parsons's emphasis on order in society. To this, Mitchell adds that the four functional problems are important to Parsons because of his view of *human nature*. A human being, to Parsons, "is an optimizing animal in terms of the gratification he seeks . . . but is faced with an environment which, at any given time, is characterized by scarcities of facilities, resources, and rewards" (Mitchell, 1967:60; Parsons and Shils, 1951:120, 197–201). Furthermore, the functional problems are real problems for human nature and society; they may be coped with, but not completely solved. In fact, to Parsons, the four problems cannot be simultaneously and optimally resolved (Parsons and Smelser, 1956:46–47).

Parsons also noted that, because of scarcity, the choices we make involve costs or trade-offs. However, having the capacity to learn, humans are capable of making better choices as time goes by. Humans change, and so does society. Most change, however, is not revolutionary; it involves strain, followed by the social system's attempt to re-equilibrate as painlessly and quickly as possible, and as closely as possible to the previous equilibrium. According to Robin Williams (1961:88), Parsons's analysis of change requires identifying its sources, identifying the affected interests, specifying what has changed, how, and how much; and relating change to the functional problems. Because of his emphasis on order and equilibrium, Parsons saw change in the system as basically disruptive and, therefore, both minimized and undesirable (Parsons, 1951).

Ideologically, it is generally agreed that Parsons was a political liberal. Order, effectiveness, and participation are important values, and his essay on "McCarthyism" (Parsons, 1955) illustrated his concern with the potential excesses of a supposedly free system. However, while he believed McCarthyism to be an illness, he did not understand why Marx and C. Wright Mills (Parsons's contemporary) considered the capitalist power elite also to be an illness.

Why do so many readers of Parsons see him as a status quo conservative, or as having a conservative, rather than a liberal, bias (Hacker, 1961:290)? First, his early book *The Structure of Social Action* (Parsons, 1937) analyzed the social science of Marshall (a conservative economist), Durkheim, Weber, and Pareto. Durkheim and especially Pareto have been viewed as status quo conservatives. Even when Parsons later incorporated others into his writing, they included Freud, whose theory of society is both elitist and based on social control, but not Marx. Thus, the radicals play almost no role in Parsons's writings.

Second, although Parsons wrote about a great variety of issues, most of them concerned leaders rather than followers. He wrote about professionals, but not their clients: the therapist, not the patient, the educator, not the student. The working classes seldom appear in his writings.

Third, even stronger evidence of his status quo conservative ideology can be found in some of his specific comments: "The role of the economy in American society and of the business element in it is such that political leadership without prominent business participation is doomed to ineffectiveness and to the perpetuation of dangerous internal conflict" (1960:247). In other words, the business elite aids capitalism in avoiding conflict. Again, in reviewing Mills's book *The Power Elite*, Parsons wrote:

> I think we can, within considerable limits, regard the emergence of the · large firm with operations on a nationwide basis as a "normal" outcome of the process of growth and differentiation of the economy. Similarly, the rise to prominence within the firm of specialized executive functions is also a normal outcome of a process of growth in size and in structural differentiation. (1954:182)

Thus, differentiation and managerialism are normal, as Spencer and Durkheim claimed. Parsons was hardly critical of the "captains of industry," as Veblen was, or of the "power elite," like Mills.

Finally, Parsons's "conception of the political system as functionally oriented toward *system* goal-attainment, rather than simply being a tool of the upper classes or of those who wield power, strongly suggests a somewhat conservative viewpoint" (Mitchell, 1967:183). Mitchell concludes:

> Parsons tends to line up with those who believe that man is religious and needs religions, that societies are natural, organic products of evolutionary growth, that man is a creature of instinct and emotion as well as reason, that men are unequal, and that class differentiation, hierarchy, leadership, and differentials in power are all inevitable. . . . Parsons views man's potentials and limitations with neither delight nor regret. The same may be said of his estimate of human institutions. (1967:183–184, 187)

Parsons, then, was certainly not among the radicals who viewed *human nature* as good and *society* as bad and in need of complete overhaul (revolution). He viewed much of what exists in social systems as at least inevitable, if not good.

Class, Gender, and Race

Class To Parsons, class inequality or "stratification is to an important degree an integrating structure of the social system" (1954:329). But what about class conflict, which Parsons admitted did occur, given the scarcity of rewards? Class conflict developed because (1) a competitive job system means that some people are losers; (2) people resist authority in organizations; (3) those in power sometimes exploit others; (4) conflicting ideologies emerge and exist; (5) attitudes and values vary across classes; and (6) the promise of equal opportunity will not be fulfilled (Hacker, 1961:297). Notice Parsons was not saying that equal opportunity has not occurred so far, but that it *will not* occur. Thus, Parsons saw both inequality and strain as inevitable.

It is important to note that Parsons spoke of strata, not classes. He pointed to widespread consensus on occupation as the primary criterion of stratification, and on the ranking of occupations (Parsons, 1940). According to one commentator, Parsons

> identified the amounts of skill, required education, and authority over others as being potentially associated with the ranking of a position. Parsons's primary emphasis, however, was upon economic reward and

⌐nsensus. Thus, his major answer to the question of what accounts
⌐n occupation's rank is: "the more highly valued jobs are the best paid."
(Abrahamson, 1978:59, quoting Parsons, 1940:857)

So, even inequality is functional for society, and is based on consensus regarding
what and who should be more highly valued and rewarded.

Gender Parsons's view of gender is most clearly expressed in his collaborative
book on family and socialization (Parsons, Bales, Olds, Zelditch, and Slater,
1955). The beginning point for this portion of Parsons's thought was his discovery of Robert Bales's research on leadership in small, task-oriented groups. Bales
had found that in most such groups two types of leaders emerge: the task leader
and the social-emotional leader. The task leader is the individual having the best
ideas and urging the group to complete the task. The social-emotional leader is
the one who keeps the group from falling apart, or from rebelling against the
task leader. Bales, incidentally, had also found that in a small fraction of cases
the same person was able to play both roles—that is, having ideas but also
cracking jokes, sometimes at one's own expense (Bales, 1949).

Parsons found Bales's results applicable to family relations. He and his coauthors reported that the task leader in families around the world is ordinarily the
male or father, and the social-emotional leader is the female or mother. For Parsons, the male "task" is economic provision, while the role of holding the family together is played by the female(s). He argued that this arrangement is functional for the social and economic system because it provides a free-floating
male labor force that follows the needs of the job market. It is functional for the
family because only one family member, the male, provides economically, while
the women and children follow the male. And it is functional or appropriate for
the two genders because it is consistent with their basic personalities.

Miriam Johnson, in her feminist review of Parsons's gender theory (Parsons,
1942a), excused his views as being simply descriptive, not prescriptive (Johnson,
1989:116). However, Parsons pointed out that women who follow a "masculine
pattern" and seek careers would, if their numbers increase, cause profound alterations in the family's structure. And since absolute equality would be incompatible with family solidarity, it seemed that Parsons was not just describing the family in 1949. Rather, given his emphasis on equilibrium, he considered such
profound alterations to be a bad thing.

The Parsons/Bales view has been criticized on several grounds. First, cross-
cultural research has found that in some societies women provide from 60 to 90
percent of what is eaten, which calls into question the generalization of male as
provider. Second, the definition of the family's "task" has been debated. If the
family's task is to raise well-adjusted children, then who is most likely to be the
task (or socialization) leader? Might it not be the mother? Third, many feminists,
from Charlotte Gilman to Dorothy Smith (see Chapter 10), have questioned the
Freudian notion that gender differences are biologically based, and that the
Parsonsian gender distinctions are innate and functional for society (Smith, 1990).

Race In his World War II writings on fascism and Nazism, Parsons (1942b) referred to racial antagonisms as having a negative effect by increasing tensions

within a social system, and in the world of nation-states. Though never becoming an important theme, he later expanded on race as a factor in group tensions. It is clear that, unlike his conservative view of class and gender, he did not see racial tensions as natural outcomes of evolution, but as problems to be solved.

Other Theories and Theorists

Power Relations   Given Parsons's conservative view of the social system, it is not surprising that he saw power as an essential integrative element. He used Hobbes's definition of power as "a man's present means to any future good," but added one qualification: "that such means constitute his power, so far as these means are dependent on his relations to other actors; the correlative is the obligation of alter to respect ego's rights" (Parsons, 1951:121). Power, according to Parsons, is both generalizable and quantifiable in social systems.

To Parsons, the two primary subsystems of power are economy and politics. Economic power is best understood through exchange, with the most obvious means of exchange being money—as in the everyday expression "purchasing power" (Parsons, 1951:124). The other subsystem that directly involves power is the political, which is primarily a matter of influence over outcomes or goals. Economic power, then, is primarily a matter of means, while political power focuses on ends (recall the AGIL scheme in Exhibit 2.2).

Parsons noted both the functional significance and potential misuse of power. Since the power of one actor is always relative to that of another, he observed,

> power can readily become the focus of disruptive conflicts. Finally, . . . force in *one* primary context, namely that of the *prevention* of undesired action, is an ultimately effective means, and force is inherently linked to territorial location because it is a *physical* means. This complex of facts is of such crucial functional significance to social systems that it is safe to say that no paramount integrative structure of a society could perform that function effectively unless it were intimately tied in with the control of power relations in general and force in particular. (1951:162)

Even technology, Parsons noted, is a facility that is useful for carrying out power relations in a social system. Thus, as with conflict, Parsons did not ignore power, but rather located it within his systemic framework as an integrative mechanism that is sometimes misused.

Modernization Theory   In his later writings, Parsons turned his attention increasingly to modernization theory. With the pattern variables Parsons had indicated that modern societies make certain characteristic choices. By 1971, he had joined those who were arguing that the entire world is moving toward the Western model. As a neo-evolutionist, Parsons saw modernization as a worldwide goal, with subgoals of industrialization, economic development, and political independence (Parsons, 1964, 1966, 1971). All this will lead to a unified world system, with shared "modern" values. In Chapter 6 you will find an expanded discussion of twentieth-century evolutionary and modernization theory.

As we have seen, Parsons borrowed from and expanded on those whose theories he found useful, but ignored those, such as the radicals, with whom he disagreed. This is again reminiscent of Herbert Spencer, who produced a comprehensive system of thought, while ignoring most of his antagonists.

Critique and Conclusions

Parsons—and functionalism in general—has been criticized on two grounds. First, he did not account for survivals or dysfunctional "leftovers" from a bygone day. Second, he did not allow much room for dissensus and conflict. Actors, according to Parsons, comply with each other's expectations because they want to (consensus) and because one's expectation is another's obligation (complementarity). Not wanting to comply and not sharing consensus on roles and obligations may lead to conflict, but as Gouldner (1970) has pointed out, this possibility has little place in Parsons's theory.

Parsons's action theory has been criticized as providing a conceptual framework but "not a theory or even a set of theories" (Mitchell, 1967:47). While acknowledging that much of Parsons's effort was spent on (often obscure) conceptualization, we might defend him by pointing out that once we have waded through the terminology and accepted his presuppositions, his thought leaves little in society unaccounted for. Action takes place between actors influenced by society's norms and their personalities; the social system has problems to solve if it is to continue ordered and in equilibrium; one of its tools is power; and the goal of much of the world is to become industrialized at the expense of its traditional cultures. We may argue that all of this results from an ideology that gives too much emphasis to order and its desirability, but it is hard to argue that it is simply incomplete.

We have criticized much of Parsons's theory as we have gone along, including his incomplete treatment of change, his conservative ideology, and his views on gender. As Mitchell commented in 1967, "when a sociologist wishes to debate, question, criticize, or rebel, it is usually Parsons who becomes the target. One often establishes his position by reference to Parsons" (1967:189). This appraisal continued to be accurate through the 1970s.

However, Mitchell made two other observations that were even more insightful, even prophetic. Parsons, noted Mitchell, had not produced a great empirical work, such as those carried out by Durkheim or Marx.[4] "Nor has there been a study equivalent to Durkheim's *Suicide*. The fact that Parsons has not guided his energies in that direction is not important in itself, but it will probably somewhat diminish his reputation" (1967:191).

The second comment on Parsons is found in Mitchell's Preface: "I doubt very much that we are yet in a position to attain a really profound analysis of the man and his work. The passage of time is a prerequisite to such understanding"

---

[4] It could be argued that Parsons's writings about hospitals, universities, and the military were, in fact, empirical studies—especially his paper on the mental hospital (1957), which included interview data. But the criticism that he never did a major empirical work still holds.

(1967:ix). And what has the passage of time done to Parsons? From the late 1970s through the 1980s, his reputation diminished substantially, kept alive by thinkers such as Jeffrey Alexander. But in the 1990s, Camic republished the early essays, including a lengthy biographical statement, and other theorists, such as Anthony Giddens and Niklas Luhmann (see Chapter 3), either re- sponded to or built upon Parsons's work.

Robert K. Merton (1910–)

Robert King Merton was born in 1910 in a South Philadelphia slum. In 1994, at the age of 84, he gave a useful autobiographical statement titled "A Life of Learning" (Merton, 1994).

The son of Jewish immigrant parents, Merton early manifested a love of learning, and spent much time at a nearby Carnegie library. He also became ac- quainted with Leopold Stokowski's world-renowned Philadelphia Orchestra, at- tending concerts for 25 cents (1994:343, 345). Thus, observed Merton, this supposedly deprived South Philly slum provided him with "every sort of capi- tal—social capital, cultural capital, human capital, and above all, what we may call public capital—that is, with every sort of capital except the personally finan- cial" (1994:346).

By the age of 14, Merton was a fairly proficient magician, with Harry Houdini as his role model. Houdini had changed his name from Ehrich Weiss, and Meyer Schkolnick decided that such a change was appropriate for him as well. And so Meyer Schkolnick became Robert Merlin, after King Arthur's fa- mous magician, and—after being reminded that this was a bit hackneyed—Rob- ert Merton. Five years later Meyer Schkolnick's name was legally changed to Robert King Merton (1994:348).

Merton earned a scholarship to Temple University, where he happened into a sociology class taught by George E. Simpson, the translator of Durkheim. Simpson saw to it that Merton attended an annual meeting of the American So- ciological Society, where Merton heard and met Pitirim Sorokin of Harvard. Merton followed his degree from Temple by daring to apply to Harvard, where Sorokin was chair. But, Merton recalled, "it was not the renowned Sorokin who most influenced my sociological thinking there; instead, it was a young instruc- tor with no public identity whatsoever as a sociologist. Talcott Parsons had then published only two articles" (1994:350). Working with Parsons and with a his- torian of science named George Sarton, Merton completed his PhD in 1936. From there he went to Tulane, where he spent two years, before joining the fac- ulty at Columbia University in New York City.

Parsons influenced Merton's theoretical stance, and, as noted previously, the two were the leading U.S. functionalists from the 1930s into the 1970s. How- ever, it was when he went from Tulane to Columbia that Merton began what he called an "improbable collaboration":

> Paul Lazarsfeld and I may have been the original odd couple in the domain
> of social science. He, the mathematically-minded methodologist, inventor
> of powerful techniques of social inquiry such as the panel method and

latent structure analysis; I, the confirmed social theorist albeit with something of an empirical bent, insisting on the importance of sociological paradigms. (1994:354)

These two became colleagues in 1941 at the Bureau of Applied Social Research at Columbia University, where they collaborated until Lazarsfeld's death in 1976.

Merton recalled that he finally convinced the mathematician that the field of sociology really existed, while "Paul's abiding concern with research methods rubbed off on me and once resulted in a codification of what I called the focussed interview," later to become the "focus group" (1994:355; Merton and Kendall, 1946). Thus, Merton stood firmly planted in both the theoretical and empirical worlds, and some of his most insightful writing was on the relation between the two (Merton, 1946). At his retirement, he became a professor-at-large and Emeritus Professor of Columbia. In the year 2000, he turned 90.

Merton's Central Theories and Methods

Parsons was gratified by Merton's apparently growing appreciation of Parsons's efforts at grand-scale theory building (see Parsons, 1961:3). However, Merton saw his own work as contributing in two multifaceted theoretical directions: middle-range theorizing and specification of functional analysis.

Theories of the Middle Range   Between grand-scale theory and the "fishing expeditions" of raw empiricists can be found theories that deal with a specific subportion of social life. Merton defined **middle-range theories** as those "that lie between the minor but necessary working hypotheses that evolve in abundance during day-to-day research and the all-inclusive systematic efforts to develop a unified theory that will explain all the observed uniformities of social behavior, social organization, and social change" (1968:39).

Such theories are in the style of Durkheim's *Suicide* and Weber's *Protestant Ethic,* and much of Merton's work was of that kind. Merton may have appreciated his mentor Parsons's theories, but considered most grand-scale theorizing to be at least premature, if not ill-conceived (Hunt, 1961). Merton wrote about deviance, role sets, political machines, and medical student attitudes; we will look briefly at the first two of these.

One of the studies that helped to make Merton's reputation was his analysis of **deviance**. Using, but altering, Durkheim's concept of anomie and the functionalist's distinction between means and goals, Merton reported four kinds of deviance; his fifth category was conformity, or the acceptance of the culture's dominant means and ends. The individual who accepts the society's goal of monetary success and strives through education and hard work to attain it, is a conformist, not a deviant at all.

The first type of deviant in Merton's analysis is the innovator—a person who accepts the goal of success but uses an alternate, or nonestablishment, means of attaining it, such as selling drugs. The second, opposite type is the ritualist—one who uses the accepted means, but rejects the goal, such as the educated person who rejects success in favor of becoming a monk. These two, innovator and ritualist, are characterized by anomie, because means and goals are inconsistent.

Merton's third type of deviant is the retreatist, who rejects both society's goals and the means of attaining them. This individual may be a drug addict, may be mentally ill, or may simply live in a hollow tree, but is clearly an outsider. The final type of deviation based on means and goals is rebellion—the substitution of another set of means and goals for the culture's dominant ones. Merton's scheme has been used to account for class, racial, and ethnic deviance, and has continued to be used and qualified in the half-century since it first appeared.

Role sets, as Merton described them in 1957, are multiple role expectations that are parts of the same position or status. For example, a high school student plays various roles vis-à-vis his or her teachers, adviser, parents, and other students. As is typical with Merton, such specification makes it possible to explain conflict, as one set of expectations—for example, getting along with other students by not being a "curve-raiser"—conflicts with another set of expectations, such as making teachers and parents happy by getting good grades.

Role-set analysis clarifies not only conflicting expectations, but also inequities. If one were to list the role sets related to the status of mother and compare it with that of father, one might discover the former to be overburdened.

> For example, does the school nurse always phone the mother when the child is sick, even when both parents work? By virtue of being a mother, is she, and not the father, automatically involved in role relationships with the school nurse? And if demands are unequal, what are the likely consequences? (Wallace and Wolf, 1986:59)

This is one of the ways in which Merton's middle-range specifying of functional theory allows for the conflict and inequities that seem to be missing from Parsons.

Specifying Functionalism   Although middle-range theories are of interest, for the purposes of this chapter Merton's contributions to functional analysis are more important. Merton recognized that, as noted early in this chapter, most functionalists answer questions such as "What does it do?" or "What purpose does it serve?" This, to Merton, is oversimplified.

Merton's first specification was the distinction between manifest and latent functions. The same action or structure may perform either or both such functions. The **manifest function** is the observed or intended outcome; the **latent function** is the unintended or unrecognized result. Other sociological observers, noted Merton, had "from time to time distinguished between categories of subjective disposition ('needs, interests, purposes') and categories of generally unrecognized but objective functional consequences ('unique advantages,' . . . 'unintended . . . service to society,' 'function not limited to conscious and explicit purpose')" (1968:116).

An example of the value of this distinction is a reanalysis of Durkheim's treatment of religion, with religion serving the manifest function of solving the human quest for ultimate meaning and the latent function of providing social identity and solidarity. Another example, referred to by Merton, was Veblen's *Theory of the Leisure Class*, where accumulation of material possessions had the manifest function of making life more comfortable and the latent function of providing status and prestige.[5]

What does this distinction accomplish? First, according to Merton, it clarifies "the analysis of seemingly irrational social patterns," or patterns that only make sense when seen in terms of their latent consequences. Second, it can help draw attention "to theoretically fruitful fields of inquiry." Third, it contributes to the sociology of knowledge, helping us understand how we know what we know. Finally, it "precludes the substitution of naive moral judgments for sociological analysis" (1968:119–126). Merton thus recognized the tendency of functionalism to slide from "What is is functional" into "What is is good."

Merton's second specification of functional analysis is found in the concept of **dysfunction**. The danger of functional analysis is its focus on structure and equilibrium. Even though, as noted earlier, Parsons referred to strains and tension management, he never attempted to incorporate them into his model of order and system. Merton, however, noted that aspects of culture and society may have "consequences which lessen the adaptation or adjustment of the system" (1957:105). Bureaucratic rules, for example, while presumably intended to increase efficiency by making things run smoothly, may be dysfunctional when they lead to "red tape" and an inability to make rational decisions.

Another use of the concept of dysfunction relates to the question "functional for whom?" Functionalists such as Parsons often assumed, without direct reference, that the need met is societal or systemic. Merton, however, noted that, to take our opening example, a casino may be functional for a rich owner while being dysfunctional for the Native American tribe. Racial discrimination may be functional for the race that controls power but extremely dysfunctional for the racial minority. Not all the parts of a social system or its culture are integrated, or work together for the good of the whole. Thus, in the same way that the manifest/latent distinction seeks to escape moral judgments, recognition of dysfunction as a structural possibility helps the observer to escape a status quo conservative stance (Merton, 1975).

Merton's third specification of functionalism is found in his view of functional alternatives. The true-believing functionalist is likely to argue that a given structure or portion of a system is functional because it is the solution to some need of the system (perhaps A, G, I, or L). It exists because it must—because it is essential or necessary. Merton, however, noted that although a structure may exist because it solves some problem, it is hardly indispensable. Thus, for example, a political machine in a big city may be functional for immigrants who do not know how to solve their own problems. But the same need could be met by education for the immigrants and taxation of the well-to-do. By turning structures into analyzable variables, into alternatives instead of indispensables, Merton has again escaped the status quo conservative trap.

Yet all this does not imply that Merton was simply a critic of functionalism. His approach to theory was still to ask the functionalist questions of ends and

---

[5] Veblen was hardly a functionalist, and Merton's use of him indicates a willingness to go "outside the camp" in order to expand and clarify functionalist assumptions and simplifications.

means, structure and consequence. Merton himself gave us a summary paradigm, or guiding framework, for what should be analyzed in functional terms: (a) items to which functions are imputed; (b) concepts of subjective dispositions (motives, purposes); (c) concepts of objective consequences (functions, dysfunctions); (d) concepts of the unit served by the function; (e) concepts of functional prerequisites; (f) concepts of mechanisms through which functions are fulfilled; (g) concepts of functional alternatives; (h) concepts of dynamics and change; (i) concepts of structural context; (j) problems of validation of functional analysis; and (k) problems of the ideological implications of functional analysis (1946:50–54). One can readily see from this list that Merton had broadened functionalism, not abandoned it.

Methods/Research/Problems   We have already noted that, while working with Paul Lazarsfeld, Merton (with Patricia Kendall) wrote a methodological piece on the focused interview. Although he was never totally oriented to methods, some of Merton's most insightful pieces concerned the relation between research and theory, and the issue of problem solving in sociology. His lengthy treatment of the interplay between research and theory is found in his collection of writings *Social Theory and Social Structure* (1968). Among his main points were (1) that different research methods are necessary for different empirical problems; (2) that research may lead to empirical generalizations, but fall short of direct theory testing; and (3) that empirical research is useful for much more than the testing of hypotheses drawn from a general theory. In short, Merton pointed out the necessary but complex links between theory and research. Merton's paper on "Problem-Finding" (1961), again showed that he had one foot firmly planted in the empirical world of research and the other in the world of middle-range theories and theoretical complexity.

In introducing a volume of papers on the current state of sociology, Merton (1961) asked, What is a sociological problem, and how does one find or formulate it? His answer was multifaceted. First, one may find it by specializing, or by becoming "more and more interested in less and less"—that is, in a smaller and smaller portion of the social world. Second, one may seek to correct errors or emphases. An overemphasis on psychological explanations, for example, led to Durkheim's sociological analysis of suicide. Third, a recurring problem may come to one's attention simply because it has never been answered adequately. Fourth, there may be conceptual obstacles to overcome. Race, class consciousness, gender, and family may all need a certain amount of reconceptualization. Fifth, inconsistent or contradictory "facts" or findings may call for new data, and new theory to explain them. Finally, a real-world problem may come to the attention of both the researcher and the theorist. It might be the authoritarian personality, identified in Nazi Germany in the 1930s (see Chapter 4), or the "cooling-out function" in education—convincing college students that they don't belong there. Numerous such sociological problems are identified simply by living in the world and observing it (Merton, 1961: xxxiii–xxxiv).

For Merton, then, theorizing was central, but it requires methodology, research, and problem identification, not just an armchair or an ivory tower.

Nature of Society, Humans, and Change

As Parsons had stated, society is a system, with a structure and parts. However, to Merton it is not in equilibrium, with the parts contributing to the good of the whole. Rather, it consists of manifest and latent functions, even dysfunctions, and, as such, is a mixture of elements, including conflict as well as order. Merton argued, then, that functionalism is not necessarily inherently conservative in its view of society.

Though he did not devote much attention to human nature, Merton made one important observation: Human nature is neither inherently good nor bad, but is changeable. It is only, he said, "with the rejection of social fatalism implied in the notion of unchangeable human nature that the tragic circle of fear, social disaster, and reinforced fear can be broken" (1948:200). He was referring to racial inequality, noting the importance to change of believing that it is possible. Clearly, Merton was a believer in changeable human nature, behavior, and attitudes.

To Merton, then, change is possible and often desirable, though that is the sort of value judgment he sought to avoid. Reading between the lines, it seems that to Merton change is best approached within the established order, by liberal means, rather than by revolution.

In terms of ideology, it should be obvious by now that Merton did not see himself as a status quo conservative. However, the questions he asked about structure and function, needs, ends, and means come from that tradition. Despite his liberalism, Merton did not completely escape the criticisms to which functional theorists such as Parsons opened themselves.

Class, Gender, and Race

Class, gender, and race were not the central topics in Merton's work. However, one of his earliest writings dealt with class. In discussing anomie and deviance, he noted that the unskilled may lack "legitimate means for becoming successful" (1938:677). Their response will be either to reject the dominant goal, or to find alternative (deviant) means for achieving it. Thus, Merton suggested, lower-class individuals are likely to "innovate," and the lower-middle classes to "conform." However, when the national ideology extols freedom and opportunity for all, it leaves some individuals with a sense of failure, even if "the cards were stacked against them." Merton's analysis of class, then, was related for the most part to his discussion of deviance.

Gender was even less a focus of Merton's attention, showing up only once in his essay on insiders and outsiders. Treating women and African Americans as out-groups, Merton noted how difficult it is for the women's movement to draw on both white and black women, and how difficult it is for black liberation movements to unite both men and women (Merton, 1972:30). With no further comment on women's liberation, Merton again avoided any sort of ideological comment on gender.

Race, like gender, was dealt with in the essay on insiders and outsiders. However, Merton also discussed race in his commentary on the self-fulfilling prophecy, which will be discussed later (Merton, 1948:183–201). He began the discussion of insiders and outsiders by noting that education is not enough to change race relations. Furthermore, a racial group may be criticized and punished for being either successful *or* unsuccessful. Thus, African Americans may be seen as inferior, so that resources are not "wasted on them," so that they continue to be less successful, which demonstrates their inferiority. Or Jews may be punished for too much success, as they were in Nazi Germany. Institutional change, not education alone, is necessary to combat ethnic and racial prejudices (Merton, 1948:200). Merton, then, saw racial inequality as a problem to be solved, not as an inevitable aspect of society.

Other Theories and Theorists

Merton's middle-range theories covered a wide variety of topics, making it impossible to introduce but a few of the more interesting and useful ones.

Self-Fulfilling Prophecy   The "self-fulfilling prophecy" was one of Merton's phrases that has been incorporated into everyday speech. Merton began with a quote from W. I. Thomas in 1928: "If men define situations as real, they are real in their consequences" (Thomas and Thomas, 1928:572). Carrying this idea further, Merton argued that if we define something as real, and act upon it, it will in fact become real.

The first illustration he presented concerns the folding of a bank. A rumor, however started, that a bank cannot cover the deposits of its customers, if acted upon will become real. No bank ever has all the money at hand that has been credited to accounts, because it reinvests most of it. Thus, "despite the comparative liquidity of the bank's assets, a rumor of insolvency, once believed (and acted upon) by enough depositors, would result in the insolvency of the bank" (Merton, 1948:184–185).

Another illustration pertained to African Americans' being kept out of unions because they are defined as "scabs" or strikebreakers. Because (in 1948) they were not allowed into the unions and needed work, they then *became* strikebreakers (Merton, 1948:187). Thus, a belief, when acted upon, may become true or factual.

Plausibility and Truth   One of Merton's most insightful comments is found in a footnote to his "Notes on Problem-Finding in Sociology" (1961). The relation between the plausible and the true, wrote Merton, leaves the sociologist

> with some uncomfortable alternatives. Should his systematic inquiry only
> confirm what had been widely assumed—this being the class of plausible
> truths—he will of course be charged with "laboring the obvious." . . .
> Should investigation find that widely held beliefs are untrue—the class of
> plausible untruths—he is a heretic, questioning value-laden verities. If he
> ventures to examine socially implausible ideas that turn out to be untrue,
> he is a fool, wasting effort on a line of inquiry not worth pursuing in the

first place. And finally, if he should turn up some implausible truths, he must be prepared to find himself regarded as a charlatan, claiming as knowledge what is patently false. (Merton, 1961:xv–xvi)

Dealing with society, about which everyone has some knowledge and many opinions, leaves the researcher and theorist open to all these possible responses.

Critique and Conclusions

Merton, then, is a theorist, researcher, and thinker about the world in which he lives. He has attempted, through many years of productive scholarship, to help us appreciate the complexities of society, and the functions performed by its various aspects. His functionalism is broad-based, and he has been able to escape many of the criticisms faced by other conservative functionalists, from Spencer to Parsons.

One scholar whose criticism Merton has not escaped, however, is Randall Collins. Merton's deviance theory, according to Collins (1981), had two advantages: first, it drew on (and altered) Durkheim, a central figure in mid-twentieth-century American sociology, and second, it rode the wave of the "great juvenile delinquency scare" of the 1950s. According to Collins, then, it was more popular than creative.

Collins's second criticism is a broad indictment of Merton's corpus of work. Merton's lack of attention to stratification and classes exemplified, in Collins's view, what was weakest in American sociology at the time. Consistent with the "great Communist scare" of that time, intellectuals such as Merton helped to drive sociology as far as possible away from Marxism. Lacking a serious theoretical and ideological dialogue, the discipline was weak and, in many ways, simply reflective of U.S. ideology. Collins's argument with Merton, and even more so with Parsons, is that, despite the interesting issues raised, the answers given lack dynamism, excitement, and dialogue.

Final Thoughts

In 1959, at the height of the dominance of functionalist theory in U.S. sociology, Kingsley Davis published a most instructive paper. In it he argued, in agreement with Merton, that a functionalist does not have to believe that everything that exists meets a need, is indispensable, or is in a system where all the parts work for the good of the whole. All that the functionalist needs to conclude is that things are interrelated, and that society is integrated or "working" (functioning) most of the time. In this sense, Davis suggested, every sociologist is a functionalist. Sociology *is* functionalism, because sociology starts from the premise that societies are real and, therefore, are integrated (Davis, 1959).

If Davis is right, then functionalism is not a theory at all, but merely a set of premises that sociologists—and non-sociologists—accept, and within which we all operate. In reading the present volume, you may want to keep Davis's point in mind, and ask yourself to what extent he has correctly stated, or overstated, the case.

References

Abrahamson, Mark. 1978. *Functionalism*. Englewood Cliffs, NJ: Prentice-Hall.

Bales, Robert Freed. 1949. *Interaction Process Analysis: A Method for the Study of Small Groups*. Reading, MA: Addison-Wesley.

Black, Max (Ed.). 1961/1976. *The Social Theories of Talcott Parsons*. Carbondale: Southern Illinois University Press.

Camic, Charles. 1991. *Talcott Parsons: The Early Essays*. Chicago: University of Chicago Press.

Collins, Randall. 1981. *Sociology Since Midcentury*. New York: Academic Press.

Cremin, Lawrence, David Shannon, and Mary Townsend. 1954. *A History of Teachers College: Columbia University*. Morningside Heights, NY: Columbia University Press.

Davis, Kingsley. 1959. "The Myth of Functional Analysis as a Special Method in Sociology and Anthropology." *American Sociological Review, 24,* 757–772.

Devereaux, Edward C. 1961/1976. "Parsons' Sociological Theory," In Max Black (Ed.), *The Social Theories of Talcott Parsons* (pp. 1–63). Carbondale: Southern Illinois University Press.

Gouldner, Alvin W. 1970. *The Coming Crisis of Western Sociology*. New York: Basic Books.

Hacker, Andrew. 1961/1976. "Sociology and Ideology." In Max Black (Ed.), *The Social Theories of Talcott Parsons* (pp. 289–310). Englewood Cliffs, NJ: Prentice-Hall.

Hunt, Morton M. 1961, "How Does It Come to Be So? " [Profile of Robert K. Merton]. *New Yorker, 36,* 39–63.

Johnson, Miriam M. 1989. "Feminism and the Theories of Talcott Parsons." In Ruth A. Wallace (Ed.), *Feminism and Sociological Theory* (pp. 101–118). Newbury Park, CA: Sage.

Kates, William. 1999, April 11. "Casino Opening Gives Mohawks Hope." *Wisconsin State Journal*, p. 6A.

Loomis, Charles P., and Zona K. Loomis. 1961. *Modern Social Theories*. Princeton, NJ: D. Van Nostrand.

Martindale, Don. 1960. *The Nature and Types of Sociological Theory*. Boston: Houghton Mifflin.

Merton, Robert K. 1938. "Social Structure and Anomie." *American Sociological Review, 3,* 672–682.

———. 1946. *Social Theory and Social Structure*. New York: Free Press.

———. 1948/1996. "The Self-Fulfilling Prophecy." In Piotr Sztompka (Ed.), *Robert K. Merton: On Social Structure and Science* (pp. 183–201). Chicago: University of Chicago Press.

———. 1957. "The Role Set: Problems in Sociological Theory." *British Journal of Sociology, 2,* 106–120.

———. 1961. "Notes on Problem-Finding in Sociology." In Robert K. Merton, Leonard Broom, and Leonard S. Cottrell (Eds.), *Sociology Today: Problems and Prospects* (pp. ix–xxxiv). New York: Basic Books.

———. 1968. *Social Theory and Social Structure* (3d ed.). New York: Simon and Schuster.

———. 1972. "Insiders and Outsiders: A Chapter in the Sociology of Knowledge." *American Journal of Sociology, 77,* 9–47.

———. 1975/1996. "Functional Analysis in Sociology." In Piotr Sztompka (Ed.), *Robert K. Merton: On Social Structure and Science* (pp. 96–100). Chicago: University of Chicago Press.

———. 1994/1996. "A Life of Learning." Philadelphia: American Council of Learned Societies. Reprinted in Piotr Sztompka (Ed.), *Robert K. Merton: On Social Structure and Science* (pp. 339–359). Chicago: University of Chicago Press.

Merton, Robert K., and Patricia L. Kendall. 1946. "The Focused Interview." *American Journal of Sociology, 51*, 541–557.

Mitchell, William C. 1967. *Sociological Analysis and Politics: The Theories of Talcott Parsons*. Englewood Cliffs, NJ: Prentice-Hall.

Parsons, Talcott. 1937. *The Structure of Social Action*. New York: McGraw-Hill.

———. 1940. "An Analytic Approach to the Theory of Stratification." *American Journal of Sociology, 45*, 841–862.

———. 1942a/1954. "Age and Sex in the Social Structure of the United States." In *Essays in Sociological Theory* (pp. 89–103). Glencoe, IL: Free Press.

———. 1942b. "Some Sociological Aspects of the Fascist Movements." *Social Forces, 21*, 138–147.

———. 1945/1954. "The Present Position and Prospects of Systematic Theory in Sociology." In Talcott Parsons, *Essays in Sociological Theory* (pp. 212–237). New York: Free Press of Glencoe.

———. 1951. *The Social System*. New York: Free Press.

———. 1954. *Essays in Sociological Theory* (rev. ed.). New York: Free Press of Glencoe.

———. 1955. "'McCarthyism' and American Social Tension: A Sociologist's View." *Yale Review, 44*, 226–245.

———. 1957. "The Mental Hospital as a Type of Organization." In Milton Greenblatt, Daniel J. Levinson, Richard H. Williams (Eds.), *The Patient and the Mental Hospital* (pp. 108–129). New York: Free Press of Glencoe.

———. 1960. *Structure and Process in Modern Societies*. New York: Free Press of Glencoe.

———. 1961. "General Theory in Sociology." In Robert K. Merton, Leonard Broom, and Leonard S. Cottrell (Eds.), *Sociology Today: Problems and Prospects* (pp. 3–38). New York: Basic Books.

———. 1962. "Richard Henry Tawney (1880–1962)." *American Sociological Review, 27*, 888–890.

———. 1964. "Evolutionary Universals in Society." *American Sociological Review, 29*, 339–357.

———. 1966. *Societies: Evolutionary and Comparatives Perspectives*. Englewood Cliffs, NJ: Prentice-Hall.

———. 1971. *The System of Modern Societies*. Englewood Cliffs, NJ: Prentice-Hall.

———. 1975. "The Present Status of Structural-Functional Theory in Sociology." In Lewis A. Coser (Ed.), *The Idea of Social Structure: Papers in Honor of Robert K. Merton* (pp. 67–83). New York: Harcourt Brace Jovanovich.

Parsons, Talcott, Robert F. Bales, James Olds, Morris Zelditch, and Philip E. Slater. 1955. *Family, Socialization, and Interaction Process*. New York: Free Press of Glencoe.

Parsons, Talcott, and Edward Shils (Eds.). 1951. *Toward a General Theory of Action*. Cambridge, MA: Harvard University Press.

Parsons, Talcott, Edward Shils, Kaspar D. Naegele, and Jesse R. Pitts. 1961. *Theories of Society* (2 vols.). New York: Free Press of Glencoe.

Parsons, Talcott, and Neil J. Smelser. 1956. *Economy and Society*. New York: Free Press of Glencoe.

Smith, Dorothy. 1990. *The Conceptual Practices of Power: A Feminist Sociology of Knowledge*. Boston: Northeastern University Press.

Thomas, W. I., and Dorothy Swaine Thomas. 1928. *The Child in America*. New York: Alfred A. Knopf.

Wallace, Ruth A., and Alison Wolf. 1986. *Contemporary Sociological Theory: Continuing the Classical Tradition*. Englewood Cliffs, NJ: Prentice-Hall.

Williams, Robin. 1961. "The Sociological Theory of Talcott Parsons." In Max Black (Ed.), *The Social Theories of Talcott Parsons* (pp. 64–99). Englewood Cliffs, NJ: Prentice-Hall.

Chapter 3

Systems, Structuration, and Modernity
Luhmann and Giddens

Nicholas Luhmann and Anthony Giddens are two encyclopedic sociological theorists of the late twentieth century. Although they differed in their responses to Talcott Parsons—Luhmann outgrew him and Giddens rejected him—they have much in common besides the volume of their writings. Neither was willing to simplify the complexity of the social world. Both addressed issues of social structure—Luhmann writing about social systems, and Giddens about the process of structuration. Both discussed problems of trust, risk, power, and reflexivity. And, because of their differences, it is interesting to compare them with each other and with the functionalists who preceded them in Chapter 2. Let us introduce them.

> *Luhmann:* Luhmann's social theory is a systemic supertheory. . . . [His] basic attitude towards the world is one of ironic distance. His . . . vision of the world is one of wonder. . . . Luhmann's social theory offers a systemic analysis of the social ordering of chaos. . . . Luhmann literally demoralizes the world. He has given up hope and given away the normative foundations of social criticism. (Vandenberghe, 1999:2)

> *Giddens:* Low-probability, high-consequence risks will not disappear in the modern world, although in an optimal scenario they could be minimized. . . . Relatively *small-scale* events, such as the dropping of atomic bombs on Hiroshima and Nagasaki or the accidents at Three Mile Island or Chernobyl, give some sense of what could happen. (Giddens, 1990:134; italics added)

The modern world consists of complex systems (Luhmann), but is not too bad a place (Giddens). It is not a Parsonsian functional system, with the parts working together as they do in an organism; it consists of numerous relatively independent systems—religious, political, economic, educational, and so on—and of people who think about themselves and their actions (Luhmann).

Looked at optimistically, that same world is moving toward global democracy, with individuals having the power to make things happen, and with the dropping of atomic bombs being but small-scale negative events (Giddens).

In this chapter we will meet the German, Niklas Luhmann, and the Britisher, Anthony Giddens.

Niklas Luhmann (1927–1998)

Max Weber, in early-twentieth-century Germany, never sought to simplify the complexity of the social world into single-factor descriptions or explanations; he did, however, attempt to make that complexity as understandable as possible. Niklas Luhmann not only saw the modern world as complicated—more so than during Weber's time—but mirrored it in his writing. The words are complex, the thoughts are complex, and his works are almost prohibitively so. He used a flexible and abstract set of concepts and propositions that could be combined in many different ways (Luhmann, 1984:xix).

The difficulty of reading Luhmann involves much more than its having been translated from German: The ideas are abstract, the sentences include new or little-known words, and they string together numerous concepts. However, it is not just his sentences that are complex—so is the overall structure of his works. Books such as *Social Systems* (1984) have no natural starting point—any order of chapters is equally reasonable and acceptable. Have you ever read a book in which it didn't matter where you started, or in what order you read the chapters? Not likely. But this is true of Luhmann's work.

Luhmann himself acknowledged that "Complicated conceptual relationships of this kind may intimidate sociologists"—and, we might add, students.[1] However, he claimed, it was not possible to convert the book "into a thoroughly plausible statement" (1984:488). Modern society is complex, and Luhmann was unwilling to simplify for the sake of accessibility. Thus, as we begin, it is logical to ask, is Luhmann "worth it"? The answer, however, must come at the end—not at the beginning—of our journey.

Niklas Luhmann was born in 1927 in Luneburg, Germany. In 1949, he completed a law degree at the University of Freiburg/Breisgau, and subsequently practiced law (Poggi, 1979:vii). However, he became disillusioned with the repetitive nature of much in the legal profession, and joined the civil service in Saxony. This he also found less than fulfilling, and during his free time he read Descartes, Kant, and the functionalist theories of Bronislaw Malinowski and A. R. Radcliffe-Brown (Knodts, 1995:xiii). His own theoretical development took place as a result both of his reading and of his civil service work on post–World War II German reparations.

---

[1]Not meaning to scare the reader away, here is one sentence from *Social Systems*: "At this functional point in the theory, the concept of ideality enters to guarantee apodictically the unconditional repeatability of thoughts, and thus the enduring richness in content of transcendental 'life'" (Luhmann, 1984:263). Got it? If not, you are not alone!

By 1960, Luhmann's administrative duties began to get in the way of his intellectual interests, and he sought and received a leave to spend a year (1960–1961) studying with Talcott Parsons at Harvard. On his return to Germany, he took an academic position at the School of Administrative Science at Speyer, where he began to expand his theoretical position beyond that of Parsons, based largely on his studies in cybernetics and biology.

The world of Luhmann's time included the rise and fall of Germany in World War II, its occupation by foreign troops during his early adulthood, and his resulting lack of confidence that modern society is a better place to live. As one commentator has observed, the way in which his

> "optimism of the intellect," is countered by a "pessimism of the will" can be seen in his almost cynical appreciation of the defeat of the Third Reich. Unlike Habermas,[2] who described himself without irony as a typical product of postwar re-education, Luhmann provocatively declares that he remembers only one thing about the liberation—that American soldiers beat him up and stole his watch. (Vandenberghe, 1999:2)

Luhmann taught in various settings from 1965 to 1968, when Helmut Schelsky invited him to join the sociology faculty at Bielefeld. The problem was that Luhmann had no formal degree in sociology. So he proceeded to get two of his early publications accepted in lieu of a degree, and in 1968 he followed Schelsky to Bielefeld, where he taught and later was Emeritus Professor until his death.

Much of Luhmann's early reputation was based on criticism of the already famous Habermas's liberal ideology. But Luhmann's later productivity was truly amazing. He wrote 40 books and 350 journal articles, a feat which he attributed to his system of cross-referenced file cards. He once stated that he spent more time "arranging and rearranging his system of file cards than writing books" (Vandenberghe, 1999:1). One reason that Luhmann is not well known in the English-speaking world may be the sheer difficulty and complexity of his systems theory. One commentator describes Luhmann's mode of presentation as "non-linear":

> One can enter the theory by a multiplicity of conceptual gates—such as complexity, contingency, system, environment, meaning, communication, self-reference, openness through closure, and so forth—but as one can never be sure to be on the right track, it is often tempting to go for the next exit. In this respect, the theory resembles more a labyrinth (or maze) than a highway to a happy end. (Vandenberghe, 1999:1)

Another commentator suggests a second reason why Luhmann may not be well known in the English-speaking intellectual world. In his work, Luhmann drew on formal logic, cybernetics, and biology, not just on the social sciences.

---

[2]Jurgen Habermas is an important contemporary German critical theorist who deals with language, and who published and debated with Luhmann. He will be discussed in Chapter 4.

Such interdisciplinary work crosses the typical intellectual boundaries, while modern scientific knowledge is compartmentalized by discipline and department. The result is that inter- or cross-disciplinary conversations and work are either ignored (being considered to be someone else's), or fragmented, dealt with like the blind men and the elephant—one inadequate piece per discipline (Savard, 1999:1). For the same reason, however, another commentator suggests that "because of the truly universal scope of his published work, Niklas Luhmann seems richly to deserve his growing reputation as the most original German sociologist since Max Weber" (Holmes and Larmore, 1982:xxxvi–xxxvii).

Luhmann's Central Theories and Methods

Luhmann's self-introduction in *The Differentiation of Society* summarizes his two most important theoretical interests:

> In recent years, I have worked on two theoretical projects that cross-fertilize one another. On the one hand, I have pursued a general theory of social systems. . . . On the other hand, I have worked extensively on a theory of modern society. We can no longer define society by giving primacy to one of its functional domains. (1982: xi–xii)

We will examine each of these themes in turn.

Systems Theory   What is a **system**? One familiar example is the solar system, which consists of a star—the Sun—with a cluster of planets revolving around it. Several of these planets also have moons around them. It is, then, a set of inter-related parts all focused on and guided by their relation to a single center. This is the sort of system that Spencer and Parsons used to characterize society.

Two other well-known systems are the interstate highway system and the telephone system. Each of these consists of interconnected parts, but neither has a single center around which it revolves. Rather, one can enter at any point and be connected to the rest. In the United States, the phone "system," while interconnected, is actually a number of subsystems, or separate carriers. And while a highway system and a telephone system are relatively independent of each other, they are both means of keeping in touch, or communicating. Telephone lines are often near highways, because a highway makes it possible to reach a telephone line to repair it. The common denominator in such systems, then, is independence with interconnectedness.

While reading Malinowski and Radcliffe-Brown and studying with Parsons, Luhmann became interested in the theory of systems. In the early stages of his theoretical development, Luhmann's view of the social system was not very different from that of Parsons. Social systems, in Luhmann's early work, consisted of real actions based upon shared meanings or interpretations. These actions and interpretations are, in turn, the result of expectations, both for one's own behavior and that of others. Such expectations are likely to be stable and consistent, or institutionalized and consensual. Thus, norms, roles, and institutions are the heart of the study and understanding of social systems (Poggi, 1979:xiii–xiv).

Words such as *systems, actions, norms,* and *institutions* are already familiar from the work of Parsons and Merton and the functionalists who preceded them. However, while indebted to Parsons, Luhmann "believes that Parsons always overestimated both the existence and the necessity of shared value commitments in modern society." Part of Luhmann's project was to explore "'alternatives to normative integration,' that is to say, ways in which modern society has maintained . . . forms of order and orderly change *without* relying on society-wide consensus about communal purposes," or relying on society-wide interconnectedness (Holmes and Larmore, 1982:xvii).

Social systems, according to Luhmann, consist primarily of communication networks. Even **socialization**, or the growth of the individual into her or his society and culture, is a result of communication: "All socialization occurs as social interpenetration; all social interpenetration, as communication" (1984:243). The gap in systems theory, claimed Luhmann, has only recently been filled with a theory of the media of communication (1982:350). Luhmann argued that systems are based on shared meanings, and shared meanings are always the result of communication. However, his departure from Parsons began when he argued that, although there are systems in the modern world, there is not a single overarching and integrated system striving for equilibrium.

Modern Society   From the beginning of his career, and increasingly later on, Luhmann emphasized two points about contemporary society: "the drastic intensification of societal complexity" and "the increasing external differentiation of the societal subsystems" (Poggi, 1979:xv). The first point means that modern society has no central institution. Aware of Marx's argument for a shift from the primacy of politics to the primacy of economics in the modern industrial world, Luhmann argued that there is *no* primary, or central, institution—politics or economics. To him modern society more closely resembles the telephone system than the solar system. As Luhmann's translators put it, "Today, a gradual process of increasing differentiation has brought into being a type of society that is relatively stable even though it has no single center and no subsector that can claim unchallenged supremacy" (Holmes and Larmore, 1982:xv). This idea is of concern to economists, and even more so to political scientists, who have fiercely criticized Luhmann's concept of a centerless or headless society (Savard, 1999:4).

His second point is that modern society is not a single social system with related parts, but several systems, including some commonly recognized institutions—such as law, religion, communication media, education, politics, and economics—and other systems consisting of organizations, personalities, and/or interactions. To Luhmann, each of these is a system, with the other systems as its environment. Society is like the telephone system and the interstate highway system: each is part of the other system's environment. The concepts of system and of function "no longer refer to 'the system' . . . but to the relationship between system and environment. . . . Everything that happens belongs to a *system* (or to many systems) and *always at the same time* to the *environment of other systems*" (Luhmann, 1984:176–177).

Luhmann's second point, about system "compartmentalization," must not be overstated. The telephone system is, after all, part of the same larger social system as the highways, and Luhmann did believe that modern society is characterized by a high degree of interdependence among social sectors. Compartmentalization was thus a relative term: Compared to preindustrial and early industrial societies, modern society exhibits much less consensual, communal, or societal solidarity. In fact, Luhmann's translators suggested,

> If we redefine the unity of society or social integration as "resistance to disintegration," it even becomes plausible to interpret compartmentalization as a palliative rather than as a threat. In one sense, at least, [this] is a mechanism for enhancing social integration. By localizing conflicts, a highly "parcelized" social order can prevent crises from spreading like brushfire from one social sector to another. In other words, or so Luhmann would have us believe, the "absence of a common life" is hardly a cause for unmitigated grief, since it may well ensure that society as a whole does not flare up like a box of matches. (Holmes and Larmore, 1982:xvi)

Thus, to continue with our analogy, when an accident occurs on the highway, the telephones are not usually affected; rather, they may be used to call for help. And when telephone lines are down, the repair truck uses the highways to go to the source of the problem. Again, a ship may be compartmentalized, so that if water enters one compartment, it can be closed off and the ship does not sink.

Trust   Luhmann's most readable work may well be his essay on trust. People put their **trust**, according to Luhmann, "in the self-evident matter-of-fact 'nature' of the world and of human nature every day," and "the necessity of trust can be regarded as the correct and appropriate starting point for the derivation of rules for proper conduct" (1979:4). Thus, we trust that a car will not lose a wheel at full speed, that a bridge will hold our car, and that the mechanic who worked on our car is knowledgeable and trustworthy. The more complex the world is, the more necessary is trust. Trust, wrote Luhmann,

> strengthens the capacity . . . for understanding and reducing complexity: it strengthens states as opposed to events and thus makes it possible to *live and to act with greater complexity in relation to events*. In terms of a well-known psychological theory, trust increases the "tolerance of uncertainty."
> This effect is not to be confused with instrumental mastery over events. (1979:15)

Mastery does not require trust, because we ourselves are determining the outcome. Ignorance, however, may require trust just as much as familiarity justifies it. We may be ignorant of the workings of an automobile, but we entrust it to a knowledgeable mechanic. "Familiarity is," wrote Luhmann, "a precondition for both trust and distrust" (1979:20). The more we know about another person (or system), the more we believe her (it) to be trustworthy or not. Thus, "familiarity and trust are . . . complementary ways of absorbing complexity": Familiarity is based on past experience, and trust on a willingness to take risks in the future (Luhmann, 1979:19).

The complexities and differential system functions of modern society demand trust, but also allow for distrust. On the system level,

> trust depends on the inclination towards risk being kept under control and on the quota of disappointments not becoming too large. If this is correct, then one could suppose that a system of higher complexity, which needs more trust, also needs at the same time more distrust, and therefore must institutionalize distrust, for example in the form of supervision. (Luhmann, 1979:89)

A large organization may have a time clock for its workers to punch in, and a floor supervisor to see to it that the work is being done. In other words, a complex world involves interpersonal and system trust and distrust. However, distrust, unless it is institutionalized—built into the rules—can be extremely exhausting or burdensome. It may "absorb the strength of the person who distrusts to an extent which leaves him little energy to explore and adapt to his environment in an objective and unprejudiced manner" (Luhmann, 1979:72).

Integrity is another word for trustworthiness. In a governmental body, for example, certain members are considered to have "personal integrity," while others are not. In addition, people may not trust an entire governmental body, causing them neither to vote nor to believe what politicians tell them. Such mass lack of trust can also be seen in relation to other subsystems of society. People trust in the value of money, and in the institutions or systems that administer it. But such system trust may be undermined by a rapid devaluing of a currency or by a bank's being unable to cover the withdrawals of its patrons (see Luhmann, 1979:50). The result of such an event may be system mistrust, resulting in a run on one or many banks.

One may trust an institution or another person for certain purposes but not for others. For example, one trusts that a bank is handling one's money well, but may not accept the bank's advice on how to invest it. Or one can "accept without question the opinion of one's colleague about a technical matter but nevertheless not risk lending him money 'personally'" (Luhmann, 1979:91).

Luhmann summarizes the role of trust in the complex modern world as follows:

> Trust reduces social complexity by going beyond available information and generalizing expectations of behavior in that it replaces missing information with an internally guaranteed security. It thus remains dependent on other reduction mechanisms developed in parallel with it, for example, those of law, of organization and, of course, those of language, but cannot, however, be reduced to them. Trust is not the sole foundation of the world; but a highly complex but nevertheless structured conception of the world could not be established without a fairly complex society, which in turn could not [function] without trust. (1979:94)

Risk   Living in the modern world requires not only trust but also the taking of risks, a subject that Luhmann examined in detail. We seek to make decisions that reduce risk;[3] we seek to ensure safety and security. In Luhmann's view, however, the best we can do is to normalize or accept it, and to calculate the likelihood of accident (1993:76).

Luhmann made an important distinction between **risk** and **danger**: We may make a decision in which we calculate or accept the risk involved; or we may be in a dangerous environment. Perhaps the simplest way to distinguish these two is to say: "I take a risk," or "I am in danger." Thus, if I drive 100 miles per hour, I am taking a risk, but I am also putting passengers and other drivers in danger. Smoking can be seen as a form of risk-taking, while asbestos in a ceiling is a danger.

Important areas involving risk and danger include technology, politics, economic life, and organizational behavior. Regarding technology, Luhmann suggested that more "than any other single factor, the immense expansion of technological possibilities has contributed to drawing public attention to the risks involved" (1993:83). Risky technologies may cause confidence to evaporate. For example, after World War II the danger of atomic and hydrogen bombs caused many people to try to reduce their danger by building "fallout shelters." Likewise, unknown technological complexities caused a fear of potential Y2K computer breakdowns.

With respect to politics, leaders may make risky decisions that bring the populace into danger. However, the closed nature of the political system—even in a supposed democracy—causes people to feel helpless about reducing risk through their own choices; they simply "leave it up to the leaders." With power, then, comes the risk of making mistakes (Luhmann, 1979:161). In addition, personified evil makes it possible to externalize blame for the dangers we feel incapable of lessening. Thus, in the Western world it has been useful to identify Mao Tse-tung, Idi Amin, Noriega, Khaddafi, Saddam Hussein, Slobodan Milosovic, and others as the risk-takers who have put us in danger (Luhmann, 1993:162, 171). However, new external threats must continually be identified, because over time the previously identified persons lose their usefulness as external personifications of evil and, therefore, danger.

In the realm of economics, Luhmann offered the analogy of the immune system, whose job it is to control disease. Deflation and inflation in the economy are immune system responses to fluctuations in money supply, demand, and so on. They are not harmless—they do affect individuals and businesses—but they are intended to reduce the risk of even greater variations (1993:177). In organizations, leaders continually make risky decisions: Should we expand, should we change to email from face-to-face contact, should we drop a line of goods, and so on. "The task of leadership would then . . . consist in weighing opportunities against risks" (1993:199).

Before writing his lengthy essay on risk, Luhmann presented in his 1984 book on *Social Systems* the following summary statement regarding modern-day risk:

> To be sure, we still have not been able to produce a theory of modern
> society. But we have experience enough with such things as: technology

---

[3] Today we attribute too much to decisions, even when the decision makers can't even be identified. One way risk is reduced psychologically (but not in reality) is to say to ourselves "they know what they are doing" (Luhmann, 1993:119).

and ecology; the volatility of international investments; . . . indispensable yet problematic political differentiation into "states," with war as the result; the acceleration of structural change; the dependence of notions of society on highly selective mass media; the demographic consequences of modern medicine; careers as the main form of the [mobile] integration of individuals and society; . . . with the consequence that the future affects the present above all in the form of risk. (1984:xlii)

Modern society, then, is so complex and so differentiated into subsystems that we live with a high level of both risk and danger, and we seek to reduce these by trust and by the control of distrust.

Power   Power, as noted above, places upon the individual or organization the responsibility of making risky decisions that may put others in danger. Luhmann's discussion of power followed to a great extent that of Weber. **Power,** he noted, has both personal and system characteristics. It may or may not involve the use of physical force or violence, but "the possibility of the use of violence *cannot be ignored* by the person affected." Power is asymmetrical, organized, and often centralized (Luhmann, 1979:149). Like the other aspects of life in modern systems, power requires communication: It is transmitted by communication, while at the same time communicating about itself—that is, about the power being asserted.

Luhmann saw power as more central to modern systems than Parsons admitted, and more open to misuse. In fact, Luhmann suggested that the twentieth century was one that "surpasses all others in the extent and efficiency of the misuse of power." Luhmann was not referring to Marx's "creaming off of surplus value by the ruling class," but to making risky decisions, obstructing needed actions by others, communicating faulty information about one's purposes, and ignoring obvious dangers (1979:162).

One complicating factor, of course, is the differentiation of society into semi-independent subsystems. It is simply impossible, Luhmann believed, even for a state—much less an educational or religious organization—to take actions that determine outcomes for everyone in a society. Power, like function, is fragmented. Although power is an important aspect of social systems, it is checked or limited by societal differentiation.

To summarize briefly, Luhmann might say that a normal or structured part of life in modern society is trusting those (persons, organizations) with power so as to reduce risks or to take risks that do not place us in unnecessary danger.

Autopoiesis   Perhaps the most difficult part of Luhmann's theoretical apparatus is what he called **autopoiesis**. The simplest definition is self-reference, or perhaps self-consciousness within one's context (Luhmann, 1984:487). With this concept, Luhmann was suggesting that human beings do not act blindly, simply on the basis of habits and norms. Rather, they are aware of their choices, of their contexts or systems, and of their environment. When I decide to go to a particular movie, for example, I am conscious of other choices I might make, such as staying home and watching TV; of what my friends are doing; of what is outside my social system, such as recreational activities I have never tried; and perhaps even of other societies that do not have such recreational activities.

The idea of self-reference enabled Luhmann to avoid the reduction of social life to the analysis of systems or norms. Self-reference, then, is at the heart of his view of social action. His theory of action includes not just the unconscious and systemic, but the self-aware, or conscious, choices that humans make. Because we live only in the present, we are continually reproducing our social worlds or systems. This self-referential reproduction, however, "would not be possible without an anticipatory recursivity" (Luhmann, 1984:446–447)—by which he meant expected response or anticipated outcome. Later in this chapter we will confront a somewhat different version of autopoiesis, or self-awareness, in Giddens's view of reflexivity.

Nature of Society, Humans, and Change

From the Middle Ages into the nineteenth century, according to Luhmann, the world was seen as a moral place. Human perfection was the goal, and *human nature* was seen as both good and evil. But this optimistic view had within it a contradiction:

> Doesn't it define the nature of humanity and its actions in a contradictory way: good and bad? . . . Materialists, moralists, utilitarians, and Rousseauists in turn called this nature good. They based their optimism on perfectibility. But this solution rests on an obvious theoretical mistake. "Good" is discussed on two different theoretical levels: within the disjuncture of good/bad and on the meta-level of nature. (Luhmann, 1984:380)

If human nature is good and perfectible, how can it also be both good and bad? Luhmann himself answered this question for the nineteenth century: Human perfection was considered socially realizable, but this "did not deny that this could founder on the general corruptibility of all nature" (1984:211). The goal was perfection and moral good, but human nature as seen in the nineteenth century was in reality dichotomous.

In terms of ideology, then, Luhmann clearly rejected the oversimplified radical nineteenth-century idea that humans were good and society was bad. The human being "is no longer the measure of society. This idea of humanism cannot continue. Who would seriously and deliberately want to maintain that society could be formed on the model of the human being" (1984:213)?

As for progressive, or liberal, and conservative thought, Luhmann recognized the existence of both in the modern world. Anything that exists, observed Luhmann, can become a theme for change in the hands of reformers or progressives, but "any proposal for change can be countered by questioning the reasons for it and by arguing for what already exists" (1979:144). Nothing in political or social life tells us which is correct.

> Whoever is in favor of something which might plausibly be characterized as "authority" or "domination" is **conservative**. Whoever wants to be "emancipated"—especially if he wants to foist "emancipation" on others—is **progressive**. Representatives of monopoly capitalism appear to be conservative. Representatives of . . . capital monopolism consider themselves progressive. (Luhmann, 1982:167, bold added)

Recalling the chapter's opening quote, Luhmann has been viewed by some as nonmoral in his view of society (Vandenberghe, 1999:2). However, others see him as leaning toward the more conservative views of his mentor, Parsons. His translators commented, "While no reader of Luhmann's work can fail to notice his ironic detachment and skepticism, neither is it possible to overlook his basic commitment to the overall advantages of functional differentiation" (Holmes and Larmore, 1982:xxxvi). Because of his emphasis on systems and functional differentiation, then, Luhmann may be interpreted as having conservative leanings, but he was hardly as conservative as Parsons.

A final word on Luhmann's ideology concerns values. Human beings evaluate people, things, and systems that matter to them. If these values are guided by an overview of the world, these values are ideological. "Values become ideological once this selective function in the orientation of action becomes conscious and is used in turn to evaluate values"—one's own or other people's (Luhmann, 1982:97).

What, then, was Luhmann's view of change? According to Luhmann, neither Parsons's theory of equilibrium nor the Darwinists' theory of evolutionary stages was, in fact, a theory of change. Luhmann characterized his own theory not as one of stable equilibrium, but as one of renewal and change—not static, but concerned with dynamic stability or instability (1984:49). Change can be planned or unplanned, but it is continuous. It can strengthen systems, alter them, or terminate them. Systems, according to Luhmann, are restless; and they are restless about their own restlessness. This can lead to self-destabilization, even to the point of self-destruction (1984:50).

Although Luhmann was critical of the evolutionary theories of developmental stages, he was in many ways an evolutionist. Much of his book *The Differentiation of Society* (1982) dealt with the way society has evolved toward greater and greater functional differentiation, and toward more and more independent subsystems. Sociocultural evolution involves the increasing complexity of society, but, claimed Luhmann, this is not a theory. It does not explain why differentiation has occurred, only that it has (1982:244).

Luhmann did not view massive and long-term social changes as necessarily requiring people's moral approval or disapproval (1982:364). Much, but not all, change up to the present can be covered by his terms "functional and system differentiation."[4] His view of change was clearly not an idealized, and certainly not a radical, one. He commented, for example, that we can "always moralize about the problem of unequal distribution. But we cannot actually advance

---

[4]Luhmann's translator summarized the many forms of differentiation mentioned in *The Differentiation of Society* (1982) as follows: (1) the privatization of religion; (2) the rise of territorial nation-states, with increasingly bureaucratic administrations; (3) the separation of property ownership and the social acceptability of individual profit-seeking; (4) the approval of "curiosity" as a legitimate motive for the pursuit of knowledge; (5) the release of art from civic and religious functions; (6) constitutional limits on political power; (7) marriage based on passionate love and personal choice, and the shrinkage of the basic kinship unit; (8) the birth of universal and compulsory public schooling; and (9) the shift in the basis of legality from immutable "natural law" to formal procedures for changing legal codes in an orderly way (Holmes and Larmore, 1982:364).

from unequal to equal distribution." Moralizing, to Luhmann, had ideological, not empirical, functions (1982:234–235). In his caustic way, he noted that the

> future is expected to bring about the communist society, an ecological disaster, emancipation from domination, or *l'homme integral*[5] extolled by Sartre and Merleau-Ponty. This, no doubt about it, is the future that cannot begin. It remains a present future and (at the very least) an infallible sign that social critics are on the scene. (1982:280)

To Luhmann, then, *human nature* was neutral, or, perhaps, unknown. Ideology was used by individuals and groups to guide their lives, but it, too, could be analyzed sociologically. And finally, change was ubiquitous and perhaps evolutionary, but hardly governable, at least not by ideology, and certainly not to be approved of or criticized.

Class, Gender, and Race

Class   Luhmann had little to say about gender and race, but he did provide some insights into class. He saw no chance "that a rebellion of the unpropertied classes against property owners could result in the utter abolition of the *difference* between owning and not owning" (1982:358). Much of Luhmann's attention to class, in fact, was focused on criticizing Marx's oversimplified view of both present and future. However, he also noted the alternate basis for hierarchy: "the fact that some persons are of better 'quality' than others and that they take precedence." This idea, noted Luhmann, had been superseded as society changed from stratified to differentiated (1984:468). In other words, in modern society, he argued, different does not mean better or worse—it simply means different(iated). Yet this does not mean that equality exists, or ever will. It simply means that hierarchy is not inherited; it is earned within one or more subsystems of society.

Was Luhmann critical of inequality, or what he called "stratified differentiation," in modern society? The following comment shows another reason why Luhmann is often identified as ideologically conservative: "Both empirical research and the critique of stratification, because of their moralistic preoccupations with domination, exploitation, and a general asymmetry in the distribution of life chances, have lost sight of this genuinely positive contribution of stratiform differentiation" (1982:264). Thus, Luhmann hardly had a theory of class or stratification, but simply said it existed, it would continue to exist, and it performed some positive functions for the modern world.

Gender and Race   On gender and race, Luhmann said surprisingly little—surprising because of the sheer volume and scope of his writings. One important point is what he did not do: He did not carry functional differentiation to the point of Parsons's gender differentiation, with males as task leaders and females

---

[5] *"L'homme integral"* is the unified or integrated or complete human being desired by these French philosophers.

as social-emotional leaders. Although most of his theory seemed to focus on male behaviors and characteristics, he did not indicate that his theory of systems, trust, and so on, was not applicable to females as well.

Luhmann noted what he called "the archaicism of race," as it was treated in the ancient world. Again, one can only infer from what he did not say. He did not indicate that race is an important factor in modern societal subsystems, and this would seem to be a serious oversight. But we must refrain from reading too much into what is missing from his writings.

Other Theories and Theorists

It has been impossible to introduce Luhmann's ideas without discussing Parsons and Marx. We have noted several times that Luhmann's systems theory began in and then outgrew that of Parsons. His debt to his mentor is made clear: "Parsons' theory is a milestone. . . . It has been the only attempt to begin with *a number of equally important functions* and then *to give a theoretical deduction of them*" (Luhmann, 1982:59).

Parsons never stated the importance of value consensus and normative orientation as strongly as his critics claimed he did, but according to Luhmann, he did overstate order. Luhmann's criticisms of Parsons involved the issues of functional primacy, complexity, and double contingency. Parsons posited primary and secondary functions; the primary ones involve mainly economics and politics. For Luhmann, however, no subsystem, such as the economic or political, determines what occurs in the other systems. Rather, each subsystem is at least somewhat autonomous and performs functions considered more or less important by a society.

The issue of complexity should be apparent by now. Schemes such as Parsons's AGIL are much too simple to deal with the subsystems of the modern industrial world (Luhmann, 1982:60). Finally, double contingency is the key factor by which Luhmann's theory of action goes beyond that of Parsons. For Parsons, social action takes place within the social system, as individuals (and whole societies) make choices governed by norms, the pattern variables, and so on. Double contingency, like autopoiesis, means that the individual thinks about the choices she or he makes, and about the contingent or reactive choices of others, or of a subsystem, to those choices. In other words, reflection makes choosing and acting much more complex than Parsons saw them. Thus, much of Luhmann's reaction to Parsons is simply that his work was too neat, unfinished, and did not go far enough (1982:47).

Luhmann's criticism of Emile Durkheim resembles one of the criticisms he raised regarding Parsons: We do not "begin with normative presuppositions. Nor, like Durkheim or Parsons, do we view the concept of norms as the ultimate explanation of the facticity or possibility of social order pure and simple" (1984:325). He also found Durkheim frustratingly oversimplified, in concepts such as organic solidarity and collective consciousness, and accused him of locking away "complex relational problems in compact concepts" (1982:17). Luhmann himself, as we have seen, was unwilling to simplify for the sake of clarity or readability.

Luhmann saw Max Weber's faults as different from those of Parsons. Whereas Parsons was too system-oriented, the "concept of system plays no important role in Weber's terminology. 'System' seems to have been inconsequential for the development of Weber's concepts of action, social action, social relation, and association" (Luhmann, 1982:41). However, he agreed with Weber that social groups consist of social actions. "It follows automatically that persons are never entirely incorporated into a social system" (1982:42). For Luhmann, then, interactional systems and social systems are separable, instead of the former simply being a subpart of the latter. Luhmann saw Weber as underemphasizing the importance of the system, and Parsons as overemphasizing it.

One further point concerns Weber's view of bureaucratic structures. Luhmann—and others—criticized Weber for outlining the characteristics of bureaucracies without doing justice to the complex interactions and behaviors within them. As Luhmann put it, "the actual difficulties of behavior and decision-making in bureaucratic organizations and the problems of making compromises between complex, competing demands within a relatively broad temporal horizon do not get discussed" (1982:46).

In his essay on trust, Luhmann referred to Merton's self-fulfilling prophecy. Distrust, noted Luhmann, "has an inherent tendency to endorse and reinforce itself in social interaction" (1979:74). In other words, if we do not trust people, we treat them as, and perhaps even make them, untrustworthy. Without referring directly to him, Luhmann also repeated an insight of Georg Simmel. In a sharply differentiated society, it is difficult to "combine a plurality of roles into a coherent life story" (Holmes and Larmore, 1982:xxi). Simmel had noted a century earlier that the modern individual sometimes plays roles that reinforced each other, but often simply "pigeonholes" incompatible behaviors. Luhmann added that "in extreme cases there are people, or social systems, who earn trust simply by remaining fixedly and immovably what they are" (1979:61). This is, to use David Riesman's language, the inner-directed individual, or John Wayne type, who has consistent, internalized orientations and does not adjust to the expectations of group or setting.

Luhmann, finally, spoke to many of the same issues as Anthony Giddens, the focus of the final portion of this chapter.

Critique and Conclusions

Luhmann may be, as one translator put it, "the most original German sociologist since Max Weber" (Holmes and Larmore, 1982:xxxvii). His central theoretical principles were (1) increasing functional and structural differentiation, (2) noncentralized, semi-independent societal subsystems, and (3) their combined outcome in complexity. Under the umbrella of systems theory, he introduced trust, risk, power, and autopoiesis—the self-awareness and self-consciousness of both individuals and systems. The modern person or group, that is, does not act just to satisfy church, government, or employer, but weighs alternatives and others' potential responses before acting. This, of course, is not entirely healthy; it reminds us of the idea of "future shock," or decision-making overload. "One of the psychological difficulties of living in modern society," admitted Luhmann, was "the disorienting abundance of choices that threaten to inundate the individual" (Holmes and Larmore, 1982:xxii).

One of the two major criticisms of Luhmann is that he never reduced the complexity of the modern world for the sake of readability. All his work was complex, but especially his "nonlinear" book on *Social Systems*. His insights seem worth grappling with, but they are almost randomly assembled, use extremely abstract concepts, and utilize few illustrations to increase the reader's understanding.

The second criticism is that Luhmann's conservatism was only partially concealed. He was highly critical of Marx, emphasized functions and systems, and argued that social inequality is permanent and performs some positive functions. Even though he was concerned about overload and future shock, critics and radicals see him as analytically beclouding his acceptance of and support for the *modern, industrial, capitalist world.*

Many of Luhmann's theoretical insights mirror, complement, and in some cases disagree with, those of the British theorist Anthony Giddens. We turn now to Giddens, and will close the chapter with comparisons of the two.

Anthony Giddens (1938–)

If any other contemporary theorist comes close to being as productive as Luhmann, it is Anthony Giddens. He has produced 31 books, now published in 22 languages, and more than 200 articles and reviews ("Anthony Giddens: Meet the Director," 1999:1). He is better known than Luhmann not only in the English-speaking world, but in most of the scholarly world.

Giddens was born in 1938 in North London. He was the first member of his family to go to the university, graduating from Hull in 1959. He completed his M.A. at London School of Economic in 1961, after which he taught at Leicester until the late 1960s. From there he went to Simon Fraser in Canada, and then to the University of California at Los Angeles (UCLA). He was at UCLA during the Vietnam War protests of the late 1960s, and his glimpse of U.S. sociology and life broadened his European view of the world of class and authority. From there he went to Cambridge, where he was a sociology lecturer, reader, and then professor from 1970 until 1997 ("Anthony Giddens: Factfile," 1999:1). At that time he became Director of the London School of Economics and Political Science, where he is at the present time.

In 1985 Giddens founded and became director of the Polity Press, which is still in operation. In 1999 he gave the Reith lectures on the BBC. He is often referred to as Britain's developer of "left-of-center politics," and as Tony Blair's guru ("Anthony Giddens: Meet the Director," 1999:1).

Giddens's first three books were on Weber, Durkheim, and the major nineteenth-century theorists, including Marx ("Anthony Giddens: Publications," 1998:1). This was hardly an atypical way to begin a career in theory, but by the mid-1970s Giddens had begun to evolve his own theoretical position, beginning with a focus on structuration. Thus, Giddens became known at first for his treatment of the "classics," before accepting the challenge of producing original contributions to sociological theory.

Giddens's Central Theories and Methods

Structuration   After his work on the nineteenth-century social theory classics, the heart of Giddens's work until the late 1980s was structuration:

> Every process of action is a production of something new, a fresh act; but at the same time all action exists in continuity with the past, which supplies the means of its initiation. *Structure thus is not to be conceptualised as a barrier to action, but as essentially involved in its production:* even in the most radical processes of social change which, like any others, occur in time. (Giddens, 1979:70)

Note that **structuration** actually describes an action: "to structurate" or "to do or produce structure." Giddens placed great emphasis on individual action: "As a leading theorem of the theory of structuration, I advance the following: *every social actor knows a great deal about the conditions of reproduction of the society of which he or she is a member*" (1979:5). As one commentator explains: "The theory of structuration is an attempt to overcome the dualism that he sees as plaguing other theories—a dualism that gives priority either to actors or to social structures. . . . Structures are created by humans, but they, in turn, constrain and enable human action" (Kivisto, 1998:148).

Giddens, then, was trying to bring the individual back into social theory. Calling his theory a "non-functionalist manifesto," Giddens argued that any theory that treats social systems as ends in themselves is invalid (1979:7), and he claimed he was trying to recover the subject or actor without lapsing into subjectivism or nonobjectivism (1979:44). Arguing that both subject and object—individual and system—exist, Giddens emphasized the "fundamentally recursive character of social life" and "the mutual dependence of structure and agency" (Giddens, 1979:69). **Recursivity** is feedback, or conscious concern with outcomes or results. Thus, it parallels Luhmann's idea of autopoiesis—self-reflection or self-consciousness.

Giddens argued that structure-functionalism ordinarily treats structure as constraint, or as opposed to freedom, and as based on agreement or consensus on the rules or norms that constrain individuals. While Giddens was perhaps overstating the constraining nature of order in functionalism, he wanted to emphasize order not as a barrier to action, but as in interplay with the actor—as a mixing of freedom and constraint (1979:70). Even the rules of interaction are reconstituted through action and interaction. Giddens, then, reconceptualized the duality of the social world from "individual and society" into the relation between "agency and structure" (Giddens, 1984:162).

To summarize many of the main points of the theory, as expressed in various sources, Giddens emphasized (1) human *agency*, or the rational/deciding actor; (2) *reflexivity*, which is not merely self-consciousness, but is "the monitored character of the ongoing flow of social life"; and (3) *structure*, or the continually reconstructed result of rules, resources, and agency (see Giddens, 1982:15–16, 1984:2–3, 376–377).

Modernity Giddens's second major concern, though less theoretical than structuration, is what he calls "late *modernity*." This has been his major interest since the beginning of the 1990s. By modernity, Giddens refers

> to the institutions and modes of behavior established first of all in post-feudal Europe, but which in the twentieth century increasingly have become world-historical in their impact. "Modernity" can be understood as roughly equivalent to "the industrialized world," so long as it be recognised that industrialism is not its only institutional dimension. (1982:15–16)

It is important to note that Giddens speaks of "late modern" society, not post-modern or post-industrial society. By this means he emphasizes historical continuity and change, rather than disjuncture (Kivisto, 1998:147).

Giddens's distinguishes between **capitalism**—a highly competitive system of production with labor markets operating on a global scale—and **industrialism**, which refers to the use of machine technology to control and transform nature (Kivisto, 1998:149). Besides industry, the most recognizable feature of this late modern world is the nation-state. In addition, though not to the same extent as Luhmann does, Giddens notes the importance of communication in tying the modern world together (1982:24).

The modern world has made possible survival, even "the good life," for an increasing proportion of its population. The nation-state provides the opportunity for democracy, for individual agency within a complex world. In *Beyond Left and Right* (1994) and *The Third Way* (1998), Giddens asserts that old "left" ideas are out of date, while those of the "right" are contradictory and even dangerous. His social democratic (liberal) "third way" is not just a theory but an action program, aimed at rekindling political activism and idealism (1994). The retreat of the gods and of tradition, he argues, has freed organizations and movements in the modern world for "reflexive self-regulation," meaning that we can contemplate and then make our own history (1984:203).

The subparts of Giddens's theory of modernity include distanciation, power, trust, and risk. **Distanciation** refers to the fact that relationships are no longer tied to specific locales. While this has been true since the invention of Morse code and the airplane, it is infinitely more so at the turn of the twenty-first century than ever before, thanks to the computer. AT&T introduced the slogan "Reach out and touch someone," and in the age of e-mail it takes only a few seconds to touch someone in Singapore, Sweden, or South Africa (Kivisto, 1998:149).

An important aspect of Giddens's theory of both structuration and modernity is **power**, or agency—the capacity to make decisions and do things (1979:69). Power is not a resource; the media are resources, and so are social connections (1984:10, 1982:39). Power both constrains and enables. Power as constraint is not force, it is restriction of choice. In other words, even without the power that goes with domination, individuals in the modern world still have a certain amount of power (or control) over the choices they make (1984:176, 257–262).

Power, then, is not only domination, but also "transformative capacity," or the ability to make things happen (1979:91). Thus, to Giddens, the modern world is "empowering," because it has freed people from the strictures of traditional, preindustrial society.

Giddens argues that the reason orthodox (structure-functional) theory does not explain social action is that it ignores the importance of power—both individual and structural (1979:253). To Giddens, power or capability is the central feature of social action, so if constraint, even by norms, is the focus of a theory, it becomes impossible to understand action.

Like Luhmann, Giddens also refers to trust and risk. As with Luhmann, trust is required in the modern world because we know so little about the systems with which we have to deal. Giddens defines **trust** as "the vesting of confidence in persons or in abstract systems, made on the basis of a 'leap of faith' which brackets ignorance or lack of information" (1991:244).

The issue that Giddens raises that is most closely related to Luhmann's theory concerns **risk**. To Luhmann, you will recall, risk involved politics, economics, technology, and other aspects of life in a highly complex and differentiated modern society. Giddens emphasizes even more than Luhmann the agency or "choice" aspect of risk. An actor may calculate the risk involved in a certain conduct in terms of sanctions "being actually applied, and may be prepared to submit to them as a price to be paid for achieving a particular end" (1979:87). For example, in the movie *A Few Good Men*, a U.S. Marine takes food to a fellow soldier who is being punished, consciously taking the risk that he too will be sanctioned if his "good deed" is found out. It is discovered, and he is expelled from the Marine Corps, having run the risk by doing what he considered right.

However, a second part of Giddens's view of risk goes beyond Luhmann's. Human beings continually try to calculate future risk. In a rapidly changing modern society, individuals attempt to lessen risk through planning. A good example is health or life insurance. Giddens calls this "colonization of the future." Thinking in terms of risk may be uncomfortable, but because nothing can be taken for granted, many individuals make decisions aimed at risk reduction and peace of mind (Giddens, 1991:133–134).

Giddens lists four risks that are more or less specific to the late modern world: (1) the surveillance, governmental and otherwise, that none can escape; (2) escalation of military power resulting in the risk of nonsurvival of the species; (3) the potential collapse of economic growth, because of capitalism's erratic qualities; and (4) the ecological and environmental limits that constrain capitalism (1990:55–63). As noted earlier,

> Low-probability, high-consequence risks will not disappear in the modern world, although in an optimal scenario they could be minimized. . . .
> Relatively small-scale [sic] events, such as the dropping of atomic bombs on Hiroshima and Nagasaki or the accidents at Three Mile Island or Chernobyl, give some sense of what could happen. (1990:134)

The Self   Giddens has devoted considerable attention to G. H. Mead's theory of the self. Although hardly an original insight, Giddens notes that Mead's view of the "I," "me," and "self" is reflexive, but their origin is not made clear. More important, Mead's theory does not situate the reflexive and reflective individual within the differentiated larger society. Giddens addresses the influence of the self on others, society, and even global strategies (1991:214). He believes that agency and structuration fill the gap in Mead's social-psychological theory.

In fact, Giddens's view of the modern self is quite different from those of Mead and Freud. In his books on self-identity (1991) and intimacy (1992), he discusses the connections between modern life and the individual. The individual exists within a structure but is also agent, meaning that the self must be created. In Giddens's view, the late modern world gives "rise to new mechanisms for forging self-identities, with the self being both object and agent in the process" (Snow and Heirling, 1992:847). One further issue in self-creation is self-actualization, or the effort to make oneself into what one wishes to be. To Giddens, self-actualization is possible because of reflexivity, or self-reflection, but is also a goal that is often impossible to attain.

Intimacy in the late modern world is often a matter of one's internal state, not constrained by external factors or demands such as the necessity of parenthood or some other role. Whether a "pure" relationship is or can be altogether satisfying is an empirical question (Giddens, 1992:3). The pure nature of relationships also causes them to be exceptionally breakable or fragile.

In summary, then, the modern world involves both human agency and constraint, which together are close to the definition of structuration. That world includes distanciation, power, trust, risk, and the created self.

Nature of Society, Humans, and Change

From Giddens's discussion of the almost overwhelming risks of modern life, one might assume that he is a pessimist regarding the future. However, as a liberal, he sees these risks as possibilities, not problems or inevitabilities. He sees the labor, peace, and environmental movements as guaranteed neither of success nor of failure. Giddens's liberalism has been described as "plausible utopian realism" (Kivisto, 1998:151).

Despite Giddens's apparent optimism regarding human agency, he does not define *human nature* as good, and certainly not as perfectible. Speaking in the same way as the twentieth-century evolutionists, Giddens notes "human control over nature." This, he says, is actually "the emergence of an internally referential system of knowledge and power." The result is that the world is now, for the most part, a created environment, consisting of humanly structured systems. Note, however, that he refers to "human control over nature," not "control over human nature" (1982:144). Though not seeing human nature as good, he views it positively enough that an increase in human agency or choice is seen as a good thing, and as capable of producing positive results in the late modern world.

Change, Giddens suggests, can be brought about through human agency. It is not evolutionary, in the sense of natural selection, or adaptation, or stages, but it is ubiquitous—the modern world can be defined as a world of change. As we have already noted, Giddens is sympathetic with—even positive toward—

this late modern world of human agency and structuration. But, surprisingly, there are times when he sounds a little like Max Weber—that is, critical of the changing world. "The sheer sense of being caught up in massive waves of global transformation is perturbing. . . . Understanding the juggernaut-like nature of modernity goes a long way towards explaining why, in conditions of high modernity, crisis becomes normalised" (Giddens, 1991:183–184). In addition, modernity creates tensions for the self: unification versus fragmentation, options versus powerlessness and meaninglessness, personal versus commodified experience, and authority versus uncertainty (1991:201). Thus, the criticism that Giddens sees the modern world "through rose-colored glasses" is at least an overstatement.

Giddens's ideology, as noted previously, is distinctly liberal and social democratic. In fact, he treats ideology as virtually synonymous with conservatism: "the capability of dominant groups or classes to make their own sectional interests appear to others as universal ones" (1979:6). Viewing himself as a liberal and critical theorist, he is also opposed to any social thought, Marxist or otherwise, that treats capitalism as evil and in need of overthrow. In summary, Giddens believes in the efficacy of human thought and action, and sees the modern world as a mixture of freedom and structure, with both negative characteristics and positive possibilities.

Class, Gender, and Race

Class   Giddens makes it clear that, in his view, "Marx's assessment of the endemic character of class conflict in capitalism is closer to contemporary industrial reality than the views which Durkheim offered" (1982:122). He agrees with Marx's view of the contradictory nature of capitalist classes, "entangled in the asymmetrical relations between class division and social or welfare rights," and that the "buying and selling of time, as labour time, is surely one of the most distinctive features of modern capitalism" (1984:144).

However, Giddens is not a Marxist. Speaking of rule by the bourgeoisie, he asserts, "we cannot today be content to leave their positive features unanalyzed" (1982:176, 178). In addition, he argues that "all social actors, no matter how lowly, have some degree of penetration of the social forms which oppress them" (1979:72). Classes are not isolated; interaction between them occurs. Even humor, he observes, can be used against the rulers in order to lessen the burden of disadvantage (1979:72). Whether humor speaks to Marx's serious issues of oppression and exploitation is at least questionable. And Giddens's emphasis on agency, even that of the oppressed, is a far cry from Sigmund Freud's argument that we are all oppressed by civilization.

Gender   As for gender, Giddens notes that modern society has dichotomized reason as a male characteristic, and emotion as female. "The identifying of women with unreason, whether in serious vein (madness) or in seemingly less consequential fashion (women as creatures of caprice), turned them into the emotional underlaborers of modernity" (1990:200). Men, as the rational gender, were seen as the logical actors in and controllers of both the extrafamilial, or larger, society and the internal society of family.

Not only was the world of rationality and politico-economic activity viewed as male, but feminism as a movement was oriented primarily toward opening that sphere to women. "Women's identities were defined so closely in terms of the home and the family that they 'stepped outside' into social settings in which the only available identities were those offered by male stereotypes" (Giddens, 1991:216). Seeing no place for emotion in his theory, Giddens fails to recognize that feminism-humanism also seeks to open emotional life to the male. As a part of his theory of modern society and its opportunities, however, Giddens is not surprised by women's seeking of new freedoms and opportunities. Change is ubiquitous, and gender roles are being freed.

Race   Although Giddens has written at some length about class and gender, he has said little about race. He has used ethnic segregation to illustrate how a social pattern results from individual motives and activities—the end result, ghetto-like areas, being an unintended consequence (latent function) of a large number of intentional individual behaviors (1984:13). But he has given little further attention to race or ethnicity as a factor in the late modern world.

Other Theories and Theorists

Perhaps more than any other recent theorist, Giddens has commented on other sociological theorists. Comte, Marx, Weber, Durkheim, Mead, Parsons, Merton, and even Luhmann are all either referred to directly or their ideas used. He criticized the early-nineteenth-century sociologist Auguste Comte for trying to use science, including social science, to "generate a moral ethos" that could replace traditional beliefs (1991:74–75). Humans, as active creators of society, are no longer likely to simply react to revelation or believe in their own creations.

We have already seen Giddens's sympathy with and disagreement with Marx, and his concern with the incompleteness of Weber's view of bureaucracy. These reactions, however, were hardly original with Giddens. He criticized Durkheim, and later Parsons, for overemphasizing the importance of constraint and order in social structure, to the neglect of agency and enablement. As Giddens puts it, "One person's constraint is another's enabling" (1984:170–176).

Having already noted the problem with Parsons's structure-functionalism, we should also note some of Giddens's responses to Robert Merton. Merton's notions of latent functions and unintended consequences may make sense of apparently irrational conduct, but "to suppose that such a demonstration of a functional relation provides a reason for the existence of a practice is mistaken" (Giddens, 1984:12). Such an argument may satisfy the observer, but it is not necessarily an explanation for behavior.

Recalling Merton's discussion of why sociological findings are ignored, Giddens observed that this is usually not because they are too outlandish or unexpected, but because they are too well known and familiar. "Where social research reveals that what actors believe about the conditions of their own action, or other features of their society, are in fact the case, its findings will necessarily appear banal or unilluminating." But, as Merton stated, when findings show commonsense beliefs to be wrong, social science can appear revelatory (Giddens, 1979:249).

Critique and Conclusions

Several commentators have argued that Giddens's attention to agency as well as structure adds an important dimension to contemporary theorizing. Structure-functionalism focused so completely on function and order as to virtually negate any sort of human control. Giddens, according to Kivisto (1998), "has played and will continue to play a singularly important role in the ongoing act of examining and reflecting on the human condition in the contemporary world" (152).

However, not all evaluations of Giddens's work are so favorable. Stjepan Mestrovic's recent book on Giddens's theory is extremely critical. Some of his criticisms, as of Giddens's view of women and his view of the modern world, are greatly overstated. However, two criticisms deserve mention. The first concerns Giddens's emphasis on human agency, and the second is on Giddens's optimistic view of the modern world.

According to Giddens, "Every competent member of every society knows a great deal about the institutions of that society: such knowledge is not *incidental* to the operation of society" (Giddens, 1979:71). For participants, this knowledge is greater closer to their day-to-day activities, rather than further away (Giddens, 1979:250). Both Luhmann and Mestrovic, however, question this assumption. According to Luhmann, citizens today are overwhelmed with information they are too busy, or too stressed, to analyze. They lose interest in the political sphere, feeling powerless to affect it, and even in their own milieu they feel incapable of controlling its complexities (Savard, 1999:3). Mestrovic adds that "most people seem to feel helpless concerning the course of world events, . . . yet they are comforted by Giddens' observations that they can still feel empowered and exercise agency in local milieux" (1998:149). And Snow and Heirling (1992) wonder "exactly what proportion of humanity . . . Giddens really address[es]"—that is, how many people in today's world actually feel and act like effective agents.

According to Mestrovic (1998:109),

> Giddens fails to explain the miracle by which human agents communicate with each other; he fails to explain how agents come to perceive social structure; and he fails to explain the origins of the agent's *faith* that his or her actions will result in specific consequences. For Giddens, all these aspects of agency and structure are seemingly self-begotten, which is not an adequate sociological explanation.

Thus, rather than a sense of agency and control, people today are more likely to feel a sense of fatalism, even apathy, about making an impact on others or on their environment (Mestrovic, 1998:206).

Giddens's theory is of a rational world in which individual actors are effective, and in which emotion and suffering apparently have little place. Although he recognizes the presence of "low-probability, high-consequence risks," such as nuclear obliteration, he seems to minimize such "relatively small-scale events" as the bombing of Hiroshima and Nagasaki (1990:134). This concerns Mestrovic greatly, and his response is full of emotion:

> After five years of dialogue, negotiation, and touting of Western human rights standards, the West essentially let the Serbs keep the spoils of their

genocide in Bosnia. It is incumbent upon Giddens to explain how this was possible despite all his lofty theorizing about dialogue, reflexivity, democracy, and globalization. (1998:142)

Had he written a year later, Mestrovic might have added that the eventual response of bombing would hardly fit Giddens's view of a rational world either.

Final Thoughts

Mestrovic's final criticism of Giddens might be raised regarding Luhmann as well. Mestrovic noted

the trouble Giddens's readers have in trying to understand him, decipher his jargon, and agree on what he means. Yet the new leisure class is satisfied with this lack of clarity, for it means that those who say they have read and understood Giddens have achieved an honor reserved for the very few. (1998:216)

Readability is not a criterion on which all the theorists in this volume necessarily rank high. But, as we asked at the beginning, are Luhmann and Giddens "worth it"? The answer is yes, on several grounds.

First, they are quite contemporary—more so than mid-twentieth-century writers such as Parsons and Merton—and as such have not tried to reduce the complexity that confronts us at the beginning of the twenty-first century. Whether that world is made up of headless subsystems as Luhmann proposed, or is as alterable and democratically viable as Giddens argues, the reader may decide. Likewise, we must think about reflexivity and risk in today's world.

Second, Luhmann and Giddens are not simply conservative and liberal, respectively. Neither is, or should be, that easy to label. Much of Luhmann's thought is demoralized, if not pessimistic, as well as conservative, while Giddens at times comes across as conservative instead of liberal.

Third, as a result of all this, Luhmann and Giddens form an excellent bridge to the radical, change, and modernist theories that lie just ahead.

References

"Anthony Giddens: Factfile." 1999. http://www.lse.ac.uk/Giddens/factfile.htm

"Anthony Giddens: Meet the Director." 1999. http://www.lse.ac.uk/Giddens/meet.htm

"Anthony Giddens: Publications." 1998. http://www.lse.ac.uk/Giddens.publications.htm

Giddens, Anthony. 1979. *Central Problems in Social Theory: Action, Structure and Contradiction in Social Analysis*. Berkeley: University of California Press.

———. 1982. *Profiles and Critiques in Social Theory*. Berkeley: University of California Press.

———. 1984. *The Constitution of Society*. Berkeley: University of California Press.

———. 1990. *The Consequences of Modernity*. Stanford, CA: Stanford University Press.

———. 1991. *Modernity and Self-Identity: Self and Society in the Late Modern Age*. Cambridge: Polity Press.

———. 1992. *The Transformation of Intimacy*. Stanford, CA: Stanford University Press.

———. 1994. *Beyond Left and Right*. Cambridge: Polity Press.

———. 1998. *The Third Way: The Renewal of Social Democracy*. London: Polity Press.

Holmes, Stephen, and Charles Larmore. 1982. "Introduction." In Niklas Luhmann, *The Differentiation of Society* (pp. ii–xxxvii). New York: Columbia University Press.

Kivisto, Peter. 1998. *Key Ideas in Sociology*. Thousand Oaks, CA: Pine Forge Press.

Knodts, Eva M. 1995. "Foreword." In Niklas Luhmann, *Social Systems* (pp. i–lii). Stanford: Stanford University Press.

Luhmann, Niklas. 1979. *Trust and Power* (Howard Davis, John Raffan, and Kathryn Rooney, Trans.). New York: John Wiley & Sons. (Two essays originally published in 1973 and 1975)

———. 1982. *The Differentiation of Society* (Stephen Holmes and Charles Larmore, Trans.). New York: Columbia University Press.

———. 1984/1995. *Social Systems* (John Bednarz, Jr., Trans.). Stanford, CA: Stanford University Press.

———. 1993. *Risk: A Sociological Theory* (Rhodes Barrett, Trans.). New York: Walter de Gruyter.

Mestrovic, Stjepan. 1998. *Anthony Giddens: The Last Modernist*. London: Routledge.

Poggi, Gianfranco. 1979. "Introduction." In Niklas Luhmann, *Trust and Power* (Howard Davis, John Raffan, and Kathryn Rooney, Trans.). New York: John Wiley & Sons.

Savard, Nelly. 1999. "Niklas Luhmann: The Political Section of His Theory." http://www.webb.net/sites/sociocyberforum//n_savard1.html

Snow, David A., and Joseph Heirling. 1992. "The Beleaguered Self." *Contemporary Sociology, 21*, 846–848.

Vandenberghe, Frederic. 1999. "Niklas Luhmann, 1927–1998." http://Rp/biog/94luhmn

SECTION II

Criticism, Marxism, and Change

In the previous section we looked at the more-or-less "official" twentieth-century conservative capitalist theory and ideology of functionalism, followed by Luhmann's and Giddens's expansions on and deviations from this theme. Now we come to three chapters emphasizing criticism and change.

The two great European wars of the twentieth century and the Great Depression of the 1930s increased Marxists' confidence in the demise of capitalism. However, critics of the Soviet Union's Stalinist socialism also raised questions about whether the Soviet model was the one to follow. In addition, many of Marx's principles, such as the labor theory of value, increasing misery of the poor, and the final revolution, were being criticized by both bourgeois economists and those sympathetic to Marxism.

Starting in the 1930s, the Frankfurt (or Critical) School, described in Chapter 4, was in dialogue with both capitalism and Marxism. Rejecting Marxist determinism and Russia's bureaucratic and totalitarian regime, this school of thought—including Max Horkheimer, T. W. Adorno, Erich Fromm, Herbert Marcuse, and others—reduced the role of economics by integrating it with political questions. In addition, criticism was broadened to include psychologized—Freudian—versions of alienation, working-class fragmentation, and even family issues (Bottomore, 1983).

Jurgen Habermas, a second-generation critical theorist, discussed the twin crises in rationality and legitimation, the former resulting from economic contradictions and the latter from a loss of popular loyalty. Together, according to Habermas (1973:49), these result in a crisis of motivation, leading to noncommitment or noninvolvement. The Frankfurt School, then, is critical of twentieth-century Western capitalism as well as of simplified classical Marxism.

The rise and fall of Russian communism, coupled with dramatic events in Western Europe, led to serious theoretical discussions and disagreements among committed Marxists. Those whose views are presented in Chapter 5 include

Nicos Poulantzas, Louis Althusser, Raya Dunayevskaya, and Erik Olin Wright. Among the issues they raise are the following: (1) Of what does societal influence or dominance consist? Is it more than control of the means of production? (2) Is Soviet socialism Marxist at all, or is it a form of state capitalism, only slightly different from that of the Western nations? (3) What is the nature of the modern nation-state? (4) What is the difference between twentieth-century monopoly capitalism and the entrepreneurial capitalism about which Marx wrote? (5) Is history predetermined toward the final revolution, is it full of contradictions unique to specific times and places, or is it a result of rational choices made by Giddens-type "actors"?

In short, then, what is the condition of Marxism at the turn of the twenty-first century, after the fall of Soviet communism and the apparent victory of capitalism's "new world order"? Erik Olin Wright, an academic Marxist, has avoided throwing the theoretical and analytical Marxist "baby" out with the Soviet "bathwater." During the 1990s, Wright spoke to many of the questions raised by the Soviet Union's collapse, and his work gives a clear view of Marxism at present.

Chapter 6 focuses on change from a world perspective. Evolutionary optimism, which seemed to disappear with World War I, reappeared, especially in the United States after World War II. The Marshall Plan and other U.S. initiatives were based on the belief that the rest of the world wants to be "just like us"—and will be, with our help. However, not all evolutionary thinking was that optimistic, nor that simplistic, as illustrated in the work of Elman Service.

Chapter 6 also introduces the "world system" theory of Immanuel Wallerstein, who notes that the peripheral parts of the world are not necessarily developing or catching up with Western industrialism—nor do they necessarily want to—but the world is a single system. At the close of Chapter 6, Theda Skocpol introduces nonevolutionary and non-Marxist views of revolutionary change. What conditions give rise to revolutions, and what are their outcomes?

Thus, by the time you complete these three chapters, you will have examined critical views of both capitalism and Marxism, as well as current theories of social change.

References

Bottomore, T. B. 1983. "Frankfurt School." In T. B. Bottomore (Ed.), *A Dictionary of Marxism* (pp. 182–188). Oxford: Blackwell.

Habermas, Jurgen. 1973. *Legitimation Crisis*. London: Heinemann.

Chapter 4

Critical Theory
The Frankfurt School and Habermas

A persistent hope for many of the Marxist theorists you will encounter was that the proletariat would eventually come to their senses and overthrow oppressive capitalist society. By the 1920s, a number of Western theorists had started to despair that this would ever occur. In fact, the 1917 socialist revolution in the semifeudal Russian state seemed to call into question the original Marxist analysis of capitalism. Many social theorists felt a return to the drawing board was in order to try to discover why the revolution was delayed, despite the persistence of inequality and alienation, and what could be done to alter the situation in order to usher in the change to a new socialist state. This was the central focus for the work of the theorists examined in this chapter.

Some social theorists have maintained their optimism about an eventual socialist transformation despite the revelations of less desirable or equitable conditions under former socialist regimes in the twentieth century. But in the view of many Western social theorists at the beginning of the twenty-first century, capitalism seems to have won, and they see little point in pursuing an old, discredited nineteenth-century dream of an equitable, planned society. However, the view from many of the countries in Africa, or Central Asia, or the Russian Republic itself, as well as among the dispossessed in capitalist states, is less celebratory about the triumph of capitalism. Consequently, it is worth considering the explanations offered by the critical theorists as to why the twentieth-century proletariat failed to transform the world as well as reflecting on the possibility that a revolutionary class can still be identified in the twenty-first century.

The Institute of Social Research

The Institute of Social Research at the University of Frankfurt was established in 1921. This was a period of turmoil and instability in Germany and in Europe in general. Despite these conditions, the revolution anticipated by many Marxist theorists did not occur. What did transpire was an increasing conservatism that in Germany culminated in the misnamed National Socialist regime.

The establishment of the Institute was made possible by an endowment from a wealthy German expatriate, Hermann Weil, who lived in Argentina. Weil had made his fortune shipping grain to Europe. His son, Felix Weil, was sent to the University of Frankfurt, where he obtained a doctorate in political science. While at Frankfurt, Felix Weil became associated with various radical groups, and he conceived the idea of an independent research institution for Marxist studies and the study of anti-Semitism (Jay, 1973:31–32). Felix Weil persuaded his father to endow the Institute, and Felix himself was associated with the venture until the onset of World War II, when he returned to Argentina to look after the family business.

In the 1930s, anti-Semitism was increasingly evident in Germany, fueled by the National Socialist fascists. One of the major research tasks for the Institute was the analysis of anti-Semitism as well as research into social and cultural conditions for an emancipated, equitable society. The Institute's financial independence was fortuitous when, in the 1930s, the Jewish members of the Institute were forced into exile. The Institute relocated to Columbia University in 1934 under the directorship of Max Horkheimer. Thus, the "revolutionary and Marxist" research Institute resettled in "the center of the capitalist world, New York City" (Jay, 1973:39).

Various theorists were associated with the Institute in addition to Max Horkheimer, including Theodor Adorno, Herbert Marcuse, Leo Lowenthal, Friedrich Pollock, Karl Wittfogel, Walter Benjamin, and Erich Fromm. The work of these theorists was voluminous and comprised a number of perspectives. For example, Lowenthal was interested in literature, Adorno in music, Pollock in the intersection of capitalism and the state, and Fromm in a synthesis of Marxism and psychoanalysis. Although everyone associated with the Institute shared a critical Marxist perspective, they did not embrace a singular theoretical stance or necessarily endorse a common view of revolutionary practice. Consequently, the reference to these critical theorists as the **Frankfurt School** is somewhat misleading because they did not represent a singular focused group (Held, 1980:15).

Max Horkheimer became director of the Institute in 1930. At his installation he emphasized that the Institute would be a place where "philosophers, sociologists, economists, historians, and psychologists must unite in a lasting working partnership . . . to pursue the great philosophical questions with the most refined methods" (Held, 1980:33). The Institute's major research focus was on alienation and domination in modern capitalist society. The Institute's research was to be **supradisciplinary** not interdisciplinary. That is, research and theoretical approaches were to transcend separate disciplinary positions to create a "supradisciplinary social theory" (Kellner, 1989:7).

The supradisciplinary nature of the research was framed by the conviction that Marxist theory was an "open-ended, historical, dialectical theory that required development, revision, and modification precisely because it was . . . a theory of contemporary socio-historical reality which itself was constantly developing and changing" (Kellner, 1989:11). The Institute's researchers saw their task as urgent because of the emergence of fascism and the lack of working-class revolutionary fervor despite the recurrent crises of capitalism.

The reassessment of Marxist theory and practice focused especially on the question of the revolutionary consciousness of the working class. Horkheimer, Adorno, and Marcuse had reached the conclusion in the 1930s that the traditional Marxist focus on a revolutionary working class had to be reformulated because false consciousness had such a grip on that class, penetrating the "innermost layers of human personality," that class-based or even individual emancipatory action was impossible in the immediate social and political context (Agger, 1979:14). This pessimism about the revolutionary potential of the working class persisted especially after the onset of World War II.

After the Nazis came to power in 1933, Horkheimer, along with other Jewish faculty members, was dismissed from the University of Frankfurt. The collection of brilliant minds at the Institute was dispersed. Most of the theorists at the Institute had Jewish backgrounds, and most of them thought of themselves as assimilated. Whatever their beliefs about assimilation, they were abruptly disabused of the notion with the rise of National Socialism, and most of the Institute members wisely chose exile. They left for Switzerland, France, Great Britain, and the United States.

Max Horkheimer went to New York, where he was joined by Pollock and Adorno. Fortunately, the private endowment from the Weil family allowed the Institute to remain relatively financially secure during the years of exile and its initial reconstitution in New York. In essence, Horkheimer, Pollock, and Adorno represented the Institute during the years of exile. In the 1940s, the three went to Los Angeles and remained there until their return to Frankfurt in 1950. Other Institute exiles found various positions. Marcuse, for example, worked for the Office of Strategic Services and the State Department, after which he went to Brandeis in 1954 and then to the University of California, San Diego, in 1965.[1]

In this chapter we concentrate on the work of Horkheimer, Adorno, Marcuse, and Fromm. The outline of their ideas sets the foundation for the examination, later in the chapter, of a contemporary critical theorist, Jurgen Habermas.

The Critical Theorists of the Frankfurt School

We had set ourselves nothing less than the discovery of why mankind, instead of entering into a truly human condition, is sinking into a new kind of barbarism. (Adorno and Horkheimer, 1944:xi)

Max Horkheimer (1895–1973)   Max Horkheimer's father was a manufacturer in Stuttgart, and Horkheimer had commercial training before doing his military service. As part of that training, with his friend Friedrich Pollock, he went to Brussels and London in the years 1913–1914 to learn French and

---

[1]One of the theorists who went to France, Walter Benjamin, committed suicide after the outbreak of World War II and the establishment of the puppet fascist regime in Vichy France.

English.[2] After 1918 he attended the universities of Munich, Freiburg, and then Frankfurt, where he obtained his doctorate in 1922 with a thesis on Kant. He became a lecturer in 1925 at the Institute for Social Research, and in 1929 he was appointed to the new chair of Social Philosophy at the Institute. He became director of the Institute in 1930.

Theodor Wiesengrund-Adorno (1903–1969)   Theodor Wiesengrund-Adorno was born in Frankfurt, the son of a successful Jewish merchant. His mother had had a successful singing career prior to her marriage, and the name Adorno was from her side of the family. She was the daughter of a German singer and a French army officer; her father's background was Corsican and Genoese. Apparently in response to Pollock's concern that there were too many Jewish-sounding names on the Institute's roster, Adorno dropped the Wiesengrund part of his name when he was in the United States (Jay 1973:22).

His mother's sister was an accomplished concert pianist who lived with the family, and Adorno's family encouraged him to take up the piano and study composition at an early age. This interest in music continued in his theoretical work on the nature of the culture industries in capitalist society (Adorno, 1984). Adorno attended the University of Frankfurt and obtained his doctorate with a thesis on Husserl's phenomenology in 1924. In 1925 he went to Vienna to study composition with Alban Berg, and it was here that he came to appreciate the atonal experiments of Schönberg. He returned to Frankfurt in 1928 and in 1931 became associated with the Institute, becoming a full member in 1938.

Herbert Marcuse (1898–1979)   Herbert Marcuse was born in Berlin to a prosperous, assimilated Jewish family. In 1918, after his military service, he was associated with the Social Democratic Party and the revolutionary Soldiers Council in Berlin. In 1919, he left the Social Democratic Party in protest over what he saw as the betrayal of the proletariat (Jay, 1973:28).

Marcuse went on to study philosophy at the universities of Berlin and Freiburg and obtained his doctorate in 1923 with a thesis on literature. Marcuse then spent six years as a bookseller and publisher in Berlin, returning to Freiburg in 1929 to study with the philosophers Husserl and Heidegger. He left Freiburg in 1932 largely because of political differences with Heidegger, whose right-wing views clashed with Marcuse's Marxist views. On Husserl's recommendation, however, he became a member of the Institute in 1933.

Erich Fromm (1900–1980)   Erich Fromm was born in Frankfurt and was brought up in an intensely religious household (Jay, 1973:88). His Orthodox Jewish parents both came from families of rabbis. In his early twenties, Fromm,

---

[2]Pollock accompanied Horkheimer and Adorno into exile in New York, and he was indispensable in maintaining the viability of the Institute despite the dispersal of most of its members. In particular, Pollock was responsible for "arranging the mundane details of their lives to allow Horkheimer the maximum time for his scholarly pursuits" (Jay, 1973:7).

along with Leo Lowenthal, who also became associated with the Institute, was active in a religious group formed around Rabbi Nobel at the largest Frankfurt synagogue. Fromm's orthodoxy lessened after his analysis in 1926 in Munich, although he never renounced his religion (Jay, 1973:89).

Fromm's doctorate, under Alfred Weber at Heidelberg, was on *Jewish Law: A Contribution to the Sociology of the Jewish Diaspora*. It was at Heidelberg that Fromm met Freida Reichmann, a Jewish psychoanalyst, who later became his wife. Fromm went on to train at the Berlin Psychoanalytic Institute and opened his own practice in 1927. In 1929 the Frankfurt Institute of Psychoanalysis was opened, and Fromm and his wife both became lecturers at the new Institute. In 1930 Fromm became director of the Social Psychology section at the Institute of Social Research. His interest in combining Marx and psychoanalysis appealed to Horkheimer and others. But by 1940 Fromm's association with the Institute came to an end, largely because of Horkheimer's disagreement with Fromm's criticisms of Freud.

Central Theories and Methods of the Frankfurt School

The theoretical backgrounds of the various members of the Institute were varied, but for most of them the work of Hegel (filtered through the work of Georg Lukacs), Marx, Weber, Nietzsche, and Freud was important. The critical stance involved the development of theory that described and analyzed the present society in relation to its past and, in doing so, enabled those who were oppressed to realize the forces that caused their oppression. In addition, the analysis would show how this oppression could be overcome with new, emancipatory conceptualizations and practices.

The critical theorists were concerned with the way in which the promise of Enlightenment rationality had been subverted in modern society. The major problem for modern society was, according to Horkheimer, the fact that "Reason has liquidated itself as an agency of ethical, moral, and religious insight" (1947:18). Reason had become rationalization that, as Max Weber had pointed out, led to a bureaucratized, controlling state rather than a liberated, equitable society.

Reason and Objectivity   Horkheimer distinguished between objective and subjective reason. **Objective reason** referred to reason as an instrument for determining social ends. Objective reason was a "force not only in the individual mind but also in the objective world—in relations among human beings and between social classes, in social institutions, and in nature and its manifestations" (1947:4).

Subjective reason was simply concerned with "means and ends, with the adequacy of procedures for the purposes more or less taken for granted and supposedly self-explanatory." Subjective reason is instrumental reason, and it "attaches little importance to the question whether the purposes as such are reasonable," just, or equitable (1947:3). Consequently, when the subjective version of reason holds there is no "reasonable" basis upon which to make ethical choices, "The acceptability of ideals, the criteria for our actions and beliefs, the leading principles of ethics and politics, all our ultimate decisions are made to depend upon factors other than reason" (1974:7).

The focus on subjective, or instrumental, reason as evidenced in positivist science meant that reason could be as easily used by the Nazi extermination industry as by institutions concerned with the elimination of poverty and suffering. Subjective or instrumental reason involved elevating the scientific "classification of facts and the calculation of probabilities" as the only "authority." In terms of subjective reason, the "statement that justice and freedom are better in themselves than injustice and oppression is scientifically unverifiable and useless," as meaningless as the statement that "red is more beautiful than blue" (Horkheimer, 1947:24).

The critical theorists maintained that disinterested, objective research was impossible because facts and values could not be separated and the researcher was always a part of the social situation being investigated. More specifically, positive methods were rejected on the basis that positivism's "exclusive faith in mathematics" was "philosophical technocracy" (Horkheimer, 1947:59). Horkheimer and Adorno maintained that positivism saw the world only in terms of "facts and things" and failed to connect these facts and things with social, and individual, needs and desires (Horkheimer, 1947:82).

Critical theory, on the other hand, not only understood the "various facts in their historical development" but also saw through the "notion of fact itself" as an historical and thus relative phenomenon. The "so-called facts ascertained by quantitative methods, which positivists are inclined to regard as the only scientific ones, are often only surface phenomena that obscure rather than disclose the underlying reality" (Horkheimer, 1947:82). The task of the critical theorist was to reveal the real conditions underlying the "facts" and, in doing so, provide a blueprint for an alternative, emancipatory reality.

The analysis of social conditions was an ethical enterprise for critical theorists. Horkheimer maintained that the Kantian ethical universals of duty and good will were abstractions that did not address the changing social context of human needs. Human nature is "continuously influenced and changed by a manifold of circumstances," and there is "no formula that defines the relationship among individuals, society, and nature for all time" (Horkheimer, 1935:152–153). The only ethical ideal should be happiness, because human beings "cannot escape from the longing for happiness and the fear of death" (Horkheimer, 1935:155).

Horkheimer believed that the transition from the hopeful promise of Enlightenment objective reason into modern subjective, instrumental reason was not an accident and could not "arbitrarily at any given moment be reversed" (1947:62). Hegel had pointed out that reason changed historically, but a progressive dialectical change toward freedom was not guaranteed. As Marcuse pointed out, the central category of the dialectic was negation (1960:449). Negation could mean that the "unreasonable becomes reasonable and, as such, determines the facts; in which unfreedom is the condition of freedom, and war the guarantor of peace" (Marcuse, 1960:vii).

Reason, in modern society, was instrumental in "sustaining injustice, toil, and suffering"; at the same time, the exercise of reason was still the best hope for the future (Marcuse, 1960:450). For example, Marxian theory took shape "as a critique of Hegel's philosophy . . . in the name of Reason," and in modern society it was only through constant critique that "Reason," and thus individuals, could come to understand the contradictions of social life and devise ways to transcend them (Marcuse, 1960:xii–xiii).

Emancipatory Theory Like Marx, the critical theorists emphasized that theoretical critique was not simply a way of making sense of the "facts"; it was also a way of helping individuals to see and understand what "is" and, in doing so, see what "might be." Methodologically, critical theory overcame the breach between theory and practice, ideas and reality, and in this way was true to its Marxist heritage.

Marx had pointed out that capitalism was a "union of contradictions. It gets freedom through exploitation, wealth through impoverishment, advance in production through restriction of consumption," so that the "very structure of capitalism is a dialectical one: every form and institution of the economic process begets its determinate negation and the crisis is the extreme form in which the contradictions are expressed" (Marcuse, 1960:311). If enlightenment and progress mean "freeing . . . man from superstitious belief in evil forces, in demons and fairies, in blind fate—in short the emancipation from fear—then denunciation of what is currently called reason is the greatest service reason can render" (Horkheimer, 1947:187). **Negative critique** "salvage[s] relative truths from the wreckage of false ultimates" (Horkheimer, 1947:183) and leads to the understanding of these contradictions because it rejects "the absolute claims of prevailing ideology" as well as "the brash claims of reality" by demonstrating their relativity (Horkheimer, 1947:182).

Theoretical critique was seen as a necessary but not sufficient condition for revolutionary change. Although theory remained primary—as Marcuse (1960:322) put it, "Practice follows the truth, not vice versa"—change required an agent. But for the Institute theorists, finding an agent under the conditions of monopoly capitalism was a problem. The alienation of the proletariat envisaged by Marx seemed to have been subverted by the ability of capitalism to satisfy an abundance of needs. The result was an "increasing distance between the consciousness of the working class and the critical individual who acts in its name" (Benhabib, 1986:157). The absence of revolutionary working-class consciousness, the entrenchment of monopoly capitalism, and the consolidation of the authoritarian state generated increasing pessimism about the possibility of emancipatory transformation in the immediate future.

Critical theorists pointed out, however, that although capitalism might satisfy many proletariat needs, increased consumption did not necessarily translate into human satisfaction and happiness, and it certainly did not compensate the proletariat for the alienation of their labor power. Capitalism, and especially monopoly capitalism, regulated consumption according to what was profitable, not according to human needs. Capitalism duped consumers into believing that they were exercising real choices among items and that these items would satisfy their needs.

Although the consumer is, so to speak, given his choice, he does not get a penny's worth too much for his money, whatever the trademark he prefers to possess. The difference in quality between two equally priced popular items is usually so infinitesimal as the difference in the nicotine content of two brands of cigarettes. (Horkheimer, 1947:99)

Even if the consumer suspected that the choice was an illusion, this would not guarantee the production of revolutionary consciousness because of the pervasiveness of reification. **Reification** refers to the process of domination whereby the products of human labor take on the appearance of things external to, and uncontrollable by, human beings. For example, economic fluctuations are often blamed on the operation of "the market." But the market is not some abstract, inevitable force; it is *people* making decisions about money, commodities, and trade.

 Georg Lukacs, a friend of Max Weber, had earlier developed the theory of reification. In *History and Class Consciousness* (1922), Lukacs suggested that the proletariat were prisoners of bourgeois ideas that encouraged the belief that capitalism and alienated labor were "natural"—that is, an inevitable part of abstract market forces that individuals could not control. Consequently, for Lukacs, it was the task of vanguard intellectuals to overcome this reification by educating the proletariat as to their "real" position in the relations of production and showing how the proletariat could control their destiny.

To the critical theorists, reification was both an objective process, being a part of the exchange relations of capitalism, and subjective because it was embedded in belief and understanding. Reification was false consciousness that was "self-inflicted alienation"—the alienation that a person and social class did to themselves (Agger, 1979:150). Consequently, it was the duty of critical theory to help generate revolutionary consciousness and practice among the proletariat.

Fromm and Freud   Simple economic determinism was not the motor of revolutionary transformation. Culture, or ideology, embedded in the consciousness, also played an important part in producing distorted personalities who reproduced the conditions of domination. This realization made Freud's work useful to critical theory because it provided an explanation for false consciousness as well as an explanation for the authoritarian personality types of modern society. Freud's libido theory also held out the promise that total domination might be subverted by the fact that basically human beings desire freedom (Alford, 1987:26).

Erich Fromm was central to the incorporation of Freud into the work of the critical theorists. Fromm maintained that psychoanalysis was compatible with Marxian historical materialism because it uncovered the unconscious forces controlling behavior. Irrational behavior had its origins in social life—in religion, customs, politics, and education.

Marxists have usually assumed that what works behind man's back and directs him are economic forces and their political representations. Psychoanalytic study shows that this is much too narrow a concept. Society consists of people . . . equipped with a potential of passionate strivings. . . . This human potential as a whole is molded by the ensemble of economic and social forces characteristic of each given society. These forces . . . produce a certain social unconscious, and certain conflicts between the repressive factors and given human needs which are essential for sane human functioning (like a certain degree of freedom, stimulation, interest in life, happiness). . . . revolutions occur as expressions of not only new productive forces, but also of the repressed part of human nature, and they are successful only when the two conditions are combined. (1965:37–38)

The psychoanalytic focus on the family was important to critical theory because it was through the family that a society put its stamp on the individual personality. Specifically, it was through the family that society reproduced the class structure. In addition, it was the family that produced the authoritarian personality type that underlay anti-Semitism.

Investigations into the way in which economic and political structures affected the psychic life of individuals resulted in the Institute projects *Studies on Authority and Family*, conducted in Germany in the 1930s, and *Studies in Prejudice*, conducted in the United States in the 1940s. The work *Dialectic of the Enlightenment*, by Adorno and Horkheimer (1944), also explored the social and historical basis for the development of the authoritarian personality and the origins of fascist society.

Nature of Society, Humans, and Change

Modern Capitalist Society The critical theorists focused primarily on the nature of modern Western society and the historical development of capitalism. A key transformation was seen to be the replacement of individual competitive capitalism with monopoly and state capitalism (see Chapter 5). With state capitalism replacing liberal capitalism after World War II, the critique of society could no longer be simply a critique of political economy.

It is no longer the norms of a bourgeois public sphere, of the liberal marketplace and of the liberal state, practicing the rule of law, to which critique can appeal. . . . Emancipatory norms are no longer immanent in public and institutional structures. Instead, they have to be searched for in the unredeemed utopian promise of culture, art, and philosophy (Adorno), or in the deep structures of human subjectivity that revolt against the sacrifices demanded by an oppressive society (Marcuse). (Benhabib, 1986:180–181)

The transformation to state capitalism is marked by the development of mass culture and the extension of social domination into the psychological as well as the economic experiences of human beings. It represents the triumph of instrumental rationality that Weber discussed. **Instrumental rationality** is concerned only with matching effective means to selected goals and thus acts as a mechanism of repression in modern society. This dehumanized exercise is contrasted with a rationality, or reason, that is concerned with the human values of happiness and justice. Horkheimer remarked that even after the defeat of fascism, the

> hopes of mankind seem to be farther from fulfillment today than they were even in the groping epochs when they were first formulated by humanists. It seems that even as technical knowledge expands the horizon of man's thought and activity, his autonomy as an individual, his ability to resist the growing apparatus of mass manipulation, his power of imagination, his independent judgement appear to be reduced. Advance in technical facilities for enlightenment is accompanied by a process of dehumanization. (1947:vi)

Weber's fears about a bureaucratized, impersonal world of "icy darkness" seemed to the critical theorists to have been realized, making it difficult to conceive of ways in which emancipatory change could be effected.

The irony is, as both Marx and Weber understood, that technological "progress" enabling human beings to control the natural world becomes "progressive enslavement" as technology and science become the singular determinants of human needs (Marcuse, 1964:144).

> The fallen nature of modern man cannot be separated from social progress. On the one hand the growth of economic productivity furnishes the conditions for a world of greater justice; on the other hand it allows the technical apparatus and social groups which administer it a disproportionate superiority to the rest of the population. . . . Even though the individual disappears before the apparatus which he serves, that apparatus provides for him as never before. (Adorno and Horkheimer, 1944:xiv)

In the early years the critical theorists subscribed to Marx's idea that technology could be harnessed for the satisfaction of human needs in a positive rather than a negative manner, but in the aftermath of the Holocaust this optimism was abandoned.

> The real individuals of our time are the martyrs who have gone through infernos of suffering and degradation in their resistance to conquest and oppression, not the inflated personalities of popular culture, the conventional dignitaries. . . . The anonymous martyrs of the concentration camps are the symbols of humanity that is striving to be born. The task of philosophy is to translate what they have done into language that will be heard, even though their finite voices have been silenced by tyranny. (Horkheimer, 1947:161)

The technological expertise the Nazis brought to bear on the elimination of whole sectors of humanity was produced by "modern" human beings. It seemed that in modern society, "conscience and personal responsibility decline 'objectively' under conditions of total bureaucratization . . . where the functioning of the apparatus determines—and overrides—personal autonomy" (Marcuse, 1970:50). The "fallen nature of modern man cannot be separated from social progress," and even though the "individual disappears before the apparatus which he serves, that apparatus provides for him as never before. In an unjust state of life, the impotence and pliability of the masses grows with the quantitative increase in commodities allowed them" (Adorno and Horkheimer, 1944:xiv–xv).

Horkheimer pointed out that the modern celebration of the "individual" is ironic. The Enlightenment dream of "machines doing men's work has now come true," but it is "also true that men are acting more and more like machines" (1974:26). False needs, satisfied by the culture industry and the increasing proliferation of commodities, extend the reach of capitalist domination. For example, the "real you" is defined in relation to the clothes you wear, the car you drive, even the toothpaste you use. Fromm (1955:133) pointed out, "We drink labels. With a bottle of Coca-Cola we drink the picture of the pretty boy and girl who drink it in the advertisement, we drink the slogan of 'the pause that refreshes'. . . least of all do we drink with our palate." Individuality is subverted by technology in the "one-dimensional society" of enslaved consumers and mass culture audiences (Marcuse, 1964). Freud's insights on subjectivity were important to critical theory because of the decline of autonomous individuality, and with it the possibility of critical reflection on society that might lead to emancipatory practice.

Human Nature Human beings are inseparable from society because the individual "is *real* only as part of the whole to which he belongs. His essential determination, his character and inclination, his avocation and view of the world all have their origin in society and in his destiny in society" (Horkheimer, 1947:9–10). The isolated individual is an illusion: "The most esteemed personal qualities, such as independence, will to freedom, sympathy and the sense of justice, are social as well as individual virtues." Consequently, the "emancipation of the individual is not an emancipation from society, but the deliverance of society from atomization . . . that may reach its peak in periods of collectivization and mass culture" (Horkheimer, 1947:135). As society changes, individual personalities change, and the "realization that young men and women today are, at bottom, different even from what they were at the beginning of the century" means that the notion of an unchangeable human essence must be discarded (Horkheimer, 1947:13). Human needs, "including sexuality," have an "historical character" (Marcuse, 1970:59).

The significance of the historical nature of human nature lies in the way repressive social forces penetrate the psyche. In advanced industrial societies, these repressive forces penetrate ever more deeply, leading to the "obsolescence of the role and autonomy of the economic and political subject" (Marcuse, 1970:59). Specifically, it is the loss of a "personal private realm" that weakens the "consciousness and conscience" and thus decreases the autonomy and rationality of the individual (Marcuse, 1970:50).

Adorno and Horkheimer used Homer's epic of Odysseus's voyage from Troy to Ithaca, which illustrated man's domination of nature, to trace modern psychic repression. They pointed out that domination of nature was necessary for man to become human, but it also marked the beginnings of man's self-repression (1944:46). A key event in Odysseus's voyage was his escape from the lure of the Sirens. Odysseus had to pass between Scylla and Charybdis while listening to the song of the Sirens. Scylla and Charybdis had the right to capture whatever came between them. They were assured of their prize because no mariner could resist the seductive songs of the Sirens. The Sirens represented the sensuous, natural world—the world of the Freudian id. Odysseus cunningly found a way to resist the temptation of the Sirens. He put wax into the ears of his rowers so they could not hear the songs and had himself bound to the mast so that he could hear the songs but could not succumb to the lure. Odysseus "has found an escape clause in the contract, which enables him to fulfill it while eluding it" so that he "as subject need not be subjected" to the Sirens (1944:59).

Odysseus was able to dominate nature, but at the price of repressing his own instinctual inner nature. He was therefore the prototype of the bourgeois whose deferment of pleasure was critical to the success of rational capitalism. Odysseus's strategy also reinforced his domination over his men, who could not hear the songs and who had to rely on Odysseus's judgment. "The oarsmen . . . are each yoked in the same rhythm as the modern worker in the factory," and their impotence, like that of modern workers, was not simply a "stratagem of the rulers, but the logical consequence of the industrial society into which the ancient Fate . . . has finally changed" (1944:37). In the long run, the taming of nature resulted in a "bourgeois commodity economy," and the conditions were established for a "new barbarism" (1944:32).

The repression of instinctual nature, necessary for individual and social progress, resulted in a transition from what Freud called the **pleasure principle** to the **reality principle** (Marcuse, 1966:12).

Pleasure principle	*Reality principle*
Immediate satisfaction	Delayed satisfaction
Pleasure	Restraint of pleasure
Joy (play)	Toil (work)
Receptiveness	Productiveness
Absence of repression	Security

The result of the transition was that the "curse of irresistible progress" became "irresistible regression" (Adorno and Horkheimer, 1944:36).

Adorno and Horkheimer became increasingly pessimistic about the possibility of any collective emancipatory project after the 1940s. Marcuse (1966), however, suggested that instinctual repression allied with supremely efficient technological rationality could be a source of liberation. That is, too much repression would invariably mean an eventual rebellion against those repressive forces.

Social Change   Marcuse suggested that Freud's libidinal repression was not a singular, static phenomenon, but varied in relation to changes in society. In modern society, repression is excessive. Basic repression has been superceded by surplus repression. **Surplus repression** occurs because capitalism can produce an abundance that can liberate humans from scarcity, but "the closer the real possibility of liberating the individual from the constraints once justified by scarcity and immaturity, the greater the need for maintaining and streamlining these constraints lest the established order of domination dissolve" (Marcuse,

1966:85). Surplus repression is repression in the interest of domination rather than in the interest of the development of civilized human beings.

Surplus repression can be undermined by the fact that the "quantitative reduction in labor time and energy leads to a qualitative change in human existence" and the "expanding realm of freedom becomes truly a realm of play" (Marcuse, 1966:222–223). In time the "distinction between rational and irrational authority, between repression and surplus-repression, can be made and verified by individuals themselves." If people do not currently make this distinction, this "does not mean they cannot learn to make it once they are given the opportunity to do so" (Marcuse, 1966:225).

The escape from the "iron cage" can be accomplished by a **"great refusal"**— the refusal to "buy into" the consumer society. Marcuse believed that this refusal would not be made by the proletariat because they have been co-opted by the ability of advanced capitalism to satisfy consumption needs and produce the semblance of the "good life" (Marcuse, 1964:18). The great refusal will be made by the "substratum of the outcasts and outsiders, the exploited and persecuted of other races and other colors, the unemployed and the unemployable" who exist outside democratic society and whose opposition is "revolutionary even if their consciousness is not" (1964:256). It is when these individuals start "refusing to play the game" that the "beginning of the end" is in sight (1964:257).

Marcuse was hopeful that the various counterculture movements of the 1960s indicated the beginnings of the great refusal. For Marcuse, love and sexual freedom were the routes to social transformation. As individuals come to recognize the excessive rationalization of society, there would be a reversion to childhood polymorphous sexuality that modern, post-Oedipul genital sexuality represses. The body would become an "instrument of pleasure," and this would hasten the disintegration of "the monogamic and patriarchal family" (Marcuse, 1966:201). Marcuse's optimistic forecast of sexual revolution as the motor of social transformation was made before STDs, including AIDS, were recognized as serious problems.

Adorno, Horkheimer, and even Marcuse realized that "transformation is objectively necessary but the need for it is not present among precisely those social strata who are defined as agents of transformation" in Marxist theory (Marcuse, 1970:99). Nonetheless, resistance was imperative, whether it took the form of a great refusal or some other form, because the "new fascism . . . will be very different from the old fascism." The new fascism will undermine democracy by repressive legislation, supported by the masses, that will "cut back . . . existing civil and political liberties" (Marcuse, 1970:100). Some theorists today maintain that this is precisely what has occurred in the late twentieth century in Western societies and that the vital sociological question remains, who can resist? If it is not the working class, maybe resistance can emerge from feminists and racial minorities.

Class, Gender, and Race

Class The critical theorists recognized the class divisions in modern society but provided no systematic analysis of class (Kellner, 1989:229). They were more concerned with the way in which Marxian class politics had been subverted by psychological as well as economic repression. A key institution in psychological repression was the family. Fromm pointed out that the family was the "medium through which the society or the social class stamps its specific structure on the child, and hence the adult. *The family is the psychological agency of society"* (1988:483).

The research *Studies on Authority and the Family*, undertaken by the Institute in the 1930s, examined the nature of the family and the psychic repression it generated under industrial capitalism. Critical theorists pointed out that the family was not a natural, unchanging form, but changed in response to external social and historical conditions. The patriarchal, bourgeois family was the particular form developed in relation to the needs of industrial capitalism. It was the ideals of this family form that tended to prevail and entrench subjective domination.

Studies on Authority and the Family was based on an empirical study of the attitudes and beliefs of German workers. Three thousand questionnaires were distributed to workers asking them their views on "the education of children, the rationalization of industry, the possibility of avoiding a new war, and the locus of real power in the state" (Jay, 1973:116).

An important methodological innovation was used in this research. The answers were recorded verbatim and then analyzed "the way a psychoanalyst listens to the associations of a patient"—that is, key words were taken as an indication of the "underlying psychological reality beneath the manifest content of the answers" (Jay, 1973:117). The study revealed discrepancies between beliefs and personality traits. The research found that approximately 10 percent of the respondents exhibited authoritarian characteristics, and about 15 percent anti-authoritarian views, with the majority being highly ambivalent.

Horkheimer and Adorno found that under state capitalism the patriarchal, bourgeois family was the foundation for the authoritarian personality. The Oedipal conflict, involving the rejection of the mother in favor of the father's authority, was the means for the child to learn to accept the authority of society. The "rational" adaptation of the child to the father's authority was internalized to produce a strong ego and superego, or conscience, adapted to the needs of capitalist society.

> The self-control of the individual, the disposition for work and discipline,
> the ability to hold firmly to certain ideas, consistency in practical life,
> application of reason, perseverance and pleasure in constructive activity
> could all be developed, in the circumstances, only under the direction of
> the father whose own education had been won in the school of life.
> (Horkheimer, 1982:101)

It is clear that the child referred to was a male child. In the early stages of capitalist, bourgeois society, the authority of the father provided the son with an object against which to rebel. This rebellion produced individual autonomy and the ability to resist domination. However, with the transformation of liberal, entrepreneurial capitalism to state capitalism, the father's economic power and family authority declined. The child still experienced the Oedipal complex but came to realize that the father did not embody total power and authority. The child then sought a father-substitute in order to develop a strong, autonomous self. But the only father-substitute was the abstract authority of instrumental reason, with the result the child became the "mass individual, a heteronomous social atom who is narcissistic, materialistic, and sadistic" and unable to resist domination (Jagentowicz Mills, 1987:98). The child learned that not "the father but the playmates, the neighbors, the leader of the gang, the sport, the screen are the authorities on appropriate mental and physical behavior" (Marcuse, 1970:52).

The foundations for capitulation to an authoritarian, fascist leader were found in the psychic fallout from these transformed family relations. From their research into the family lives of German workers, the critical theorists concluded that the "German working class would be far less resistant to the right-wing seizure of power than its militant ideology would suggest"—a conclusion borne out by the general enthusiasm for National Socialism (Jay, 1973:117).

Gender Horkheimer and Adorno focused on the problems for the male child in state capitalist families. The mother, "as representative of nature," was, in the early stages of bourgeois capitalism, a source of security and comfort for the male child. Women in general were "the enigmatic image of irresistibility and powerlessness" (Adorno and Horkheimer, 1944:71–72). The mother provided a refuge from the father's authority, and her unconditional love was a source of emotional sustenance that provided the child with a vision of an alternative, utopian reality—a vision of instinctual Eros in contrast to rational authority, the pleasure principle as opposed to the reality principle.

This idyllic situation, according to the critical theorists, changed as women entered the productive sphere and many of their socialization tasks were taken over by other institutions. The mother ceased to offer a refuge from the authoritarian world of the father because she became more and more like a man. For Adorno and Horkheimer, as well as Marcuse, this was a negative step. For example, Marcuse believed that the feminine principle, based on the "promise of peace, of joy, of the end of violence" natural to women, was the foundation for emancipation of both men and women (1972:77).

The celebration of the feminine principle was a blind spot in the work of the critical theorists. The principle merely restated the gender dichotomies that support capitalist patriarchy (Jagentowicz Mills, 1987:116). The mother might represent the promise of liberation for sons, but this promise did not extend to daughters. Daughters, in the Freudian account, had to reject the mother in favor of the father in order to develop a mature femininity. At the same time, like their mothers, daughters must embody the same liberatory promise for men.

There was some nostalgia for the nineteenth-century bourgeois family among the critical theorists. They saw the destruction of this family form as the destruction of the sphere of love, and thus of any possibility of resistance to the instrumentality of mass society. But the emotional support it offered its male members obscured the damage this family form did to mothers and daughters. Adorno and Horkheimer concluded that "Fatherlessness creates a mass individual or an authoritarian personality" but a motherless society meant a "loss of a vision of the future lived in freedom," a society "without love or hope" (Jagentowicz Mills, 1987:109). A motherless society was one that was primed for anti-Semitism, and for racism in general.

Race   Horkheimer and Adorno argued that "race is not a naturally special characteristic" but was a potent sign in certain social contexts (1944:169). Anti-Semitism, for example, projected repressed fears and wants onto the despised other, most especially the fear of impotence in the face of overwhelming social and economic forces. They saw Nazism as a "psychological problem, but the psychological factors themselves have to be understood as being molded by socio-economic factors" (Fromm, 1941:208).

In capitalist society, anti-Semitism was economically important to the bour-geoisie because it concealed the nature of domination in productive relations. Adorno and Horkheimer pointed out that Jews had historically been denied ac-cess to manufacturing so they often found their livelihood in commercial and fi-nancial enterprises. Thus, "commerce was not their vocation but their fate" (Adorno and Horkheimer, 1944:175). The actual nature of productivity in these occupations was often concealed, and the merchant and banker appeared to profit on the backs of productive workers. They were, however, simply middle-men who concealed the reality of the capitalist manufacture's appropriation of surplus wealth. The Jew became the "bailiff of the whole system and takes the hatred of others upon himself" (1944:174). Under monopoly capitalism, wealth was concentrated in the hands of a few and the middleman role became redun-dant. The Jew, however, remained a handy scapegoat for the resulting eco-nomic problems that monopoly capitalism produced.

Jews, and others who were similarly stigmatized, were easy targets for per-secution. They could be used to expiate the social dislocations of capitalism as well as the unconscious antisocial forces that were barely repressed under sys-tems of instrumental domination.

In the 1940s, an ambitious study dealing with prejudice, and specifically with anti-Semitism, was launched in the United States.[3] *Studies in Prejudice* was a five-volume collaborative work, with Adorno and the members of the Berke-ley Public Opinion Study Group, R. Nevitt Sanford, Daniel Levison, and Elsie Frankel-Brunswik, as the main researchers. Horkheimer was the overall coordi-nator of the project. The main theoretical underpinning for the discovery of the subjective manifestations of prejudice came from psychoanalysis.

The studies employed both qualitative techniques, such as interviews, and quantitative techniques. The five studies were *Dynamics of Prejudice*, which ex-amined the personality traits and prejudicial attitudes of war veterans; *Anti-Semitism and Emotional Disorder*, which consisted of case studies of psychotherapy patients who demonstrated anti-Semitism; *Prophets of Deceit*, which examined the techniques of mass persuasion; *Rehearsal for Destruction*, which described the historical origin of anti-Semitism in Germany; and *The Authoritarian Personality*, which examined the correlations between prejudice and personality traits.

---

[3]The study was funded by the American Jewish Committee.

The Authoritarian Personality (Adorno et al., 1950) was specifically concerned with outlining the personality traits of the potentially fascist individual. Extensive questionnaires and interviews were conducted, and an F scale was developed that measured anti-Semitism and antidemocratic attitudes. The study concluded that prejudiced individuals had distinctive personalities as a result of their socialization. Prejudiced, antidemocratic personalities came from authoritarian families in which conformity was the rule, discipline was strict but often arbitrary, and any deviations from rigidly held but conventional values were severely punished. The authoritarian personality had a strong resemblance to the sadomasochistic personality discussed by Fromm in the earlier *Studies on Authority and the Family*.

The Authoritarian Personality revealed the familial psychosocial dynamic of authoritarianism and prejudice, but "the authoritarian family did not produce authoritarian children solely because of what it did—provide a model for arbitrary domination—but equally for what it could not do—protect the individual against the claims made on his socialization by extra-familial agencies" (Jay, 1973:247). As Fromm (1955:237) pointed out, "Fascism, Nazism and Stalinism have in common that they offered the atomized individual a new refuge and security. These systems are the culmination of alienation." Prejudice was a persistent social problem because the authoritarian personality type was as much a product of society at large as it was of family dynamics.

Adorno concluded *The Authoritarian Personality* with the observation that if "fear and destructiveness are the major emotional sources of fascism, *eros* belongs mainly to democracy" (Adorno et al., 1950:976). Education, therefore, had to be tied to democratic politics if prejudice was to be curtailed and eros furthered.

After the Second World War, Horkheimer reflected on the situation of German Jews and concluded that the trauma of the Nazi era had yet to be overcome. He believed that protection from repeating the past lay in knowledge of that past and, more important, in education that made individuals "critical in the face of demagogy" so that they could distinguish "demagogy from a truly rational politics" (1974:117–118).

Other Theories and Theorists

We have concentrated on four key members of the Institute because of space limitations, but several other important theorists were associated with the Institute in its early years. Among them were Leo Lowenthal and Walter Benjamin, who were interested in a sociology of literature; Karl Wittfogel, whose interest was in comparative sociology; Karl Mannheim, who developed the sociology of knowledge; and Paul Lazarsfeld, who became important to communications research in U.S. sociology (see Chapter 2). In addition, Adorno produced a considerable amount of work on art and culture, specifically critiques of mass culture.

The major focus for the diverse work of the critical theorists was on **domination** in capitalist and, during the war years, fascist society. They suggested that because domination penetrated into the innermost core of the personality, domination was often unrecognized and unrealized. This made it difficult to conceptualize how the world should be; that is, it made it difficult to mount a rational critique of the present and formulate possibilities for an emancipated future.

Critique and Conclusions

A major criticism of the critical theorists is that they simply replaced economic analysis with cultural analysis and, in doing so, weakened, if not eliminated, the possibility of revolutionary praxis on the part of the proletariat. But the critical theorists from the outset maintained that the former division between political economy (base) and culture/ideology (superstructure) no longer held in twentieth-century society. The two were critically interconnected, and it was the interconnections that made emancipation difficult. The focus on ideology, culture, and the damaged psyche in a capitalist society was part of a continuing concern with how capitalism changed historically and how the impulse to a better world could be promoted. After the 1930s, however, Adorno and Horkheimer became pessimistic about the possibility of radical transformation, and neither participated in any direct way with the radical student protests of the 1960s.

Another criticism of critical theory is that it remained a philosophical, unscientific enterprise that did not come to grips with the "real" conditions of modern repression and domination. This criticism has some validity, but it should be recalled that the immediate postwar situation of the original Institute members could not, and did not, approximate those of the 1930s origins. After the Institute's reconstitution in Germany, the work of critical theory remained focused on revealing the structures of domination underlying the seeming benevolence of state capitalism. This focus influenced the work in the critical theoretical tradition of students such as Jurgen Habermas.

Jurgen Habermas (1929–)

Jurgen Habermas was born in Gummersbach, near Düsseldorf, and grew up during the Nazi regime and the Second World War. The early experience of the Nazi era had a profound effect on his thinking. As a teenager, Habermas was shocked by the Nuremberg trials and the "discovery of the horrors of the Nazi regime" (Bernstein, 1985:1). In the 1950s he became concerned about the "continuities between the Nazi regime and the emergent West German state" (Outhwaite, 1994:2). His work has been a search for a social framework that can ensure that fascism will not reappear.

Habermas studied philosophy at Göttingen, Zurich, and Bonn. He obtained his doctorate from Bonn in 1954. For a couple of years he was a journalist, and from 1956 until 1959 he was Adorno's assistant at the Frankfurt Institute. In 1961 he was appointed Professor of Philosophy and Sociology at the University of Heidelberg. He returned to the Institute in 1964, where he assumed Horkheimer's Chair in Philosophy and Sociology.[4] In 1971 he assumed the directorship of the new Max Planck Institute for the Study of the Conditions of

---

[4]Horkheimer had not been very supportive of Habermas when he was a student. Kellner (1989:207) suggested that this was because Horkheimer became more conservative after his return to Germany and he found Habermas's work too left wing. Adorno, however, did support Habermas for the Chair position.

Life in the Scientific-Technical World. He returned in 1982 to the Chair of Sociology and Philosophy at the University of Frankfurt, where he remained until his retirement.

Habermas's Central Theories and Methods

Charting the intellectual influences on Habermas is a daunting task because of his encyclopedic knowledge of contemporary philosophical and social theories (Outhwaite, 1994:5). Central to his work, however, have been the theorists of the Frankfurt Institute and the classical theorists, Marx, Freud, and Weber. His main focus is on transforming the negative critique of original critical theory into a positive program for emancipatory practice.

Communication   Like his critical theory predecessors, Habermas is concerned with reformulating Marxian theory in the light of twentieth-century social changes, and most especially in light of the expansion of state power into all spheres of social life. Habermas expands Marx's conception of humanity by adding **language** (communication) to **work** (labor) as a distinct feature of species-being.

The introduction of language as a significant part of human development led Habermas to concentrate on how undistorted communication might be possible and how it could lay the foundation for emancipatory practice. **Distorted communication** is the equivalent of Marx's false consciousness. **Undistorted communication** refers to the conditions under which social goals and values can be discussed on a rational, egalitarian basis so that a consensus can be reached on the ends and values to be pursued. Undistorted, rational communication only occurs when the "peculiarly constraint-free force of the better argument" prevails (1984: 1:26).

Habermas's model for undistorted communication is psychoanalysis. In Freudian psychoanalysis the patient is encouraged, through a process of self-reflection, to become aware of previously repressed needs. Recovery (freedom) results from the patient's recognition of this self-imposed repression. As with the psychoanalyst, the role of the critical theorist is to assist the repressed to recognize and understand their collective social situation and, as a result, formulate emancipatory practices. Habermas regards this endeavor as particularly important today because of the extent to which science and technology distort communication in the interest of technological rationalization and the political reinforcement of repression.

Domination and Communication   In his analysis of current forces of domination, Habermas turned to Weber's analysis of purposive rational action. Habermas extended Weber's recognition of the penetration of purposive rationality in the economy to the knowledge spheres of science, art, and political/legal/moral theory. His main point is that purposive rationality penetrates everyday practices, especially everyday communications, and contributes to the loss of meaning in everyday life. In a modern society governed by purposive rationality, everything "has a price." Everything can be justified in rational, means-end terms. As a result, the normative sphere is sidelined, or even made obsolete, and emotional desires and subjective intuitions are relegated to the irrational sphere.

But Habermas claims that it is possible to find a way out of the "disenchantment" of modernity through the construction of an ideal speech community. The **ideal speech community** presupposes that (1) all individuals capable of speech can participate in the debate; (2) all individuals have equal rights to give their reasons for their stated position; and (3) no individual can be denied the right to participate in the debate. These are the necessary and universal conditions for the ideal speech community because they guarantee that the force of better (rational) argument will prevail.

The ideal speech community is Habermas's way of maintaining critical theory's injunction to link theory and practice. The ideal speech community connects with Marx's idea that ideology can be understood as distorted communication (Held, 1980:277). The ideal speech situation is therefore politically important in providing the foundation for the full realization of human needs and interests. The very nature of communication in the ideal speech community is one of mutual trust and comprehension rather than the achievement of rational, instrumental ends.

Positivism and Communication   According to Habermas, a critical part of modern distorted communication, and hence domination, is the value placed on science and technology. Like his critical theory predecessors, Habermas maintains that science and technology are not neutral or objective procedures without any evaluative weight. Habermas recognizes that science in the early nineteenth century was a progressive force, but by the twentieth century science, in its positivist form, had become a form of ideological domination. Positive science became a means for the manipulation of both the natural and social world in the interest of technical rather than social progress. Furthermore, Habermas claims that science is "no longer understood as *one* form of knowledge"; rather, knowledge is now identified as science (1971:19).

"Scientism"—the belief that all problems have a technical solution apart from any political or moral considerations—is the new ideology of advanced capitalism. The individual becomes powerless in the face of technical experts, whose presumed efficiency in solving social and economic crises is presented as being in the best interests of the individual. The result is "the depoliticization of the mass of the population" as "reified models of the sciences . . . gain objective power" over individuals' self-understanding (Habermas, 1970:374). For example, the advertisers' catchphrase "Studies show . . ." acts as a powerful persuader of a commodity's value, or recommendation for certain behaviors as desirable. Critical reflection and protest are eliminated by the idea that experts know best.

Habermas claims that the dominance of technological rationality and positivist science over all spheres of life is not an inevitable process, although ideologically it might be presented as such (1976:11). Habermas sees science as having an instrumental place in modern society, freeing individuals from the constraints of external nature, but argues that this place must be balanced by a politics that is enlightened and emancipatory. A basic distinction needs to be made between purposive rational action, on the one hand, and communicative action taking account of values and beliefs, on the other.

The interrelationship of productive forces and normative structures is, in Habermas's view, important to the legitimation problems of the state. Habermas is particularly concerned with the legitimacy of the state in advanced capitalist societies because of the state's special position in its "role as corporate actor, not only making decisions affecting the whole society, but doing so in the name of society itself" (Wuthnow, Hunter, Bergesen, and Kurzweil, 1984:218). These decisions, in fact, promote the interests of elites, but this is obscured by the ideological appeals to technical expertise.

Nature of Society, Humans, and Change

Society   Habermas analyzed the historical nature of the steering problems and crises in four types of society: primitive, traditional, capitalist, and postcapitalist. In the postcapitalist designation, Habermas included "state-socialist societies—in view of their political-elitist disposition of the means of production" (1976:17). With the exception of primitive societies, he considered all of the societal types to be **class societies**.

Steering problems are those that involve system integration and social integration. Habermas defines **social integration** as "*life-worlds* that are symbolically structured" (1976:4)—normative structures concerned with integration and pattern maintenance (Talcott Parsons's terminology). **System integration** refers to controlling or "steering performance of a self-regulated *system*" (1976:4). System integration involves adaptation and goal attainment.

According to Habermas, crises occur (1) when "members of a society experience structural alterations as critical for continued existence and feel their social identity threatened"; and (2) when social integration is "at stake, that is, when the consensual foundations of normative structures" are impaired and society becomes "anomic" (1976:3). Habermas's evolutionary model of social change departs from the Marxist emphasis on the economy to stress the importance of normative legitimations in the process of social change.

Primitive societies were based on a kinship system, with age and sex as the "organizational principle." In this type of society, change occurred as a result of external factors that undermined "familial and tribal identities" (Habermas, 1976:18). The usual sources of social change were "demographic growth in connection with ecological factors—above all, interethnic dependency as a result of economic exchange, war, and conquest" (1976:19).

In **traditional** societies, the basic organizational principle was "*domination* in political form." The centrality of the kinship system characteristic of primitive society gave way to the "power and control of the state" (1976:19). In traditional societies, differentiation and functional specialization began to appear. Social change or crises occurred as a result of the "contradictions between validity claims of systems of norms and justifications that cannot explicitly permit exploitation, and a class structure in which privileged appropriation of socially produced wealth is the rule." The result was "heightened repression" in order to maintain system integration, but such repression led to "legitimation losses, which for their part result in class struggles." These struggles could, over time, lead to "the overthrow of the political system and to new foundations of legitimation—that is, to a new group identity" (1976:20).

When looking at capitalist societies, Habermas distinguishes between **liberal capitalist** society and **organized** or **advanced capitalist** society. The organizational principle of liberal capitalism is "*the relationship of wage labor and capital, which is anchored in the system of bourgeois civil law*" (1976:20). In this type of society, "economic exchange becomes the dominant steering medium" and the state's power is limited to "(a) the protection of bourgeois commerce in accord with civil law (police and the administration of justice); (b) the shielding of the market mechanism from self-destructive side effects (for example, legislation for the protection of labor); (c) the satisfaction of the prerequisites of production in the economy as a whole (public school education, transportation, and communication); and, (d) the adaptation of the system of civil law to needs that arise from the process of accumulation (tax, banking, and business law)" (1976:21).

The key transformation in liberal capitalist society, according to Habermas, is the "uncoupling," or separation, of the economic system from the political system. This separation allows for a sphere in "bourgeois society that is free from traditional ties and given over to the strategic-utilitarian action orientations of market participants" (1976:21). The result is that the "relations of production can do without traditional authority legitimated from above" (1976:22).

But when legitimacy rests on the operations of the market, Habermas argues, the inevitable fluctuations of the market become a threat to social integration. These fluctuations, with their consequences of increased unemployment and/or inflation, make the inequities of economic relations clearly evident despite the ideology that the marketplace is a meeting place of equals. "Economic crisis is immediately transformed into social crisis; for, in unmasking the opposition of social class, it provides a practical critique of ideology of the market's pretension to be free of power," and this critique threatens social integration (1976:29).

The crisis in liberal capitalist systems differs from that in previous social types because the conflicts take on the "appearance of natural catastrophes" and lose the "character of a fate accessible to self-reflection," acquiring the "objectivity of inexplicable, contingent, natural events" (Habermas, 1976:30).

The transformation of liberal capitalism to organized or state-regulated capitalism occurs with the rise of multinational corporations. The state, observes Habermas, is increasingly called upon to intervene in the economy because of the steering problems caused by economic fluctuations. As a result, the distinction between the economic and political systems tends to disappear when, for example, the state offers subsidies to industry, sets up job creation schemes, and offers tax relief to attract industry.

The "re-coupling," or interdependence, of the economic and political systems increases legitimation problems for the state. But, argues Habermas, the legitimation problem is not solved democratically with the "genuine participation of citizens in the process of political will-formation," which might reveal the "contradiction between administratively socialized production and the continued private appropriation and use of surplus value" (1976:36). The contradiction is concealed by making the administration independent of the democratic political system. Consequently, the needs and desires of the citizens can be ignored, especially when the administration claims to be exercising scientific expertise in the "best interests" of the citizens. The result is democracy in form only (1976:37).

Economic/political interdependence is unstable, however, because the manipulation of the normative structure often has unintended effects of highlighting meanings and norms previously taken for granted. Turning the spotlight on these meanings and norms subjects them to public scrutiny, and the resulting public discussion and discontent raise the possibility that change will be demanded (Habermas, 1976:47–48). That the state will have legitimation problems is almost guaranteed because, according to classical free enterprise ideology, the state is damned if it does intervene in the economy but, given the inevitable social problems, the state is damned if it does not intervene (Wuthnow et al., 1984:220).

Legitimation crises can only be avoided, in Habermas's view, by the development of new ways of reaching normative consensus through communicative competence. **Communicative competence** refers to the everyday world of taken-for-granted assumptions that structure understanding of how the world is and how individuals can act in that world. Communication is different from instrumental action. In modern society, however, the taken-for-granted assumptions are increasingly tied to the rationalization of the everyday world because of the reliance on technical rules and scientific knowledge. For example, marriage becomes a contract; family members seek legal redress against each other; education is tied to employment; universities are required to act like businesses; and political debate becomes 30-second sound bites of slogans fueled by vast sums of campaign "donations" (Waters, 1994:165).

Rationalization is in competition with understanding, and social relations are "regulated only through money and power" (Habermas, 1984, 2:154). But "money and power can neither buy nor compel solidarity and meaning" (1984, 2:363). The construction of an ideal speech community to reclaim the right of citizens to determine their own fate becomes imperative, in Habermas's view, in the face of the loss of meaning caused by the rationalization of everyday life.

Humans   Communicative competence, to Habermas, is bound up with identity formation. Habermas turned to George Herbert Mead's idea that reason is based on the communicative relations between individuals. That is, identity can only develop in interaction with others, and individuals know themselves only through the eyes of others (1984, 1:390).

Socialization is therefore the internalization of a society's grammatical as well as normative rules governing communication. This internalization occurs, according to Habermas, in four stages of cognitive and moral development.

- The **symbiotic** stage occurs in the first year of life, when the child's dependency means a lack of differentiation from the surrounding world of people and objects.

- The **egocentric** stage begins when the child learns to distinguish self from the surrounding environment of people and objects but judges the significance of that environment in terms of his or her own needs and desires.

- The **sociocentric-objectivist** stage, from about age four to adolescence, involves the child's learning to differentiate the environment of people and objects using complex and abstract symbols and categories. At this stage, the child learns to distinguish objects from their symbolization, and her or his understanding from the understanding of others.

- The **universalistic** stage involves the ability to think abstractly and to reflect critically on the self and its place in the world. At this stage, autonomy, especially from the immediate agents of socialization, is achieved. Also at this stage, altruism prevails as individuals transcend their private needs and desires to take account of communal needs and goals.

Socialization produces "individuals." However, individual identity does not occur as a result of individual efforts, claims Habermas, but as a result of intersubjective recognition (1990:130). In the stages of development, therefore, the most significant one is the development of cognition, the egocentric stage. Cognition is the basis for the development of competent communicative abilities, which in turn produce intersubjective recognition. Communication is therefore not simply about reaching understanding; it is also about social interaction and social integration. Communication involves interactions that "develop, confirm, and renew" an individual's group membership and personal identity. Communication involves not only social interaction and integration but also "processes of interpretation in which cultural knowledge is 'tested against the world'" (Habermas, 1984, 2:139).

According to Habermas, human beings organize themselves in terms of **knowledge-constitutive human interests** as a result of their work and symbolic communication about work activities (1971:311). Three types of knowledge interests guide human action:

- **Technical interests** give humans control over nature and are represented in the social organization of work.

- **Practical interests** enable human beings to act in relation to common traditions and rest on language competence.

- **Emancipatory interests** have to do with power and the need to free human beings from domination by abstract, hypostatized powers.

All of these interests depend on communication. But for the third, emancipatory interest, to be an effective critique of domination, argues Habermas, the communication must meet certain validity criteria.

When individuals communicate, they make validity claims that are either accepted or rejected. Three types of **validity claims** determine whether a communication is understandable:

- An objective scientific claim that the communication is true.

- A normative claim that the communication is in accordance with legal requirements and social norms.

- A subjective, ethical claim that the communication sincerely expresses the individual's feelings.

The intention in communication is to reach a consensus about validity claims. This is achieved when all speakers have equal, unconstrained access to the dialogue so that the "force of the better argument" prevails (Habermas, 1984:26).

Habermas recognized that communication could be systematically distorted, either consciously or unconsciously. But whether the communication represents conscious lying and manipulation or unconscious delusion, both speaker and audience assume that the claims made are true, right, and sincere.

Communication and Change   For Habermas, the key to social change lies in the development of the ideal speech situation. The ideal speech situation is not a physical place. It is an outline of the "necessary but general conditions for the communicative practice of everyday life" that will enable the participants to realize "concrete possibilities for a better, less threatened life, on *their own* initiative and in accordance with *their own* needs and insights" (1989:69). The ideal speech community is not simply a "talking shop" of endless discussion and interpretation. Emancipatory critique is not arbitrary, but rests on the rational justification of normative statements.

New social movements represent one of the ways in which the ideal speech situation might materialize. Habermas regards contemporary social movements, such as the environmental movement, the peace movement, the gay rights movement, and the women's movement, as sources for emancipatory transformation. These movements are quite unlike the class conflicts of labor and capital because they are concerned with the quality of life, self-realization, and normative expectations. These movements not only protest the domination of capital and state power, but they also develop alternative practices to the rationalized, technological world ruled by money and power.

Habermas's ideal speech situation presupposes that if the correct procedural norms are followed, consensus will be possible because reason will prevail. The outcome will be defensible because it is true, right, and sincere. A key requirement for this ideal situation is that all the participants be free and equal and genuinely desire to reach rational agreement on the issue(s) involved. These requirements may be problematic when race and gender are taken into account, at least in the short term.

Class, Gender, and Race

Class   Habermas argues that capitalist society has changed so drastically that the "two key categories of Marxian theory, namely class struggle and ideology, can no longer be employed as they stand" (1971:107). State-regulated, advanced capitalism suspends class conflict by buying off the workers with improved access to goods and services. The probability that the stark differences between the owners of capital and the nonowners will become more obvious, promoting a revolutionary consciousness among the dispossessed, is circumvented by the glitter of consumer society.

Class distinctions persist, but according to Habermas, they are not central to social conflict. Conflict in modern society involves underprivileged groups who are not classes as such and certainly do not represent the majority in the society. The disenfranchisement and pauperization of groups such as single mothers or homeless youth, "no longer coincides with *exploitation*, because the system does not live off their labor." Although these groups may "react with desperate destruction and self-destruction," as long as they are marginalized from other, more privileged groups in the society, there is little possibility that their protests will translate into general revolutionary action (1971:110). In fact, the state may use these groups to consolidate its power by encouraging potential allies to see them as social misfits, lazy bums, and welfare cheats.

Like the earlier critical theorists, Habermas has abandoned the proletariat as a potentially emancipatory force, and he has problems finding another group to replace them. He also tends to overlook the situation in non-Western countries and the possibility that emancipatory transformation may arise as a result of the obvious inequities of global capitalism. He has suggested that the only truly revolutionary group in Western societies is the women's movement (1971:112).

Gender   Habermas has actually said little about gender in his work, overlooking the gender implications in relations between public and private institutions in capitalist societies. For example, the public economic sphere is linked in Habermas's account to the private sphere of the nuclear family. Exchanges between the family and the economy are "channeled through the 'roles' of worker and consumer." Similarly, the public sphere of politics is linked with the administration system of the state, and the exchanges between the two are linked through the "role" of citizen and, "in late welfare state capitalism, that of client" (Fraser, 1989:123). These "roles" are, however, gendered. For example, the child-rearing role is generally a feminine role that is unpaid but produces the next generation of workers and consumers. Similarly, the role of citizen is frequently compromised by the fact that it is women as single mothers, for example, who comprise the majority of the clients of state welfare.

Critical theory generally needs to be more attuned to the issues of gender. Most especially, the possibility of the emancipatory transformation through the ideal speech situation envisaged by Habermas requires a consideration of the way in which women's voices and opinions can be heard when there has been little change in gender relations. As Fraser (1989:137) puts it, "From a feminist perspective, there is a more basic battle line between the forms of male dominance linking 'system' to 'life world' *and us*."

This battle line is not eased by Habermas's observation that the "historical legacy of the sexual division of labor, to which women were subjected in the nuclear bourgeois family, . . . gives them access to virtues, to a set of values that are both in contrast and complementary to the male world and at odds with the one-sided rationalized praxis of everyday life" (1987, 2:394). Separate but equal, with the suggestion that women's moral superiority can usefully temper male rationality, is hardly a revolutionary or emancipatory observation.

Race   Habermas's work has similar problems of omission with respect to race. Habermas has addressed the issue of race largely in the context of immigration and citizenship issues regarding "guest" workers in Europe. He sees the right-wing opposition to these workers as resting on the idea that they threaten national identity—that different cultural values, religious beliefs, and ethnic identities challenge conceptions of citizenship. Habermas's call for civic-minded debate about social issues is thus compromised by the conflict between legal and ethnic conceptions of citizenship (Pensky, 1995:90).

As Warnke (1995:140) has pointed out, the possibility of normative consensus on issues such as "liberty, equality, sanctity of life, and human rights in general" as a result of participating in the ideal speech situation can still be "impeded by power, wealth, race, or gender" and the coexistence of different cultures. Habermas has not successfully addressed these issues to date.

The importance of these issues can be seen in the vote of a Swiss suburb in March 2000 on the acceptance or rejection of recent immigrant requests for citizenship. In a process that approximated the full information requirement of Habermas's ideal speech community, the voters were give a booklet containing information on the salary, tax status, background, and hobbies as well as family photographs of the individuals seeking citizenship. Out of fifty-six families, only four, all of Italian origin, were accepted. Those rejected were largely of Yugoslavian origin ("Who's Swiss? City Votes Against Most Foreigners," 2000).

Other Theories and Theorists

Habermas's consistent focus throughout his work has been on the relation among reason, modernity, and democracy, with the aim of providing an outline of an emancipated, rational society. Habermas himself has stated that his "research program has remained the same since about 1970" (1993:149). He has pursued the development of a theory of communicative action as the means to continue critical theory's injunction to connect theory and practice.

Critique and Conclusions

The work of Habermas and the earlier critical theorists was predicated on the idea that theory is central to the practical transformation of society. But for Habermas and earlier critical theorists, the revolutionary agent of such transformation was difficult to identify. Critical theory stresses the "importance of fundamental transformation which has little basis in social struggle" but tends to lose sight of "important social and political struggles both within the West and beyond it—struggles which have changed and are continuing to change the face of politics" (Held, 1980:399–400). For example, it is difficult to imagine the possibility or the conditions for the beginnings of free, unconstrained dialogue and discourse among the current ethnic and racially based contenders in Africa, South America, the Balkans, the Middle East, and Asia, let alone the members of politically extreme parties and movements in Western democracies. In fact, Habermas's optimistic, evolutionary assumption that moral consciousness evolves and that norms and values become more universalistic seems unconvincing in the face of the barbarism of the past century.

Habermas's ideal speech community assumes a singular public sphere rather than a multiplicity of publics and carries the implication that democratic politics revolves around a unitary state. But the voices of women, gay activists, and racial and ethnic minorities that are often excluded from formal political structures of debate and dialogue suggest the need to recognize the multiplicity of public spheres. Furthermore, individuals discuss a lot of things in public contexts that do not resemble Habermas's "classical Enlightenment sphere." Such public discussions, taking place in "churches and self-help groups, among filmgoers and on talk-radio, among parents waiting for their children after school dances," are about "childbearing and childrearing, marriage and divorce, violence of various sorts"—everyday topics of immediate concern to the body politic (Calhoun, 1996:460).

Axel van den Berg (1980:476) is scathing in his judgment of the critical theorists, claiming "they have chosen the comfortable heights of philosophical abstraction and obscurity far away from the daily concerns of the rabble" and that "to expect any public support for a philosophy whose only distinction is its sheer obscurity, for a notion of reason lacking all substance, for a utopia without any indication of its features or feasibility has absolutely nothing to do with emancipation of any kind." In fact, however, Habermas's intentions are somewhat more modest than the grand utopian solution against which van den Berg takes aim.

Habermas sees critical theory that is true to its Marxist origins as providing the means to analyze the abstractions of social life that conceal the real relations of exploitation and domination. To accomplish this, the analysis must concentrate on the "grammar of forms of life" (Habermas, 1984, 2:576). Habermas sees critical theory as therefore true to the origins of sociology.

> *Sociology* originated as a discipline responsible for the problems that politics and economics pushed to one side. . . . Its theme was the changes in social integration brought about within the structure of old-European societies by the rise of the modern system of nation states and by the differentiation of a market regulated economy. Sociology became the science of crisis par excellence; it concerned itself above all with the anomic aspects of all the dissolution of traditional social systems and the development of modern ones. (1984, 1:4)

Critical theory's importance remains clear, in Habermas's view, because the legacy of National Socialism lives on in European neoconservatism and neo-Nazism (1989).

Final Thoughts

Sociology, as a critical theoretical enterprise, still has a place in the twenty-first century. The global crises that threaten the freedom of citizens, the fragility of democratic institutions in the face of global market forces, and the various siren calls for ideological purity in the name of a race, religion, or nation, all need to be critically and publicly analyzed. Sociology is a critical resource at the individual level also in its analysis of the everyday/everynight threats to human dignity and self-esteem. There are no guarantees, no "ultimate redemption" guaranteed by the "laws of history," but redemption remains, as Habermas puts it, a "practical hypothesis" from which a critical sociology can start (McCarthy, 1989:xiv).

References

Adorno, Theodor. 1984. *Aesthetic Theory* (C. Lenhardt, Trans.). London: Routledge and Kegan Paul.

Adorno, Theodor, Else Frenkel-Brunswik, Daniel J. Levison, and R. Nevitt Sanford. 1950. *The Authoritarian Personality*. New York: Harper.

Adorno, Theodor, and Max Horkheimer. 1944/1979. *Dialectic of Enlightenment*. London: Verso.

Agger, Ben. 1979. *Western Marxism: An Introduction*. Santa Monica, CA: Goodyear Publishing Company.

Alford, Fred, C. 1987. "Habermas, Post-Freudian Psychoanalysis and the End of the Individual." *Theory, Culture and Society*, 4(1), 3–29.

Ashenden, Samantha. 1999. "Questions of Criticism: Habermas and Foucault on Civil Society and Resistance." In Samantha Ashenden and David Owen (Eds.), *Foucault Contra Habermas*. London: Sage.

Benhabib, Seyla. 1986. *Critique, Norm, and Utopia*. New York: Columbia University Press.

Bernstein, Richard J. (Ed.). 1985. *Habermas and Modernity*. Cambridge, MA: MIT Press.

Calhoun, Craig. 1996. "Social Theory and the Public Sphere." In Bryan S. Turner (Ed.), *Social Theory* (pp. 429–470). Oxford: Blackwell.

Delanty, Gerard. 1997. "Habermas and Occidental Rationalism: The Politics of Identity, Social Learning, and the Cultural Limits of Moral Individualism." *Sociological Theory*, 15(1), 30–59.

Fraser, Nancy. 1989. *Unruly Practices: Power, Discourse and Gender in Contemporary Social Theory*. Minneapolis: University of Minnesota Press.

Fromm, Erich. 1941. *Excerpt from Freedom*. New York: Holt, Rinehart and Winston.

———. 1955. *The Sane Society*. New York: Holt, Rinehart and Winston.

———. 1960. *The Fear of Freedom*. London: Routledge and Kegan Paul.

———. 1965/1981. *On Disobedience and Other Essays*. New York: Seabury Press.

———. 1979/1980. *The Greatness and Limitations of Freud's Thought*. New York: Harper and Row.

———. 1988. "The Method and Function of an Analytic Social Psychology." In Andrew Arato and Eike Gebhardt (Eds.), *The Essential Frankfurt Reader* (pp. 477–496). New York: Continuum.

Habermas, Jurgen. 1970. *Towards a Rational Society* (Jeremy J. Shapiro, Trans.). London: Heinemann.

———. 1971. *Knowledge and Human Interests* (Jeremy Shapiro, Trans.). Boston: Beacon Press.

———. 1974. *Theory and Practice* (John Viertel, Trans.). London: Heinemann.

———. 1976. *Legitimation Crisis* (Thomas McCarthy, Trans.). London: Heinemann.

———. 1984. *The Theory of Communicative Action* (vol. 1) (Thomas McCarthy, Trans.). Boston: Beacon Press.

———. 1987. *The Theory of Communicative Action* (vol. 2) (Thomas McCarthy, Trans.). Boston: Beacon Press.

———. 1989. *The New Conservatism* (Shierry Weber Nicholsen, Ed. and Trans.). Cambridge, MA: MIT Press.

———. 1990. *Moral Consciousness and Communicative Action* (Christine Lenhardt and Sherry Weber Nicholsen, Trans.). Cambridge, MA: MIT Press.

———. 1993. *Justification and Application: Remarks on Discourse Ethics* (Ciaran P. Cronin, Trans.). Cambridge, MA: MIT Press.

Held, David. 1980. *Introduction to Critical Theory*. London: Hutchinson.

Horkheimer, Max. 1935/1993. *Between Philosophy and Social Science* (C. Frederick Hunter, Matthew S. Kramer, and John Torpey, Trans.). Cambridge, MA: MIT Press.

———. 1947. *The Eclipse of Reason*. New York: Oxford University Press.

———. 1974. *Critique of Instrumental Reason*. New York: Seabury Press.

———. 1982. *Critical Theory: Selected Essays*. New York: Continuum.

Jagentowicz Mills, Patricia. 1987. *Woman, Nature and Psyche*. New Haven, CT: Yale University Press.

Jay, Martin. 1973. *The Dialectical Imagination: A History of the Frankfurt School and the Institute of Social Research 1923–1950*. Boston: Little, Brown.

Kellner, Douglas. 1989. *Critical Theory: Marxism and Modernity*. Baltimore: Johns Hopkins University Press.

Lukacs, George. 1922/1968. *History and Class Consciousness*. Cambridge, MA: MIT Press.

Marcuse, Herbert. 1960. *Reason and Revolution*. Boston: Beacon Press.

———. 1964. *One-Dimensional Man*. Boston: Beacon Press.

———. 1966. *Eros and Civilization*. Boston: Beacon Press.

———. 1970. *Five Lectures: Psychoanalysis, Politics, and Utopia*. Boston: Beacon Press.

———. 1972. *Counterrevolution and Revolt*. Boston: Beacon Press.

McCarthy, Thomas. 1989. "Introduction." In Jurgen Habermas, *The Structural Transformation of the Public Sphere* (pp. xi–xiv). Cambridge: Polity Press.

Outhwaite, William. 1994. *Habermas: A Critical Introduction*. Stanford, CA: Stanford University Press.

Pensky, Max. 1995. "Universalism and the Situated Critic." In Stephen K. White (Ed.), *The Cambridge Companion to Habermas* (pp. 67–94). Cambridge: Cambridge University Press.

van den Berg, Axel. 1980. "Critical Theory: Is There Still Hope?" *American Journal of Sociology, 86*, 449–478.

Warnke, Georgia. 1995. "Communicative Rationality and Cultural Values." In Stephen K. White (Ed.), *The Cambridge Companion to Habermas* (pp. 120–142). Cambridge: Cambridge University Press.

Waters, Malcolm. 1994. *Modern Sociological Theory*. London: Sage.

White, Stephen K. (Ed.). 1995. *The Cambridge Companion to Habermas*. Cambridge: Cambridge University Press.

"Who's Swiss? City Votes Against Most Foreigners." 2000, March 13. *Globe and Mail*, pp. 1, 3.

Wiggershaus, Rolf. 1994. *The Frankfurt School* (Michael Robertson, Trans.). Oxford: Polity Press.

Wuthnow, Robert, James Davison Hunter, Albert Bergesen, and Edith Kurzweil (Eds.). 1984. *Cultural Analysis*. Boston: Routledge and Kegan Paul.

Chapter 5

Marxism Since 1930
Poulantzas, Althusser, Dunayevskaya, and Wright

Struggles for freedom continue, whether by workers experiencing near depression levels of unemployment, women confronting attacks on their right to control their own bodies and minds, black people and other minorities combating resurgent racism, or youth protesting environmental destruction, militarism and a decaying educational system. . . .

How, then, can it be that despite the persistence of such aspirations for freedom, we are witnessing a breakdown in the effort to articulate a concept, a goal, an *idea* of human liberation that speaks to the realities of our time?

Part of the reason lies in the fact that all too many revolutionaries failed to grasp the *class* divide separating Marx's Marxism from its absolute opposite, Communist totalitarianism. (Hudis, 1992:viii)

What has become of Marxism at the turn of the twenty-first century? Did it die with the Soviet Union? Is it on the defensive, regrouping, purifying, or explaining its theory? Is it still waiting for capitalism to self-destruct, or is it merely an academic discourse? In this chapter we will attempt to speak to these issues as we follow Marxist theory and practice from Lenin's death to the twenty-first century. We will begin with a brief review of early Marxism, then discuss a series of theoretical issues, and close the chapter with a look at Erik Olin Wright's contemporary Marxism.

An outstanding two-volume work, *A History of Marxian Economics*, edited by Howard and King and published in 1992, summarizes classical orthodox Marxism-Leninism. By 1900, the central pillars of Marxism were three: First, capital was being concentrated in ever larger and more powerful economic units. This led "to a rising rate of exploitation and to the relative (if not absolute) immiseration of a rapidly increasing and class-conscious proletariat." Second, "economic crises were inescapable under capitalism and would tend to become more severe." This resulted not just from exploitation, but from the inherent contradictions within capitalism. "Third, and as a consequence of all this, capitalism itself was ripe for replacement." A corollary to this third proposition was that "socialism offered a viable, and in every way preferable, alternative to the capitalist mode of production" (Howard and King, 1992:387).

Somewhat later, in the writings of Lenin and Luxemburg, a fourth claim was advanced: "Theories of imperialism asserted that the struggle for economic territory was the fundamental impulse behind the political and military rivalries of the various capitalist states" (Howard and King, 1992:387). The other addition to Marxism in the early twentieth century was the existence of an avowedly Marxist state—the Soviet Union.

Marxism from 1930 to 1980

Since 1930, many important world events have needed interpretation: the Great Depression of the 1930s in the United States and much of the world, the Second World War, the political independence of former colonies, the spread of transnational corporations, and the eventual fall of Marxism in the Soviet bloc countries. "Uneven development entailed the underdevelopment of backward and dependent, or Third World, regions and not . . . their rapid assimilation as more or less equal partners in the world system" (Howard and King, 1992:388). Thus, the language used to describe Third World countries changed from "developing" to "underdeveloped."

In addition, the safeguards produced by capitalism itself—such as the federal reserve system—have at least called into question the potential severity of economic crises. Although the crisis principle has not been completely rejected, it is being debated by Marxists today. Likewise, the notion that capitalism is ripe for overthrow also seems questionable. This is not simply because of the capitalist world's military might, which Marx and Engels recognized, or because of **false consciousness**—the identification of the oppressed with the system that oppresses them. It is also because capitalism continues to "deliver the goods." Even relative immiseration is hard to recognize in the advanced capitalist countries, though it can certainly be found in the Third World (Howard and King, 1992:388).

As for capitalist conflicts and socialism's readiness to take over (as it supposedly did in Russia), two issues have arisen. On the one hand, U.S. economic and military dominance after 1945 produced a new (capitalist) world order, and on the other hand, the Stalinist model of socialist development failed to live up to its own Marxist ideology, in Russia and elsewhere (Dunayevskaya, 1958; Howard and King, 1992:389). In the face of all these changes, critics have been only too eager to announce Marxism's demise.

In this chapter we will examine at length some of the major currents in Marxism since 1930, closing with Erik Olin Wright's "no frills" Marxism in which ideology and utopia are minimized. Wright's analytical Marxism is important because it embodies a broad spectrum of today's academic Marxism, the "Left Academy," which in the past 30 years has attempted to give Marxism intellectual credibility, while not succumbing either to the glorification of communist states or to defeatism in confronting the capitalist world order.

Central Theories and Methods of Post-1930s Marxism

In this section we will examine several important Marxist theoretical concepts developed during the period between 1930 and 1980, approximately in the order in which they appeared. Several of them, such as hegemony, in the 1930s, and the state and structuralism, in the 1960s, were discussed in ways that emphasize their complexity. Next, the concept of state capitalism sought to explain the non-Marxist nature of the Soviet Union and Eastern Bloc states, while the concept of monopoly capitalism built on Thorstein Veblen and Lenin in demonstrating the large-scale, neo-imperialistic nature of modern capitalism. We will close this section with several miscellaneous but valuable Marxist insights.

Hegemony   **Hegemony** is leadership or authority. According to Marx, throughout human history hegemony has been determined by control of the means of production and exploitation of the workers. For Vilfredo Pareto, such hegemony was a matter for the political ruling elite. However, the key figure in an expanded twentieth-century Marxist understanding of hegemony was Antonio Gramsci, an Italian who lived from 1889 to 1937. Gramsci joined the Italian Communist Party in 1913, and throughout the rest of his life was a dedicated Marxist revolutionary. He was in prison for more than a decade at the end of his life, having questioned Mussolini's fascist control over Italy. He was also critical of Stalin's government in Russia, and, of course, of capitalism. While in prison, he produced his most important theoretical writings, despite long periods of ill health (Gramsci, 1937).

For Gramsci, hegemony was not just structural domination through economics or politics. It was a combination of political, intellectual, and moral leadership (Mouffe, 1979:179), meaning that it involved superstructure or ideology and private institutions as well as politics. Although dictatorship may or may not be one element, wrote commentator Jacques Texier, Gramsci's formulations were important

> precisely because they stress the unity of consensus and dictatorship. This is the case with the definition of the **integral state** as follows: "State = political society + civil society, in other words, hegemony protected by the armour of coercion." A social group exercises its hegemony over subordinate social groups which accept its rule so long as it exercises its dictatorship over the hostile social groups which reject it. (Texier, 1979:64, quoting Gramsci, 1937:263)

Hegemony, then, is exercised through the commitment of those who are persuaded and through control of any opposition.

The hegemonic apparatus of a society includes, according to Gramsci, "schools, churches, the entire media and even architecture and the names of streets" (1937:332). Hegemony, then, involves persuasion or consensus, as well as coercion. Leadership and power have to be explained as they function in the "real world," not in some simplified economic or political portion of it (Paggi, 1979:138). And hegemony in the real world involves creation of a higher synthesis, a general interest or collective will (Mouffe, 1979:184, 194). Note that Gramsci was not saying that the hegemony of those in power is the general interest, but that it incorporates ideology, institutions, and power in order to appear that it is.

What can the working classes do to offset such broad-scale hegemony by the bourgeoisie? In Gramsci's view, it is

> vital for the working class not to isolate itself within a ghetto of proletarian purism. On the contrary, it must try to become a "national class," representing the interests of the increasingly numerous social groups. In order to do this it must cause the disintegration of the historical bases of the bourgeoisie's hegemony by disarticulating the ideological bloc by means of which the bourgeoisie's intellectual direction is expressed. (Mouffe, 1979:197)

This process is much more complex and difficult to effect than the working-class uprising described and preached by early Marxists. Gramsci thus sought to reincorporate ideological issues into the Marxist discussion of bourgeois control and proletariat revolution.

State Capitalism   In the early twentieth century, Rosa Luxemburg criticized Lenin's centralized Russia. But by the 1940s, Marxist criticisms of the Soviet Union as not having lived up to its supposed embodiment of communist thought had increased dramatically. If Stalin's totalitarian regime exemplified Marxism in action, capitalist ideologues needed to do very little to discredit it, except to point out its characteristic failings. In the early 1940s, Raya Dunayevskaya, formerly the Russian-language secretary to Leon Trotsky, began to describe the Soviet Union not as a Marxist state, but as "state capitalism." This was, of course, 50 years before Russia gave up the trappings of Marxist ideology in favor of capitalism.

When Dunayevskaya began writing about the Soviet Union, it was still being held up by Marxists as an example—albeit an imperfect one—of a Marxist state. Even during the radical activity of the "New Left" in the 1960s, criticism of Russia was often muted. Peter Hudis, in introducing Dunayevskaya's book, wrote that the '60s radicals were convinced that their effectiveness would make it possible to pick up Marxist theory on the way to the revolution. "This skipping over of theory," noted Hudis, "only made it easier for the New Left to fall into the trap" of glorifying a nation-state "masquerading as Communism, since the Stalinist rulers continued to use 'Marxist' language" (Hudis, 1992:xx).

When Lenin's Bolshevik party took over the government as the vanguard of a proletarian dictatorship, he claimed that he was carrying out Marxist doctrine. When he instituted the New Economic Policy of a mixed economy as a necessity, he argued that it would eventually wither away into true communism. And when Stalin transformed the Soviet Union into a bureaucratized totalitarian state, he defended the necessity of "purification"—of getting rid of the misguided.

However, Dunayevskaya claimed in the 1940s that the Soviet Union was never really Marxist, and certainly not communist. To understand it, she suggested, one had to combine the realities of (1) Lenin's party dictatorship, (2) Russia's mixed economy, and (3) Stalin's bureaucratic totalitarian state, while (4) ignoring the Marxist "smoke-screen." Dunayevskaya carried out a meticulous analysis of the Russian economy in 1942–43 and carried it further in 1946–47 (Dunayevskaya, 1951:35–82). In these analyses, she noted the ownership of property by the state, the surplus value being extracted by the state intelligentsia, the "fight for profit," and the class system of the Soviet Union. Connecting her analysis back to Marx's *Capital* (Volume 3), she concluded that the Soviet Union was simply **state capitalism**, far removed from Marx's theory. The Soviet bureaucracy was, in fact, the "bodyguard of capital," making it an "absolute contradiction" between theory and practice. Such state capitalism was not the highest stage of capitalism in its contradictions; it was "the *transformation* of monopoly capitalism into its opposite" (Dunayevskaya, 1951:98).

On this view, the Soviet Union did not *become* capitalist at the beginning of the 1990s; it simply confessed to what it already was. It had been a combination of socialism and capitalism since its inception, and had become more so during Stalin's time.

Monopoly Capitalism and Imperialism   Two central figures in twentieth-century U.S. Marxism were Paul Baran and Paul Sweezy. Both were born in 1910, the former in Russia and the latter in New York City. They met in the early 1940s at Harvard, and began their long collaboration. The centerpiece of their collaboration was the best-selling book *Monopoly Capital*, which appeared in 1966, two years after Baran's death.

The first major issue for Baran and Sweezy concerned underconsumption and waste. Observing a lengthy post–World War II growth in capitalist production, Baran, and later Sweezy, reported that capitalism's problem is that so much of its productive capacity is wasted on the military, on advertising, and on product differentiation. Despite Marx's observation about capitalism's need for new, esoteric goods and services, Baran saw much of the supposed boom as using up or wasting profits. Baran and Sweezy criticized capitalism for wasting instead of promoting a higher standard of living for the masses.

As the economic boom of the 1940s and 1950s began to wane, and especially as former colonies became politically independent, Baran and Sweezy turned their attention to underdevelopment in the Third World. Using terms such as *neo-imperialism* and *neocolonialism*, Baran noted that economic neo-imperialism has "effortlessly replaced colonial [political] control and brought about sustained underdevelopment. Surplus continues to be drained off, principally through the repatriation of profits from foreign" investments in the Third World (Howard and King, 1992:171). Even the class structures of such peripheral societies, which are primarily proletarian, are products of neo-imperialism. Advanced capitalist societies dominate not only by investment, but by their control of technological expertise and of money through the World Bank, International Monetary Fund, and other sources. **Monopoly capitalism** includes all of this.

Though it was not central to their argument, Baran and Sweezy took note of racism when they connected Third World peoples with the marginalized peoples of the advanced capitalist societies. Looked at worldwide, they observed that race is highly correlated with class, meaning that the revolution, when it comes, will involve both.

Sweezy's Marxist enthusiasm eventually changed its focus from Eastern Europe and Russia to Cuba. Although Baran died too soon after the Cuban revolution to follow Sweezy's lead, it is possible he might never have done so. Baran's "traditional Marxist contempt for the peasantry" and his allegiance to heavy industry as central to the socialist revolution might have kept him from ever viewing the Third World as a primary locus of revolution (Howard and King, 1992:175). In fact, unlike Dunayevskaya, Baran was so impressed by the command or socialist economies of Russia, Eastern Europe, and China that at his death he was still convinced that neither capitalist reform nor peasant uprising could accomplish what could be done by a centrally planned industrial politico-economic system.

Once North American Marxism turned away from the underconsumption argument, in only "two respects did the ideas of Baran and Sweezy have a more permanent impact upon Marxian economics throughout the world. This was in their treatment of armaments expenditure . . . and in their theory of underdevelopment in the Third World" (Howard and King, 1992:124).

The last important issue in monopoly capitalism is imperialism and the multinationals. Present-day Marxism takes two views of capitalism and development. The older view, found in some parts of Marx's own writing, is that capitalism creates the material preconditions for a better (socialist) society, as well as the class forces that will bring it about. This is the classical Marxist position stating that society must pass through a capitalist phase on the way to socialism. The second, more recent, view is that "it is precisely the failure of capitalism to generate economic development that makes revolution necessary," especially in the Third World (Brewer, 1980:16). This second position is found in the work of Immanuel Wallerstein, who argues, as we will see in Chapter 6, that capitalism is now a world system, with some nations at the core and others on the periphery. (On these two versions of Marxism, see Blomstrom and Hettne, 1984:33–38.)

An important feature of imperialism today, as Baran and Sweezy noted, is the multinational or transnational corporation—a result of the centralization and then the internationalization of capital. Manufacturing where there is cheap labor, and distribution close to the markets, make it rational to locate enterprises in more than one setting, sometimes in several advanced societies, and sometimes also in less developed countries. Some have argued that multinationals indicate a lessening of the importance of the nation-state. However, Anthony Brewer and Nicos Poulantzas assert that, although national economies may be less relevant, "this is quite different from arguing the irrelevance of the national governments as a site of class conflict, of political integration, and of a state apparatus that has at its command more potent weapons than those of monetary and fiscal policy" (Brewer, 1980:279). In short, "capital that operates internationally needs the support of a home state to protect its interests" (1980:280).

Marx and Engels wrote at a time of relative peace among the advanced capitalist nations. Engels, for example, witnessed the Berlin conference of 1885, in which Africa was carved up into colonies by the European powers. Lenin and Luxemburg, on the other hand, wrote during World War I, when these same nations were at each other's throats. The present "world order" under U.S. dominance seems to again represent capitalism's "peaceful" hegemony, with conflicts concentrated largely in the Third World or involving ethnic rivalries.

Before the turn of the twentieth century, transport improved, organizational forms made the international flow of capital easier, and the international transfer of technology became possible. A century later, the computer has advanced the technology of communication even more dramatically, potentially making core dominance—economic and military—over the periphery easier than ever. However, underdevelopment does not necessarily support or strengthen neo-imperialism. The other two potential outcomes are increasing capitalist development in the periphery, or socialist/communist revolution.

So far, we have looked at Gramsci's theory of hegemony, Dunayevskaya's view of the Soviet Union as state capitalism, and twentieth-century monopoly capitalism as expressed particularly in economic neo-imperialism. We come now to Poulantzas's view of the state in relation to Marxism.

Poulantzas and State Power   Nicos Poulantzas was born in Athens and in 1968 joined the faculty at the Sorbonne in Paris. Perhaps more than any other late-twentieth-century Marxist, Poulantzas developed a Marxist theory of the state. Although his thousands of words on this subject were not always consistent, it is possible to bring together and summarize his key ideas: "as his work developed during the 1970s, Poulantzas increasingly emphasized the nature of the state as a system of *strategic selectivity* and the nature of political struggle as a field of *competing strategies for hegemony*," or dominance and control (Jessop, 1990:221).

Marx's and Engels's theory of the state was primarily that it is the mechanism (structure) whereby the owners of the means of production rule a society. Others had treated the state as little more than the expression of control in a society, or, as Gramsci put it, an expression of both political and ideational hegemony. For Poulantzas the **state** is even more complex:

> a *strategic field and process* of intersecting power networks, which both articulate and exhibit mutual contradictions and displacements. . . . This strategic field is traversed by tactics which are often highly explicit at the restricted level of their inscription in the State: they intersect and conflict with one another, finding their targets in some apparatuses or being short-circuited by others, and eventually map out that general line of force, the State's "policy," which traverses confrontations within the State (1978:136)

Poulantzas went on to say that these tactics are not merely detachable and oppositional parts. They exhibit a unity of state power, which is both unified and contains inconsistencies. One, but only one, of the inconsistencies involves class interests, to which we shall return. To follow Poulantzas, we must discard the view of the state as completely unified.

Demonstrating his ability to explain complexity, Poulantzas noted that the state is more than a combination of repression and ideological false consciousness. Even fascist or totalitarian societies must control unemployment and introduce social legislation to meet the needs of the population (1978:31). In fact, Poulantzas argued that even from the micro-political standpoint, much state behavior is incoherent and chaotic (1978:135).

Furthermore, the state apparatus includes more than state power; it includes everything from the postal service to the road system. Such services are not, of course, independent of power, because those in power need such mechanisms themselves. "Thus, while all the State's actions are not reducible to political domination, their composition is nevertheless marked by it" (1978:14). In summary, then, for Poulantzas the state was neither completely unified nor free-standing. It was, rather, a complex mixture of class and group struggles, including ideological and economic issues, interest group goals and desires, services, and cross-national connections.

Poulantzas (1978) also laid out the relations among state, nation, language group, and class. Noting that there was no Marxist theory of the nation, he argued that the nation, defined by its territory, preceded both capitalism and the modern state. Moreover, it will outlast capitalism: The state will wither away, but not necessarily the nation. Language groupings overlap imperfectly with the state, although modern "nation-states" work very hard—legally and otherwise—to construct national languages. Whether it be Hindi in India or English in the United States, there are state- and power-based reasons for constructing a dominant language, a language of government and education.

The state and its power, then, were Poulantzas's central theoretical interest. Breaking out of the mold of both dogmatic Marxism and Louis Althusser's structuralism (discussed next), he was willing to deal with complexity, to admit that state, power, and economic classes overlap but are not synonymous. This was a major contribution to Marxist thought.

Althusser's Marxist Structuralism   Defining **structuralism,** Edith Kurzweil asserted that "ultimately all social reality" is "the interplay of the as yet unconscious mental structures" (1980:4). Based primarily on the work of the French anthropologist Claude Levi-Strauss, structuralism was adopted by French psychoanalysts, linguists, sociologists, and even Marxists. It dominated French scholarship from the 1950s into the 1970s, and even though it waned after that, structuralist language continued to be used.

Most of Louis Althusser's Marxist structuralism was published in the 1960s, especially in two books: *For Marx* (1965) and, with Etienne Balibar, *Reading Capital* (1968). A key aspect of Althusser's thought was separating Marx's writings into four periods: "1840–1844: the Early Works; 1845: the Works of the Break; 1846–1857: the Transitional Works; and 1857–1883: the Mature Works" (Althusser, 1965:35). In so doing, Althusser was able to downplay the importance of Marx's early humanistic concerns—"alienation, the abstraction (in the Hegelian sense) that unites the opposites, the negation of the negation"—and simplified economic determinism (Althusser, 1965:199). The "mature Marx," according to Althusser, should be the focus of attention and theory 100 years after Marx's death.

Of what did the mature Marx consist, according to Althusser? Society is a "structured whole," consisting of complex mental and physical conditions. This complexity includes the contradictions of which Marx spoke. These contradictions constitute the

> conditions of existence. As an example, take the complex structured whole that is society. In it, the "relations of production" are not the pure phenomenon of the forces of production; they are also their condition of existence. The superstructure is not the pure phenomenon of the structure, it is also its condition of existence. (Althusser, 1965:205)

Such complexity includes structures of dominance or hegemony (a concept for which Althusser gave Gramsci credit), uneven development, economics, politics, and superstructure or ideology (Althusser, 1965:114, 217). Calling himself a scientific Marxist rather than a structuralist, Althusser rejected humanistic Marxism, simplified "upside-down" Hegelianism, the notion of the inevitable revolution growing out of capitalism, historically specific Marxism related to a single time and place (such as Italy in the 1930s), and, as we have noted, simple economic determinism. He also rejected the notion of mental continuity (Levi-Strauss) and of change growing out of equilibrium (functionalism). Rather, he argued that the structural complexity and unevenness of capitalism must be understood and not simplified, and the revolution must be prepared for and organized (Kurzweil, 1980:36).

According to François Dosse, it was Poulantzas's 1968 work on power and the state that brought Althusser to the attention of the French intelligentsia and other Marxists. Poulantzas argued that Althusser's insights included criticism of two "misreadings of Marx: the one historical, and the other economist." The historical mistake was in a simplified viewing of social class as the subject of history. Class is but one portion of societal complexity, one bearer of social structure. The other misreading of Marx reduced classes to relations of production. Poulantzas, expanding Althusser into the realm of power and the state, had, according to one commentator, "the merit of proposing a new way of thinking about power conceived of as a vast and encompassing strategic realm, a far more complex approach than the usual references to a state-class instrument" (Dosse, 1967:173).

Althusser's attempt to both purify and complexify Marxism began to wane almost as soon as it became popular. French demonstrations and riots in 1968 received little support from Althusser, which left him open to criticism by other French Marxists. Even more important, in 1974 Althusser wrote *Elements of a Self-Criticism*. In this book, he stated that he had overemphasized ideology or the structure of ideas: "Our 'flirtation' with structuralist terminology certainly went beyond acceptable limits" (1974:57).

What, then, was Althusser's contribution? "By complexifying Marx's work, paying the price of a system of rigorous, synthetic [structural] thinking that wanted to totalize, Althusser managed to stave off Marxism's decline—a random spark . . . [in a] century in which Marxism was to lose itself in its fatal destiny, in the tragedy of totalitarianism" (Dosse, 1967:188).

Technology, Functionalism, Rational Choice: G. A. Cohen and Others

One oversimplification of Marx leads to economic or technological determinism.

G. A. Cohen, in his analytic and quasi-functionalist reformulation of historical materialism, comes close to this oversimplification.

Central to history, according to Cohen, are productive forces and technological change, founded on three premises: (1) humans are somewhat rational; (2) human history is one of scarcity; and (3) human intelligence enables us to improve our situation (1978:152). As a whole, this means that human beings have the capacity to solve scarcity problems. Production is only one pole of the solution, however; distribution is the other.

The other two elements in Cohen's thinking, both of them tied to the three premises noted above, are functionalism and rational choice. To Cohen, class oppression, not just differentiation, is necessary to the growth of surplus, because some people have to make other people work. The nonproducers have to see to it that the producers produce a surplus. At early historical stages, the surplus was not yet such that all could survive comfortably. It is only at what Cohen called "stage 4" that the surplus is sufficient for redistribution to be "functional" for everyone's comfortable survival.

Cohen spent two full chapters of his book explaining functionalism in general and then Marxist functionalism. The functional explanation of a societal ritual, for example, might show what it does for a people, without claiming that some other ritual might not meet the same need (Cohen, 1978:276). Thus, one can state the function of something without explaining it by referring to its function (1978:283). Cohen, like Robert Merton, questioned whether functional explanation is inherently ideologically conservative. Cohen argued that not only class oppression but class conflict may be historically functional, in the sense of meeting an important societal need for change and equality.

As for rationality, Cohen is one of several rational choice Marxists. Sometimes referred to as "analytical Marxism," this strand of theorizing begins with Cohen's premise that humans are at least somewhat rational. This school of thought, which arose and grew in the 1970s and 1980s, has three main features:

> First, rational choice Marxists have shown a concern for rigour and clarity to a degree unusual in Marxian theory. . . . Second, . . . the concepts and ideas of non-Marxists have figured prominently, and especially those of analytical philosophy, mathematical model-building, modern psychology and neoclassical economics. . . . Although critical . . . of Marx's central claims, rational choice Marxists have frequently demonstrated that much of his analysis is correct, and that this can be demonstrated by using non-Marxian theory.
>
> Third, there is a pronounced tendency to deduce Marxian propositions about socio-economic systems from the rational behaviour of decision-makers. It is this feature which makes analytical Marxists also rational choice Marxists. (Howard and King, 1992:335)

Cohen, John Roemer, and Jon Elster are important figures in this school of Marxist thought. However, Cohen has contributed little except his statement of the principle of rationality. Roemer, whose major concern is not history but values and ethics, argues that the distribution of property is more central to capitalism than is labor exploitation (Roemer, 1986). It is property and, as Cohen noted, technology about which choices are made, and on which capitalism is based. Roemer and Elster both depart from Marx in their **methodological individualism**, meaning that explanation is always in terms of individual, rather than class or nation-state, actions. Such micro-level explanation, depending on the choices individuals make in society, is said to be the foundation for understanding societal action and change.

Since Roemer reduces explanation to the individual level, one is left to wonder if theory or explanation actually requires one further reduction—to the biological level. Of course, Marxists do not make this final reduction. Besides, Roemer and Elster do not consistently reduce explanation to the individual, and Elster notes that individual decisions are often governed by Darwinian evolutionary processes and group norms (Elster, 1985, chap. 1).

However, these theorists argue that structuralist explanations, like those of Louis Althusser and Nicos Poulantzas, restrict individual choice to the point that it is virtually inconsequential. Cohen's writing, discussing as it does both functionalism and rational choice, bridges the gap between societal structures and the individual will, showing that neither should be carried so far as to become a caricature. It is worth noting that these theorists seldom refer to Marxists other than Marx himself, and they often correct his logic. Finally, Chapter 9 will expand on the theme of rational choice as an important late-twentieth-century non-Marxist theoretical position.

This section has covered a broad spectrum of twentieth-century Marxist perspectives. Dunayevskaya criticized the Soviet Union as not being Marxist at all, but as state capitalism. Baran and Sweezy carried the theory of monopoly capitalism and imperialism beyond Veblen's and Lenin's early-twentieth-century views. Gramsci presented his complex view of hegemony, which was then employed by Althusser in his structuralist theory, and by Poulantzas in his theory of state power. Finally, Cohen and others added technological determinism, functionalism, and rational choice to Marxist thought.

Nature of Society, Humans, and Change

Marxism has been consistent over the past 150 years in its views of society and change. *Capitalist society* is seen as exploitative and coercive. However, according to Gramsci and Althusser, its exploitation is a complex mix of political domination, control over economic production and property, and ideological hegemony. Its oppressive character means that it requires change—a change involving revolution, not just gradual, continuous evolution. Present-day Marxists disagree on the likelihood, location, and timing of the revolution, but they continue to argue for its necessity.

It is much too simple to say that Marxists today believe that human nature is good. Rather, human nature, according to Gramsci, is the "complex of social relations." This, he says,

> is the most satisfying answer because it includes the idea of becoming . . . and because it denies "man in general." Indeed, social relations are expressed by various groups of men which each presupposes the others and

whose unity is dialectical, not formal. Man is aristocratic in so far as man is a serf, etc. (1937:355)

In other words, *human nature* is defined by one's membership in society, in relation to other humans. This is somewhat reminiscent of Merton.

To Althusser, human nature is freedom. "It is the essence of man just as weight is the essence of bodies" (1965:224). Thus, the oppression of humans goes against human nature. Existence under capitalism is "man dispossessed, alienated." Liberal reform is not enough; human nature requires "the revolt of man against his inhuman conditions" (1965:226). The essence of humanity is freedom, which can only be achieved by the overthrow of an inhuman, oppressive society.

Class, Gender, and Race

Class, gender, and race have all been important to Marxists, generally in descending order of importance.

Class   As a major issue in Marxist theory, class was referred to often in the "Central Theories" section of this chapter. Here we will look at class in the writings of Poulantzas, for whom this topic was a second major focus of attention (after state power).

Poulantzas disagreed with classic Marxism that classes can be "in-themselves" and later become "for-themselves." Classes are, by their nature, for themselves; that is, they are self-aware, and exist only in and for the class struggle (Poulantzas, 1974:14). Furthermore, much of the state apparatus (though not all) is also a function of class. This apparatus includes repression (police, prisons, army); ideological institutions (religious, media, educational, entertainment); conservative trade unions; and even monogamous bourgeois families. Of course, the most direct aspects of class domination are the elements that Marx himself discussed: means and relations of production.

Poulantzas noted that individuals occupy places within a class structure. However, for Poulantzas individual position is secondary to the reproduction and continuation of the class system itself (Poulantzas, 1974:28–29).

The single most important contribution of Poulantzas to class theory is found in his discussion of the **petit bourgeoisie.** In classic Marxism the petit bourgeoisie were the owner-workers, who both own and work their own means of production. However, according to Poulantzas, the new petit bourgeoisie are what non-Marxists might call the lower middle class. This group results from the decomposition in capitalism of the role of entrepreneur into two separate roles: creator-owner, on the one hand, and clerks and service workers, on the other. These wage earners lack both ownership and control, and the criterion used to distinguish them is the lack of power and authority, in Max Weber's sense of those terms. What they have in common with the old petit bourgeoisie is that they are neither bourgeoisie nor proletariat.

One criticism of Marxism is that the rise of the middle class means that Marx's two-class opposition is not just incomplete, but wrong. Poulantzas, however, uses "group" instead of class for the petit bourgeoisie, continuing to emphasize the Marxist struggle between proletariat and bourgeoisie.

What happens to the petit bourgeoisie? Marx assumed that the old petit bourgeoisie would eventually be driven out in the competition with big capitalism, ending up in the proletariat. As for the new petit bourgeoisie, Poulantzas's conclusion is that a few will move up into the bourgeoisie, while most will fall into the proletariat. He reminds us of Robert Michels's point about the ideology of mobility: "the ideology of 'promotion' and of 'climbing' up into the bourgeoisie. . . . This upward transfer is in fact very restrained, but it continues to feed the illusions and hopes that these agents have for themselves and especially for their children" (Poulantzas, 1974:284). The majority, as in the case of the old petit bourgeoisie, end up in the working class or proletariat.

We have seen that for Poulantzas the state is more than a "tool" of the ruling class, and classes are more complex than the classic twofold division. However, struggle is still central to understanding classes, and the final revolution is still to be worked and hoped for. Is Poulantzas optimistic about the future? Does he believe in the revolution's inevitability? We will examine this important issue in "Final Thoughts" at the end of this chapter.

Gender Poulantzas makes several important comments on gender, especially in *Classes in Contemporary Capitalism* (1974). Class barriers impose inequalities on certain groups of people—old and young, but especially on women. The complexity of their position results from the fact that they are influenced by both a class and a gender division of labor. Women, he argues, are double victims of their position both as nonproductive, or domestic, workers and as exploited members of the workforce. "It is well-known how detrimental a factor it can be for the struggles of women . . . that their wages may be thought of in the family apparatus as simply providing a little extra for housekeeping," not as breadwinner, but as supplementer (1974:306).

Another insight on gender is his observation of the difference between what happens when working-class men are upwardly mobile and when working-class women are upwardly mobile. Male workers, notes Poulantzas, "who leave the working class go chiefly into the 'independent' sector," or bourgeoisie, "while female workers move above all into . . . the petty bourgeoisie," becoming clerks and service workers (1974:319). And these workers, in turn, are more likely to be "downsized" by automation/computerization.

Although Poulantzas hardly provides a complete theoretical explanation for patriarchy or for women's subordinate role in the societal and familial division of labor, his Marxist concern with inequality is expressed in his recognition that women face gender-based, as well class-based, difficulties (see Jessop, 1990: 238–239).

Raya Dunayevskaya (1981) wrote at greater length than did Poulantzas on women under capitalism. Speaking first about Rosa Luxemburg, she observed: "Luxemburg rightly refused to be pigeonholed by the German Social-Democracy into the so-called Woman Question, as if that were the only place she belonged" (1981:89). For twenty years, she noted, Luxemburg and Clara Zetkin worked closely. Zetkin chose to concentrate on organizing working-class women, while Luxemburg focused on more general Marxist issues.

Luxemburg and Zetkin played leadership roles in the Stuttgart Women's Conference of 1907. Although they supported women's suffrage, they made it clear that the larger issues were the general strike and the revolution itself. Thus, while "everything merged into the proletarian revolution, . . . always thereafter, woman as revolutionary force revealed its presence" (Dunayevskaya, 1981:95). Luxemburg understood the important role of women in the revolution—a role that could not be played in the patriarchal world of her time.

Dunayevskaya did more than indicate Luxemburg's support for the liberation of women. She spoke to the issue herself at the beginning of the 1980s in her appropriately titled essay, "The Task That Remains to Be Done: The Unique and Unfinished Contributions of Today's Women's Liberation Movement" (1981:99–112). Fifty years after Luxemburg's contribution to the woman question, Dunayevskaya noted that the women's liberation movement of the 1960s not only opposed capitalistic patriarchy but also "directed the male-chauvinist epithet at the male left" (1981:99). In other words, male radicals themselves were rightly accused of sexism. In many countries around the world, noted Dunayevskaya, spokeswomen began to enunciate the need to involve women both before and during the organizing phase of the revolution.

What happened in Russia was certainly not good enough: To assume that the revolution led by the Bolshevik party would somehow, in the long run, take care of women's needs and problems automatically was to make a serious error. According to Dunayevskaya, as we have seen, that first workers' state turned into its "opposite, the state-capitalist monstrosity we know today" (1981:109).

Women's liberation, then, is an important Marxist issue. The oppression of women is explained by patriarchal structures and attitudes, both in the capitalist world and in radical organizations.

Race   Race is an issue that Marxists often speak of tangentially, as being subsumed under class. However, Dunayevskaya introduced her discussion of women's liberation with an essay titled "An Overview by Way of Introduction: The Black Dimension" (1981:79–87). She began the essay with references to Mary Wollstonecroft (1792) and to an African American woman, Maria Stewart, who spoke thus in 1831:

> O ye daughters of Africa, awake! awake! arise! No longer sleep nor slumber but distinguish yourselves. Show forth to the world that ye are endowed with noble and exalted faculties. . . . How long shall the fair daughters of Africa be compelled to bury their minds and talents beneath a load of iron pots and kettles? (Dunayevskaya, 1981:79)

Tracing the history of black women in the United States through the nineteenth and into the twentieth century, Dunayevskaya noted that they had been ignored throughout much of Western history. This was true not only in the United States; "take Africa, whose history, especially as it concerns women, has hardly been touched" (1981:84). So the revolution, as it spreads, must involve women and the nonwhite races, as well as the working class. We will see more on African American women in the writings of Patricia Hill Collins (Chapter 10).

Other Theories and Theorists

We have introduced Poulantzas's and Dunayevskaya's ideas on classes, gender, and race. A few insights on other topics are also worth noting.

Besides the ideology of upward mobility, Poulantzas referred to another issue that concerned Michels: reformist and conservative unions, particularly trade unions. Like Michels, he criticized them as anything but revolutionary, hardly representing working-class needs and interests (Poulantzas, 1978:225).

Poulantzas also commented on the similarities among political parties in modern nation-states:

> These parties never offered a real political alternative to the reproduction of capitalism; yet they made it possible to choose between centres that formulated bourgeois policy in different ways. Today, they differ over little more than the aspect of administrative-executive policy that should be popularized. (1978:230)

The differences are not simply fictitious, but—whether Tories and Labor in Britain, or Republicans and Democrats in the United States—they certainly do not represent clear-cut ideological cleavages.

Both Poulantzas and Luxemburg criticized Lenin—though not as strongly as did Dunayevskaya—as having laid the groundwork not for rank-and-file democracy, but for the exact opposite. Without general elections, Lenin's organization of the Soviet Russian state led directly to Stalin's bureaucratization (Poulantzas, 1978:253). The popular masses remain outside the state looking in, with even the practice of representative democracy leaving the masses far from the seats of power. Thus, mass movements and infiltration of government by the working class are important, and both are difficult to effect (Poulantzas, 1978:259).

Poulantzas had much to say about the possibilities and limitations of U.S. global hegemony. Writing in 1974, he concluded that the European nations, Japan, and the Vietnam War had all conspired to weaken U.S. dominance. (Whether he would have said the same thing 25 years later is questionable.) However, he added that 60 percent of all foreign investments come from the United States. He also noted that U.S. dominance of the computer industry has made for worldwide standardization (Poulantzas, 1974:66)—an insight that today could be expanded to include CNN, movies, and other aspects of U.S. culture disseminated around the world. Hegemony, as Gramsci pointed out, is not restricted to multinational corporations and military interventions; it includes a great variety of cultural elements, all of which serve to spread capitalist products and ideas.

Critique and Conclusions

Our criticisms and conclusions regarding Marxism will be held until the end of the chapter, after we have introduced Erik Olin Wright's theoretical contributions that begin the twenty-first century. In his analytic and academic approach, Wright argues that Marxism has not been defeated by the transition of Eastern Europe's "quasi-Marxist" states to avowed capitalism. In fact, as you will see, his contributions to Marxist theory increased during the 1990s, after the breakup of the Soviet Union.

Marxism Now: Erik Olin Wright (1947–)

Erik Olin Wright was born in 1947 in Berkeley, California, to an academic family. He completed BA degrees at Harvard and at Oxford and a PhD in sociology at the University of California, Berkeley. Since 1976 he has been on the sociology faculty at the University of Wisconsin–Madison, except for one year as a visiting professor at Berkeley.

Wright has been a productive Marxist scholar for more than twenty years, but his important recent works are three books published in the 1990s, since the collapse of the Soviet Union and the East European bloc of communist countries: *Reconstructing Marxism* (1992, with Levine and Sober), *Interrogating Inequality* (1994), and *Class Counts* (1997).

In his 1994 book, Wright speaks of what has been called the "crisis of Marxism": (1) the above-mentioned changes in countries formerly ruled by nominally communist parties; (2) the lack of coherent programs for change in communist, socialist, and social democratic parties in the capitalist world; (3) the exit of intellectuals from Marxism toward liberalism or post-Marxism; and (4) the decline in consensus among Marxist intellectuals over the core principles of Marxism (1994:175). Wright's task, then, as he sees it, is to "contribute to this reconstruction of Marxism as a theoretical framework for radical social science." He believes "that the Marxism which will emerge from the present period of theoretical transformation will not only be more powerful theoretically than the Marxism of the heyday of the New Left, but will also be of more political relevance" (1994:175–176, 179).

Wright is an analytical Marxist who is also an empirical and an academic Marxist. His empiricism is clearly stated in his most recent book:

> Research pushes social theory forward in two basic ways. Where there is a controversy between contending theoretical claims about some problem, research potentially can provide a basis for adjudication between the alternatives. . . . The goal of research can [also] be to find interesting surprises, anomalous empirical results that go against the expectations of a theory and thus provoke rethinking. (1997:519–520)

His goal in this book is to try to convince non-Marxists that class analysis is useful, and to convince Marxists that quantitative analysis is useful (1997:546).

Wright's primary focus of attention is classes, to which we will turn later. First, however, we will discuss his analytic and antireductionist approaches to Marxist thought.

Wright's Central Theories and Methods

Wright's contributions to Marxist theory are in midstream, and can be expected to continue into the twenty-first century. However, we will begin this discussion with his antireductionism.

Antireductionism   Wright and his coauthors contrast their approach with **methodological individualism**, which is "the view that all social phenomena are best explained by the properties of individuals who comprise the phenomena" (Wright, Levine, and Sober, 1992:108). Though critical of it, they believe that Jon Elster's (1985) book *Making Sense of Marx* is the most insightful one written by an individualist. Elster seeks explanation only at the individual level, and argues that radical holism or "methodological collectivism" is teleological and lacking in credibility. Likewise, Wright and his colleagues question Althusserian structuralism, asserting that "structures cause structures and individuals are only 'supports' of social relations" (1992:114).

Wright and his coauthors are "**antireductionists**," meaning that not all phenomena can or should be reduced to the individual level. Their approach, they believe, is a good one if Marxism seeks to deal with the real—that is, the empirical—world. In other words, antireductionists have room for both irreducible social- or structural-level phenomena and for micro- or individual-level explanations (1992:124, 127).

Analytical Marxism   Analytical Marxism was spurred by a London conference in 1979, the year of Poulantzas's death, that included Cohen, Elster, and Roemer—a group Wright joined in 1981. Wright argues that four specific commitments justify considering Analytical Marxism as a distinct "school" of contemporary Marxist thought. First is its commitment to conventional scientific norms. Second is an emphasis on systematic conceptualization, especially of core concepts. Third is a concern with fine-grained specification of the steps in the theoretical linking of concepts, whether they are about causal processes in explanatory theories or about logical connections in constructing normative theories. Finally, attention is paid to the intentional action of individuals within both types of theories (Wright, 1994:181–182).

Marxism has often been hostile to conventional science; even what has been called "scientific socialism" has abused the canons of science (for example, Althusser's work). Wright believes that if Marxism aspires to be more than an ideology, to be a genuine social scientific perspective, it must engage relevant data from empirical research. But what makes Analytical Marxists "Marxist"? (1) Their questions come from the Marxist tradition; (2) their agenda (such as Wright's research on class) is Marxist; (3) their language is Marxist; and (4) they share a core normative orientation to Marxism (Wright, 1994:192–193).

One of the subfields of Analytical Marxism to which Wright does not subscribe, and which has caused much controversy among contemporary Marxists, is the rational choice model discussed earlier in this chapter, especially in the work of Roemer. This view states that, at the very least, Marxist theory should incorporate as one element a concern with conscious choice (Roemer, 1981, 1982). Wright does not ignore such choice, but he does not use it as a prime explanatory tool.

Nature of Society, Humans, and Change

Wright is committed to the Marxist view of societal inequality and exploitation. He is also committed to research on class as a (not the) factor explaining the nature or characteristics of society. He does not, however, hold to a firm belief in a postcapitalist socialist/communist world. These issues are treated at length in his 1994 book.

Wright cites three conceptual nodes within Marxism's view of society: class analysis; a theory of historical trajectory, or the direction of history; and an emancipatory theory and ideology. Marxism, Wright summarizes, "is above all about using *class analysis* to understand the political processes for the realization of *historically* possible *emancipatory* goals" (1994:239).

Human nature is mixed, and change is necessary, but not inevitable. In all that Wright says about society, class is the central concept. He agrees ideologically with much that Marxists have said about the ills of capitalism, but he is not an optimistic Marxist—not convinced of the feasibility, much less the inevitability, of the final revolution or cure. As an empirical researcher, Wright argues that the motivator is the reduction of the class factor in society, not classlessness; he emphasizes the process, not an ideal endpoint (1994:245). To this we will return in the concluding section.

Class, Gender, and Race

Class   It is impossible to discuss Erik Olin Wright's view of society without raising the issue of class. Class analysts, according to Wright, can study anything they want: religion, war, crime, cultural tastes, and so on. However, the dependent variable is history, and the emancipatory ideology is the vision of a classless society in which exploitation has been eliminated. Thus, says Wright, "Marxism as class emancipation identified the disease in the existing world. Marxism as class analysis provided the diagnosis of its causes. Marxism as the theory of historical trajectory identified the cure" (1994:240). Few Marxists today, notes Wright, believe that class is the sufficient cause explaining capitalism, and even fewer believe that the historical trajectory is toward socialism as the result of capitalism's development, ills, and contradictions.

Traditional Marxist treatments of classes, in Wright's view, have suffered from two problems: They have been too abstract and too macro—meaning that they have viewed classes in structural terms, but have not mapped class in the lives of individuals. He sees three potential foci of attention within class analysis: structure, formation (how they come into being), and individuals within the class struggle. Wright emphasizes structure and individuals-in-classes (1994).

Class is the empirical and theoretical subject of his latest book, the 500-plus page cross-national analysis titled *Class Counts* (1997), in which he analyzes structure, change, permeability, consciousness, gender, and race. We will begin with the first two, then move on to gender and race.

With regard to class structure, Wright notes that if the only criterion used is relation to the means of production, 85–90 percent of most developed countries are in one class. Therefore, he sees the need to include skills and authority in the definition. These, of course, are similar to the criteria Poulantzas used to define the new petit bourgeoisie. Looking at cross-national data, Wright concludes that all three dimensions are appropriate for defining class structure, though authority is not as independent, nor its boundary as clear, as the other two. At present, Wright sees a total of six locations in class relations: capitalists, petty bourgeoisie, expert managers, experts (such as scientists and engineers), nonskilled managers, and workers (1997:24, 525–526).

The "middle class" are those who are in a contradictory structural location. In some ways they are exploiters, and in some ways exploited. Although this is reminiscent of Poulantzas's discussion of the petit bourgeoisie, Wright does not indicate that the middle class will eventually end up in either the bourgeoisie or the proletariat (1994:251).

In discussing class change, Wright notes that the working class in the United States declined in the last third of the twentieth century, and the decline appears to be accelerating. Some would argue, he says, that this is an indication of deproletarianization, while others would argue from a global perspective that "the transnational character of capitalism in the world today makes it inappropriate to study" class transformations "within single national units." Wright's data seem to point to the second explanation, which, of course, is consistent with those who have claimed that the working classes of the developed countries are actually among the exploiters—that is, part of the international bourgeoisie (1997:108–109).

So what are the chances that change will lead to a classless society? In his 1994 book, Wright gives the arguments against such an outcome, and then those that support it. First, the arguments against:

1. Incentives and sanctions [are] needed for efficiency of complex economies.
2. Skepticism about the possibility of democratic control of the means of production in large firms.
3. Information problems make centralized planning of production impossible. (1994:218–219)

Support for the possibility of eliminating class inequities rests on the following arguments:

1. Incentives need not threaten classlessness, especially when public goods replace the need for some private consumption.
2. More education, fewer work hours, and other reforms make democratic control more possible.
3. Market mechanisms could allocate capital with a strong state neutralizing the classist effects. (1994:219)

As we have noted, Wright is not completely convinced of the validity of the second set of arguments, or of the potential for a classless society.

Gender and Race   Wright adds both gender and race to his analysis of class, recognizing that some Marxists argue that both of these can be subsumed under, or reduced to, class.

In *Interrogating Inequality* (1994), Wright compares the premises of Marxist and feminist emancipation:

> Marxists have often treated the viability of communism—a society without class oppression—as problematic; . . . . Feminists generally take it for granted that social life does not *require* male domination; Marxists are

forced to defend the claim that social life under conditions of developed technology does not need some form or other of class domination. . . . One hundred years ago it was quite different. Radical class theorists took it as obvious that class inequality and domination were becoming increasingly unnecessary and could be superseded in a post-capitalist society. . . . Feminists in the last century, on the other hand, rarely envisioned a society without a quite substantial gender division of labor and even gender inequality. (1994:211, 220)

Gender, notes Wright, is seen by some as reducible to class, by some as reciprocal to class, or as a sorting mechanism for class, or as a linkage to class, or as causally related to class (1997:243–247). His empirical analysis of gender and class adds much to our understanding of these potential relationships. Labor force participation in the six countries he studied does little to explain gender involvement in household tasks. Though Wright was not the first to discover this, whether women have high-status jobs, low-status jobs, or no jobs, they do the large majority of housework. "Feminists," notes Wright, "have long argued for the autonomy of gender mechanisms in explaining the production and reproduction of male domination," and that is in fact what his data show for the United States, Canada, the United Kingdom, Norway, Sweden, and Japan (1997:304).

Wright's insights into gender and class are reinforced when race is added to the data mix. In 1992 he noted that functionalist Marxists, such as Cohen, usually translate non-class interests, such as race, into class interests. Whites, it is said, have class "'interests' in dominating blacks," and this is explained by bourgeois interest in dominating workers (Wright et al., 1992:75). However, his six-country data show that "race is a salient feature of the social structure only in the United States." His U.S. sample contained no black capitalists, only one black small employer (a woman), and only a handful of black petty bourgeoisie (all men) (Wright, 1997:67).

What happens when employer/authority/expertise are combined and related to race and gender? Wright finds that in the United States 33 percent of white males are in this "privileged" class location, compared to 12.5 percent of white women, 8.4 percent of black men, and 3 percent of black women. Looked at from the working-class perspective, Wright's data show that 87 percent of black women, 77 percent of black men, 67 percent of white women, and 51 percent of white men are in the extended working class. In short, today's U.S. working classes are mostly women and racial minorities (Wright, 1997:69).

A word on class consciousness by race and gender is instructive. The anti-capitalism of the black working class is much greater than that of the white working class, but gender differences in class consciousness are negligible. This can be explained, Wright believes, by the fact that the black experience of slavery in the United States heightened racial consciousness, whereas the sharing of households by men and women makes for more of a common cross-gender expression of class. One further insight from Wright's data is that gender inequality and consciousness are greater in countries where class inequality is less and where racial inequality is not a factor (1997:544).

Wright's conclusion is that the independent effects of race and gender seem to mean that the struggle for equality in these two ascribed statuses is worth pursuing within capitalism, rather than strictly as a subpart or by-product of the class struggle (1997:545).

Other Theories and Theorists

Wright, of course, responds to some of Marx's ideas, as well as those of recent Marxists, such as Roemer. However, he offers a lengthy evaluation and critique of Cohen's reconstruction of historical materialism. The notion of the long-term nonviability of capitalism, endorsed by Cohen, is based on the labor theory of value and on the tendency of the rate of profit to fall. However, this trend is debatable, according to Wright's data. A more likely basis for internal contradiction in capitalism is its ultimate inability to keep the social connections and organization of workers from leading to their acting as a class. But Wright questions whether a "radical egalitarian alternative" might not be possible, rather than Cohen's (and Marx's) revolutionary outcome (Wright, 1994:229).

As have others, Wright notes that class consciousness depends to a great extent on the individual's perception of his or her future class situation. This, of course, recalls again Michels's argument that the ideology of mobility reduces class antagonism, because individuals believe that they can make the system work for them.

Finally, Wright refers to Giddens, Theda Skocpol, and Ann Orloff. Giddens (see Chapter 3) argued that there is no fundamental dynamic in society that explains its trajectory. Although Wright is hardly a "true believer," he does emphasize class as a central component of history and change. Skocpol (see Chapter 6) and Orloff argue that the emergence of social insurance is explained by the institutional capacities of states, but Wright believes that a 100-year period would show that classes and other Marxist dynamics can explain social insurance at least as well as the action of the capitalist state.

Critique and Conclusions

Though we will not try to summarize all the issues raised in this chapter, concluding comments on Wright and Poulantzas are in order. Wright's own conclusion is that "it is unlikely that fine-grained assessments of the relative importance of different causes can be made" (Wright et al., 1992:174). Class is a cause, but not *the* cause, for society's structures and for individual choices—pervasive, yes; primary or single, probably not. His empirical work has turned Marxism into measurable variables instead of dogmatic dichotomies. And Wright's task is hardly complete, as he himself admits.

Where does Wright's work leave Marxism at the turn of the twenty-first century? Is it in crisis because of the collapse of avowedly Marxist governments, or because of its historical failure thus far to truly emancipate according to its dogma? That seems at least partially correct. But as a scientific and theoretical perspective from which to analyze international neocolonialism, technology, the role of the state, and the class factor, it is very much alive.

Bob Jessop, the main biographer and critic of Poulantzas, claims that Poulantzas never utilized either Althusser's structuralism nor Michel Foucault's micro-power perspective (see Chapter 11) to the extent that they would have been useful to him. Whether he would have done so had he lived longer is only conjecture. Despite Poulantzas's complex views of the state and classes, Jessop concludes that he "failed to develop an adequate account of hegemonic strategies, to consider their relation to accumulation, and to connect them to the process of class formation. He continued to refer to hegemony and its crises as if these involved processes of class leadership" (1985:326). While these points may be correct, it is perhaps unfair to complain about the loose ends left dangling by Poulantzas at his death at the age of 43.

Final Thoughts

Though they do not agree on all major points, Marxists agree on the exploitative and oppressive nature of the capitalist world order. But the complexity and hegemony of that world is daunting. Dunayevskaya criticized the Soviet Union as 70 years of state capitalism, not Marxist socialism. Gramsci, Althusser, and Poulantzas addressed the complexity of capitalist hegemony, seeing it as difficult to combat. Baran and Sweezy showed how large-scale capitalism controls the world through neocolonialism. And the personal stories of Althusser and Poulantzas are disturbing, as we shall see. A powerful commitment can also mean a profound discouragement.

What about the future—the final revolution? In 1974 Poulantzas stated that we "must rid ourselves once and for all of the illusions . . . that an objective proletarian polarization of class determination must necessarily lead in time to a polarization of class positions" (1974:334). Four years later he stated this position even more strongly. History, he asserted, has provided us no example of a successful experience of the democratic or revolutionary road to socialism, but only "negative examples to avoid and some mistakes upon which to reflect" (1978:265). Does this mean it is impossible?

> Maybe. We no longer share that belief in the millennium founded on a few iron laws concerning the inevitability of a democratic-socialist revolution. . . . What is more, optimism about the democratic road to socialism should not lead us to consider it as a royal road, smooth and free of risk. (Poulantzas, 1978:265)

Just how pessimistic was Nicos Poulantzas about the revolution required to bring justice and equality to the world he was committed to changing? All we know is that a few months after writing the above, in 1979, he gave up the fight and committed suicide. A year later, Althusser ended a life of depression and intellectual uncertainty by killing his wife, spending the last ten years of his life in an asylum. On the other hand, Marxists today, such as Erik Olin Wright, are optimistic about the value of Marxist analysis and categories, and continue to contribute greatly to understanding and explaining capitalism—even though Marx's own optimism about the final revolution is hardly reflected in his followers today.

References

Althusser, Louis. 1965/1969. *For Marx*. London: Allen Lane/Penguin Press.

———. 1974. *Eléments d'autocritique [Elements of Self-Criticism]*. Paris: Hachette.

Althusser, Louis, and Etienne Balibar. 1968/1970. *Reading Capital*. London: New Left Books.

Baran, Paul, and Paul Sweezy. 1966/1970. *Monopoly Capital*. Harmondsworth, England: Penguin.

Blomstrom, Magnus, and Bjorn Hettne. 1984. *Development Theory in Transition: The Dependency Debate and Beyond: Third World Responses*. London: Zed Books.

Brewer, Anthony. 1980. *Marxist Theories of Imperialism: A Critical Survey*. London: Routledge and Kegan Paul.

Cohen, G. A. 1978. *Karl Marx's Theory of History: A Defense*. Princeton, NJ: Princeton University Press.

Dosse, François. 1967/1997. *History of Structuralism*. Minneapolis: University of Minnesota Press.

Dunayevskaya, Raya. 1951/1992. *The Marxist-Humanist Theory of State-Capitalism*. Chicago: News and Letters.

———. 1958/1971. *Marxism and Freedom: From 1776 Until Today*. London: Pluto Press.

———. 1981/1991. *Rosa Luxemburg, Women's Liberation, and Marx's Philosophy of Revolution*. Urbana: University of Illinois Press.

Elster, Jon. 1985. *Making Sense of Marx*. Cambridge: Cambridge University Press.

Gramsci, Antonio. 1937/1971. *Selections from the Prison Notebooks*. London: Lawrence and Wishart.

Howard, M. C., and J. E. King. 1992. *A History of Marxian Economics: Vol. 2. 1929–1990*. Princeton, NJ: Princeton University Press.

Hudis, Peter. 1992. "Introduction." In Raya Dunayevskaya, *The Marxist-Humanist Theory of State-Capitalism* (pp. i–xxvi). Chicago: News and Letters.

Jessop, Bob. 1985. *Nicos Poulantzas: Marxist Theory and Political Strategy*. London: MacMillan Publishers.

———. 1990. *State Theory: Putting Capitalist States in Their Place*. University Park: Pennsylvania State University Press.

Kurzweil, Edith. 1980. *The Age of Structuralism*. New York: Columbia University Press.

Mouffe, Chantal (Ed.). 1979. *Gramsci and Marxist Theory*. London: Routledge and Kegan Paul.

Paggi, Leonardo. 1979. "Gramsci's General Theory of Marxism." In Chantal Mouffe (Ed.), *Gramsci and Marxist Theory* (pp. 113–167). London: Routledge and Kegan Paul.

Poulantzas, Nicos. 1974. *Classes in Contemporary Capitalism*. London: New Left Books.

———. 1978. *State, Power, Socialism*. London: New Left Books and Verso.

Roemer, J. E. 1981. *Analytical Foundations of Marxian Economic Theory*. Cambridge: Cambridge University Press.

———. 1982. *A General Theory of Exploitation and Class*. Cambridge, MA: Harvard University Press.

———. 1986. *Analytical Marxism*. New York: Cambridge University Press.

Texier, Jacquies. 1979. "Gramsci, Theoretician of the Superstructures." In Chantal Mouffe (Ed.), *Gramsci and Marxist Theory* (pp. 48–79). London: Routledge and Kegan Paul.

Wright, Erik Olin. 1994. *Interrogating Inequality*. New York: Verso.

———. 1997. *Class Counts: Comparative Studies in Class Analysis*. Cambridge: Cambridge University Press.

Wright, Erik Olin, Andrew Levine, and Elliot Sober. 1992. *Reconstructing Marxism*. London: Verso.

Chapter 6

Sociocultural Change: Evolution, World System, and Revolution
Service, Wallerstein, and Skocpol

Sociology has a tradition of macro theories of change. Nineteenth-century examples include Herbert Spencer's and W. G. Sumner's evolutionary theories, Durkheim's discussion of society's change from mechanical to organic solidarity, and Marx's analysis of the need for a revolutionary transformation. In the mid-twentieth century Parsons and the functionalists argued that change does take place, but it is usually minimal and with a view to reinstating the former equilibrium as closely as possible.

We focus in this chapter on three twentieth-century perspectives on change, using one U.S. theorist as the center point of each discussion, but bringing in others as needed. We begin with Elman Service and the various elements of evolutionary thinking today, including modernization theory. Then we look at Immanuel Wallerstein's world system theory, as a reaction to modernization theory, and also introduce its critics. Finally, we examine Theda Skocpol's non-Marxist theory of revolution, comparing it briefly with other non-Marxist theories.[1]

---

[1]In this chapter we cannot introduce all the theories of cultural and social change that might interest you. However, in this footnote we touch briefly on two.

One kind of theory uses personality and family to explain change toward development and modernization. Everett Hagen (1962) argues that race, religion, climate, urbanization, and environment are all causal, but are preceded in their effects by a change in personality. This change, in turn, is influenced by social structure, parental behavior, and childhood. Most traditional societies produce an authoritarian personality, but some produce an innovative one, which leads to change. David McClelland's (1962) argument is close to Hagen's. Of the various characteristics related to change, McClelland argues, a need for achievement (n-ach) is central. N-ach results from societal contacts and comparisons, giving rise to entrepreneurship and the desire for improvement or betterment. Each of these is a subtheory of modernization, but they seem to beg the question of what causes traditional families and societies to produce such personalities.

Twentieth-Century Evolutionism: Elman Service (1915–)[2]

Looking back at nineteenth-century thinking, we recall that the dominant belief in Europe was not just in biological evolution, but in social and cultural evolution as well. In the 1800s, wrote V. Gordon Childe,

> "progress" was an accepted fact. Trade was expanding, the productivity of industry was increasing, wealth was accumulating. Scientific discoveries promised a boundless advance in man's control over Nature, and consequently unlimited possibilities of further production. Growing prosperity and deepening knowledge inspired an atmosphere of unprecedented optimism throughout the Western world. (Childe, 1936:9)

Both Lewis Henry Morgan and Edward Tylor, writing independently in 1871, saw "technology, science, and material culture generally, as undergoing a progressive, cumulative evolution, independent from religion and 'intellectual and moral' progress" (Service, 1971:8).

According to Robert Nisbet (1969), the key elements of classic nineteenth-century social evolutionary thinking were the following:

1. Change is *natural*. It is as much a part of a social entity—whether a civilization, an institution, or a cluster of cultural elements—as is structure or equilibrium.

2. Though not an observable fact, change is *directional*. It has a beginning, a middle, and an end—or, metaphorically, birth, growth, and death.

3. Change is *immanent*. It is internal to societies, their structures and cultures, and not ordinarily induced from the outside.

4. Change is *continuous*, consisting of small gradations or steps within a single series. The problem with this, of course, was that Darwin's geological evidence found gaps and apparent reversals in the record, and so did accounts of peoples. Nonetheless, nineteenth-century writers tended to assume natural, continuous, incremental change.

Godfrey and Monica Wilson's 1958 book, *Analysis of Social Change*, is neither an economic nor a psychological theory of change, but a demographic one. Change occurs when there is either an increase or decrease in the scale or density of a society. This can be a result of inadequate space (exhaustion of land supply), conquest by (or of) a society, or various other causes.

Three comments are necessary: First, these theories are more complex than we have indicated. Second, they are versions of modernization theory, which dominated the 1950s and 1960s. Third, they are not incompatible with other theories presented in this chapter, but seem to require explanations that push the causal chain further back toward the individual.

[2]We have selected Service, rather than V. G. Childe, Leslie White, or Marshall Sahlins, for discussion in this chapter not because he is necessarily the most creative, but because he introduces a broader spectrum of issues than the others. Also, Service confronts several unique evolutionary problems that connect him to other theorists in this volume. Like Erik Olin Wright in the previous chapter, Service raises the important contemporary issues in his particular school of thought.

5. Change is *necessary*. There is a logical necessity in evolution and progress. Not only conservative thinking, but some of Marx's early arguments, despite the language of revolution, were based on the necessity of change through capitalism to socialism.

6. Finally, nineteenth-century evolutionists believed in *uniform causes*, traceable to a beginning point in natural history, rather than to a cataclysm, crisis, or God-directed event. (Nisbet, 1969:166–188)

All this changed in the twentieth century. During and after World War I, many European thinkers lost confidence in evolutionary progress. In addition, the Depression of the 1930s and worldwide discontent affected European sociological theorizing. Within the social sciences themselves, two non- (sometimes anti-) evolutionary viewpoints spread. One was that of Franz Boas, Robert Lowie, and other U.S. cultural anthropologists who stated that civilization involves a variety of elements, some borrowed, some internal, and some "leftovers." Thus, culture is a "planless hodgepodge, [a] thing of shreds and patches" (Lowie, 1920, quoted in Service, 1971:149). In praising Lowie's book, *Culture and Ethnology*, one reviewer wrote: "The theory of cultural evolution [is] to my mind the most inane, sterile, and pernicious theory in the whole . . . of science" (quoted in White, 1960:v).

The other nonevolutionary viewpoint is found in the writings of Malinowski and Radcliffe-Brown, British social anthropologists, who argued in the 1920s and 1930s that explanation comes from getting inside a society and its culture and understanding the current interrelations of its parts, and not from concerning oneself with its history. Thus, for more than 30 years nonevolutionary thinking dominated the West—a result of world upheaval, Lowie's "fragmentary" cultural perspective, and British functionalism.

Elman Service was born in 1915. In his 1975 book, he recounts his intellectual history:

> The problem of the origins of civilization and primitive states has been a preoccupation of mine since I simultaneously discovered anthropology and Marxism in the late 1930s. . . . I eventually became dissatisfied with Marxism and, I hope, with all forms of "systematic" thought. (1975:xvi)

Service explains that in the 1940s, at the University of Michigan, Leslie White's evolutionary teaching and writing helped him focus his long-term interests. To this was added the influence of Julian Steward at Columbia, with whom Service did graduate work in the late 1940s. He then returned to the University of Michigan, where he did his early scholarly work with Marshall Sahlins.

Service's Central Theories and Methods

Despite Childe's brief 1936 book, published in Britain, only in the 1950s was there any noticeable shift of opinion toward an evolutionary outlook again. Following World War II, European thinking continued to be pessimistic, but optimistic evolutionary thought reemerged in the United States, as a result of victory without internal destruction, and in the nonwhite world, as a reaction against the dominance of Western nations and the white race (Service, 1971:9).

Cultural Evolutionism   By 1959, there were already two major distinctions within twentieth-century cultural evolutionary thought. One was between directed and nondirected evolution; the other was between supra-historical and historical evolution.

In the nineteenth century, the dominant view was clearly that evolution was **nondirected**—a "natural," or uncontrolled, process. Evolution results from competition, from natural selection or the survival of the fittest, or else from cooperative adaptation, with competition as secondary. Leslie White (1949) agreed, arguing that culture determines what people do, not vice versa. He gave little credence to free will, claiming that if one person does not synthesize cultural elements in a new way, someone else will. Thus, White agreed with Herbert Spencer and William James that history is not the story of the doings of great individuals, but of cultural and social forces, neither guided by human endeavor, nor headed toward a predetermined goal.

Although it may seem only a matter of emphasis, Childe titled his 1936 book *Man Makes Himself*. The main difference, according to Childe, between biological and cultural/social evolution is that humans can look back, can think through problems, and can even imagine and then construct or **direct** future evolution. "Changes in culture and tradition can be initiated, controlled, or delayed by the conscious and deliberate choice of their human authors and executors" (1936:21). It is the brain, in Childe's view, that makes humans different from other animals and makes it possible for humans to control their own cultural evolution (1936:28).

Others, such as Charles Erasmus in his 1966 book *Man Takes Control*, later took the same position. They argued that cultural, especially technological, evolution is not a natural process, but is guided by the thought and action of specific human beings. The building of a "better mousetrap" or a better computer is not a matter of the natural selection of elements, but results from human thought, planning, and development.

Throughout his scholarly career, Service agreed with White and the "social forces" or nondirected school of evolution, rather than with Childe and Erasmus. For example, in 1975 he quoted favorably Max Gluckman's view of the rise of Shaka to power among the Zulu in South Africa. While Shaka may have been endowed with military genius, his "rise to power was probably also a result of tides that had been running in the life of the African peoples for two centuries," including population growth, emigration, crowding of land, and contact with Europeans (Gluckman, 1960:158). Later Service generalized this point: Individuals make decisions and do things, but we "welcome, for the more general purposes of this book, a sophisticated grasp of the structural leverages and constraints that plot the actors' actions in general ways" (Service, 1975:164).

The second important distinction is between unilinear and multilinear, or supra-historical and historical, evolution. The dominant position on this issue remains, as it was in the nineteenth century, **unilinear**—the idea of a single path along which human societies, cultures, and technology have moved and are moving. Complexity, cross-cultural differences, and even speed of change are irrelevant to the overall course of human history. Also called "universal" or "general" evolution, this view sees a "passage from less to greater energy transformation, lower to higher levels of integration, and less to greater all-around adaptability" (Sahlins and Service, 1960:38).

Although this is the dominant position, Julian Steward, one of Service's teachers, introduced the multilineal concept. Noting that diffusion or borrowing has often been used to explain how cultural elements got from one part of the world to another, Steward disagreed. Why, he asked, would not the same environmental conditions give rise to the same inventions and adjustments independent of one another, without the necessity of culture contact? The **multilinear** view, first, "postulates that genuine parallels of form and function develop in historically independent sequences or cultural traditions. Second, it explains these parallels by the independent operation of identical causation in each case" (Steward, 1955:14).

It is possible that Childe and White as unilinear and Steward as multilinear evolutionists are not in substantial disagreement. Childe spoke of urban civilization, with its cultural characteristics, as "not simply transplanted from one centre to another, but . . . in each an organic growth rooted in the local soil" (Childe, 1936:135). Service, referring to his teachers White and Steward, declared: "I never felt that the two approaches were incompatible" (Service, 1962:viii).

In 1959, a symposium was held on "Principles of Culture Evolution." The outcome was the 1960 volume *Evolution and Culture*, written by several scholars, including Sahlins and Service, who served as editors. In this small work they solved the debate by simply saying that evolution is both. That is, the two writer/editors utilized the concepts of **general** and **specific** evolution. By specific they meant historically specific, which included Steward's notion of independent origins (Sahlins and Service, 1960:38).

Two years later, however, Service claimed that the "general" and "specific" distinction was basically Marshall Sahlins's. He added that some of his own ideas "were precipitated out of discussions (and arguments) with Sahlins, with whom I have been collaborating off and on for some time" (Service, 1962:viii). By 1975, when he published his most important book, Service was still interested in the history of specific societies, but only as they contributed to a general understanding of the origin and development of civilization and the state.

Civilization and the State   Childe (1936) claimed that the first civilizations originated in what he called an "urban revolution." Its important aspects included specialists, such as craftsmen and priests, food surplus from the countryside, public buildings, a ruling class, writing, arithmetic, long-distance trade, and controlled force—the state (Service, 1975:7).

In his 1962 book, *Primitive Social Organization*, Service argued that urbanization itself had to be explained, and that the primary change was from agricultural tribes to centralized chiefdoms. This centralization, he observed, took place in environments consisting of dramatically different climates in fairly close proximity. A seacoast, a fertile lowland, and highland forests might be characterized by fishing, agriculture, and animal hunting, respectively. At first people were nomadic, moving from region to region as seasons changed. However, Service proposed, at some point certain individuals settled "in the middle," and traded the mountain and seacoast produce between the now-settled peoples, keeping some for themselves. The outcome, in these climatically varied parts of the world, was "specialization in production and redistribution of produce from a controlling trade center. The resulting organic base of social integration made possible a more integrated and differentiated society, and the increased efficiency in production and distribution made possible a denser society" (1962:144).

Thus, Service's argument was that in Central America, China, and elsewhere, environmental or climatic diversity and productive specialization gave rise to redistribution, which in turn gave rise to urban agglomerations. He stated this point again in 1975: "A chiefdom in good working order seems to be held together because it can accomplish the above functions [specialization, worship, etc.] well, especially redistribution—here, in fact, is the organismic model of society so beloved of the classical sociologists" (1975:79).

But by that year (1975), his explanation was changing and becoming more complex. Looking at a variety of societies around the world, he argued that

> those of the New World were unrelated to those of the Old World. This is a most significant fact, for it affects our perspective. Were it one single development that spread to the other areas by conquest, diffusion, emulation, or whatever, then the problem would be "historical"—that is, our concern would be simply, what happened? When? But since it happened several times independently we immediately wonder, even if it only happened twice, . . . what *causes* or repetitive *processes* were at work. (1975:5)

Was this general evolution a result of economic redistribution, as he had argued previously? No. Political "power organized the economy, not vice versa." Administration came first; it included economic redistribution, but much more than that. These first governments, argued Service, "seem clearly to have reinforced their structure by doing their economic and religious jobs well—by providing benefits—rather than by using physical force," or being acquisitive (1975: 8). When violence was used, it was against either "princes" or other pretenders to power, or else against external forces. In fact, he says, "neither urbanism nor state violence is a necessary factor in the *development* of civilization" and the state (1975:185). This, of course, is very different from Lenin's and Poulantzas's views of the state.

The stages of evolution included the hunting-gathering band, the agricultural tribe, the diversified chiefdom, and finally the state, whose functions included religious leadership, economic redistribution, class control (à la Marx), specialization (à la Durkheim), bureaucracy (à la Weber), and control of force if necessary. Viewing this evolution in terms of leadership or authority, it is from the agricultural big-man to the traditional chiefdom to the bureaucratized and civilized state. This, Service reminds us, coincides with Weber's three types of authority: charismatic (big-man), traditional, and rational-legal or bureaucratic (Service, 1975:306).

Another of Service's concerns was the fall, as well as the rise, of societies and states. Although the terminology of growth and decay is metaphoric, there is no question that societies go through some such process. Adaptation is functional up to a point, fostering adjustment to and even control over one's environment. However, "there are both positive *and* negative aspects of adaptation to environment. . . . More adaptation equals less adaptability" (Service, 1975:319). Here Service referred, as he had in 1971, to Thorstein Veblen's efficiency principle, described as "the penalty of taking the lead" (Veblen, 1915). Thus, "newly civilized societies of the frontier have an increasing evolutionary potential that the original center steadily loses in the very act of successfully dominating [and adapting to] its own local environment" (Service, 1975:314). This might be labeled the "leap-frog" principle.

For Service, then, evolutionary explanation includes (1) the primacy of beneficial administration, (2) economic redistribution, (3) specialization, and (4) evolutionary potential in inverse relation to successful adaptation. Together these are the prime factors in explaining the rise of civilizations as well as the fall of specific societies. Service, like Weber, recognized that the real world is much more complex than such principles: "Numerous other factors are ultimately involved in the actual history of the rise and fall of a civilization. Disease, fire, flood, drought, earthquakes, overpopulation, soil depletion—who knows what else?—may have been involved in the fall of real societies." But, he argued, "such findings would have no bearing on the general relevance of the administration/adaptation/potentiality factor in evolution" (Service, 1975:322).

Nature of Society and Humans

Since change is the theme of this chapter, we will leave it out of this heading. As for society and humans, complexity is again the theme.

> Human beings do have varying abilities directed and powered by different motives and values (ideally they would be self-serving at the same time that they are socially useful); but the high offices and positions of power, wealth, and authority as institutional *structures* are real, too, and we need analysis of their evolution and functional connections and purposes. Both radical and conservative positions are important and interesting and in our case it would be nice to know the rulers' ego-structures as well as the social structure. (Service, 1975:288)

However, "to guess at the underlying motives and personalities of leaders, and then offer the guess as an explanation, is to be reductionistic. . . . Let us then, at this point, desist from Hobbesian or Rousseauian guesswork about the bad and good in human motives" (1975:289). Furthermore, although we believe that our explanation of the origin and rise of civilization, the state, and society, may be fairly accurate, we must not assume that the study of origins "somehow reveals that entity's *true nature*" (1975:286).

In short, Service was unwilling to hazard a guess as to the goodness or bad-ness of either human nature or society. Once again, we must conclude that he believes complexity allows for neither simplification nor reductionism.

Class, Gender, and Race

With his focus on evolutionary change at the societal level, Service did not speak to issues of class, gender, and race. Even when he used the term *class*, it referred not to the Marxist or Weberian socioeconomic categories, but to tradi-tional Australian kinship divisions or moieties (Service, 1971:115–133).

Other Theories and Theorists

Closely related to evolutionary thinking is modernization theory. Sahlins and Service hypothesized, in 1960, why evolutionary theory was reviving: "Is it be-cause we now find ourselves observing a world-wide conflict between older, en-trenched social orders and once-lowly and dominated peoples whose awaken-ing has made 'progress' again the slogan of the day?" (1960:2). The answer in the 1960s was clearly yes. The political independence of former colonies, their push for economic development, and the Western societies' economic "evange-lization" and neocolonialism were seen in the writings of Talcott Parsons, Daniel Lerner, and others as leading to "modernity," or stated in terms of process, "modernization" (Janos, 1986:42; Lerner, 1958). "Heavily influenced by the evolutionary theory, American social scientists conceptualized modernization as a phased, irreversible, progressive, lengthy process that moves in the direction of the American model" (So, 1990:261).

What, precisely, is this *modernity,* viewed by the West as giving it the status of a worldwide "vanguard" (to use Lenin's term)? Nisbet defined it as "technology, industrialism, democracy, secularism, individualism, equalitarianism, and, for a few, socialism. Counterposed to these were the attributes of *traditionalism* or . . . 'backwardness' or 'primitivism,'" including kinship, religion, and ruralism (1969:191). The expected changes, then, included moving from small-scale to large-scale societies, from simple to complex technology, and from personal to impersonal or anonymous relationships. In theories about worldwide evolution, terms used interchangeably included "civilized," "modern," and "developed."

Just how dominant was such evolutionary thinking, when applied to worldwide change? One volume, *Modernization: The Dynamics of Growth*, pub-lished in 1966, included the writings of 25 Western scholars (Weiner, 1966). The underlying assumption was that, over time, the rest of the world would become "just like us." Modernization was not only an evolutionary theory, it was an action program. Advisers were sent to various parts of the world to oversee change, development, and Westernization. Capitalists, critics (such as Veblen), and Marxists all agreed that the world was headed toward large-scale capitalism. However, capitalists saw it as the end or completion of the process, while Marxists saw it as the semi-final stage, to be followed by the worldwide revolutionary overthrow of capitalism.

Critique and Conclusions

Service used his "leap-frog" approach to change in hypothesizing about the future. He believed that the country most likely to leap over the United States and the West is China. To do so, however, it must choose not to simply allow itself to be incorporated in a subordinate role to the West-dominated world order (Service, 1975:323–324). Were he writing 25 years later, he might conclude that China is already foregoing this opportunity and opting for Western influences.

Modernization theory of the 1950s–1970s was basically a sub-branch of twentieth-century evolutionary theory. It included as a major value judgment the concept of progress. Sahlins and Service defined progress as "improvement in 'all-around adaptability.'" Speaking of cultures, they asserted that the higher forms "are again relatively 'free from environmental control,' i.e., they adapt to greater environmental variety than lower forms" (1960:38). And, other evolutionists added, higher forms adapt their environment to meet their needs. Nisbet noted that belief in such progress "calls plainly for a gigantic act of faith." But, he added, most of us cannot live without such faith (Nisbet, 1969:223).

Nisbet remarked in 1969 that the theory of social evolution had been a justification for the ascendancy of the West, and that, aside from empirical research, the theory had changed little since the 1800s (1969:202). In the final quarter of the twentieth century, however, both the definition of modernity and the belief in progress came to be questioned. Much recent thinking on modernization has given a more positive role to tradition and suggested a complex relationship between tradition and modernity. In fact, the language of multilinealism is now being used to describe differentiated paths into the so-called "modern world" (So, 1990:86–87). At the beginning of the twenty-first century, the notion of uniformity or a single path is being criticized by Immanuel Wallerstein and others.

Other doubts have also been raised. Sahlins and Service spoke of the "passage from less to greater energy transformation, lower to higher levels of integration" (1960:38). But how does the evolutionist or modernization theorist deal with the using up of energy sources, polluting of the environment, and ever-increasing inequalities both within and between societies? These issues must be ignored if the term "progress" is to be used. Marx and Engels, of course, warned that these were inherent characteristics of capitalism; but observers have so far been able to overlook them in the light of ever-increasing productivity, at least in the advanced capitalist societies.

The term "advanced capitalist societies" leads us to alternative theoretical views regarding economic development and evolutionary progress. After some 20 years, evolutionary modernization theory was challenged by dependency, underdevelopment, and world-system theories.

World System Theory: Immanuel Wallerstein (1930–)

Much of the background for world system theory is the same as that for evolutionary and modernization theory. The post–World War II period of U.S. confidence in a single path to development waned and was followed by several alternate attempts to explain what was happening in the world.

Immanuel Wallerstein began in the 1960s as an Africanist and Marxist (So, 1990:171) and has taught for many years at the State University of New York at Binghamton. His research in Africa convinced him that interdependence was such that a society or state could not be understood in isolation. Noting the economic difficulties faced by the newly independent African countries, he attacked the central features of modernization theory: reification of the nation-state, belief in a single path to development, and disregard for the "development of transnational structures that constrain and prompt . . . diverse as well as parallel paths" (Skocpol, 1994:55–56). He proposed an analytic framework that is worldwide, with the nation-state as but "one kind of organizational structure among others within this single social system" (Wallerstein, 1974:7).

In introducing Wallerstein's world system, we should note that he has never abandoned the Marxist view of exploitation and oppression. He does not, however, speak of a final revolution, and his analysis of oppression does not focus on classes within nation-states, but primarily on the world capitalist system.

Wallerstein has stated more than once that he is doing "world-system analysis," not writing world system theory. However, his efforts at explanation from this perspective justify treating it as a theory.

Wallerstein's Central Theory and Methods

Wallerstein's multivolume historical project is still in progress. He began in 1974 with *The Modern World-System*, a treatment of the emergence of capitalist agriculture and a European-dominated world economy in the sixteenth century. That his view involves change is seen in an essay published the same year, "The Rise and Future Demise of the World Capitalist System."

According to Wallerstein, three factors were essential to the establishment of a world economy during and after the sixteenth century:

an expansion of the geographical size of the world in question, the development of variegated methods of labor control for different products and different zones of the world economy, and the creation of relatively strong state machineries in what would become the core-states of this capitalist world-economy. (1974:38)

Why did the world capitalist system emerge in Europe, instead of in China or, earlier, in Rome? In the sixteenth century, says Wallerstein, China had a population and technology equivalent to Europe's, and was equally involved in exploration. However, as a political empire, China's centralization discouraged entrepreneurship, and its focus (as Rome's had been) was control of people, rather than Europe's concern with space and resources (1974:63). This is, in short, the "structural advantage" of world economy over world empire (1974:179).

Since then the world has increasingly become a single system, with an international division of labor. As one commentator describes Wallerstein's orientation, "the focus of political inquiry shifted from the narrower Durkheimian concept of the division of labor within a society to the division of labor on a larger, global scale and, as a corollary, from the concept of social stratification to stratification among national societies" (Janos, 1986:71). This modern world system, notes Wallerstein, is capitalist, meaning that it "is based on the priority of the ceaseless accumulation of capital. Such a system is necessarily inegalitarian, indeed polarizing, both economically and socially" (1999:87).

According to Wallerstein, at the outset this was an economic system with fairly independent subparts, not a political empire. However, it became a system in which different world regions played different roles, and still do. The **core** comprises those economic interests and nation-states that control productive activities. They have money to invest, expect a large return on investment, involve a free-floating labor force, and exploit the resources of the periphery. The **periphery** is the opposite. For much of its history it was neither economically nor politically independent. Its resources are controlled by the core, and its labor supply is controlled by either its own bourgeoisie or that of the core, or both. By trading with the core at a disadvantage, "the peripheral ruling class contributes to regional income disparity and undermines its own political position in the international system" (Janos, 1986:77).

The **semiperiphery** is the "halfway house" between the other two, but it is more than that. It serves as a buffer between core and periphery, keeping the system from disintegrating. It is also a location to which production is transferred when costs increase in the core (for example, Mexico and Indonesia). It has capital of its own, but is nevertheless dependent on the core for much of its infrastructure.

An interesting question is how a nation moves from periphery to semiperiphery, or even from semiperiphery to core. Wallerstein speaks of three mechanisms for moving from periphery to semiperiphery. The first is "seizing the chance," when an aggressive state "takes advantage of the weakened political position of core countries and the weakened economic position of domestic opponents of such policies" (1979:76). The second is "by invitation," when a transnational corporation simply moves into a less developed part of the world, and in so doing brings that area into the semiperiphery (1979:80). The third, riskiest approach is "self-reliance"—distancing one's economy from the world system, perhaps by nationalizing a resource, thereby chancing both the loss of foreign investment and core pressure for reincorporation into the periphery (1979:81).

Wallerstein makes no secret of the fact that much of his analysis continues to have a Marxist orientation. He uses Marx's terminology of exploitation, mode of production, conflict, bourgeoisie, and so on. The four Marxist ideas that Wallerstein finds useful are class struggle, polarization, the socioeconomic determination of ideology, and alienation as an evil to be eliminated (1995:226–231). Worldwide class distinctions are between states as well as within them. Exploitation is an international phenomenon, but it is also overt in the periphery, "where the elites exercise and institutionalize it in order to extract surplus from their own populations and thereby to import luxuries" (Janos, 1986:76).

The mark of the modern world, says Wallerstein, "is the imagination of its profiteers and the counter-assertiveness [docility, fatalism] of the oppressed." However, exploitation "and the refusal to accept . . . [it] as either inevitable or just constitute the continuing antimony of the modern era, joined together in a dialectic which has far from reached its climax in the twentieth century" (1974:357).

At the same time, Wallerstein notes the inadequacy of Marxist analyses of racial, ethnic, and gender struggles (1995:228). And he adds that his view of the avowedly socialist countries is quite un-Marxist: He sees them as semiperipheral, seeking access to the core. This view seems to have been corroborated by the collapse of the Soviet Union, the changes in Eastern Europe, and these countries' desired incorporation into the capitalist "new world order." However, Wallerstein does not agree with Dunayevskaya's view that these countries have always been covertly capitalist. In fact, he speaks of 1917 to 1991 as "the period in which there were states governed by Communist, or Marxist-Leninist, parties." In his view, the Russian revolution of 1917 was actually "one of the first, and possibly the most dramatic, of the national liberation uprisings in the periphery and semiperiphery of the world-system" (1999:7, 11).

Wallerstein and others have written thousands of pages on his world system analysis, but let us attempt to summarize its major tenets: (1) The division of labor and of classes is a worldwide phenomenon. Although Marx and Engels noted this in the *Manifesto*, Wallerstein details its historical development, observing the expansion of the capitalist system, especially in the twentieth century. (2) Economics is the predominant factor, not politics. Political divisions serve economic needs, and political dominance may even thwart development. (3) The world system is made up of three types of units: core, semiperiphery, and periphery. Although these are agglomerations of nation-states, they are more regional than national. (4) Change is continuous, but it is neither Marxist nor a matter of modernization. It is not unidirectional, or even directional, and is not likely to be revolutionary, in the traditional sense of the word. We will return to this issue later.

Nature of Society, Humans, and Change

Wallerstein is, in many ways, a disillusioned Marxist. On the positive side, he gives capitalism credit for having created the world system, since, "for all its cruelties, it is better that it was born than that it had not been" (1974:357). On the negative side, however, capitalism "has been more exploitative (that is, extractive of surplus labor value) and destructive of life and land, for the vast majority of persons located within the boundaries of the world-economy, than any previous mode of production in world history" (1984:9).

It is the vigor of capitalism that exacerbates its contradictions. Capitalists are successful at amassing profit, and in so doing they continue to increase the inequities of the world they control. Wallerstein's criticism of this social world or society, however, is not necessarily opposed to a view of human nature as good.

Echoing Marx's "to understand in order to change," Wallerstein argues that "our intellectual responsibilities are moral responsibilities" (1984:113). Social scientists—that is, those most capable of understanding capitalism and its world system—are those most responsible for making the world a better place. Without action, the social scientist becomes irrelevant. Stated positively,

> social science really does have something to offer the world. What it has to offer is the possibility of applying human intelligence to human problems

and thereby to achieving human potential, which may be less than perfection but is certainly more than humans have achieved heretofore. (1996:24)

In Wallerstein's view, the *world capitalist system* and its human alienation are essentially evils in need of correction. The intellectuals (Marx) or the social scientists (Wallerstein) can and must do something about it, not because they are perfect, or even good, but because they understand. We will return to the role of the social scientist in the section on "Other Theories."

Wallerstein presented his views on social change at the opening of the Third Portuguese Congress of Sociology in 1996 (Wallerstein, 1999:118–134). He began with the opening sentences of his 1995 book: "Change is eternal. Nothing ever changes." He explained this theme as follows: "That change is eternal is the defining belief of the modern world. That nothing ever changes is the recurrent wail of all those who have been disabused of the so-called progress of modern times" (1999:118).

Looking at technology, it is obvious that planes circle the globe, keeping up with time zones; we e-mail friends in Sweden or Singapore, and receive a response in minutes; a sale of stocks in Tokyo affects Wall Street a few hours later. At the same time, we are being told that the modern world is in terminal crisis, that we may soon resemble the fourteenth century more than the twentieth-first, that our infrastructure "may go the way of the Roman aqueducts" (1999:119). Technological change, yes, but progress? There are those, says Wallerstein,

> who look back on the multiple hunting and gathering bands that flourished . . . as structures in which humans worked many fewer hours per day and per year to maintain themselves than they do today, whose social relations were infinitely more egalitarian, and that operated in an environment that was far less polluted and dangerous. . . . The past ten-thousand years may therefore be said to constitute one long regression. (1999:119)

Not surprisingly, Wallerstein claims that neither the language of change nor of non-change is valid as stated; nor is the language of progress. A deceptive way of looking at change is in terms of functionalism. If a system is working well, it is described as superior in its functioning; if it dies, it is because it was inferior in its functioning (Wallerstein, 1999:126). However, these statements are tautological, or circular.

The major changes that have taken place in the twentieth century are, according to Wallerstein, (1) the self-determination of nations, especially resulting from decolonization—although political freedom has not been coupled with economic freedom, and certainly not with democracy; (2) a dramatic growth in economic capability or productivity, resulting in increased inequality rather than more equal distribution (1995:269); (3) the rise and fall of avowedly Marxist nation-states, which, in their time, did not live up to their own ideology.

Where is the world headed in the future? In his post-USSR book (1995), Wallerstein made predictions about the period 2000–2025. Japan, the United States, and the European Economic Community will continue to form a powerful core economy, while "the overall share of the South," meaning the population below the Equator, "in world production and world wealth will go down," with a decline in their health, education, and other social indicators. The North-South confrontation "will be at the center of the world political struggle from now on" (1995:20, 24). Wallerstein was unwilling to predict a favorable outcome, stating the changes that *should* take place, but not assuming they will.

Change, in Wallerstein's view, should be approached by looking at systemic, historical, and social change, but not looking for progress. The change from feudalism to capitalism was systemic and historical. However, the replacement of the Ming Chinese empire by the Manchu was not a systemic change, or a change in essential form. And, says Wallerstein, although we are going through a systemic transformation at present, it is not clear what this will mean in terms of long-term social change (1999:133).

Liberalism dominated the world system during the middle third of the twentieth century. Liberalism emphasizes liberty; democrats want equality. The demand for democracy, according to Wallerstein, "is stronger than it has been at any time in the time of the modern world-system" (1999:98). Liberal reformism—the managing of change by competent people, as seen in the social programs of Scandinavia and to a lesser extent in the United States—is on the defensive in the face of conservative pressures to reduce government spending and increase private control. Whether the result will be a new growth of fascism or new kinds of radical movements, Wallerstein is not sure.

Class, Gender, and Race

Class Not surprisingly, as a quasi-Marxist, Wallerstein considers class to be a crucial analytic category. Using a somewhat broader, even vaguer, definition than Marx, Wallerstein defines classes as "groups that have a common relationship to the economy" (1984:8). He seeks to explain "why, in the history of the capitalist world-system, the bourgeoisie and proletariats have often defined their class interests in status-group terms and expressed their class consciousness in national/ethnic/religious forms" (So, 1990:229). The reason, says Wallerstein, is that

> class represents an antinomy [opposition], as a dialectical concept should. On the one hand, class is defined as relationship to the means of production, and hence position in the economic system which is a *world*-economy. On the other hand, a class is a real actor only to the extent that it becomes class-*conscious*, which means to the extent that it is organized as a *political* actor. But political actors are located primarily in particular national *states*. (1979:196)

But, according to Wallerstein, the existence of national economies within the world system is more rhetoric than reality. Classes are "real" in the world economy, not in nation-states. Since class consciousness is produced by and for nation-states, most of it is a false or fake consciousness, to use Marxist terminology (Wallerstein, 1984:8). "Hard-hat" workers support their flag and government, unaware that their common interest is actually at the sub- or supranational class level. Wallerstein also notes, as have Michels and others, the way in which the prospects for upward mobility weakened any sense of class solidarity in the early twentieth century (So, 1990:192). Thus, international classes, national false class consciousness, and the ideology of mobility are Wallerstein's main contributions to the discussion of class.

Gender   Wallerstein notes that in the twentieth century, "those oppressed by racism and sexism insisted on claiming the rights that liberals said they theoretically had" (1995:155). But capitalist liberalism, he suggests, may actually be an oxymoron: Liberals assert human rights and a belief in equality, while living in and supporting a world system that is, and always will be, based on inequality (1995:160–161). In other words, much of what poses as gender equality is rhetoric, not action intended to reduce or wipe out the oppression of women.

However, says Wallerstein, feminism is a real challenge not just to liberalism, but to the classic sociology of Marx, Weber, and Durkheim. Both the world and the world of knowledge have been male biased in many ways. As Charlotte Gilman noted, the perspective of women has been ignored. But, adds Wallerstein, feminism is not a united viewpoint: White women, women of color, and Third World women often have decidedly different interests and goals.

Race   Wallerstein has written a considerable amount about race and ethnicity in the world capitalist system. In his analysis, race and ethnicity are tools used by the capitalist world economy for two purposes: (1) to justify and enforce unequal benefits from the world system, and (2) to keep the working classes from uniting (Campbell, 1999:12).

Ethnicities (nations, peoples) are actually social constructs; they are shaped, reshaped, created, and destroyed as they are found to be useful or detrimental to individual or societal goals (Wallerstein, 1984:20). An ethnic Meru professor at the University of Nairobi was once asked if he was both Meru and Kikuyu—a larger ethnic category under which the Meru are sometimes subsumed. His answer was: "When it is to my advantage, I am Kikuyu; when it is disadvantageous, I am just Meru." Even the terminology used serves a purpose:

> To the extent that these "peoples" are defined by themselves (and by others) as controlling or having the "moral" right to control a state-structure, these "peoples" become "nations." To the extent that a given "people" is not defined as having the right to control a state-structure, these people become "minorities" or "ethnic groups." (Wallerstein, 1984:20)

In other words, not only national class consciousness and identification, but ethnicity, nation, minority, and even race are to some extent concocted, and therefore false, labels.

Quijano and Wallerstein (1992:551) note that during slavery, African Americans were kept legally in inferior positions. However, in the postslavery period, ethnicity was not sufficient to maintain the advantages of whites, especially white males. A large amount of upward mobility made informal boundaries insufficient to maintain the ethnic/racial hierarchy. Thus, racism, both prejudicial and discriminatory, was institutionalized to reinforce ethnic stratification. Then, with formal changes toward equality, advantage continued for those in the upper strata of society, with less need for explicitly racist controls.

Some have argued, notes Wallerstein, that because of busing and reverse discrimination, we now live in a world of multiculturalism. In his view, however, we have barely scratched the surface of historic racial/ethnic inequities. "Blacks, women, and many others are still getting the short end of the stick, by and large, whatever the marginal improvements here and there" (1999:100).

Race and ethnicity apply to the entire world economy. They are not the only categories used to divide people, but they are significant; if anything, they are becoming more important in maintaining the world system. And, as noted above, ethnicity is flexible enough to be changed to meet the occupational and social needs of those in control (Wallerstein, 1987:386). As one commentator has pointed out, Wallerstein's "analysis of race is quite consistent with his previous assertions about the nature of science and society" (Campbell, 1999:15). To Wallerstein, it is important that race be examined in the context of the world system. As a social construct, it is central to the power and economic relations of the world, and—as in the case of gender—an understanding of race is necessary for those who would change society.

Other Theories and Theorists

So far in this chapter we have looked at evolutionary modernization theory and world system theory. To these two we need to add theories of dependency/underdevelopment/dependent development—that is, theories that have questioned both the evolutionists and Wallerstein's world system.

Dependency Theory   While Wallerstein was developing his world perspective, beginning with Africa, dependency theory arose in and focused on Latin America. There are many parallels between Wallerstein's early work and the Latin American dependency theory of Andre Gunder Frank—a most important "voice from the periphery" (Blomstrom and Hettne, 1984).

Earlier we noted that modernization was not just a theory but an action program, aimed by the United States especially at Latin America. Alvin So (1990) has described how this gave rise to dependency theory:

> The dependency school first arose in Latin America as a response to the bankruptcy of the program of the U.N. Economic Commission for Latin America (ECLA) in the early 1960s. . . . Many populist regimes . . . tried out the ECLA development strategy of protectionism and industrialization through import substitution in the 1950s, and many Latin American researchers had high hopes for a trend toward economic growth, welfare, and democracy. However, . . . in the early 1960s, Latin America was plagued by unemployment, inflation, currency devaluation, declining terms of trade, and other economic problems. Popular protests were followed by the collapse of popular regimes and the setting up of repressive military and authoritarian regimes. (1990:91)

In 1969, Frank wrote an influential paper, "The Sociology of Development and the Underdevelopment of Sociology," in which he criticized American writers on modernization. He characterized such change as "(1) empirically untenable, (2) theoretically insufficient, and (3) practically incapable of stimulating a process of development in the Third World" (Blomstrom and Hettne, 1984:50).

Arguing particularly with Talcott Parsons's pattern variables,[3] Frank asserted that the developed nations are often less universalistic, less based on achievement, and not as functionally specific as Parsons would lead us to believe; likewise, the underdeveloped nations are not as particularistic or ascriptive as this theory claims (Frank, 1969). Also, according to Frank, "underdevelopment was not an original stage, but rather a created condition; to exemplify he points to the British deindustrialization of India," as well as the negative effects of the European invasion of Africa and Latin America (Blomstrom and Hettne, 1984:52). In other words, contact with and oppression by Europe "underdeveloped" the Third World.

Fernando H. Cardoso joined Frank and others in spelling out the theoretical principles of the dependency school. As we have noted, much of their earliest thought paralleled very closely Wallerstein's world system perspective. A summary of dependency theory must include the following: (1) Obstacles to development arise not so much from a lack of capital or skills, but from the international division of labor; that is, they are external, not internal. (2) Surplus is transferred from underdeveloped to developed countries, so that the former lack the surplus necessary to develop. (3) Self-reliance and dissociation from the developed nations offer the only path to development (Blomstrom and Hettne, 1984:76).

During the 1970s and 1980s, dependency theory was both criticized and made more complex. Some societies were seen as characterized by national control of their own development, having produced their own technological expertise and goods internally.[4] Others were seen as having "export enclaves," or centers linked to the developed world, and still others as simply underdeveloped. These types were explained and further specified according to various configurations of politics (fascist, socialist, democratic), of resources (many/few, diverse/specific), of technological capability and training, and of available capital.

Knowledge and the Future Wallerstein spent the 1990s analyzing the future of both society and social science. He claims that the next 50 years will see more upheavals in both the periphery and the core. Just where today's world system will be in A.D. 2050 he is unwilling to predict. As for social science, Wallerstein argues that we must do two things: (1) break down so-called disciplinary barriers, and (2) accept the responsibility of proposing changes that will

---

[3]As discussed in Chapter 2, these pattern variables are (1) diffuseness/specificity, (2) affectivity/affective neutrality, (3) particularism/universalism, (4) ascription/achievement, and (5) self-orientation/collectivity orientation. According to Parsons, the first of each is found in traditional societies, and the second in modern, industrial societies. Furthermore, the worldwide change toward modernization is toward the second of each pair (Parsons, 1966:22–23).

[4]For example, Anthony Brewer wrote, "I see no reason why an independent capitalist class should not be formed on the basis of export-led industrialization or copying of techniques" (1980:289).

make the world a better place. The task of social science, he concludes, is greatest precisely

> when the historical social system is . . . furthest from equilibrium, when the fluctuations are greatest, when the bifurcations are nearest, when small input has great output. This is the moment in which we are now living and shall be living for the next twenty-five to fifty years. (1999:217)

Critique and Conclusions

Although it would be interesting to go into dependency/underdevelopment theory in greater detail, the point has been made that multiple theories of world economics and economic change now exist. In summary, the four major schools of thought are (1) the modernization school, focusing on the "developed" societies and aimed at making the rest of the world "just like us" by bringing them along a single evolutionary path; (2) the Marxist view, discussed in the previous chapter, focusing on capitalist exploitation, imperialism, and the eventual socialist revolution; (3) Wallerstein's quasi-Marxist world system view, which sees the world as a three-tiered system, with oppression and contradictions but little hope of an overall revolution to correct its ills and inequalities; and (4) the underdevelopment/dependency view, which focuses on the Third World and proposes a more complex relationship among the factors making for economic change.

To return now to world system theory, Marxist critics have argued that Wallerstein does not explain as well as Marx did the transition from feudalism to capitalism. They have also rejected his focus on production for the market, rather than on relations of production. Finally, they assert that "class is afforded only a peripheral role in Wallerstein's conceptual apparatus, and is therefore, like the mode of production, of little importance [to Wallerstein] as an analytical tool" (Blomstrom and Hettne, 1984:188–189). Some critics simply state that Wallerstein provides a world stratification analysis, not a class analysis.

In response to these critics, Wallerstein and his followers have "conceded that the concept of 'world-system' is merely a research tool, that the world-system perspective can be used to study local historical developments, and that social class should be conceptualized as a dynamic historical process" (So, 1990:230).

Another criticism of Wallerstein is that his theory has only one new idea: that the world is a single system. Everything else he presents is either borrowed or is (often massive) descriptive detail. A final, quite intricate criticism comes from Theda Skocpol, whose theory of revolution is the focus of the third section of this chapter. Wallerstein responds directly to her criticism, but we will save their exchange until we have looked at Skocpol's theory.

Revolution: Theda Skocpol (1947–)

So far in this chapter on change, we have examined evolutionary theory and theories of world system and development (or the lack thereof). We turn now to non-Marxist theories of revolution, especially that of Theda Skocpol.

In the early 1970s, as the Vietnam War was winding down, Theda Skocpol was a politically involved graduate student at Harvard. "The times certainly stimulated my interest in understanding revolutionary change," she says. "And it was during these years that my commitment to democratic socialist ideals matured" (Skocpol, 1979:xii).

After finishing her degree at Harvard, Skocpol remained as a member of the nontenured faculty from 1975 to 1981. From 1981 to 1985, she taught sociology and political science at the University of Chicago, before returning to Harvard as Professor of Sociology, subsequently becoming jointly tenured in the Harvard Department of Government.

Skocpol studies both sociology and comparative history, and her dissertation compared the French, Russian, and Chinese revolutions. This became the focus of her first pathbreaking book, *States and Social Revolutions* (1979).

Skocpol's Central Theories and Methods

Skocpol was influenced by Barrington Moore's 1966 book on democracy and dictatorship, which we will look at under "Other Theorists" below. However, her viewpoint is very much her own, and involves understanding the state as well as revolutions.

The State   A **state**, says Skocpol, is not simply created and manipulated by a dominant class, nor is it just an arena for socioeconomic or class struggles.

> It is, rather, a set of administrative, policing, and military organizations headed, and more or less well coordinated by, an executive authority. Any state first and fundamentally extracts resources from society and deploys these to create and support coercive and administrative organizations. . . . These fundamental organizations are at least potentially autonomous from direct dominant-class control. (1979:29)

In fact, Skocpol asserts, while performing its own functions the state may even create conflicts of interest within the dominant class. "The state normally performs two basic sets of tasks: It maintains order, and it competes with other actual or potential states" (1979:30).

Skocpol's non-Marxist view of the state is interesting when compared with those of Nicos Poulantzas and Elman Service. Poulantzas, though a committed Marxist, also noted that the state was, from time to time, an independent actor in the capitalist world—related to the ruling class, but not to be analytically subsumed under it (Poulantzas, 1978; Skocpol, 1979:28). Service's view of the origin of the state was that it was primarily an administrative structure whose task was to organize and control a region, with economic redistribution occurring later and secondarily. Thus, there is much similarity among the three, and all contrast in some degree with orthodox Marxism.

States, according to Skocpol, are actual organizations whose primary functions are to control their populations, collect taxes, and recruit for the military. Given these functions, "international military pressures and opportunities can prompt state rulers to attempt policies that conflict with, and even in extreme cases contradict, the fundamental interests of a dominant class." A state must deal both with its own class-divided socioeconomic structures and with an international system of other states. If a state deals efficiently with these primary functions, it will be considered legitimate by most people within its territory (Skocpol, 1979:31).

Revolution   Why study revolutions, and why discuss them in this volume? Skocpol claims that they "deserve special attention, not only because of their extraordinary significance for the histories of nations and the world but also because of their distinctive pattern of sociopolitical change" (1979:4). And change is what this chapter is about.

> **Social revolutions** are defined as rapid, basic transformations of a society's state and class structures; and they are accompanied and in part carried through by class-based revolts from below. Social revolutions are set apart from other sorts of conflicts and transformative processes above all by the combination of two coincidences: the coincidence of societal structural change with class upheaval; and the coincidence of political with social transformation. (Skocpol, 1979:4–5, bold added)

Rebellions, in contrast, do not result in structural change, and neither do riots.

Where and why do revolutions take place? According to Skocpol, "Modern social revolutions have happened only in countries situated in disadvantaged positions within international arenas" (1979:23). The causal factors include (1) an organized landed class that can stand up to the state; (2) peasant discontent with both land and state policies; and (3) a rigid leadership, such as a hereditary monarchy, and/or a state under pressure from other stronger nations. According to Skocpol, these are the conditions that held in France in the 1780s and in Russia and China in the twentieth century. Political crises emerged in all three countries because their old regimes were unable to implement basic reforms, and because of external pressures from Britain, Germany, and Japan, respectively.

Inflexibility and external threat are only part of the explanation. Peasant revolts, argues Skocpol, "have been the crucial insurrectionary ingredient in virtually all successful social revolutions to date," certainly in those of France, Russia, and China (1979:113). Here Skocpol draws a distinction between serfs who work on large estates and those who farm their own land. The latter, she says, are much more likely to be able to organize and revolt. Thus, the original propositions in her theory of revolution were (1) external threat, (2) state rigidity and weakness, (3) fairly independent and discontented communities, and (4) peasant insurrection. Skocpol later summarized her 1979 position as follows:

1. State organizations are central to social revolutions because they can only occur when administrative and coercive powers break down.

2. International/world historical context is crucial because context has often created the precipitating crisis/breakdown.

3. A structural, non-voluntarist approach is necessary because purposive action alone does not create and structure a revolution—it is no use trying to explain revolutions in terms of mass psychology or class interests or ideological leadership. (1994:7–9)

However, while Skocpol was writing her 1979 book, the Shah of Iran was toppled, and it was incumbent on her to explain the Iranian revolution from her theoretical perspective.

> What should I say about a massive old-regime state whose bureaucracies and armies crumbled *without* first facing defeat in war or strong military competition from abroad? Even more pressing, what should I say about a revolution that apparently was "made"—quite deliberately—by urban social movements, in the absence of either peasant revolts or a rural guerrilla movement? (1994:17)

External threat and peasant discontent seemed to be missing from the Iranian revolution. However, external influence through multinational oil companies and through the Shah's acceptance of Westernization may have played the same role as a military threat. More important, she later wrote, "I became convinced that this social revolution, like others, occurred through a conjuncture of state weakness and popular revolts rooted in relatively autonomous communities" (1994:17). That these communities were urban instead of rural simply broadened her theory, reducing peasant insurrection to a subspecies of autonomous-community discontent. That the Shi'a Islamic clerics took control and made the Iranian government into a conservative Islamic state is not very different from Lenin's Bolsheviks taking control in Russia after the state had already been overthrown/fallen.

As noted earlier, Skocpol rejects a factor that has been treated as central in some other theories. Ideological hegemony is often important in postrevolutionary society, she argues, but it does not provide a predictive key to either the occurrence of revolution or the postrevolutionary organizational activities of the revolutionaries (1979:170). Her analysis emphasizes "the clear importance not only of political consolidation but also of state structures in determining revolutionary outcomes" (1979: 163–164).

Skocpol recognizes that there are failed or unsuccessful revolutions, such as those in England in the seventeenth century and Germany in the mid-1800s. Her argument is that these revolutions failed because the monarchy (the state) was strong and flexible enough to withstand internal and external pressures, and that enough power was delegated to the landlords that they were able to withstand peasant discontent (1979:140).

Finally, Skocpol discusses common postrevolutionary features. One is the creation of a centralized, bureaucratized state; a second is the loss of old upper-class control and privilege; a third is the transformation of the class structure (1979:161). However, she notes that, despite similar causal factors, the results are different because the revolutions occur in different world-historical contexts. In other words, she is more willing to theorize about causal factors than about common consequences (1979:233–234).

Social Policy   In the past decade, Skocpol's work has moved from revolutions to social policy. Four theories, she suggests, have been offered to explain social policy programs in Western societies. First is the logic of industrialism approach, which argues that cities and industrial development have forced societies to do something about the problems produced thereby. A second theory is based on national values. Belief in independent versus group action in problem solving is used to explain differences in the speed with which industrializing, urbanizing societies develop social policies. Third, welfare capitalism theory argues that social policy is a result of ideological divisions between conservatives and liberals, who disagree on the extent to which social insurance measures should be instituted by corporations themselves. Finally, the political class struggle approach is based on the ruling class's "doing good things" for those in need in order to keep the class structure under control—as Marx posited (Skocpol, 1995:17–18).

Nature of Society, Humans, and Change

Skocpol makes no judgments either about human nature or about society. And her theory avoids the rational radicalism of Rousseau and those who followed him, who claimed that through ideology and human thought one could envision, and then construct, a better world.

Skocpol's entire theory pertains to one kind of change: the dramatic, radical overthrow and rebuilding of a society's structures. She does not argue that there are no other forms of change, or even that there is a single combination of factors leading to revolution (recall her discussion of Iran).

Class, Gender, and Race

Although Skocpol is not primarily a theorist of class, much has already been said about her view of the relationship between class and revolution. Classes and class conflict are not the "prime movers" in revolutions, though they may be actors. According to Skocpol,

> class forces, whether capitalist classes that retain control over strategic
> means of production and economic linkages, or popular classes whose
> revolts or military mobilization contribute to the revolutionary struggle, are
> bound by ties of conflict and cooperation, command and mobilization to
> the dynamic and partially autonomous activities of states and state builders.
> (1979:291–292)

Thus, classes play a complex role in revolutionary activity, but to Skocpol, unlike Marx, they are not the prime movers in society.

Skocpol says little about race and gender in her theory of revolutions. However, in her recent work on social policy she speaks briefly to each of these factors. In discussing the U.S. War on Poverty, she notes the importance of race as an issue that is sometimes treated as unique, and sometimes subsumed under class or poverty (1995:251).

Skocpol's discussion of gender and social policy (1995:72–135) focuses on explaining the differences between British and U.S. social policies. Calling them paternalistic and maternalistic, respectively, she shows how British policies have been for the most part subsumed under labor movements. In the United States, in contrast, women were excluded from party politics, resulting in separate movements on their own behalf (1995:114–135). This distinction is reminiscent of the early-twentieth-century contrast between Beatrice Webb's socialist but nonfeminist activity in Britain and C. P. Gilman's clearly feminist writing and action in the United States.

Other Theories and Theorists

Current theories of revolution, according to Skocpol, can be divided into four categories: Marxist, aggregate-psychological, systems/value consensus, and political conflict (1979:8–9). All these theories are voluntarist, meaning that revolution is seen as the result of beliefs, consciousness, and planning on the part of individuals and groups. None of them, notes Skocpol, recognizes the state as an actor and reactor, and all ignore "*inter*national structures and world-historical developments" (1979:14). The Marxist theory, involving class consciousness and the actions of revolutionaries, we are already familiar with. Let us here look briefly at some of the others.

The theory that most influenced Skocpol's ideas was that of Barrington Moore. Moore's *Social Origins of Dictatorship and Democracy* (1966) was quasi-Marxist and in direct opposition to the single-path theory of modernization (Blomstrom and Hettne, 1984:21). For Moore, the two key factors that explain the recent histories of the world's societies are commercial transformation and violent revolution (or lack thereof). These two factors can combine in any of four ways, with the following results: "Commercialization and revolution together breed democracy; commercialization without revolution results in fascism; revolution without commercialization leads to communis[m]; . . . and, finally, the absence of both commercialization and revolution is the harbinger of political stagnation and decay" (Janos, 1986:61). Revolutions from above ordinarily result in bourgeois democracy, while those from below are more likely to produce socialism/communism.

Moore's fairly simple and straightforward theory left several loose ends dangling. First, commercialization was treated as either synonymous with or precedent to industrialization. But the discussion of dependency and underdevelopment, you will recall, indicated that it is possible to have large-scale commercial/market activity without industrialization, resulting in dependence on the more industrialized societies. Second, commercialization and revolution, which resulted in bourgeois democracy in France and the United States, has produced other outcomes—such as a socialist/capitalist mix or a semiperiphery position—at other times and places.

Lest we become too critical of Moore's simple and elegant theory, however, Skocpol reminds us that in the mid-1960s there were two primary views of the world: Marxism and modernization. To Moore's credit, he broke social scientific thinking out of this dichotomous debate.

A second view of revolution is that people become angry and frustrated and, as a result, bring about change (Gurr, 1970). This frustration-aggression school of thought opposes, but is analogous to, the theory of development/modernization that says personality and achievement orientation of individuals modernize societies (see footnote 1). The problem with frustration-aggression theory is that so many different life circumstances can give rise to feelings of frustration and relative deprivation. "To extrapolate from sums or proportions of individual attitudes to the occurrence of structural transformations . . . is to accept a naive additive image of society and its structure" (Portes, 1971).

A third approach, the ideology school of thought, argues that a well-worked-out set of alternative ideas leads to organization and then to change (Johnson, 1966). One of Skocpol's major debates has been with Bill Sewell, who represents the ideological school. Looking primarily at the French Revolution, Sewell argues that Skocpol has over-reified the concept of structure. The Enlightenment, says Sewell, contradicted the ideology of the Old Regime, insisting on natural law rather than divinity and revelation, and universalism rather than the ideology of privilege. After coexisting peacefully for a time, ideological oppositions were polarized by economic crisis, leading eventually to revolutionary upheaval (Sewell, in Skocpol, 1994:176–178). In this view, ideology is a causal focus for revolution that cannot simply be subsumed within structural analysis. Though it is more complicated than this, Skocpol's response is that it is a matter of emphasis: For her, structure is more important, while for Sewell, ideology is primary.

A fourth approach is the political-conflict perspective, best articulated by Charles Tilly. Tilly criticized other theorists for concentrating "on individual attitudes or on the condition of the social system as a whole" (Tilly, Tilly, and Tilly, 1975:488). Political violence, including revolution, "tends to flow directly out of a population's central political processes, instead of expressing diffuse strains and discontents within the population" (1975:436). Mobilization of discontent, or political conflict, is the focus of Tilly's ideas. However, one is left wondering what it is that mobilizes discontent. Is it class interest, or group frustration, or something else?

It should be noted that not all of these theories are mutually exclusive. Frustration might be channeled within existing structural divisions, or ideology might reinforce class interests. So let us move to our conclusions, first on Skocpol and Wallerstein, and then on the chapter as a whole.

Critique and Conclusions

One of the more interesting debates involving those discussed in this chapter has been between Wallerstein and Skocpol. Skocpol was asked to contribute to a review symposium on Wallerstein's *Modern World-System* (1974), and she took the opportunity to again think through her own ideas in relation to his. Her major criticisms were of his focus on economics to the exclusion of politics, and his focus on the world system to the exclusion of states and regional subdivisions.

> Wallerstein's insistence on a world-historical approach to development was to be welcomed, . . . but not his economic reductionism or his teleological treatment of the whole world as a single seamless "system." . . . I advocated the analysis of states as administrative and military organizations embedded in international geopolitical systems of military competition. (Skocpol, 1994:12)

Comparative historical studies of states and regions seem to Skocpol most useful in making appropriate comparisons. She is also critical of Wallerstein's attempted explanation of the rise of capitalism in the fifteenth and sixteenth centuries; earlier we noted that his view of origins is indeed the weakest part of his theoretical framework. Skocpol also argues that Wallerstein, while rejecting modernization theory, makes some of the same mistakes in treating certain changes as inevitable; he is, after all, quasi-Marxist and, as such, views the world as having traveled along a certain socioeconomic path. But having said all this, it is obvious that Skocpol's major criticism is that Wallerstein deemphasizes national class divisions and nation-states too much.

By way of response, Wallerstein argues that Skocpol's notion of states as having a life of their own misperceives their character. All institutions, including states, have staffs and rules that give them a life of their own. However, this "life" is used for various purposes by its members and those who support it. It is not independent of other parts of a regional and world system. In other words, the state is not unimportant, but as part of an explanatory framework it must be subsumed under the larger, more important world structure (Wallerstein, 1984:30–35). And, he might have added, he does not represent the world system as seamless, but as comprising three subparts playing different but complementary roles.

Once again, then, it may be a matter of emphasis, with Skocpol's primary unit of analysis being the state, but not simply as an independent actor, and Wallerstein's primary unit being the world economic system, while recognizing that its subparts include nation-states. It is worth noting that Skocpol's dependent or outcome variable is revolution, whereas Wallerstein's is world economic change. Wallerstein and Skocpol, of course, would argue that the difference is much more than emphasis—that their central variables are in fact the beginning point for understanding the changing social world in which we live.

Final Thoughts

We have covered a large amount of theoretical material in this chapter. First, we have examined evolutionary theories of change, including the "modernization" idea that the whole world should and will develop toward the Western/European model. Although modernization theory is clearly questionable, some of Service's evolutionary insights into the origins of states and redistributive networks seem correct.

In the second part of the chapter, we looked at Wallerstein's world system approach, which he painted with such broad strokes that it was (like Marx's ideas) bound to have loose ends. Skocpol's questioning of Wallerstein's ignoring the state, Wallerstein's weak explanation of the origins of capitalism, and the dependency/underdevelopment view of stagnation and world antagonisms have left some questioning much of Wallerstein's framework. Then, in the final section, we became acquainted with Theda Skocpol's theory of revolutions, and compared it with several other such theories.

The overall concern of this chapter has been change—evolutionary, developmental, and revolutionary. Some explanations (Marxist, Wallerstein) have treated the entire world as an economic system, while others have reduced it to personality characteristics. Many changes are in fact incremental, resulting from small internal alterations in technology or organization; they are handled with as little social change as possible, in order to get back to equilibrium, or "business as usual." Others are revolutions on a massive, perhaps even worldwide, scale. You might find it interesting to try combining several theories that are complementary instead of contradictory. We have already noted, for example, how Service's theory of the origin of the state can be combined with Skocpol's on the role of the state in revolutions. The rest is up to you.

References

Blomstrom, Magnus, and Bjorn Hettne. 1984. *Development Theory in Transition: The Dependency Debate and Beyond: Third World Responses*. London: Zed Books.

Brewer, Anthony. 1980. *Marxist Theories of Imperialism: A Critical Survey*. London: Routledge and Kegan Paul.

Campbell, Mary E. 1999. "An Exploration of the Theories of Immanuel Wallerstein." Unpublished paper, University of Wisconsin–Madison.

Childe, V. Gordon. 1936/1951. *Man Makes Himself*. New York: Mentor Books.

Erasmus, Charles J. 1966. *Man Takes Control*. Minneapolis: University of Minnesota Press.

Frank, Andre Gunder. 1969. *Latin America: Underdevelopment or Revolution*. New York: Monthly Review Press.

Gluckman, Max. 1960. "The Rise of a Zulu Empire." *Scientific American, 201,* 157–168.

Gurr, Ted Robert. 1970. *Why Men Rebel*. Princeton, NJ: Princeton University Press.

Hagen, Everett. 1962. *On the Theory of Social Change*. Homewood, IL: R. D. Irwin.

Janos, Andrew C. 1986. *Politics and Paradigms: Changing Theories of Change in Social Science*. Stanford, CA: Stanford University Press.

Johnson, Chalmers. 1966. *Revolutionary Change*. Boston: Little, Brown.

Lerner, Daniel. 1958. *The Passing of Traditional Society*. New York: Free Press.

McClelland, David. 1962. *The Achieving Society*. Princeton, NJ: Princeton University Press.

Moore, Barrington, Jr. 1966. *Social Origins of Dictatorship and Democracy: Lord and Peasant in the Making of the Modern World*. Boston: Beacon Press.

Nisbet, Robert A. 1969. *Social Change and History: Aspects of the Western Theory of Development*. New York: Oxford University Press.

Parsons, Talcott. 1966. *Societies: Evolutionary and Comparative Perspectives*. Englewood Cliffs, NJ: Prentice-Hall.

Portes, Alejandro. 1971. "On the Logic of Post-Factum Explanations: The Hypothesis of the Lower-Class Frustrations as the Cause of Leftist Radicalism." *Social Forces, 50,* 26–44.

Poulantzas, Nicos. 1978. *State, Power, Socialism*. London: Verso Editions.

Quijano, Anibal, and Immanuel Wallerstein. 1992. "Americanity as a Concept, or the Americas in the Modern World-System." *International Social Science Journal, 44,* 549–557.

Sahlins, Marshall D., and Elman Service. 1960. *Evolution and Culture*. Ann Arbor: University of Michigan Press.

Service, Elman R. 1962. *Primitive Social Organization: An Evolutionary Perspective*. New York: Random House.

———. 1971. *Cultural Evolutionism: Theory in Practice*. New York: Holt, Rinehart, and Winston.

———. 1975. *Origins of the State and Civilization: The Process of Cultural Evolution*. New York: W. W. Norton.

Skocpol, Theda. 1979. *States and Social Revolutions*. New York: Cambridge University Press.

———. 1994. *Social Revolutions in the Modern World*. Cambridge: Cambridge University Press.

———. 1995. *Social Policy in the United States*. Princeton, NJ: Princeton University Press.

So, Alvin Y. 1990. *Social Change and Development: Modernization, Dependency, and World-System Theories*. Newbury Park, CA: Sage.

Steward, Julian H. 1955. *Theory of Culture Change: The Methodology of Multilinear Evolution*. Urbana: University of Illinois Press.

Tilly, Charles, Louise Tilly, and Richard Tilly. 1975. *The Rebellious Century, 1830–1930*. Cambridge, MA: Harvard University Press.

Veblen, Thorstein. 1915. *Imperial Germany and the Industrial Revolution*. New York: Macmillan.

Wallerstein, Immanuel. 1974. *The Modern World-System: Capitalist Agriculture and the Origins of the European World-Economy in the Sixteenth Century*. New York: Academic Press.

———. 1979. *The Capitalist World-Economy*. New York: Cambridge University Press.

———. 1984. *The Politics of the Capitalist World-Economy*. Cambridge: Cambridge University Press.

———. 1987. "The Construction of Peoplehood: Racism, Nationalism, Ethnicity." *Sociological Forum, 2*, 373–388.

———. 1995. *After Liberalism*. New York: New Press.

———. 1996. "Social Science and Contemporary Society: The Vanishing Guarantees of Rationality." *International Sociology, 11*, 7–25.

———. 1999. *The End of the World As We Know It*. Minneapolis: University of Minnesota Press.

Weiner, Myron (Ed.). 1966. *Modernization: The Dynamics of Growth*. New York: Basic Books.

White, Leslie A. 1949. *The Science of Culture*. New York: Farrar, Straus and Giroux.

———. 1960. "Foreword." In Marshall D. Sahlins and Elman Service (Eds.), *Evolution and Culture* (pp. v–xii). Ann Arbor: University of Michigan Press.

Wilson, Godfrey, and Monica Wilson. 1958. *Analysis of Social Change*. Cambridge: Cambridge University Press.

SECTION III

Transitions and Challenges

A number of late-twentieth-century views have challenged the Durkheim-Marx-Weber core of sociology. Two of these—feminism and Freudianism—were already active in theoretical circles by the turn of the twentieth century. In the next five chapters, we will introduce our own set of transitions and challenges, beginning with a review of mid-twentieth-century sociology in Chapter 7.

Chapter 7 notes the hegemony of structural-functional thinking at mid-century (see Chapter 2) and the strong belief within sociology that value-free knowledge is possible. This position was questioned by Alvin Gouldner and C. Wright Mills from a Marxist perspective, and by the 1960s it was also challenged by student and "New Left" protests. In addition, outstanding Third World, feminist, and African American thinkers were challenging the marginalization of women and minorities.

The four challenges introduced (or reintroduced) in Chapters 8–11 are symbolic interactionism (Chapter 8), rational choice and exchange (Chapter 9), feminism (Chapter 10), and Michel Foucault's view of power, sex, violence, and science, along with its feminist critics (Chapter 11). Finally, although not really part of Section III, Chapter 12 will present a recapitulation and some final thoughts.

Chapter 8, on symbolic interactionism, picks up where George Herbert Mead left off in his theoretical treatment of the development of the self, and of the use of symbols in interpersonal communication. You will meet briefly the disciple of Mead who coined the term "symbolic interactionism"—Herbert Blumer. Next is Erving Goffman, who was both indebted to and distinct from the Mead-Blumer tradition. His dramaturgical approach explained interaction as analogous to behavior on a theatrical stage, in which "appropriate" lines are delivered, with "backstage" behavior being less scripted. Goffman also studied total institutions, such as asylums and prisons, in which individuals live their entire lives. The other major figure you will meet in Chapter 8 is Arlie Hochschild. Her work on emotions adds to the hyper-intellectualized version of symbolic interactionism presented by the male scholars. Her application to family is also an important part of her work.

Chapter 9 introduces rational choice and exchange theories, focusing on James Coleman's version of each. "I think, therefore I choose or decide" and "I think, therefore I choose what is in my best interest" are simplified versions of these two theories. The notions of making rational decisions and of maximizing profit are old ideas, but they are important in current theorizing. Those who disagree argue either from the premise that humans are irrational and emotional, or else from Pareto's view that humans are rationalizers, not rational.

In the nineteenth and early twentieth centuries, male scholarship did an effective job of obliterating females from the core of sociological theory. In Chapter 10 we note that by the 1970s, many feminists and female sociologists were active, often having to rediscover the answers produced a half-century or more earlier—but also asking new questions. Dorothy Smith and Patricia Hill Collins are the central figures in this chapter.

One issue that arose in the 1960s and 1970s was that the radical movements of that period kept women "in their place," playing secondary roles. Smith sought to bring women's experience into what must be explained, and she has helped to clarify both the similarities and differences between women's and men's lives in today's world. Collins adds an important dimension to the discussion by comparing not only women's experience with men's, but black women's experience with white women's. Her insights draw together many earlier concerns of Charlotte Gilman, W. E. B. Du Bois, the Marxist Raya Dunayevskaya (Chapter 5), and recent feminists.

Chapter 11 presents a serious expression of doubt regarding the traditional core of sociology. Foucault represents a number of sociologists who have questioned the very meaning of the texts we read. What is sociological knowledge, and what is its relation to power? Does power simply create so-called "knowledge"? Even more than those who raise issues of irrationality and rationalization, Foucault seeks to explain punishment, violence, and madness in today's world—meaning that we live in anything but a rational modern world. Feminist scholars have seen Foucault in two ways: On the one hand, they appreciate his interest in discipline and punishment as referring to much of women's historical experience; on the other hand, they are not convinced that his treatments of sex and pleasure comprehend women's lives.

Chapter 7

Mid-Twentieth-Century Sociology

The late 1950s and 1960s have been regarded, in historical hindsight, as significant years of momentous changes in the social and cultural life of most Western societies. From Elvis and an explosion of popular culture to a proliferation of experimental transformations in the arts in general; from mechanical worlds to the wired worlds of media and microchip; from love and marriage connected like a horse and carriage to "free," experimental, and cosmic love and later, with the prevalence of AIDS, dangerous love; from political reformism/conformity to the politics of protest and violence; from "father knows best" to the rise of the feminist movement—the period was marked by critical changes, most especially in embodying a general "crisis of authority" and "movements of dissent" (Owram, 1996:171).

A major part of the transformation was related to the baby boom that altered, numerically and culturally, most Western societies. The idea of radical transformations that affected all aspects of social life has given the period its historical "identity" in the West. Of course, in the same time period, many non-Western societies were neither peaceful nor conformist, and the independence movements in Africa were defining non-Western events. What set the Western world apart was the scale of the changes and challenges that the baby boomers generated. Among those changes and challenges we can include the questioning of sociological orthodoxy, especially the idea of a structural-functionalist hegemony so important in North American sociology.

Ideological Disputes

As you saw in Chapter 1, sociological theory tries to understand and explain what goes on between people. By the 1960s, this exercise had become a fragmented, fractious enterprise. The internal sociological disputes over theory and

141

methods were often played out in the meetings of various national and international sociological associations as well as in the pages of journals and reviews.

A frequent accusation used by the protagonists was that their opponents' stance was "ideological." This accusation usually meant that the opposing position was either radical (even revolutionary) or conservative (or possibly neo-fascist). The accusations of ideological bias were complicated by the political upheavals of the era in various parts of the world. Sociological radicals were implicitly (and in some cases explicitly) associated by their opponents with radical political aims and even accused of associating with, or at least condoning, so-called terrorist organizations such as the Black Panthers. Conservative sociologists were associated, again implicitly if not explicitly, with repressive state and corporate institutions and were often accused of being tools of the military-industrial complex (Mills, 1959).

We have pointed out that ideological content is part of any theory and its presence does not necessarily invalidate the theory. But in many of these disputes over the "correct" way to theorize and practice sociology, ideology as bias was the weapon of choice to invalidate an opponent's stance. The dissatisfaction with the dominant sociological paradigm took a "quasi-ideological form" in the 1960s when "system theory, particularly the Parsonsian variety, was seen simply as providing justification for the conservative impulse dominating the postwar period" (Friedrichs, 1970:25).

In hindsight we can recognize that many of the debates were "tempests in an academic teapot" and that the presumed practical political importance of sociology's and sociologists' "taking a stand" was overdrawn. For example, the opposition of a considerable number of sociologists to the Vietnam War provided moral comfort but had little practical effect on the nature and duration of the war. The disputes did, however, highlight the fact that sociology has always been "political" in the sense of assuming that the discipline could in some way make a difference to society. This assumption has often meant that sociology has been "an 'oppositional science' despite its establishment as an academic subject" (Shils, 1985:175). What was important in the 1960s were the new sociological directions that spun off from many of the disputes, and it is these new directions that comprise the content of the rest of this volume.

To understand the various theoretical positions that have characterized sociology in the second half of the twentieth century, some discussion of the debates and disputes is useful. The vicissitudes of these debates will be discussed under the headings of facts and values, macro/micro perspectives, feminism and feminist theory, and race relations, recognizing that in fact the debates overlapped these divisions.

Facts and Values

In Howard Becker's 1960 presidential address to the American Sociological Association, he insisted that "There is no substitute for remaining in close touch with the empirical evidence, with the 'damned facts'" (Becker, 1960:809). The post–World War II sociological generation in the United States had been carefully trained in empirical research methods and were "dedicated to the gospel that value judgments were to be described and not made" (Friedrichs, 1970:77). This stress on research methods, especially statistical research, was less prevalent in European circles and in Britain. Empirical work there remained outside the university context, being largely undertaken by governments. In most cases, sociology in Europe and Britain was more social philosophy than empirical research (Bulmer, 1985:5).

But the view that it was empirical evidence, purged of any evaluative content, that formed the bedrock of the sociological enterprise was already the subject of contention in the U.S. sociological community by the 1950s. Alfred McClung Lee and Elizabeth Briant Lee, Alvin Gouldner, C. Wright Mills, and Robert S. Lynd were some of the dissenters from the idea of a value-free sociology. The dissent was muted at first by the institutional dominance of the value-free perspective. In a 1953 recording played at the annual American Sociological Association meeting, containing advice from 20 former presidents on the nature of the sociological enterprise, only one, Harry Pratt Fairchild, "mentioned a concern for social justice." All of the others stressed "the need for a value-free science" (Galliher and Galliher, 1995:27).

Mid-twentieth-century sociology in North America was dominated by a small set of theoretical positions (Collins, 1981:1). Collins characterized the sociological profile for North America at that time as functionalism—the "main pretender to being general theory"—with social change taking the form of an "ethnocentric evolutionist developmentalism" and, at the micro level, the "narrow positivism of social behaviorism" or the "loyal opposition of symbolic interactionism." Kingsley Davis, in his presidential address to the American Sociological Association in 1959, asserted that sociology equaled functional analysis (recall the "Final Thoughts" in Chapter 2).

The most influential of the functionalist theorists was Talcott Parsons (see Chapter 2). Parsons's *The Social System* (1951) was a key text in establishing the paradigmatic status of system and functionalism, which were "deemed by the well-informed professional to represent sociological orthodoxy in the 'fifties" (Friedrich, 1970:19). Hinkle (1994:336) asserts that by 1950 the "ascendance of structural functionalism seemed to be assured" and various alternative theoretical orientations from the past had become residual.

The general indifference to alternative sociological perspectives in U.S. sociology in the 1950s was, according to Hinkle, the result of the institutionalization of the discipline in the academy. Gouldner (1963:45) saw the problem more specifically as the compulsive trend to transform an institutionalized sociology into a "profession." In a discussion of Parsons's paper "Sociology as a Profession," Gouldner remarked that Parsons's description had been rejected by E. C. Hughes. Hughes (1963:45) claimed that the American Sociological Association was not a "professional but, rather, a learned society." Gouldner, however, pointed out that professionalism seemed to have taken hold, resulting in "the growth of technical specialists" and a "diffusion of the value-free outlook to the point where it becomes less of an intellectual doctrine and more of a blanketing mood" (Gouldner, 1963:48).

Value-free Sociology

The push for professionalism and value-free sociology and the codification of sociological orthodoxy as structural functionalism were accompanied by an increase in the number of sociology students in the 1940s and in the membership of the American Sociological Association, which grew from 1,651 in 1946 to 3,241 in 1950. The entrenchment and expansion of sociology within academia consolidated the idea that the only viable sociological enterprise was a **scientific** enterprise and that it was "statistically-oriented, qualified empiricist neo-positivism" that formed the "legitimating criteria (or norms) for undertaking valid sociological research" (Hinkle, 1994:62).

In a review of the state of sociology in the 1950s, Lipset and Smelser proclaimed the "complete triumph since World War I of the new 'scientific sociology'" (1961:40). George Lundberg (1961:40) stated confidently that, like physical scientists, social scientists could produce scientific knowledge with "impersonal, neutral, general validity for whatever purposes man desires to use it." Lundberg went on to point out that the "services of *real* social scientists," as value-free scientists, "would be as indispensable to Fascists as to Communists and Democrats, just as are the services of physicists and physicians" (Lundberg, 1961:57).

The claims to value neutrality did not go unchallenged. Gouldner pointed out that the segregation of reason and passion (or sociological scientific techniques and social ethical positions) *"warps reason by tingeing it with sadism and leaves feeling smugly sure only of itself and bereft of a sense of common humanity"* (1963:51, emphasis in the original). Despite such criticisms, the majority of North American sociologists believed that the discipline had made progress toward becoming a science of society.

The triumphalism of North American commentators on the state of the discipline at that time was only minimally echoed in other sociological centers such as Europe, Asia, Britain, and South America, but there was *seeming* consensus on the nature of the sociological enterprise as necessary, worthy, and scientific. Structural and functional perspectives were current in other sociological centers, but they were often given national interpretations that had to do with the particular development of sociology in those centers. A significant divergence from the structural-functional perspective was the retention of a Marxist or conflict perspective in European sociology, and C. Wright Mills at Columbia was a persistent critic of North American sociology from the 1950s. Mills's *The Sociological Imagination* (1959) critiqued structural functionalism and abstract empiricism and contrasted these perspectives with what he saw as the more sociologically relevant European critical tradition.

Nonetheless, in both the European and North American context, there was a "widely shared dream that sociology could and would produce the objective truth of modern society" (Lemert, 1992:65). Lundberg (1961) asked the question "Can Science Save Us?" and concluded that, yes, science—both natural *and* social science—could alleviate physical and social problems. There were no other alternatives to placing "faith in social science" for "social solutions" (1961:134).

This "agreeable" sociological atmosphere was to undergo considerable disruption as the decade of the 1960s progressed. As Friedrichs (1970:25) euphemistically remarked, sociology "entered a time of troubles." This period resembled the crisis stage that Kuhn (1970) saw as the "necessary prologue to the emergence of a new paradigm." The time was ripe for a transformation of the nature, grounds, and methods of sociology. It was the value-free, scientific claim that was a target for young "dissenters."[1] A particular focus for opposition was the theoretical hegemony of Parsons's structural functionalism (Alexander, 1987:111).

Protests and Challenges

The claims of *any* scientific enterprise to be the agent of progress, social well-being, and in the West at least, democracy had come under increasing scrutiny in the aftermath of World War II and Hiroshima. The irony of sociology's adoption of the "value-free posture . . . informed by the image of natural science" was that the claim was "at least a generation out of date," as most Western spokesmen for natural science saw "creative work in science as riddled by personal, idiosyncratic factors" (Friedrichs, 1970:137).

In the 1960s, the discussions and dissent over sociology as a value-free science became more evident and insistent. The internal sociological malaise was situated in, and affected by, the more general social and political upheavals of the decade. The mid-sixties saw protests aimed at postindustrial society and the upheavals of "race, poverty and the Vietnam War" (Eisenstadt and Curelaru, 1976:335). Much of the protest was centered in universities and colleges, fueled by the huge increases in postsecondary student populations.

Among the radical protesters, "from Berkeley and New York to Paris and Berlin," sociology students were usually in the forefront, if not the leaders, of student protest and revolts (Collins, 1981:316). Lipset and Ladd (1972) showed that sociologists in general were more predisposed to political radicalism than other members of the professoriate. Janowitz (1972:114) reported that, on the central issues of the 1960s—the Vietnam War, race relations, and civil liberties—data collected for the Carnegie Commission of Higher Education showed that "sociology professors had the highest concentration of 'left of center' attitudes on these related issues." A large proportion of the more radical sociologists were young graduates and newly minted PhD's rather than the structural-functional old guard in North America or the old left-leaning partisans in Great Britain and Europe.

The radicalism of this period has often been subsumed under the term New Left. The description does not refer to any singular, specific political party or movement, but refers more generally to the fact that the ideas of Marx and Lenin, as well as Mao, were regarded as relevant to the necessary, revolutionary, global struggle against the forces of any entrenched institutional repression.

---

[1]Friedrichs (1970:24) pointed out that Bell's "end of ideology" thesis was dated by the revolutionary events of the 1960s almost as soon as it appeared in 1960.

The Marx who was relevant was not, however, the Marx of class conflict but the Marx of alienation. For the whole counterculture, "of which the New Left was a part, the whole notion of existential angst was essential" (Owram, 1996:230). Indeed, many of the radicals of the 1960s maintained a tenuous, usually remote, relationship with the members and organizations of the traditional "working class." For example, Maoists maintained that the more interesting and necessary tactics were motivating and assisting peasant uprisings.

What these interrelated movements, ideologies, and activities meant for sociology was a more eclectic approach to what counted as a foundational theoretical past. For North American sociology in particular, it meant a more systematic incorporation of Marx's work into the sociological mainstream after its subterranean existence in the 1950s in various conflict theories. Part of the reason for the neglect of Marx in North American sociology had to do with the political tenor of the times, in particular the postwar reaction to Stalin and McCarthy's witch-hunts for communists in U.S. government service. In North American sociology, it was New Left sociologists, using Marx's legacy, who criticized structural functionalism by accusing it of neglecting the socially significant forces of "inequality, power, coercion, conflict and change" (Turner and Turner, 1990:168).

Marx's work had always been important to European and British sociology, but the nature of that importance was reinterpreted, focusing on the "humanist" Marx, the "young" Marx, or the Hegelian legacy in Marx's work. Freud also found a new audience as an important theorist of sex/gender constructions that differed from the previous clinical, psychiatric utilization of his work. Freud's new audience was, however, a radically critical audience of new-wave feminists.

The radicalism of sociology students and young faculty encountered resistance. In some cases, military force was used to quell student protests. From the 1964 free-speech agitation at Berkeley to the Paris student riots in May 1968, including numerous strikes and occupations at universities and colleges around the world, civil disobedience was met with increasing intolerance by established state authorities. The use of force to control and contain the protests was partly in response to the increasing violence of the protests themselves, as the romanticism of "flower power" gradually gave way to the Realpolitik of, for example, the guns and bombs of the Weathermen, the Red Brigade, and the Front de la Libération du Quebec.

Negative reactions and resistance were also found in the various institutional supports for academic sociology—the journals, association meetings, and faculty committees. The central concern was the future course of the discipline, especially the issue of value-free sociology. Some of the tenor of the debate can be gleaned from American Sociological Association presidential addresses of the late 1960s and 1970s.

Presidential Addresses

In his 1964 presidential address, George C. Homans criticized the structural-functional perspective that had been dominant "for a whole generation" but which, in his view, "had run its course, done its work, and now positively gets in the way of our understanding of social phenomena" (Homans, 1964:809). Homans's main criticism was that structural-functional explanations were not in fact scientific, largely because they failed to provide explanations for empirical relations. According to Homans, the perspective did not take "the job of theory seriously enough," and it never "produced a functional theory that was in fact an explanation" (1964:818). More specifically, as the title of his address, "Bringing Men Back In," indicated, the structural functional focus on the social system at the expense of social action produced a theory that "appeared to have no actors and mighty little action" (1964:817). Homans's own theoretical perspective, which concentrated on the nature of social action in terms of rational choice, is discussed in Chapter 9 of this volume.

The growing chorus of criticism of the structural-functional perspective, and of the work of Talcott Parsons in particular, continued, and a pluralism of perspectives developed. Some of the fiercest critics were feminists, who saw Parsons's work as the codification of patriarchal attitudes and practices. For example, Betty Friedan (1963:121–123) took Parsons to task for his promotion of the segregation of sex roles as "functional" to the maintenance of the patriarchal status quo. Other departures from the mainstream paradigm included ethnomethodology and phenomenological sociology as well as feminist sociology.

The resulting pluralism was not greeted with delight by all members of the sociological community. Coser's presidential address in 1975, titled "Two Methods in Search of a Substance," was a critique of both ethnomethodology and the search for technical precision at the expense of theory. In Coser's view, these two developments were representative of the "growth of narrow, routine activities" that produced "sect-like, esoteric ruminations," and together they reflected "crisis and fatigue within the discipline and its theoretical underpinnings" (Coser, 1975:691). Despite the seeming difference, even antagonism, of the two methods, Coser detected a common thread in their "preoccupation with method" that led to the "neglect of significance and substance." Coser maintained that sociology would be judged in terms of the "substantive enlightenment" it was able to bring to the "social structures in which we are enmeshed and which largely condition the course of our lives." If this was neglected, sociology would forfeit its birthright and degenerate into "congeries of rival sects and specialized researchers who will learn more and more about less and less" (Coser, 1975:698).

Coser was not alone in his criticism of sociological pluralism, especially as represented by the methodological debates around statistical research and theoretical significance.[2] Gouldner, in *The Coming Crisis of Western Sociology* (1970), had also launched an attack on the theoretical mindlessness of statistical research and the limitations of structural functionalism, as well as ethnomethodology—which he characterized as psychedelic anarchism. Collins (1981) maintained that Gouldner's focus on Western sociology was somewhat misleading, however. It did not address other traditions such as Marxist or neo-

---

[2] The idea that mathematical functions should be developed to express social relationships and thus establish sociology as a genuine scientific enterprise was promoted by a small number of sociologists in the early years. See, for example, Dodd (1942).

Weberian conflict theory, phenomenology, or the "European idealist-historicist tradition," so that in Collins's view, a more apt title for the book would have been "The Crisis of Functionalist Theory" (Collins, 1981:317).

The debunking of the value-free proposition, exemplified by structural-functionalist perspectives and the instrumentalism of "pure" empiricism, was deemed vital because, according to the critics, social and political conditions of the late 1950s and 1960s made sociology vulnerable to manipulation by prag-matic, but often unscrupulous, politicians. Galliher and Galliher (1995:28–32) have documented some of the positions taken by prominent sociological advo-cates of value-freedom on the McCarthy era, fascism, and racism. For example, Parsons helped U.S. military intelligence and the State Department find univer-sity appointments for "experts on the Soviet Union, who had assisted the Nazi government during WW II," and Edward Shils thought the Vietnam War was justified and expressed regret that "it had to be halted without success."

The way in which the presumed neutrality of statistical "facts" could make sociological work amenable to misuse by nonsociologists was the subject of Alfred McClung Lee's 1976 presidential address. Lee's election had been the re-sult of a write-in campaign, and the "candidacy of such an anti-establishment candidate was aided by the widespread alienation generated by the war in Viet Nam" (Galliher and Galliher, 1995:113). Lee had long been opposed to the idea of value-freedom, seeing it as simply moral bankruptcy on the part of sociolo-gists. He and his wife, the sociologist Elizabeth Briant Lee, founded the Society for the Study of Social Problems in 1951 and, in 1976, the Society for Humanist Sociology. Their concern was that sociology address "real life problems of peace, equality and social justice" (Galliher and Galliher, 1995:126).

Lee's address was titled "Sociology for Whom?" His answer was a "sociology for the service of humanity" (1976:925). Lee had always been concerned that strict empiricism and a value-free perspective would simply prepare sociologists "for employment by social manipulators" (1973:36). He maintained that the "great challenge of social science is the development and wide dissemination of social wisdom and social action techniques that will enable more and more people to participate in the control and guidance of their group and their soci-ety" (1973:6). In Lee's view, the integrity of sociology and its founding prin-ciples was at stake.

Lee's concern reflected Peter Blau's disquiet, expressed in 1974. Blau had warned that the "growing concentration of resources and powers in large orga-nizations and their top executives poses a serious threat of structural consolida-tion in contemporary society" that was fundamentally "incompatible with de-mocracy, which depends on checks and balances to protect the sovereignty of the people." Blau's conclusion was that the "challenge of the century" was to "find ways to curb the power of organizations in the face of their powerful op-position, without destroying in the process the organizations and democracy it-self." The alternative, he believed, was that "democratically instituted recurrent social change" would be replaced by "alternate periods of social stagnation and revolutionary upheaval." In his view, the "threat is serious, and the time is late" (Blau, 1974:633–634).

Ethical Sociology

The call for sociological ethical responsibility exemplified what Friedrichs has called the "prophetic stance" characteristic of some earlier positions in U.S. sociology, found in the work of, for example, Pitrim Sorokin, Robert S. Lynd, and C. Wright Mills. A key feature in the work of these sociologists was a "critical diagnosis of existing social institutions combined with a highly optimistic image of the contribution that sociology might make to a more intelligent reordering of human affairs" (Friedrichs, 1970:74). Most of these sociologists did not involve themselves directly in the political realm, but their position was akin to that endorsed by Max Weber, who had pointed out that although party politics had no place in research or the classroom, this did not mean that sociologists should adopt a posture of moral indifference to the events of their time. Indeed, indifference could be dangerous in that it supported established powers by default and produced a sociology in which "research is typically utilitarian and consideration of ethics is proudly eschewed," and there is no concern for the subjects who are studied (Galliher and Galliher, 1995:176).

An ethical sociology is important, but as Becker and Horowitz (1972:64) pointed out, "radical rhetoric or ideological posture does not inevitably result in politically useful sociological work." Furthermore, ideology is no substitute for "cogent, empirically verified knowledge of the world as a basis for effective action." In their view, there was, sociologically speaking, no substitute for the "damned facts." But this does not mean that factual investigations are, or ever could be, devoid of values, or that the "facts" exist apart from interpretation. More recently, Alan Sica has suggested that "sociological work of the highest order began as, and continues to be, an exercise in *applied ethics*" and the "self-abnegating "scientist," aloof from values or political freight, fools no one anymore" (1997:3).

The debates and disputes that characterized the 1960s and early 1970s were often bitterly fought, but the result was constructive in pushing theoretical and research enterprises in new directions. Levine (1995:271–272) lists 18 different approaches that are currently pursued in sociology, some of which are new departures on old themes, such as ethnomethodology, structuralism, phenomenology, sociobiology, rational choice theory, and world systems theory. The proliferation of approaches, characterized by different presuppositions about the nature of the social, has often been simplified by the idea of a macro/micro divide (Ritzer, 1983). The divide refers to some theorists' concentration on the "macro" level of total social systems while others concentrate on the "micro" level of analysis of social action and social relations.

Macro/Micro Perspectives

The macro/micro (or in European sociology, structure/agency) conceptualization was a shorthand way of acknowledging the multiparadigmatic character of sociology. In *The Structure of Scientific Revolutions*, originally published in 1962, Thomas Kuhn defined **paradigms** as "universally recognized scientific achievements that for a time provide model problems and solutions to a community of practitioners" (1970:57). Paradigms define "what should be studied, what questions should be asked, how they should be asked, and what rules should be followed in interpreting the answers obtained" (Ritzer, 1983:7).

Kuhn's work criticized the traditional idea that progress in the physical and natural sciences was cumulative and that each scientific breakthrough was based on previous scientific work in the manner implied by Isaac Newton's comment, "If I have seen further, it is because I stood on the shoulders of giants." Kuhn maintained that, although accumulation of knowledge in "normal science" did occur and progress was made, the more significant breakthroughs were the result of scientific revolutions. **Normal science** he defined as research "based upon one or more past scientific achievements, achievements that some particular scientific community acknowledges for a time as supplying the foundation for its further practice" (1970:10). Dominant paradigms, or common frames of reference, enable normal science to accumulate knowledge, but at some point the paradigms prove insufficient to explain all that needs explaining.

Kuhn pointed out that all science is continually confronted with exceptions and anomalies that cannot be explained in terms of the dominant paradigm. Initially, scientists either ignore these anomalies or attempt to incorporate them into the established paradigm. When the anomalies persist and it becomes apparent that the established paradigm cannot explain them, the foundations for a scientific revolution are established.[3] When anomalies cannot be overlooked or denied, the scientific discipline enters a state of crisis. Dissent increases within the scientific community, until the old paradigm is rejected and a new one takes its place. Such revolutions, or paradigmatic shifts, are usually the work of young scientists, less bound by tradition, who are able to formulate new conceptualizations that make better sense of the evidence (the facts) and thus transform the way in which the subject matter, or scientific "reality," is perceived and understood.

Sociology and Paradigm Conflicts

Sociology is also characterized by paradigmatic conflicts. The facts/value debate, for example, was a paradigmatic debate about the role of the sociologist and the subject matter of sociology. Another paradigmatic divide concerns the appropriate object, or unit of analysis, for sociology. Should the sociologist study society, as Durkheim suggested, or should the appropriate unit of analysis be the interactions and symbolic meanings of social actors, as advocated by Mead and Cooley? That is, is sociology the **macro** study of total social systems and their structures and institutions, or is it the study of **micro** social interactions with an emphasis on the autonomy of the social actor?

---

[3] Kuhn points out that the anomaly "appears only against the background provided by the paradigm," and the fact that "a significant scientific novelty so often emerges simultaneously from several laboratories is an index both to the strongly traditional nature of normal science and to the completeness with which the traditional pursuit prepares the way for change" (1970:65).

The institutionalization of the macro/micro dichotomy occurred at the Tenth World Congress of Sociology, held in Mexico in 1983. The title for the conference was "Macro- and Micro-Sociological Analysis." The general tenor of the Congress was to try to heal the divide and lay to rest the idea that there were two separate theoretical pursuits in sociology. Many of the papers delivered at the Congress saw the dichotomy as resulting from "partisan, selective and one-sided readings of the classics" (Eisenstadt and Helle, 1985, 1:3).

Despite the efforts of scholars at the World Congress, the dichotomy tended to linger on in sociological discourse and sociological textbooks. One reason was that, as you have seen in the previous chapters, classical sociologists often used different paradigms, and these subsequently became the basis for overgeneralized differentiations among the theorists and their theories. For example, Durkheim's focus on social facts is often contrasted with Weber's verstehen approach. Durkheim's insistence on the distinction between sociology and psychology, with sociology having a subject matter all its own, has also been used to justify the macro/micro division. Similarly, Durkheim's or Spencer's focus on social systems may be contrasted with Simmel's focus on the intricacies of social interaction.

The division of the work of the classical sociologists into rigid macro/micro categories misrepresents their work. For example, Simmel's (micro) studies of the forms and types of interaction are complemented by his monumental (macro) analysis of the history and development of monetary systems. In the 1960s, however, the division seemed entrenched, as did the often acrimonious relations between "interactionists" and "system" theorists over the "correct" unit of sociological analysis.

Some of the acrimony was related to the entrenchment of sociology in the academy and the boom in sociology enrollments, with the consequent competition for legitimacy and students (and their fees). Lemert (1992:66) suggests that the divisions were apparent in the 1950s and early 1960s, but there was a "mutual nonaggression pact by which the parties agreed simply to keep silent about their differences" for the "greater good of sociology." By the late 1960s, the pact fell apart. "Differences were not just allowed but passionately desired," and "ethnomethodology, constructionism, phenomenology, critical theory, Marxisms of various kinds were the rage in many departments, at least among graduate students. Some survived; some did not. But none had any particular intention of respecting official orthodoxy other than their own" (Lemert, 1992:66).

Contemporary Paradigmatic Divisions

Despite our belief that the macro/micro dichotomy is a misguided division of the sociological endeavor, we use it here because it remains descriptive of the divided focus of much contemporary sociological work and, despite the valiant efforts of many contemporary theorists, the desired synthesis seems elusive. In 1984, Collins still saw sociology split into "separate cocoons that scarcely occupy the same intellectual universe." He singled out statistical sociology in particular, claiming that it "makes no concessions of intelligibility toward outsiders and shows almost no interest in linking up with larger theoretical concerns" (Collins, 1984:330). Collins maintained that it was a mistake to regard statistics as "neutral method," arguing that "statistics is not method but theory" or rather, "*substantive theory* of how chance processes operate in the social world" (1984:331). Collins also saw "anti-positivists" militantly promoting their own programs of "interpretive, historical, Marxist, structuralist, or ethnomethodological sociology" and condemning their "positivist opponents *in absentia*" (Collins, 1984:330–331).

In 1990, Turner and Turner (1990:139–140) called sociology an "impossible science" because any synthesis of the various paradigms remained elusive. They saw the lack of synthesis as resulting from the encouragement of "enormous intellectual diversity" by the American Sociological Association (ASA) during the expansive years of the 1960s. Turner and Turner suggested that the problem became serious when student enrollments and financial support began to decline in the 1970s. The fragmented sociological community and the ASA did not have the control or resources to cope with the decline by reorganizing the discipline or mobilizing the "profession toward a more coherent conception of itself as a discipline" (1990:140). Their conclusion was that "it will be difficult for American sociology to become theoretically unified like the natural sciences" (1990:171).

Turner and Turner's pessimism can be qualified by Kuhn's point that no scientific endeavor remains static or is more than briefly unified in its understandings of the content and methods appropriate to its subject matter. Indeed, the vitality of much physical and natural science in the later twentieth century would appear to be the result of a variety of competing paradigms, and the same applies to late-twentieth-century sociology.

The search for synthesis/coherence/unity is itself an ideological project. Scientific revolutions rejuvenate, and the proliferation of perspectives might just as well be seen, in Kuhn's terms, as a "pre-paradigm shift" in which "several schools compete for the domination of a given field." Over time, however, a "post-paradigm" period emerges, the number of schools is reduced, and a "more efficient mode of scientific practice begins" (Kuhn, 1970:178). Thus, Turner and Turner's "impossible science" is probably only a temporary phenomenon.

Indeed some of the more recent theoretical work attempts to bridge, if not eliminate, the various divides as well as incorporate extra-sociological disciplinary perspectives. Two sociological developments that address and attempt to bridge these divides are feminist sociological theory and theories of race and colonialism.

Feminism and Feminist Sociological Theory

A student of sociology in the 1950s would have assumed that the discipline, like most other academic pursuits, was almost entirely a masculine activity. This assumption was accurate with respect to the academy. Despite the increased number of women students in sociology graduate programs from the late 1950s on, and despite the significant contributions of women in the past to the establishment of sociology, research and academic appointments remained masculinist.

Women's Marginality

The situation for women in the sociology department at Berkeley was representative of most sociology departments prior to the 1960s. From 1948 through 1970, the university hired no women in tenure track positions, although between 1952 and 1972 one-third of its graduate students were women (Orlans and Wallace, 1994:6). In 1940, before the establishment of the Department of Sociology at Berkeley in 1946, Dorothy Swaine Thomas (1899–1977) was hired as a lecturer in rural sociology on the understanding that she would eventually chair the Department of Sociology when it was established. Thomas's reception at Berkeley was less than cordial among male sociologists; Nisbet was particularly opposed to her potential leadership of the department, claiming that Thomas was "personally and professionally . . . a menace to a liberal arts college" (Murray, 1979:72). Despite this opposition, Thomas became the first woman elected president of the American Sociological Society (now the ASA) in 1952. When the department was formed and Thomas was excluded, she left for the University of Pennsylvania, where she remained until her retirement in 1974.

Similarly, Deegan (1995:325) notes that the Sociology Department at the University of Chicago had a total of 11 untenured, and thus marginal, female faculty members between 1892 and 1960. The first woman to obtain tenure at the University of Chicago was Evelyn Kitagawa in 1975. Deegan's figures are particularly telling because it was at the University of Chicago that North American sociology really became recognized as an academic discipline. The first sociology graduate program was established at the University of Chicago in 1892, and in the early years, from 1892 to 1920, women made significant contributions to the department.[4]

The marginality of women at the University of Chicago and Berkeley was echoed in other sociological centers, despite the important contributions made by many women to the establishment of the discipline. Morgan (1980) listed 117 women sociology graduates from North American colleges and universities in the nineteenth century, but noted that only 6 of the 117 obtained academic positions. The marginality of women sociologists was not simply their failure to obtain academic positions; their work was also overlooked in books and discourses about the sociological canon. For example, Charlotte Perkins Gilman was regarded as a utopian novelist rather than an important sociologist, despite her four major sociological books.

A similar historical amnesia affected European women sociologists. Harriet Martineau wrote the first methods text for sociology and introduced Auguste Comte's work to the English-speaking world with her translation and condensation of his six-volume *Cours de philosophie positive* into two volumes in 1853, yet

---

[4]Mary Jo Deegan (1991) has produced a valuable reference book documenting the lives and work of 51 women sociologists, from Harriet Martineau (1802–1876) to more contemporary sociologists such as Dorothy Smith and Alice Rossi. In addition, she lists 64 other significant women sociologists whose biographies are not included in the book. The numbers are impressive, especially as Deegan's work does not include the women sociologists who would have been part of the graduate cohorts of the 1990s.

her contributions have, until recently, been ignored. Marianne Weber's socio-logical work is usually overlooked, especially when that of her husband is dis-cussed. And in Britain, Beatrice and Sydney Webb, who formed a lifelong socio-logical team and were prime movers in the establishment of the first social science institution, the London School of Economics (LSE), in 1895, did their own sociological work outside the academy. In fact, there were no women soci-ologists of any note in Britain before the late 1950s. When sociology at LSE be-gan to expand in 1950 with the enrollment of 12 graduate students, only one was a woman—Olive Banks, who went on to a distinguished career at the Uni-versity of Leicester (Halsey, 1985:152).

The absence of women from the new sociological institutions in the late nineteenth and early twentieth centuries is all the more remarkable when you recall that this was the period of the first women's movement and many of the classical sociologists had something to say about women and the "woman question."

The marginality of women in the institutionalization of sociology in North America in the 1950s was attributable partly to their role as wives and mothers and partly to institutional impediments, such as nepotism rules, that made it impossible for faculty wives to obtain faculty positions—other than temporary, part-time, and untenured positions. More insidious was the invisibility of women's contributions to their husbands' publications. Many women sociolo-gists were effectively coauthors of their husbands' work, but many did not re-ceive recognition in print. An exception was Alfred McClung Lee, who included his wife, Elizabeth Briant Lee, as coauthor of *The Fine Art of Propaganda* (1939). This acknowledgment was, as one commentator observed, "almost unheard of at the time . . . even if the woman did most of the writing and research" (Galliher and Galliher, 1995:57).

The invisibility of women and their intellectual contributions was not pecu-liar to sociology. Spender (1982) noted that men had often claimed credit for the intellectual labor of women, or had discredited the scholarship because of the sex of the author rather than on the basis of the content of the work. The result was that the legacy of women's intellectual work was lost, and women were often in the position of "reinventing the wheel." This was certainly the case in the early years of the second women's movement, when women researchers began to look into the archives and to unearth the work of women in the past, only to discover that many of the issues they currently identified and confronted had been ad-dressed by their foremothers, often in the same terms. In the 1960s, feminists in the academy began to challenge this masculine hegemony.

Feminist Transformations

The process of recovering women's social realities, as well as women's past so-ciological contributions, began in conjunction with the second women's move-ment in the 1960s. Classical sociologists frequently had a great deal to say about women's roles and behaviors, but in twentieth-century text summaries and evaluations of their work, their comments on women as well as on race were usually omitted. The elimination of these often misogynist comments on women by the classical theorists tended to reinforce the idea that the development of sociology was a heroic male quest.

The initial feminist transformations of sociology were directly connected with the women's movement. As one feminist sociologist noted, "The women's movement has struggled to make women's voices heard in universities and colleges, and within academic disciplines," and researchers "took seriously in practice and in theory the universality lent our project by the category 'women'" (Smith, 1999:16, 18). For second-wave feminist sociologists, experience was privileged as a source of knowledge. The claims of objectivity, or a value-free science, were rejected as unattainable and, when pursued, productive of distorted knowledge and oppressive practices.

The origins of the second wave of feminism were in the various political protest groups of the New Left, the civil rights movement, and colonial liberation movements. The feminist movement was also fueled by the increased population of female students in colleges and universities. Many of these female graduates became the young, educated suburban housewives whose discontent Betty Friedan called the "problem with no name." Friedan (1963:13) found that the "dream image" offered American women, which was believed to be the envy of women "all over the world"—the suburban housewife—was profoundly unsatisfying to many of these women. Women were discovering that they were, as Simone de Beauvoir (1961:xvi) put it, the "Other":

> Thus, humanity is male and man defines woman not in herself but as relative to him: she is not regarded as an autonomous being . . . she is simply what man decrees; thus she is called "the sex," by which is meant that she appears essentially to the male as a sexual being. For him she is sex—absolute sex. . . . She is defined and differentiated with reference to man and not he with reference to her; she is incidental, the inessential as opposed to the essential. He is the Subject, he is Absolute—she is the Other.

The "problem with no name" was not confined to suburban housewives; women in the New Left movements were confronted with a similar experience. As Lydia Sargent (1981:xii) observed, "They were doing important, valuable work: stopping a war, fighting for civil rights; they were taking risks, learning and growing." But movement women also knew that the "men in the movement (and in some cases the women) saw women's function and legitimacy primarily through their participation in traditionally 'feminine' ways, i.e., as movement wives, mothers, sisters, mistresses, secretaries, maids, waitresses, nurses, and sex objects." The discovery of persistent inequities, even in movements devoted to freedom and equality, and the realization that change would have to start with women themselves, produced a variety of women's movements devoted to the analysis of women's conditions and the search for social change.

The early movements were often dominated by young women students, and especially young women sociologists. What they discovered was that the sociological subject was normatively a white male, with women, as well as blacks, making an appearance in restricted contexts of marriage and family or race relations. When women were included in sociological accounts, the information was often ideological rather than based on careful empirical investigation. Broverman and associates, for example, documented the double standard that prevailed in judgments of mental health. From a clinical point of view, a "healthy" woman accepted the behavioral norms for her sex, although these same norms were considered unhealthy for a competent, mature adult. The norms governing healthy adult behavior matched those that defined the healthy, mature *male* (Broverman, Broverman, Clarkson, Rosenkrantz, and Vogel, 1970).

Women's Issues

The identification of women's issues under the general rubric that the "personal is political" began to transform traditional sociological content, methods, and theoretical perspectives. The feminist recognition of the political significance of "private" matters helped a demographer, Harriet Presser, generate a "research agenda that reflected both my personal experiences and my political concerns." This research agenda had the effect of enhancing her "commitment to the field," which in turn helped to "broaden the field itself" (1994:142). For Presser, the personal was not only political "but also professional."

For many other young women sociologists, the "everyday world" became "problematic," which generated studies of sex/gender social divisions (Smith, 1987). Ann Oakley, for example, did a sociological analysis of housework as work. Her *Sociology of Housework* (1974) documented women's dissatisfaction with the nature and conditions of housework that paralleled, in many respects, the dissatisfactions expressed by male assembly-line workers. Oakley's work was initially greeted with disbelief by mainstream, mostly male, sociologists, for whom the idea that housework was work, only differentiated from their own studies of work by being unpaid, was absurd and certainly unsociological!

The women's movement linked together the inequities of home and work and brought women's concerns into the political arena. Housework, sexuality, and "daily life in the community and the family" were seen as "sites of struggle and consciousness" and, therefore, as significant issues for sociological research (Rowbotham, 1992:273). More important, feminist research was not research *on* women, but research *for* and *by* women.

As the access to the sociological establishment remained difficult for women, they set about forming their own networks, associations, and publishing outlets, just as Gilman had done 60 years earlier with the *Forerunner*. Several journals devoted to feminist research were established, many of them interdisciplinary in nature and focused on social change. An example of interdisciplinarity and the productive results of the crossing of boundaries is the journal *Signs: Journal for Women in Culture and Society*, first published in 1977.

Mainstream sociology was slow to recognize the profound transformation that feminist research involved for a comprehensive analysis of the nature of the social. But as you will see, in most contemporary theory, feminism is having an impact on the discipline, if only in making sex/gender issues theoretically important and not easily relegated to "nature." Beginning in the early 1970s, courses and research on gender have burgeoned. In these developments, the interrelationship of theory and practice—so central to the initial stages of the feminist movements, historically and in the present—has been retained in the theoretical focus and empirical research of feminist sociologists.

The focus on "women" as an undifferentiated social category quickly gave way to the recognition of differences among women, and the resulting debates have been a source of considerable intellectual and practical progress and change. For many women sociologists, feminism, and the scholarship it has generated, has been personally significant in their lives and careers. For many academic and professional women, second-wave feminism has been the most intellectually challenging and exciting development of the twentieth century, whether in sociology or any other discipline.

Feminist Sociology and Race

For disadvantaged women, especially women of color, feminism has occasionally been a source of support in the pursuit of social change, but in other ways it has been seen as an impediment. The early feminist movements tended to be dominated by young, white, Western, middle-class women and to reflect the lives and aspirations of these women. Women of color and lesbian women often felt excluded not only from the movements but also from the feminist sociological work.

The invisibility of race in the early feminist movements was akin to the invisibility of women and blacks in the early years of sociology. Historically, the relation of white feminists to racism has been ambiguous. Early-twentieth-century feminists often expressed racist sentiments. The fact that most pre–Civil War white women advocates of equal rights for women in the United States were abolitionists does not mean, in bell hooks's view, that they were antiracist (1981:124). Hurtado maintains that "white feminist theory has yet to integrate the facts that for women of color, race, class, and gender subordination are experienced simultaneously and that their oppression is not only by members of their own group but by whites of both genders" (1994:138–139).

Women of color have faced a persistent dilemma in opposing inequalities of race and gender. Opposition to the dominance of white society involves a particular opposition to white men, who have historically exploited women of color in more brutal and unthinking ways than their exploitation of white women. But women of color also have to contend with the ambiguity of identifying with men of color in their collective oppression. The recognition that these same men are themselves implicated in a patriarchal culture means that women of color experience a double subordination.

It was not only in the context of feminism that race became a salient sociological issue in the post–World War II years. In the 1960s especially, race relations became a focal point in the perceived "failure" of mainstream sociology to address the critical issues of the day.

Race and Colonialism

Women and racial minorities may have been topics of sociological research, but the "perspectives of sociology—its basic premises, concepts, and explanations—reflected the experience, social interests, and values of predominantly White, middle class men" (Seidman, 1994:97). Politically, according to Seidman, the "exclusion of an African-American and feminist perspective . . . made sociology more acceptable because it was more in line with the mainstream of liberal America." He suggests that the "painless institutionalization of sociology" in the United States was accomplished by excluding those "movements and perspectives that were threatening to middle America, e.g., feminism, Black nationalism, socialism, sexual radicalism" (1994:98).

British and European sociology always had, at least marginally, a socialist perspective. However, feminism, sexual radicalism, and nationalism in relation to colonial empires were relegated to the sociological sidelines in British and European as well as North American sociology.

The 1950s and 1960s saw a proliferation of liberation movements nationally and internationally. The nationalist movements against colonialism in Africa, Asia, and Latin America were paralleled by internal racial conflicts that were especially violent in the United States. Frantz Fanon's *The Wretched of the Earth* (1963) was a powerful and influential account of the psychopathology caused by racism and colonialism. Fanon concluded that shaking off colonial oppression meant repudiating the white, European philosophical heritage of the Enlightenment and formulating indigenous solutions to social problems and inequities. Fanon was appealing to indigenous Algerian rebels against French colonial rule, but his work resonated internationally. He called on the rebels to "Leave this Europe where they are never done talking of Man, yet murder men everywhere they find them" (1963:252). In the 1960s, "the term 'racist' became, with 'fascist,' the ultimate epithet . . . replacing the increasingly ineffectual term 'communist'" (Owram, 1996:167).

Black Militancy

For African Americans, the independence of many African states by 1960 fueled impatience with their own second-class standing in the United States. C. Eric Lincoln (1961:9–10) remarked that "Many Negroes for whom Africa seemed as remote as the planet Jupiter" began to find themselves "exhilarated and encouraged by the emergence of black national states in the once 'dark' continent." The assimilationist position of the National Association for the Advancement of Colored People (NAACP) was overshadowed by the increasing militancy of the Black Muslim movement and its pursuit of an independent, segregated Black Nation in the late 1950s.

Militancy increased with the formation of the Black Panther party, whose goal was to "exert organized force in the political arena" to satisfy the needs and desires of black people and whose leaders spoke of "political power growing out of the barrel of a gun" (Cleaver, 1969:84–85, quoting Huey P. Newton). The motto of the Black Panther party, taken by Huey Newton from Mao Tse-tung's *Little Red Book*, stated, "We are advocates of the abolition of war; we do not want war; but war can only be abolished through war; and in order to get rid of the gun it is necessary to pick up the gun" (Cleaver, 1969:89).

The Black Panthers were the revolutionary offshoot of the Black Power movement of Malcolm X and the security force, the Fruit of Islam, set up to protect (as well as discipline) the members of the Black Muslim Nation. The militancy of young black men became even more evident after the death of Malcolm X, who was shot in 1965. There was some justification for the increasingly violent tenor of the protests, given the violence of state forces in reaction to peaceful protests, sit-ins, and voter registration in the southern states.

The increasingly violent response of young black men was at odds with the longstanding integrationist policies of the NAACP. Martin Luther King had delivered his "I Have a Dream" speech in Washington, DC, in August 1963, and in 1964 Congress passed the Civil Rights Act and the Voting Rights Act. The militant Stokely Carmichael, however, claimed that by 1964 it had become clear to many young blacks that nonviolent demonstrations and the passage of laws did nothing to alleviate the underlying poverty and despair of the majority of the black population. In 1965, one of the most violent demonstrations erupted in the largely black community of Watts in California (1969:93).

Carmichael regarded the civil rights movement as a "bourgeois" movement. He maintained that it did not address the international issue of U.S. colonial domination, which was of critical concern to the Black Power movement. Carmichael pointed out that white society calls blacks "niggers," Spanish-speaking people "spics," Chinese "chinks," and Vietnamese "gooks." This dehumanization justified colonial and neocolonial enslavement, exploitation, and oppression. Furthermore, enslavement was made easier because the oppressed began to "believe in [their] own inferiority" (Carmichael, 1969:97). Carmichael's solution was not simply the destruction of racism but also the destruction of economic exploitation represented by imperialistic capitalism. Black Power meant that blacks had to see themselves as "part of the Third World; that we see our struggle as closely related to the liberation struggles around the world" against white imperialism (1969:101–102).

Sociology and Race

In the academic sociological community, reactions to the protests and violence were ambiguous. Robert E. Park had studied race relations in the 1930s and had recognized that all "national minorities" would want to "control and direct their own destinies" in situations of oppression (1950:114). But Park's work was itself a minority effort. In 1961, John Howard Griffin published *Black Like Me*, an account of his (a white man's) sojourn in the southern United States disguised as a black man. The book was a powerful sociological account of the character of racism and its social and cultural consequences. The book also garnered African American criticism of a white man in "blackface."

Griffin's book did not become influential in mainstream sociology, which tended to examine race through the lens of the functions of social conflict. Himes, whose work was characteristic of this approach, examined what he called the rational conflict responses of black Americans to social abuses (1966). But the conflict he examined focused on relatively peaceful acts of protest and political action; he ignored the violent conflicts more characteristic of that period. In fact, Himes's analysis was a form of bourgeois sociology that matched Carmichael's indictment of the NAACP.

A more divisive controversy arose within the sociological community in response to James Coleman et al.'s 1975 report *Trends in School Segregation, 1968–73*. The report claimed that the racial desegregation of white schools through compulsory busing had resulted in a white flight to the suburbs. The result was that racial imbalance in the schools—which the busing was intended to combat—had increased rather than decreased. This report came as a shock, given that in 1966 Coleman had reported test results showing positive effects of racial desegregation. However, several sociologists questioned the nature and interpretation of the statistical evidence in the 1975 report.

Among the critics was Alfred McClung Lee who, as president of the American Sociological Association, raised questions about the findings and asked for an investigation. The ASA council rejected the request for an investigation, but several critical responses essentially called into question the way in which the data had been interpreted. Most especially, the critics focused on the political conclusions drawn from the supposedly value-free report of statistical trends. These critics maintained that it was "false to assume that the use of statistical techniques would automatically take care of the value questions" (Galliher and Galliher, 1995:122–123) and concluded that "the allegedly value-free social scientist was not so value-free after all" (1995:120). Galliher and Galliher (1995:122–123) report that Coleman was "hurt" and "stunned" by the criticisms of what he claimed were issues of "scientific fact," and for a number of years he dropped his membership in the ASA. The Coleman–Lee controversy illustrated the dilemmas generated by opposing views on the ethical and scientific responsibilities of sociologists, especially when important political issues are involved.

Race relations were the subject of sociological concern, but it was a concern that seemed to be generated "after the fact." In 1963, Everett Hughes asked, "Why did social scientists—and sociologists in particular—not foresee the explosion of collective action of Negro Americans toward immediate full integration into American society?" (1963:879). Hughes's answer was that sociologists had failed to use their sociological imaginations because "our conception of social science is so empirical, so limited to little bundles of fact applied to little hypotheses, that we are incapable of entertaining a broad range of possibilities, of following out the madly unlikely combinations of social circumstances" (1963:889). More generally, Hughes argued that the very professionalization of sociology was responsible, limiting creative sociology and curbing "that utopian imagination which can conceive of all sorts of alternatives to the way things are" (1963:890). He encouraged sociology to be more "playful," to break out of the straightjacket of academic sociology and be open to new, innovative perspectives.

The variety of different perspectives, the interdisciplinary collaborations, and a renewed emphasis on comparative, historical research that emerged from the turbulent decades of the 1960s and early 1970s, which we examine in the rest of this volume, certainly broke out of the straitjacket in interesting ways.

Final Thoughts

Gender and race, as well as the international legacy of colonialism, brought into clear view the divisions that had animated sociology from its inception. During the 1960s and early 1970s, the divisions were often generational, pitting young against old, and fought in the public domain as well as in the academic context.

In sociology, themes of "conflict, power, diversity, and inequality" became almost as prevalent as the former stress on integration and shared belief systems characteristic of structural functionalist theory (Seidman, 1994:133).

But mainstream academic sociology did not turn totally "outward to engage public life, it turned inward to focus on the making of scientific knowledge" (Seidman, 1994:133). The maverick spin-offs already mentioned, such as ethnomethodology, phenomenology, and gender and cultural studies, attempted to retain the classical sociological conception of the discipline as an objective theoretical enterprise as well as a socially responsive and responsible one. Consequently, in the 1990s, "theory in American sociology has never encompassed such a range of diversity," although some perspectives have "only a fringe existence" (Hinkle, 1994:341).

The "new" directions are often critical reassessments and reinterpretations of past classical sociological work. These classical theoretical supports are generally used as foundations in an attempt to bridge—or, more hopefully, to transcend—the sociological divisions and conflicts that became so clear in the disruptive period of the 1960s and early 1970s. In the rest of this volume, we will examine the trends in late-twentieth-century sociology in terms of the search for at least a temporary agreement in theory and practice, given the inescapable multiparadigmatic, and ultimately political, nature of the sociological enterprise.

References

Abrams, Philip. 1968. *The Origins of British Sociology, 1834–1914.* Chicago: University of Chicago Press.

Alexander, Jeffrey C., 1987. *Twenty Lectures: Sociological Theory Since World War II.* New York: Columbia University Press.

Becker, Howard. 1960. "Normative Reactions to Normlessness." *American Sociological Review, 25,* 803–810.

Becker, Howard S., and Irving Louis Horowitz, 1972. "Radical Politics and Sociological Research: Observations on Methodology and Ideology." *American Journal of Sociology, 78*(1), 48–66.

Bell, Daniel. 1960. *The End of Ideology.* Glencoe, IL: Free Press.

Bendix, Reinhard. 1970. "Sociology and the Distrust of Reason." *American Sociological Review, 35,* 831–843.

Blau, Peter M., 1974. "Parameters of Social Structure." *American Sociological Review, 39,* 615–635.

Bourdieu, P., and J. C. Passeron. 1970. *Reproduction: In Education, Society and Culture.* Beverley Hills, CA: Sage.

Broverman, I. K., D. M. Broverman, F. E. Clarkson, P. Rosenkrantz, and S. R. Vogel. 1970. "Sex-Role Stereotypes and Clinical Judgments of Mental Health." *Journal of Consulting and Clinical Psychology, 34,* 1–7.

Bulmer, Martin. 1985. "The Development of Sociology and of Empirical Social Research in Britain." In Martin Bulmer (Ed.), *Essays on the History of British Sociological Research.* Cambridge: Cambridge University Press.

Carmichael, Stokely. 1969. "Black Power and the Third World." In Tariq Ali (Ed.), *The New Revolutionaries: A Handbook of the International Radical Left.* Toronto: McClelland and Stewart.

Clark, Terry. 1973. *Prophets and Patrons: The French University and the Emergence of the Social Sciences*. Cambridge, MA: Harvard University Press.

Cleaver, Eldridge. 1969. "Letter from Jail." In Tariq Ali (Ed.), *The New Revolutionaries: A Handbook of the International Radical Left*. Toronto: McClelland and Stewart.

Coleman, James S., Sara D. Kelly, and John A. Moore. 1975. *Trends in School Segregation, 1968–73*. Washington, DC: The Urban Institute.

Collins, Randall. 1981. *Sociology Since Mid-Century*. New York: Academic Press.

———— (Ed.). 1984. *Sociological Theory*. San Francisco: Jossey-Bass.

Coser, Lewis A. 1975. "Two Methods in Search of a Substance." *American Sociological Review, 40,* 691–700.

de Beauvoir, Simone. 1961. *The Second Sex*. New York: Bantam Books.

Deegan, Mary Jo. 1987. "An American Dream: The Historical Connections between Women, Humanism, and Sociology, 1890–1920." *Humanity and Society, 11,* 353–365.

———— (Ed.). 1991. *Women in Sociology*. New York: Greenwood Press.

————. 1995. "The Second Sex and the Chicago School." In Gary Alan Fine (Ed.), *A Second Chicago School? The Development of Postwar American Sociology* (pp. 322–364). Chicago: University of Chicago Press.

Dodd, Stuart S. 1942. *Dimensions of Society*. New York: Macmillan.

Eisenstadt, S. N., with M. Curelaru. 1976. *The Form of Sociology: Paradigms and Crises*. New York: John Wiley and Sons.

Eisenstadt, S. N., and H. J. Helle, 1985. *Perspectives on Sociological Theory. Volume 1: Macro Sociological Theory. Volume 2: Micro Sociological Theory*. London: Sage.

Fanon, Frantz. 1963. *The Wretched of the Earth*. New York: Grove Press.

Friedan, Betty. 1963. *The Feminine Mystique*. Harmondsworth, England: Penguin.

Friedrichs, Robert W. 1970. *A Sociology of Sociology*. New York: Free Press.

Galliher, John F., and James M. Galliher. 1995. *Marginality and Dissent in Twentieth Century American Sociology*. New York: State University of New York Press.

Gouldner, Alvin W. 1963. "Anti-Minotaur: The Myth of a Value-Free Sociology." In Maurice Stein and Arthur Vidich (Eds.), *Sociology on Trial*. Englewood Cliffs, NJ: Prentice-Hall.

————. 1970. *The Coming Crisis of Western Sociology*. New York: Basic Books.

Griffin, John Howard. 1961. *Black Like Me*. Boston: Houghton Mifflin.

Halsey, A. H. 1985. "Provincials and Professionals: The British Post-War Sociologists." In Martin Bulmer (Ed.), *Essays on the History of British Sociological Research*. Cambridge: Cambridge University Press.

Himes, Joseph. 1966. "The Functions of Racial Conflict." *Social Forces, 45,* 1–10.

Hinkle, Roscoe C. 1994. *Developments in American Sociological Theory, 1915–1950*. New York: State University of New York Press.

Homans, George C. 1964. "Bringing Men Back In." *American Sociological Review, 29,* 809–818.

hooks, bell. 1981. *Ain't I a Woman? Black Women and Feminism*. Boston: South End Press.

Hughes, Everett C. 1963. "Race Relations and the Sociological Imagination." *American Sociological Review, 28,* 879–890.

Hurtado, Aida. 1994. "Relating to Privilege: Seduction and Rejection in the Subordination of White Women and Women of Color." In Anne C. Herrman and Abigail J. Steward (Eds.), *Theorizing Feminism: Parallel Trends in the Humanities and Social Sciences* (pp. 136–154). Boulder, CO: Westview Press.

Janowitz, Morris. 1972. "Professionalization of Sociology," *American Journal of Sociology, 78,* 105–135.

Kuhn, Thomas. 1970. *The Structure of Scientific Revolutions* (2nd ed.). Chicago: University of Chicago Press.

Lee, Alfred McClung. 1973. *Toward Humanist Sociology.* Englewood Cliffs, NJ: Prentice-Hall.

———. 1976. "Sociology for Whom?" *American Sociological Review, 41,* 925–936.

Lee, Alfred McClung, and Elizabeth Briant Lee. 1939. *The Fine Art of Propaganda.* New York: Harcourt Brace.

Lemert, Charles. 1992. "Subjectivity's Limit: The Unsolved Riddle of the Standpoint." *Sociological Theory, 10,* 63–72.

Levine, Donald N. 1995. *Visions of the Sociological Tradition.* Chicago: University of Chicago Press.

Lincoln, C. Eric. 1961. *The Black Muslims in American,* Boston: Beacon Press.

Lipset, Seymour Martin. 1972. *Rebellion in the University: A History of Student Activism in America.* London: Routledge and Kegan Paul.

Lipset, Seymour Martin, and Everett Carl Ladd, Jr. 1972. "The Politics of American Sociologists." *American Journal of Sociology, 78*(1), 67–104.

Lipset, Seymour Martin, and Neil J. Smelser (Eds.). 1961. *Sociology: The Progress of a Decade.* Englewood Cliffs, NJ: Prentice-Hall.

Lundberg, George. 1961. *Can Science Save Us?* New York: Longmans, Green.

Madge, John. 1962. *The Origins of Scientific Sociology.* New York: Free Press.

Mills, C. Wright. 1959. *The Sociological Imagination,* New York: Oxford University Press.

Morgan, J. Graham. 1980. "Women in American Sociology in the Nineteenth Century." *Journal of the History of Sociology, 2,* 1–34.

Murray, Stephen. 1979. "Resistance to Sociology at Berkeley." *Journal of the History of Sociology, 2,* 61–84.

Oakley, Ann. 1974. *The Sociology of Housework.* New York: Pantheon Books.

Orlans, Kathryn P. Meadow, and Ruth A. Wallace (Eds.). 1994. *Gender and the Academic Experience.* Lincoln: University of Nebraska Press.

Owram, D. 1996. *Born at the Right Time.* Toronto: University of Toronto Press.

Park, Robert E. 1950. *Race and Culture.* Glencoe, IL: Free Press.

Parsons, Talcott. 1951. *The Social System.* New York: Free Press.

Presser, Harriet B. 1994. "The Personal Is Political *and* Professional." In Kathryn P. Meadow Orlans and Ruth A. Wallace (Eds.), *Gender and the Academic Experience* (pp. 141–156). Lincoln: University of Nebraska Press.

Ritzer, George. 1983. *Contemporary Sociological Theory.* New York: Alfred A. Knopf.

Rowbotham, Sheila. 1992. *Women in Movement.* London: Routledge.

Sargent, Lydia (Ed.). 1981. *Women and Revolution.* Montreal: Black Rose Books.

Seidman, Steven. 1994. *Contested Knowledge: Social Theory in the Postmodern Era.* Cambridge, MA: Blackwell.

Shils, Edward. 1985. "On the Eve: A Prospect in Retrospect." In Martin Bulmer (Ed.), *Essays on the History of British Sociological Research.* Cambridge: University of Cambridge Press.

Sica, Alan. 1997. "Ethical Culture." *Perspectives, 19*(1), 1–3.

Smith, Dorothy. 1987. *The Everyday World as Problematic: A Feminist Sociology.* Toronto: University of Toronto Press.

———. 1999. *Writing the Social.* Toronto: University of Toronto Press.

Spender, Dale. 1982. *Women of Ideas and What Men Have Done to Them.* London: Ark Paperbacks.

Turner, Stephen Park, and Jonathan H. Turner. 1990. *The Impossible Science.* Newbury Park, CA: Sage.

Chapter 8

Symbolic Interactionism
Blumer, Goffman, and Hochschild

The theorists discussed in the earlier chapters of this volume might be classed as "grand theorists." The theorists discussed in this and the following two chapters represent important divergences from and qualifications to the grand theory tradition. However, these theorists still owe debts to the structural-functional and critical theorists of the twentieth century. We begin this chapter with a general overview of the interactionist tradition and a short exposition on the work of Herbert Blumer, and then move on to discuss the work of Erving Goffman and Arlie Hochschild.

The Interactionist Tradition

The interactionist tradition has been associated with the work of a varied group of sociologists described as the "Chicago School," including George Herbert Mead, W. I. Thomas, and Robert E. Park. Mead's social psychological approach was foundational for the interactionist tradition, but the empirical work of Thomas and Park in urban and race relations generated the critical methodological characteristics of the tradition. Field research, ethnographic studies, interviewing, case histories, documentary sources, and ecological analysis were used in a variety of important studies that emerged from the Sociology Department at the University of Chicago during the early years of the twentieth century. These methods remain important to any current interactionist research.

One of the strengths of the Chicago "school" in the early years was the encouragement of interdisciplinary links. Although the term "school" has "connotations of clique or cult," this was not the case for the Chicago sociologists. Interdisciplinarity was encouraged by the "interest in local research on the city of Chicago" and the "pragmatist orientation widely diffused through the university" (Bulmer, 1984:190). Robert Park, for example, was particularly interested in adopting ideas from a variety of disciplines to help in his research (Bulmer, 1984:215).

The overriding character of early interactionist research was its empirical nature and its pragmatic focus. Interactionism was a radical sociology that attempted to provide the means for people to improve their lives (Deegan and Hill, 1987:xi). This focus was quite unlike that of most classical sociologists, for whom "first- or even secondhand acquaintance with the contemporary world was not seen as a necessary requirement for fruitful sociological generalization," and empirical work, such as census taking and social surveys, was not the major concern (Bulmer, 1984:5). It was assumed that social surveys and social research were different enterprises. Survey research was seen as primarily focused on social problems and social planning, whereas social research had a broader focus, formulating "hypotheses or propositions about social action" and attempting to produce "theories and laws to explain social phenomena" (Bulmer, 1984:65).

In the early twentieth century, Chicago sociologists set a precedent with an impressive body of empirical work. A new direction was established for American sociology. Theorists became more aware of the vital importance of the empirical research. Some of the important work produced during the early years included Thomas and Znaniecki's *The Polish Peasant in Europe and America*, Johnson's *The Negro in Chicago*, and a whole series of empirical urban studies such as *The Hobo, The Gold Coast and the Slum, The Gang, The Taxi-Dance Hall, The Natural History of a Delinquent Career*, and *Social Factors in Juvenile Delinquency*. All of these works, focusing on the social problems of the city, were major contributions to the development of specialized fields such as criminology, the sociology of the family, the sociology of social problems, and urban sociology (Bulmer, 1984:89).

Some critics have suggested that interactionism is good at empirical research but bad at theory. Others contend that the early Chicago school "successfully bridged the gap between, and combined together, theory and empirical research" (Bulmer, 1984:224).

The theorists we discuss in this chapter certainly combined the two approaches. Blumer set out the terms of the interactionist tradition, Goffman extended the tradition in important ways, and Hochschild continues the innovative research tradition, building on Goffman's work in her examination of the sociology of emotions.

Herbert Blumer (1900–1987)

It was Herbert Blumer who coined the term **symbolic interactionism**. Blumer's work focused on the ways human beings took control of their lives, as "acting people" in a society that is a "complex of ongoing activity" (Blumer, 1969:85). The two parts—symbol and interaction—produce meaningful interaction. That is, interaction involves giving social objects symbolic value. Social objects can be anything—physical objects, animals, history, language, ideas, emotions—as well as self and other people. According to Blumer (1969:80), the individual in all of his or her everyday acts "is designating different objects to himself, giving them meaning, judging their suitability to his action, and making decisions on the basis of the judgment." People interpret and act on the basis of symbols.

Symbols are abstract meanings attached to things, people, and behavior so that they can have different meanings for different individuals. The important point is that individuals consciously and creatively evaluate, make decisions, and act. Whether the evaluation, decision, and action are "functional" or even ethically commendable is not necessarily an issue. However, given the legacy of George Herbert Mead, there is an assumption that individuals will progress toward a more democratic society and that this progress will be helped by sociology.

Interaction involves the self engaged in communicating with self: selecting, checking, suspending, regrouping, and transforming meanings in terms of the social context and the individual's intentions and interests (Blumer, 1969:5). But for Blumer, the most significant feature of all "human association is that the participants *take each other into account*" as a basis of conduct (1969:194). Society is a "complex of ongoing activity" involving collectively initiated "joint actions" (Blumer, 1969:85). **Joint actions** are "constituted by the fitting together of the lines of behavior of separate participants" as, for example, in a trading transaction, family dinner, wedding, games, or war (1969:70). Joint actions have a history that is "orderly, fixed and repetitious" because the participants have a common definition of the situation (1969:71).

Social interaction is an interaction between people, not between roles. "It is ridiculous," argued Blumer, "to assert, as a number of eminent sociologists have done, that social interaction is an interaction between social roles" (1969:75). Roles may affect, in some degree, the "direction and content of action," but "this is a far cry from asserting action to be a product of roles" (1969:75).

Blumer took the position that social structures, like roles or status, are important but not determinant in the way that structural functionalists maintain. In his view, "grand theory" that "orders the world into its mold" provides little information about the nature of social life (1969:14). For Blumer, sociology involves examining and interpreting the empirical evidence in order to develop an inductive understanding of human behavior and human society.

In summary, the premises of symbolic interaction are as follows: (1) "human beings act towards things on the basis of the meaning things have for them"; (2) "the meaning of such things is derived from, or arises out of, the social interaction one has with one's fellows"; and (3) "these meanings are handled in, and modified through, an interpretative process used by the person in dealing with the things he encounters" (Blumer, 1969:2). Individual and joint actions are framed by historical and cultural meanings, but there is always room for creativity and improvisation. It is "the social process in group life that creates and upholds the rules, not the rules that create and uphold life" (Blumer, 1969:19).

Blumer's methodology was inductive. "The isolation of relations, the development of propositions, the formulation of typologies, and the construction of theories are viewed as emerging out of what is found through constant observation of that world instead of being formed in an *a priori* fashion through deductive reasoning from a set of theoretical premises" (Blumer, 1975:62). This approach to research is qualitative rather than quantitative. It begins with an **exploratory stage,** in which the investigator looks closely at a "sphere of life that is unfamiliar and hence unknown to him" in order to develop a research focus. Once the research focus is achieved, the investigator moves to the **inspection stage,** which involves an "intensive focused examination of the empirical content of whatever analytical elements are used for purposes of analysis" (1969:43). The investigator uses **sensitizing concepts** that "suggest directions along which to look," which in turn will lead to **definitive concepts** that provide "prescriptions of what to see" (1969:148–149).

Blumer's theoretical and methodological focus provides a part of the background to the work of Erving Goffman. However, Goffman did not claim membership in any "school." Goffman himself "did his best to avoid being classified . . . even to the point of declaring a belief in conceptual eclecticism" (Burns, 1992:6). According to Fine (1990:121), however, although Goffman never labeled himself a symbolic interactionist, if he is excluded from the perspective "we exclude our soul."

The link with interactionism lies in Goffman's analysis of the "interaction order" and his development of a theory of face-to-face interaction. Goffman's focus also extended the symbolic interaction tradition in his examination of patterns, or rules of social interaction that apply in a variety of situations. In Goffman's ASA presidential address, he pointed out that "pedestrian traffic rules can be studied in crowded kitchens as well as in crowded streets, interruption rights at breakfast as well as in courtrooms, endearment vocatives in supermarkets as well as in the bedroom" (1983b:2). In this development of a theory of the **interaction order,** Goffman moved beyond and away from the interaction roots exemplified by the Chicago school.

Erving Goffman (1922–1982)

Erving Goffman was born in Manville, Alberta, Canada, in 1922. He graduated from the University of Toronto in 1945 and went to the University of Chicago for graduate work in sociology and social anthropology. He obtained his master's degree in 1949. His master's thesis was a "protracted and ultimately vain attempt to use statistics to understand an audience's responses to a then popular American radio soap opera called 'Big Sister'" (Manning, 1992:7).

Goffman's subsequent work was a drastic departure from the quantitative focus of his master's thesis. One of his pieces, "On Cooling the Mark Out" (1953), published prior to his PhD dissertation, foreshadowed his subsequent work. In this essay, Goffman studied the art of the con man and illustrated the procedures the con artist used to reconcile people to their realization that they had been conned. "Cooling out" refers to the efforts of the con artist to control the anger of the "mark" (the person who has been "taken") in order to defuse the risk of police intervention or other forms of retaliation on the part of the person who has been wronged.

Goffman pointed out that being conned is not an unusual event that only happens to gullible people. Everyone, at some time, is a potential mark. Any venture runs the risk of failure and thus the loss of self-esteem. When this happens, repair work is necessary to restore "face"—that is, to restore the image of the self and thus restore social order. This examination of the ostensibly "trivial and commonplace, or peripheral or bizarre" as a means to reveal the nature of "normal behavior" in society as a whole was to remain Goffman's style and method (Burns, 1992:16).

Goffman's PhD thesis was based on fieldwork on a remote Shetland Island. The thesis was initially conceived of as a participant observation study of the social structure of the island. Goffman's "cover" for his stay on the island was an interest in agricultural techniques. He also worked as a part-time dishwasher at the island's one hotel. Shortly after his arrival, Goffman became fascinated by the various stratagems and rhetorics used by the islanders in their interactions among themselves and with strangers and visitors. The island was a small, barren place, with only 300 families as permanent residents. Everyone lived in almost constant sight of one another. This provided Goffman with an ideal social microcosm in which to study face-to-face interactions. His PhD study of social interaction and self-presentation, titled "Communication Conduct in an Island Community" (1953), was published in 1959 as *The Presentation of Self in Everyday Life*.

In 1954 Goffman became a visiting scientist at the National Institute of Mental Health in Bethesda, Maryland. As a ward orderly at the hospital, Goffman did participant observation research on the interactions among patients, doctors, and administrators, recorded in his work *Asylums* (1961a). In 1957 he joined the Department of Sociology at Berkeley, and in 1968 he moved to the University of Pennsylvania, where he remained until his early death at age 60.

Goffman's Central Theories and Methods

Goffman's work was the observation and analysis of individual conduct "as an attribute of social order, of society, not as an attribute of individual persons" (Burns, 1992:23). Goffman was indebted to, but stood apart from, the interactionist, and later symbolic interactionist, tradition fostered at the University of Chicago. In addition to the heritage of George Herbert Mead at Chicago, Goffman was also influenced by Everett Hughes, who is best known for his studies of occupations. Hughes's view that "basic patterns of behavior and institutional structures were best looked for in the analogies which underlie seeming incongruities"—such as finding out about doctors by studying plumbers, or prostitutes by studying psychiatrists—was applied to great effect in Goffman's early essay "On Cooling the Mark Out" (Burns, 1992:11). Goffman also used Hughes's concept of "total institution" in his study of mental hospitals.

The influence of W. Lloyd Warner, a social anthropologist, was also significant to Goffman's work (Collins, 1986:109). Goffman's graduate work was in social anthropology as well as sociology, and he was Warner's research assistant at Chicago when Warner was working on his analysis of social stratification. As an anthropologist, Warner maintained that more was known about the ceremonies and rituals of tribal peoples than about modern urban individuals, and he set out to chart the ceremonies and rituals of status in modern American society (Collins, 1986:109). In his early work, Goffman combined Warner's social anthropology with the Chicago empirical tradition to produce his own "studies of the rituals of everyday life" (Collins, 1986:110).

Goffman was concerned with the composition of the "self" at the "micro" level of social action and interaction. However, he also placed these interactions within a more "macro" moral context. In Goffman's view, "universal human nature is not a very human thing. By acquiring it, the person becomes a kind of construct, built up not from inner psychic propensities but from the moral rules that are impressed on him from without" (1967:45). He focused on the individual as a product of social interaction, not on the individual whose existence predated society.

For Goffman, the connection between the individual and society was through ritual. Goffman's use of ritual was indebted to Emile Durkheim; he argued that the "self" in modern society becomes a sacred object in the same way that the collective symbols of more primitive societies operated in Durkheim's *The Elementary Forms of Religious Life*. The "self" as "sacred object . . . must be treated with proper ritual care and in turn must be presented in a proper light to others" (1967:85). The rituals of modern social life that individuals perform for each other, to maintain "civility and good will on the performer's part" and acknowledge the "small patrimony of sacredness" possessed by the recipient, are "stand-ins" for the power of supernatural entities described by Durkheim (Goffman, 1961b:62). As Goffman (1967:95) put it, "Many gods have been done away with, but the individual himself stubbornly remains as a deity of considerable importance."

Among the classical theorists, Goffman was also influenced by Georg Simmel. Like Simmel, Goffman looked at the details of everyday life not simply as illustrations or data for theoretical abstractions but to provide an accurate description of the social world. Simmel's concept of "pure sociation" established the study of interaction as basic to sociological analysis. Goffman continued this tradition in his insistence that face-to-face interaction comprised an autonomous area of sociological analysis. "My concern over the years has been to promote acceptance of this face to face domain as an analytically viable one" (1983b:1).

Goffman's methods of incorporating the Simmelian micro level of interaction and the macro-level analysis of Durkheimian ritual behavior have been described as empirically eclectic: a "bricolage" (Fine, 1990:124). For example, in *Behavior in Public Places*, Goffman noted that the data he used came from "a study of a mental hospital . . . some from a study of a Shetland Island community . . . some from manuals of etiquette, and some from a file where I keep quotations that have struck me as interesting" (1963:4). His approach was basically **inductive**, identifying the ways in which individuals in a variety of social contexts accomplished interaction. Goffman thus paid attention to speech as well as silence, and to "bodily appearance and personal acts" such as "dress, bearing, movement and position, sound level, physical gestures such as waving or saluting, facial decorations, and broad emotional expression," selecting his material in a seemingly unorganized manner (1963:33).

Goffman's seemingly eclectic methods were not really new, unusual, or unorganized; they represented basic sociological methods, if sociology is understood as the interpretation of "events, actions, reported experiences" that are a part of everyday life. Sociological discoveries are thus not about the "discovery of previously unknown facts," but about "re-ordering what is already known" (Williams, 1988:73).

For Goffman, reordering starts from a "small observational base" and moves toward "more and more comprehensive conceptual frameworks for the description of that base" (Williams, 1988:73). Using this procedure, Goffman's methodology was "simultaneously theoretical and empirical." That is, he proceeded to "borrow, beg and build concepts," seeking the "interrelationship between them" and at the same time making discoveries "consisting of new ways of organizing data" (Williams,1988:82). For example, in observing the ways in which individuals attempt to control the impressions they make on others in any interaction, Goffman used drama as a metaphor, describing such impression management as a "performance" involving "stage-craft and stage management" (1959:15).

Goffman cautioned, however, that the **dramaturgical** approach was "in part a rhetoric and a maneuver" and that the language of the stage was a "scaffold . . . [that] should be erected with an eye" to being demolished (1959:254). Goffman was careful to make a distinction between theoretical abstractions and the real world to which they referred. Conceptual abstractions are "exhaustible where reality is not," and there is no "simple correspondence . . . between the knowable and the real such that the former directly reflects the latter" (Williams, 1983:101).

The theater metaphor was a handy means of illustrating the "structure of social encounters" that occur in all social life (Goffman, 1959:254). As a means to illuminate the nature of social life, drama has been used by a number of other theorists in the Western social theory tradition, beginning with Plato. Although Goffman used this metaphor, he did not regard it as inevitable or universal in all interactions. The idea that people "behave *as if* they are scripting their own roles" was, however, insightful and theoretically significant (Fine, 1990:124). Goffman claimed that sociology did not provide "a ready framework" that could order the sort of data he examined. Although "many of these data are of doubtful worth, and my interpretations . . . may certainly be questionable," he maintained that "a loose speculative approach to a fundamental area of conduct is better than a rigorous blindness to it" (1963:4).

Goffman acknowledged the criticism that sociology had produced little of value in its short career and that sociologists might well trade what they had produced "for a few really good conceptual distinctions and a cold beer." However, he maintained that sociologists should not trade in their calling, but instead should "sustain in regard to all elements of social life a spirit of unfettered, unsponsored inquiry, and the wisdom not to look elsewhere but ourselves and our discipline for this mandate" (1983b:17).

Nature of Society, Humans, and Change

Society as Frame   In *Frame Analysis*, Goffman stated that he was concerned with "the structure of experience individuals have at any moment of their lives" and made "no claim whatsoever to be talking about the core matters of sociology—social organization and social structure" (1974:13). This does not mean, however, that Goffman or interactionists generally ignore society and social structures. Goffman's position was that the nature of society and its structures or institutions is discovered in the behaviors of individuals. This theoretical perspective is consistent with Durkheim's definition of social fact: "every way of acting, fixed or not, which is general throughout a given society, while existing in its own right, *independent of its individual manifestations*" (quoted in Burns, 1992:25). As Goffman (1967:43) suggests, "If persons have a universal human nature, they themselves are not to be looked to for an explanation of it. One must look rather to the fact that societies everywhere, if they are to be societies, must mobilize their members as self-regulating participants in social encounters."

According to Goffman, society frames interaction, but interaction is not dependent on macrostructures. Furthermore, interaction can have a transformative impact on social structures. The key point in Goffman's work is that he rejected the classical sociological opposition between the individual and social structure that still retains credibility in current sociological theory. For Goffman, "individual and social structure are not competing entities"; they are "joint products of an interaction order sui generis" (Rawls, 1987:138).

Goffman saw the interaction order as a "substantive domain in its own right" and argued that "isolating the interaction order provides a means and a reason to examine diverse societies comparatively, and our own historically." He noted that all of us spend time "in our daily life . . . in the immediate presence of others" and all that we do is *"socially situated."* This social situatedness gives rise to "indicators, expressions or symptoms of social structures such as relationships, informal groups, age grades, gender, ethnic minorities, social classes and the like," and these "effects" should be treated as "data in their own terms" (1983b:2). The "forms of social life" that these effects illustrate can be "catalogued sociologically" to expose the intrinsic nature of "interactional life," or the distinctive features of face-to-face interaction. Furthermore, social structures are "dependent upon, and vulnerable to, what occurs in face-to-face contacts" (1983b:246).

Although social structures "don't 'determine' culturally standard displays," such as rituals and ceremonies, they do "help select from the available repertoire of them" (1983b:251). Thus, there is a "loose coupling" between interaction and social structure. As an example, Goffman notes that a small number of males, "such as junior executives, . . . have to wait and hang on others' words" in a manner similar to that of women involved in informal cross-sexed interaction (1983b:252). This observation of cross-gender similarities allows Goffman to formulate a role category of subordination that "women and junior executives (and anyone else in these interactional circumstances) share." But this subordinate "role . . . belongs *analytically* to the interaction order, which the categories women and junior executives do not" (1983b:252).

Goffman does not provide any clear definition of society or social structure other than to point to their constructed and "framing" nature. **Frames** are basic background assumptions that enable us to understand what is going on in any encounter or situation. These prior assumptions make sense of the situation and the interaction and enable the individual to respond appropriately. Frames are the organizational principles that define everyday situations (1974:11). There are two kinds of frames: natural and social.

Natural frames refer to events in the physical world that do not seem to involve human intervention, such as the weather.[1] **Social frames** are the basic understandings individuals bring to any interaction that provide the means to comprehend the motives, intentions, and desires of others. Social frameworks are not simply an understanding of the other's actions; they also involve an appraisal of those actions as to their "honesty, economy, safety, elegance, tactfulness, good taste, and so forth" (1974:22). Frames anchor social life and make it predictable most of the time. But frames can be undermined, and it is when they are undermined that we become aware of them. For example, Goffman points to media stories of visits from aliens or demonstrations of levitation as being outside the conventional beliefs about reality, and thus illuminating the taken-for-granted, everyday assumptions that frame behavior.

The predictability of everyday life is based on primary frameworks, but that predictability can be precarious. Primary frameworks can be "keyed"; that is, they can be transformed into something different. A **key** is defined as a "set of conventions by which a given activity, already meaningful in terms of some primary framework, is transformed into something patterned on it but is seen by the participants as something quite else" (1974:43–44). For example, sports and some games involve the keying of combat into a more restrained, less consequential activity.

Keying transforms experiences, but it is not always or necessarily a benign transformation. Keying can also involve fabrications such as hoaxes, illusions, satire, "frame-ups," and so on, in which some people are "in the know" and others are duped. Fabrications undermine frames and make people uneasy, and in this respect they can produce social disruptions and disorder. Direct fabrications, if they are harmful to the duped, can usually be countered, but indirect fabrications are more troubling. Indirect fabrications occur when an individual claims that a definition or a rumor told to another is untrue, but the recipient of the information refuses to believe that it is a lie (1974:107).

These discussions of frames and fabrications are part of Goffman's attempt to illustrate the nature of the "self" and the way in which that self has some modicum of security in social interaction. Individuals are able to progress through their everyday lives on the basis that the self they present to others in any particular situation will be accepted by others as a sincere and competent "me" that the "I" reacts to, usually creatively.[2]

Goffman moved from a central concern with the "self" as dramatic performance to the analysis of the structures and strategies of interaction in his later works, *Strategic Interaction* (1969) and *Frame Analysis* (1974). In these studies, Goffman moved from more concrete analysis of self to "more abstract analysis

---

[1]The weather *seems* to be an example of the extra-human, but of course the activities of human beings, such as clear-cutting forests or using ozone-depleting fuels, do affect the weather.

[2]Goffman's debt to G. H. Mead is evident here, especially Mead's conception of the knowledgeable creativity of human beings.

of principles that organize our experience" (Lemert and Branaman, 1997:lxxiv). *Frame Analysis* is an investigation of the "organization of experience"—what occurs when individuals ask themselves and others, "What is going on here?" (1974:153). Goffman is not dealing here with the "structure of social life" but with the "structure of experience that individuals have at any moment of their social lives." The film *Rashomon* is an ideal representation of such framing. When individuals believe they understand "what is going on," they will "fit their actions to this understanding and ordinarily find that the ongoing world supports this fitting" (1974:158).

The organizational premises of everyday life are what Goffman calls the "frame of the activity," and everyday life contains many "quickly changing frames." For example, "a man finishes giving instructions to his postman, greets a passing couple, gets in his car, and drives off" (1974:161). All of these activities are "framed" in different ways, although they are performed sequentially. The instruction "belongs to the realm of occupational roles," and the greeting is "part of the ritual order in which the individual can figure as a representative of himself." Although all these various activities could be "subsumed under the term 'role'—for example, the role of suburbanite— . . . that would provide a hopelessly gross conceptualization" of what was going on (1974:161).

The frames within which individuals organize experience are cultural constructs, prefabricated by the society or cultural group. They "buttress" in real life "what people understand to be the organization of their experience," so that actions are performed "self-fulfillingly" (1974:162). People develop a "corpus of cautionary tales, games, riddles, experiments, newsy stories, and other scenarios which elegantly confirm a frame-relevant view of the working of the world" and then "comport themselves so as to render this analysis true" (1974:162–163). Thus, there is no original behind the frame.

Humans as Performers   In *The Presentation of Self in Everyday Life*, Goffman used the theatrical metaphor of performance to illustrate how human beings present themselves in their various social roles in face-to-face interactions with others. According to this analysis, individuals play parts, and observers are "asked to believe that the character they see actually possesses the attributes he appears to possess, that the task he performs will have the consequences implicitly claimed for it, and that, in general, matters are what they appear to be" (1959:17).

The individual is both performer, who fabricates impressions in the "all-too-human task of staging a performance," and a character, "typically a fine one, whose spirit, strength, and other sterling qualities the performance was designed to evoke" (1959:252). The **impression management** that is involved in the presentation of a self is not intrinsic to the individual, but derives from "the whole scene of his action" that hopefully convinces the audience of the self being presented. Thus, a "correctly staged and performed scene leads the audience to impute a self to a performed character, but this imputation—this self—is a *product* of a scene that comes off, and is not a *cause* of it" (1959:252). The self "as a performed character, is not an organic thing—the product of some intrinsic nature—with a specific location, whose fundamental fate is to be born, to mature, and to die; it is a dramatic effect arising from the scene that is presented, and the characteristic issues, the crucial concern, is whether it will be credited or discredited" (1959:252–253).

Goffman suggests that the presentation of a performance involves front and back stage behaviors. **Front stage** refers to actions that in a "general and fixed fashion . . . define the situation for those who observe the performance" (1959:22). The props to maintain the front include physical settings; personal possessions such as "clothing; sex, age, and racial characteristics; size and looks; posture; speech patterns; facial expressions; bodily gestures; and the like" (1959:24). **Back stage** is a place "where the impression fostered by the performance is knowingly contradicted as a matter of course" (1959:112). It is the place in which the performer "can relax; he can drop his front, forgo speaking his lines, and step out of character" (1959:112). As an illustration, Goffman quotes Simone de Beauvoir on women's relationships in the absence of men: "With other women, a woman is behind the scenes; she is polishing her equipment, but not in battle; . . . she is lingering in dressing-gown and slippers in the wings before making her entrance on the stage." A woman prepares back stage for her confrontation with men, in which she is "always play-acting; she lies when she makes believe that she accepts her status as the inessential other" and at all times with her "husband or with her lover, every woman is more or less conscious of the thought: 'I am not being myself'" (quoted in Goffman, 1959:113).

Maintaining the separation of front and back stage is important for impression management. This separation is found in all areas of social life—for example, the bedroom and the bathroom are "places from which the downstairs audience can be excluded. Bodies that are cleansed, clothed and made up in these room can be presented to friends in others" (1959:123). But the separation can break down, and when it does, it can result in "embarrassment and dissonance" and seriously undermine the credibility of the previous performance.

Impression management, whether successful or unsuccessful, involves an audience that also has a stake in ensuring a successful performance. Consequently, in some cases where the performance slips or something unexpected occurs, the audience may attempt to "save the day" by ignoring the faux pas or providing excuses for the untoward behavior. However, there are situations in which the audience makes the successful performance of a role difficult, as Goffman illustrated in *Asylums* (1961a) and *Stigma* (1965).

In his dramaturgical approach in *The Presentation of Self in Everyday Life*, Goffman suggests that the performer has considerable control over the image of the self, but in *Stigma* this control is compromised. Whatever the stigma— "abominations of the body" or "blemishes of individual character," usually inferred from records of "mental disorder, imprisonment, addiction, alcoholism, homosexuality, unemployment, suicidal attempts, and radical political behavior," or the "tribal stigma of race, nation, and religion"—there is likely to be a gap between an individual's virtual and actual social identity. **Virtual identity** refers to what an individual is supposed to be in the eyes of others—the "character we impute to the individual." **Actual identity** refers to the "category and attributes" an individual can be "proved to possess" (1965:2, 4).

Social identity is spoiled when there is a discrepancy between the virtual and the actual identity, as is often the case for individuals with a stigma. Indeed, many "normals" believe that "the person with a stigma is not quite human" and will practice various forms of discrimination that, unthinkingly or not, reduce the stigmatized individual's life chances (1965:5). The stigmatized individual also tends to "hold the same beliefs about identity" as the "normals." As a result, the stigmatized individual perceives "that whatever others profess, they do not really 'accept' him and are not ready to make contact with him on 'equal grounds'" (1965:7).

Goffman's point in discussing the ways in which stigma affects social identities, along with the various interactional practices used to conceal, accommodate, or even flaunt stigma, is that all individuals at some point are subject to stigma. He suggested that possibly the only nonstigmatized individual in U.S. society was a young male "married, white, urban, northern, heterosexual Protestant father of college education, fully employed, of good complexion, weight and height, and a recent record in sports." Any male who "fails to qualify in any of these ways is likely to view himself—during moments at least —as unworthy, incomplete, and inferior" (1965:128). In sum, "stigma management is a general feature of society," and Goffman suspected that the "role of normal and the role of stigmatized are . . . cut from the same standard cloth" (1965:130). Furthermore, as "interaction roles are involved, not concrete individuals," in many instances "he who is stigmatized in one regard nicely exhibits all the normal prejudices held towards those who are stigmatized in another regard" (1965:138).

The stigmatized are not without resources to resist their typification, as Goffman demonstrated in his study of asylums. Asylums, like prisons, concentration camps, nunneries, or monasteries, are **total institutions**—that is, they are totally, or almost totally, closed to the outside world. The closure, bureaucratization, and rationalization of everyday life characteristic of such institutions diminish the identity, the "self," of the inmate. The new inmate of such institutions confronts a "series of abasements, degradations, humiliations and profanations of self" designed to produce a "self" that the institution can deal with and control.

In total institutions, the self is "systematically, if often unintentionally, mortified" (1961a:55). Various indignities are constantly visited on the inmates, such as having to ask for the most mundane things. For example, asking permission to use the toilet or the telephone may result in teasing or having "the request denied" or being "questioned at length, ignored, or put off" by those in authority (1961a:41).

> In a total institution, minute segments of a person's line of activity may be
> subjected to regulations and judgments by staff; . . . Each specification robs
> the individual of an opportunity to balance his needs and objectives in a
> personally efficient way and opens up his line of action to sanctions. The
> autonomy of the act itself is violated. (1961a:38)

Individuals in total institutions make a primary adjustment to the organization when they identify and cooperate with the organizational demands and become "normal" or "programmed" members. However, individuals may also make secondary adjustments that "represent ways in which the individual stands apart from the role and the self that were taken for granted for him by the institution" (1961a:189). Individuals may use the resources of the institution in creative ways to reestablish the self and claim some autonomy and status. Goffman suggests that this "underlife" of the institution, by which "participants decline in some way to accept the official view of what they should be putting into and getting out of the organization and, behind this, of what sort of self and world they accept for themselves" represents a "movement of liberty" (1961a:305). For example, he observed that mental hospital inmates created "free places" for themselves, such as the woods on the hospital grounds that were used as a cover for illicit drinking or for playing poker. Free places enabled the inmates to escape, for a short time, the surveillance of the staff and affirm a personal sense of self in the face of institutional impositions.

This analysis of the production and constitution of the self in total institutions again illustrates the central concern found in all of Goffman's work: the self as a dramatic performance accomplished in the context of, and constrained by, social expectations or rituals of social life. Whatever the constraints, however, social interaction is creative action, and this is the key to the issue of social change.

Social Change   Goffman does not address the issue of social change directly; there are no accounts of dramatic or revolutionary social change in his work. But his discussions of the ways in which individuals "modify their conduct in many normatively guided ways" (1963:243) provide a clue to the nature of social change. It is from the multiplicity of everyday social interactions that the "gossamer reality of social occasions is built" (1963:247), and social change effected.

The reproduction and transformation of social institutions is accomplished through the creative interactions of individuals. All social interaction entails risk or "fatefulness." Risky or fateful activity is "activity that is both problematic and consequential," and although such fatefulness is minimized as much as possible in any social context, "the human condition is such that some degree of fatefulness will always be found" (1967:164). As Anthony Giddens (1984:139) observed, social changes "of a deep-rooted kind, by their very nature, involve alterations in the character of day-to-day social practices." The rituals of social interaction control and contain the unexpected and disruptive, but they are never totally successful, and it is from these disruptions that social change occurs.

Class, Gender, and Race

Goffman only referred obliquely to issues of class and race. He did point out that his focus on the "nature of personal experiencing" had political implications and that they were "conservative ones" (1974:157). He acknowledged that the analysis of personal experiences does not "catch at the differences between the advantaged and the disadvantaged classes" and in fact could be said "to direct attention away from such matters." Like the critical theorists, Goffman believed that "he who would combat false consciousness and awaken people to their true interests has much to do, because the sleep is very deep." His work was not intended "to provide a lullaby but merely to sneak in and watch the way people snore" (1974:158).

Goffman was more forthright in his discussions of gender. He pointed out that sex differences are assumed to be invariable and, therefore, significant. But, in his view, sex differences are only significant because the culture makes them so. For example, the fact that women can breast-feed and men cannot is a "temporary biological constraint" that is "extended culturally" to encompass a whole complex of rights and duties that are sex typed.

In *Gender Advertisements*, Goffman maintained that gender relations in Western society reproduce parent–child relations. When a male confronts a female or a subordinate male, "some mitigation of potential distance, coercion, and hostility is quite likely to be induced by application of the parent–child complex." This means that, "ritually speaking, females are equivalent to subordinate males and both are equivalent to children" (1979:5). This effect originates in the "home training of the two sexes" (1977:202).

Children acquire normative gender interaction patterns because of the differential treatment by parents depending on the sex of the child. In North American family life, Goffman observed, "whatever the economic or class level and however well or badly off a female sees she is when compared to children in other families, she can hardly fail to see that her male sib, equal to her when compared to children in other families and often equal, too, in regard to ultimate claims upon the family resources, is yet judged differently and accorded different treatment from herself by their parents" (1977:202–203).

Goffman pointed out that the differentiation of the sexes is a cultural artifact produced by the "interactional field." He gives the example of "toilet segregation," which is "presented as a natural consequence of the difference between sex-classes, when in fact it is rather a means of honoring, if not producing, this difference" (1977:205). Gender is displayed in ritual ways, and the presumed "naturalness" of the displays is often anchored by comparisons with animal life. But Goffman (1977:214–215) maintained that the animal analogy as "a source of imagery" was simply a "cultural resource." The animal kingdom only provides "mimetic models for gender display, not necessarily phylogenetic ones" (1977:214–215).

Male and female "human nature" is the "capacity to learn to provide and read depictions of masculinity and femininity and a willingness to adhere to a schedule for presenting these pictures and this capacity they have by virtue of being persons, not females or males" (1977:224). Thus, according to Goffman, "one might just as well say there is no gender identity. There is only a schedule for the portrayal of gender." Why gender is selected as primary rather than some other attribute is "an open question," but gender "in close connection with age-grade, lays down more, perhaps, than class or other social divisions an understanding of what our ultimate nature ought to be and where this nature ought to be exhibited" (1977:225).

Gender is thus constructed in the rituals of everyday interaction, and the sociologist's task is not to uncover "real, natural expressions, whatever they might be," but to illustrate the "capacity and inclination of individuals to portray a version of themselves and their relationships at strategic moments" (1977:223). Nothing "biological or social-structural" lies beneath the expressions of femininity and masculinity, although these same expressions "function socially . . . to support belief that there is an underlying reality to gender" (1977:226).

However, the recognition of the cultural construction of masculinity and femininity does not provide any easy political answer to sexism. Goffman pointed out that gender stereotypes "run in every direction, and almost as much inform what supporters of women's rights approve as what they disapprove" (1977:225). He believed that the problem with any social change in gender relations was that the very actions and relations that denote male domination are also the expressions that define the "gentlest, most loving moment." Unlike other disadvantaged groups, who can "turn from the world to a domestic scene where self-determination and relief from inequality are possible, the disadvantage that persons who are female suffer precludes this" (1977:226). The home is not a refuge from gender hierarchy and inequality, but rather the place in which such hierarchy is reaffirmed. Indeed, the "gentling of the world" as a result of the extension of the parent–child complex of "intimate, comfortable practices" is what produces female subordination (1977:226).

Changes in gender relations cannot be effected simply by altering institutional structures. Attention must be paid to the variety of everyday, taken-for-granted interactions that denote gender power relations. Goffman's somewhat pessimistic conclusion with respect to change in gender power relations has been criticized by Burns (1992:236), who contends that Goffman's caution regarding the significance of structural changes is contradicted by the historical evidence. Burns claims that the "partial emancipation gained by women's movements over the past century and a half is surely the result of the direct assault on 'structural arrangements,'" and the "greater liberty, more social acceptance on an equal footing with men . . . have all *followed* the gains registered in structural reforms" (1992:236).

In fact, both Goffman and Burns are correct. Structural changes have mitigated some of the disadvantages women experience, but the household division of labor remains skewed even in the most professedly egalitarian relationships. Many studies have indicated that housework remains primarily a female task, especially after the birth of the first child (Meissner et al., 1975; Coltrane, 1989; Hochschild, 1989). Furthermore, the occupational locations of women and men indicate that the gender rituals of everyday life are indeed hard to change.

Other Theories and Theorists

In later years, Goffman moved into the analysis of conversation. In this analysis, he maintained that meaningful, or "felicitous," conversation depended on the sharing of a common stock of knowledge. Correct speech, or "talk," is essential if the speaker is to demonstrate sanity and a well-meaning attitude toward the other. "Felicity's Condition" (1983a) refers to the "requirement to demonstrate the sanity behind our actions"—the common rule that underlies all face-to-face interaction (Manning, 1992:93). All communication must address the "other's mind, that is, . . . the other's capacity to read our words and actions for evidence of our feelings, thoughts, and intent" (1983b:192).

Goffman's interest in conversational analysis links up with the work of the ethnomethodologists, such as Dorothy Smith, whose work is examined in Chapter 10. However, Goffman's major focus, even in conversational analysis, remained a fascination with the self as performance and strategic impression management (Lemert and Branaman, 1997:lxiii).

Critique and Conclusions

Goffman's work cannot be easily "placed" in any one theoretical tradition. Goffman himself maintained that such genealogies were sterile exercises that detracted from an engagement with sociological practices and debates. His work was and remains a constant source of renewal in many different directions for sociological theory, as you will see in subsequent discussions in this volume.

Goffman's major achievement was to direct the attention of sociology to the significance of the "infinitely small, to the things which the object-less theoreticians and concept-less observers were incapable of seeing and which went unremarked because they were too obvious." As a result, the "guardians of positivist dogmatism assigned Goffman to the 'lunatic fringe' of sociology." This judgment has proved erroneous, as Goffman has become "one of the fundamental references for sociologists, and also for psychologists, social psychologists and socio-linguists" (Bourdieu, 1983:112).

In his ASA presidential address, Goffman described his work as the promotion of the "face-to-face domain as an analytically viable one—a domain which might be titled . . . the *interaction order*—a domain whose preferred method of study is microanalysis" (1983b:2). His work was an important corrective to the seeming dominance in U.S. sociology of the structural functionalist orthodoxy. Anthony Giddens (1984), however, has pointed out that sociological analysis still needs to bridge the divide between the micro and the macro, between face-to-face interaction and social structures; he claimed that his own structuration theory (see Chapter 3) was an attempt to use Goffman's work, as well as that of ethnomethodologists, to close the divide. Goffman's work was particularly valuable to many feminist sociologists, as you will see in Chapter 10.

Arlie Russell Hochschild (1940–)

Arlie Hochschild entered graduate school at Berkeley in 1962 and completed her MA and PhD there. She taught at the University of California at Santa Cruz for two years and then returned to Berkeley, where she is currently a Professor of Sociology.

Hochschild has recorded her ambivalence about her graduate studies and the problems she faced by attempting to combine graduate study, an academic job, and child care during the late 1960s and early 1970s. Like many other women graduate students at the time, she found few female role models in academia. At Berkeley there were no female professors other than Gertrude Jaeger, who was a lecturer, although "one fifth of the graduate students were women, hoping one day to become professors" (Hochschild, 1994:136).

Hochschild records that in 1968 the women graduate students began to meet and talk about their problems, both academic and personal, questioning the "basic concepts in sociology and trying to picture what sociology would look like if women's experiences counted as much as men's" (1994:136). The women's caucus that emerged out of the initial meeting was duplicated during that period at other universities and in other disciplines. The central theme for all of them was to take women's experience "and the public perceptions of that experience seriously." It was this perspective that led Hochschild to make the study of emotions central to her work.

Hochschild indicates that her focus on emotions was inspired by the "collective consciousness" of the second women's movement and by Goffman's work. Goffman's "focus on the have-nots of dignity" and "the poetry in his viewpoint" were important, but she was also aware that his description of the social world was from a male point of view. Although Hochschild did not take courses from Goffman during her period at Berkeley, she did come to know him through his visits to a Berkeley faculty study group after he had moved to Pennsylvania. Hochschild sent him some of her articles, and he responded with "trenchant comments and warm human support"; indeed she described his responses as akin to "God himself calling" (1994:137)!

Hochschild's Central Theories and Methods

Hochschild's work on emotions has extended Goffman's work in important ways. First, she has expanded on his studies of embarrassment and shame to incorporate a whole range of emotional responses. Second, she examines the outward signs of emotional response and work as Goffman did, but unlike Goffman, she also examines the inner emotional life of the self. Goffman looked at the emotions registered in social situations, but according to Hochschild, ignored the self as "subject of emotive experience"—the self that "introspects or dwells on outer reality without a sense of watchers" (1983:216). In contrast to Goffman, Hochschild is interested in "how people try to feel," rather than how "people try to appear to feel" (1979:560).

Freud has also had an impact on Hochschild, although she finds his work wanting. In contrast to Goffman, Freud "proposed a self that could feel and manage feeling," but in Hochschild's view, Freud's work was limited by his singular focus on anxiety. Hochschild is interested in how people "consciously feel" and not, "as for Freud, how people feel unconsciously" (1979:560).

Hochschild proposed looking at both the "social and psychological side" of emotion by asking how "institutions control how we 'personally' control feeling" rather than simply looking at how "institutions influence personality." She points out that emotion is the most important "biologically given sense" because it provides the means to know how to act in the world and, more important, enables us to understand self in that world—it is an "orientation toward *action*" and also "an orientation toward *cognition*" (1983:219).

Hochschild's first major work, *The Managed Heart* (1983), was a study of the emotional labor required by two occupations, flight attendant and bill collector. The two occupations represent opposite poles of emotional labor. Flight attendants are asked to feel "sympathy, trust, and good will" toward their clients, whereas bill collectors have to feel "distrust and sometimes positive bad will" (1983:137). The study of the two occupations was a mixture of interviews, participant observation, and documentary analysis. Her general focus was on the links between "feeling rules, emotion management, and emotive experience" as a corrective to the "tacit assumption" in social psychology that "emotion because it seems unbidden and uncontrollable, is not governed by social rules" (1979:551).

Class, Gender, and Race

Goffman (1961b:23) pointed out that individuals control "psychological states and attitudes" because they are aware of the general rule that "one enter into the prevailing mood in the encounter." In other words, people manage their emotions. Emotion management assumes that individuals are "capable of feeling, capable of assessing when a feeling is 'inappropriate,' and capable of trying to manage feelings" (Hochschild, 1979:557). The sociology of emotions is therefore concerned with the "theoretical junctures—between consciousness of feeling and consciousness of feeling rules, between feeling rules and emotion work, between feeling rules and social structure" (1979:560). It is concerned with **emotion work** and **emotion management**.

There are two general types of emotion work: "*evocation*, in which the cognitive focus is on a desired feeling which is initially absent" and "*suppression*, in which the cognitive focus is on an undesired feeling which is initially present" (Hochschild, 1979). These types of emotion work are managed by three general techniques: "*cognitive*: the attempt to change images, ideas, or thoughts in the service of changing the feelings associated with them"; "*bodily*: the attempt to change somatic or other physical symptoms of emotion"; and "*expressive* emotion work: trying to change the expressive gestures in the service of changing inner feeling" (1979:562). These three techniques are often found together in practice.

Emotion work is usually accomplished without too much conscious effort; it is when feelings do not fit the situation that individuals become conscious of the "work" involved in emotion. There are guidelines, or social "feeling rules," about the appropriate fit between a situation and displayed emotion. For example, it is expected that people will be sad at funerals, happy at weddings. These feeling rules are "implicit in any ideological stance" and often become clear when the definition or meaning of situations change. For example, Hochschild points to the different feeling rules that traditionally were ascribed to men and women on the assumption that they have different natures. Women were supposed to be more sensitive and emotional in contrast to manly stoicism.

Hochschild points out, however, that these ideological assumptions about men and women have been transformed to some extent by the feminist movement, which has attempted to change gender-based feeling rules. For example, when the "same balance of priorities in work and family now ideally applies to men as to women," women can "as legitimately (as a man) become angry (rather than simply upset or disappointed) over abuses at work, since her heart is supposed to be in that work and she has the right to hope, as much as a man, for advancement." Similarly, "a man has the right to feel angry at the loss of custody if he has shown himself the fitter parent" (1979:567).

Class Hochschild does not discuss class directly, but her discussion of emotional labor is connected to class distinctions. Hochschild distinguishes emotion work and emotion management from emotional labor. **Emotional labor** refers to the commoditization of emotion work—the "management of feeling to create a publicly observable facial and bodily display." This labor is "sold for a wage and therefore has exchange value," in contrast to the use value of emotion work and management (1983:7). The smile and solicitous demeanor of the flight attendant is an essential part of the job. And just as the assembly-line worker can be estranged from work and self, so the emotional laborer can suffer estrangement. But whereas the alienating labor of the assembly line can be mitigated by the emotional sanctuary of the home, estrangement resulting from emotional labor is not easily left on the job.

The physical laborer and the emotional laborer are both "subject to rules of mass production. But when the product—the thing to be engineered, mass-produced, and subjected to speed-up and slowdown—is a smile, a mood, a feeling, or a relationship, it comes to belong more to the organization and less to the self" (1983:198). Emotional labor "becomes a public act, bought on the one hand and sold on the other"; feeling rules are "no longer simply matters of personal discretion, negotiated with another person in private but are spelled out publicly . . . in training programs, and the discourse of supervisors" (1983:118–119). As a result, "there is much less room for individual navigation of the emotional waters" (1983:119). In jobs that require emotional labor, the strain that often results from feeling, and feigning feeling, results in "emotive dissonance."

Emotional labor, with its accompanying emotive dissonance, is most characteristic of the middle classes and women. Women, especially middle-class women, are expected to, and in fact do, manage feeling more than men. Hochschild indicates that some working-class jobs, such as prostitution or personal service, also require emotion work, but generally emotional labor as opposed to physical labor is much less prevalent in working-class than in middle-class jobs. Furthermore, middle-class parents tend to control their children through appeals to and management of feeling, in contrast to working-class parents who tend to control their children through management of behavior. Consequently, "middle class parents prepare their children for emotional management" and emotional labor more than working-class parents do (1979:570–571).

Gender Hochschild states that because women in general still "depend on men for money," one of the ways of repaying their debt is to do "extra emotion work—*especially emotion work that affirms, enhances, and celebrates the well-being and status of others*" (1983:165). Because the "world turns to women for mothering . . . this fact silently attaches itself to many a job description" (1983:170). Hochschild looked at the gender characteristics of standard occupational groups in the U.S. Census and found that of the twelve major occupational groups, five required emotional labor. The five groups were professional and technical workers, managers and administrators, sales workers, clerical workers, and service workers. In these five occupational categories, women were "overrepresented . . . about half of all working women hold such jobs," whereas men were "underrepresented; about a quarter of all working men are in emotional labor jobs" (1983:234–235).

The gender discrepancy in emotion work and emotional labor was an important part of the problems Hochschild observed in her next project: an examination of the way in which dual-career or dual-job couples handle their domestic and child-rearing responsibilities. In *The Second Shift* (1989), Hochschild reported her study of more than 50 dual-career or dual-job couples. She also focused in depth on the strategies of ten of the couples in the management of their home and work responsibilities. She found that although women may have changed, workplaces have "remained inflexible in the face of the family demands of their workers" and, on the home front, "most men have yet to really adapt to the changes in women." The result has been a "stalled revolution" (1989:12).

Most of the couples maintained a compromise between "traditional and egalitarian ideals" of domestic and paid labor, but generally the women assumed far more of the burden of the "second shift" than did the men. Hochschild noted that many married men made a single action the "substitute for a multitude of chores in the second shift." The man offered a "token"—for example, "Evan took care of the dog"—which came to symbolize his contribution to the second shift. But Evan, like the other men in the study, had the "male norm" on their side: Because men "out there" did even less than they were doing, their wives should feel "lucky" that they did what they did, no matter how minimal (1989:47, 51).

Hochschild observed a cycle that tended, over time, to reinstate women's "traditional" responsibilities for most domestic and child-rearing work—the "backstage stage" work. Men are expected to (and do in the general case) "put more of their 'male' identity in work" so that their "work time is worth more than female work time—to the man and to the family" (1989:254). The greater "worth of male work time makes his leisure more valuable, because it is his leisure that enables him to refuel his energy, strengthen his ambition, and move ahead at work." The result is that "his aspirations expand. So does his pay. So does his exemption from the second shift" (1989:254).

The lack of "backstage support" women experienced for their paid labor, in contrast to men, raised the "emotional price of success impossibly high" for most women (1989:256). The emotional price women paid in the burden of the second shift became clearer when, in a later study, Hochschild examined the family and work arrangements in an organization that had instituted "family-friendly" policies. The corporation, called Amerco in her study *The Time Bind* (1997), had introduced flextime, job sharing, and parental leave, and ran an excellent day-care center for employees' children.

Hochschild discovered that of the family-friendly policies, "only flextime, which rearranged but did not cut back on hours of work, had any significant impact on the workplace" (1997:26). In general, the majority of workers, both men and women, worked more hours. In addition, the "best-paid employees—upper-level managers and professionals—[were] the least interested in part-time work or job sharing," and few men "at any level expressed interest in part-time work" (1997:28). The "first shift (at the workplace)" tended to take more and more time, with the result that the "second shift (at home) becomes more hurried and rationalized" (1997:214). Generally, the more that work—with its "deadlines, its cycles, its pauses and interruptions"—shapes the lives of workers, the more "family time is forced to accommodate to the pressures of work" (1997:45). Child care was especially difficult, and parents held out the hope that "quality time"—that is, "scheduling intense periods of togetherness"—could compensate for the loss of time and possible loss of quality in the parent–child or family relationship. However, what quality time usually entailed was simply "transferring the cult of efficiency from office to home" (1997:50).

Hochschild observed that juggling domestic, especially child-care and spousal, relations often produced difficulties and conflict, largely for women. She found that problems at home upset women more than problems at work, and that both types of problems upset women more than men. Many of her respondents, both women and men, indicated that work, in contrast to the home, became a "haven" as a "tired parent flees a world of unresolved quarrels and unwashed laundry for the reliable orderliness, harmony, and managed cheer of work" (1997:44). Hochschild found, however, that women, more than men, sought support mechanisms at work where they could complain about domestic, spousal, and child-care problems and seek solutions from coworkers. Furthermore, work as the "haven" from domestic turmoil seemed to produce longer hours on the job the more domestic responsibilities increased. Hochschild noted that single parents at Amerco averaged 45 hours a week—hourly female single parents 43 hours and hourly single male parents 48 hours a week. Women with children in dual-earner marriages averaged 51 hours a week, and men with children in dual-earner marriages averaged 53 hours a week (1997:261).

The "third shift" of emotional work that resulted from the compression of the second shift was especially difficult for women. Generally, the "time-starved mother" was forced into choosing between "being a good parent and buying a commodified version of parenthood from someone else" (1997:232). The "commodification of home life" in turn tended to make "children's protests" worse. Generally, children's "resentment, resistance, passive acquiescence . . . frustrations . . . stubborn demands or whining requests," resulting from the "damage done by the reversal of worlds," caused considerable emotional turmoil, especially for mothers (1997:218). This third, "unacknowledged" shift of emotional work, carried mainly by mothers, reinforced the feeling that "life at home is hard work" compared to life in the workplace.

In the traditional focus on cognition and behavior, Hochschild argues, sociology has ignored a critical dimension of social life—emotions. Hochschild's work seeks to correct this critical blind spot in sociological research. Her work demonstrates that emotional display is learned behavior, and points to the importance of emotion work in "bridging . . . traditional interactionist concerns with self and situation" (Fine, 1990:134). In addition, Hochschild makes an important contribution to bridging the micro/macro divide in her studies on the organization of "feeling work" in social institutions.

Other Theories and Theorists

After Blumer, suggests Fine (1990:119), interactionism could generally be divided into two perspectives. The first perspective, following Mead, focused on the "self." This perspective was social psychological with a "heavy overlay of cognitive imagery." To some extent, Hochschild's work falls more in this tradition. The second focus owed more to the Park and Thomas survey research tradition at Chicago, with its concentration on a "situation." This perspective was micro sociological, with "strong ties to social and cultural anthropology and a focus on 'behavior,' not 'cognition.'" Goffman's work is more attuned to this second perspective. However, neither Hochschild nor Goffman can be totally subsumed under either of these perspectives.

Recent work in the interactionist tradition is more diverse, involving combinations of these foci. In fact, some theorists claim that the interactionist perspective is not limited to micro sociological analysis, but can also deal with macro issues. The main areas in which interactionists have contributed in recent years are "(1) self and identity theory; (2) dramaturgy, accounts and presentation of self; (3) collective behavior and collective action; (4) culture and art; (5) sociolinguistics approaches ; and (6) social problems theory" (Fine, 1990:121).

Critique and Conclusions

The work of Hochschild and others on emotion extends the focus of interactionism in important ways. As Hochschild has noted, the work of Mead and Blumer on "conscious, active and responsive gestures" might have been even more fruitful if they had also attended to the "importance of feeling" (1979:555).

The social psychological focus of interactionism takes seriously the premise that people are active, creative interpreters of their social worlds. In this sense, interactionism stands in contrast to the formulation of the abstract "actor" of "grand theory." But although interactionism may be contrasted with grand theory, it is nonetheless important to such theory. The focus on the micro relations of social life, and the inductive and qualitative nature of the methodology generally employed, provides a rich source of data and raises important, usually overlooked, issues that can put the proverbial "meat" on the bones of abstract theoretical constructions.

Final Thoughts

Interactionism has been associated with phenomenology and ethnomethodology on occasion, but these approaches represent a somewhat different view of what constitutes the sociological object. Interactionism is "*at its core* social and relational, whereas the phenomenological approach emphasizes the individual construction of the world, a world of discrete and separate actors" (Fine, 1990:139). The ethnomethodological approach also differs, focusing more on conversational analysis. Phenomenological sociology and ethnomethodology also represented challenges to the structural functional tradition in American sociology, and we touch on these approaches in Chapter 10.

References

Blumer, Herbert. 1969. *Symbolic Interactionism: Perspective and Method*. Englewood Cliffs, NJ: Prentice-Hall.

———. 1975. "Comments on Parsons as a Symbolic Interactionist." *Sociological Inquiry, 45*, 59–62.

Bourdieu, Pierre. 1983. "Erving Goffman, Discoverer of the Infinitely Small." *Theory, Culture and Society, 2*(1), 112–113.

Bulmer, Martin. 1984. *The Chicago School of Sociology*. Chicago: University of Chicago Press.

Burns, Tom. 1992. *Erving Goffman*. London: Routledge.

Collins, Randall. 1986. "The Passing of Intellectual Generations: Reflections on the Death of Erving Goffman." *Sociological Theory, 4*, 106–113.

Coltrane, Scott. 1989. "Household Labor and the Routine Production of Gender." *Social Problems, 36*, 473–491.

Deegan, Mary Jo, and Michael R. Hill (Eds.). 1987. *Women and Symbolic Interaction*. Boston: Allen & Unwin.

Drew, Paul, and Anthony Wooton (Eds.). 1988. *Erving Goffman: Exploring the Interaction Order*. Cambridge: Polity Press.

Fine, Gary Alan. 1990. "Symbolic Interactionism in the Post-Blumerian Age." In George Ritzer (Ed.), *Frontiers of Social Theory* (pp. 117–157). New York: Columbia University Press.

Giddens, Anthony. 1984. *The Constitution of Society*. Cambridge: Polity Press.

Goffman, Erving. 1953/1997. "On Cooling the Mark Out: Some Aspects of Adaptation to Failure." In Charles Lemert and Ann Branaman (Eds.), *The Goffman Reader* (pp. 3–20). Oxford: Blackwell Publishers.

———. 1959. *The Presentation of Self in Everyday Life*. Garden City, NY: Doubleday Anchor Books.

———. 1961a. *Asylums*. Garden City, NY: Doubleday Anchor Books.

———. 1961b. *Encounters: Two Studies in the Sociology of Interaction*. Indianapolis: Bobbs-Merrill.

———. 1963. *Behavior in Public Places*. New York: Free Press of Glencoe.

———. 1965. *Stigma: Notes on the Management of Spoiled Identity*. Englewood Cliffs, NJ: Prentice-Hall.

———. 1967. *Interaction Ritual: Essays on Face-to-Face Behavior*. Garden City, NY: Doubleday Anchor Books.

———. 1969. *Strategic Interaction*, Philadelphia: University of Pennsylvania Press.

———. 1974. *Frame Analysis*. New York: Harper Colophon Books.

———. 1977/1997. "The Arrangement between the Sexes." In Charles Lemert and Ann Branaman (Eds.), *The Goffman Reader* (pp. 201–227). Oxford: Blackwell Publishers.

———. 1979. *Gender Advertisements*. Cambridge, MA: Harvard University Press.

———. 1981. *Forms of Talk*. Philadelphia: University of Pennsylvania Press.

———. 1983a. "Felicity's Condition." *American Journal of Sociology, 89*, 1–53.

———. 1983b/1997. "Frame Analysis of Talk." In Charles Lemert and Ann Branaman (Eds.), *The Goffman Reader*. Oxford: Blackwell Publishers.

———. 1983c. "The Interaction Order." *American Sociological Review, 48*, 1–17.

Hochschild, Arlie Russell. 1979. "Emotion Work, Feeling Rules, and Social Structure." *American Journal of Sociology, 85*, 551–573.

———. 1983. *The Managed Heart: Commercialization of Human Feeling.* Berkeley: University of California Press.

———, with Anne Machung. 1989. *The Second Shift.* New York: Viking.

———. 1994. "Inside the Clockwork of Male Careers." In Kathryn P. Meadow Orlans, with Ruth A. Wallace (Eds.), *Gender and the Academic Experience.* Lincoln: University of Nebraska Press.

———. 1997. *The Time Bind.* New York: Henry Holt.

Lemert, Charles, and Ann Branaman (Eds.). 1997. *The Goffman Reader.* Oxford: Blackwell Publishers.

Manning, Philip. 1992. *Erving Goffman and Modern Sociology.* Stanford, CA: Stanford University Press.

Meissner, Martin, et al. 1975. "No Exit for Wives: Sexual Division of Labor and Cumulation of Household Demands." *Canadian Review of Sociology and Anthropology, 12*, 424–439.

Rawls, Ann Warfield. 1987. "The Interaction Order Sui Generis: Goffman's Contribution to Social Theory." *Sociological Theory, 5*, 136–149.

Scheff, Thomas J. 1986. "Micro-Linguistic and Social Structure: A Theory of Social Action." *Sociological Theory, 4*, 71–83.

Williams, Robin. 1983. "Sociological Tropes: A Tribute to Erving Goffman." *Theory, Culture and Society, 2*, 99–102.

———. 1988. "Understanding Goffman's Methods." In P. Drew and A. Wooton (Eds.), *Erving Goffman: Exploring the Interaction Order.* Cambridge: Polity Press.

Chapter 9

Rational Choice and Exchange
Coleman

What is "rationality"? Often the term is used in a purely evaluative sense: decisions I make are "rational"; those of which I disapprove are not. Occasionally, we adopt a broader perspective, and judge rationality not just in terms of approval but in terms of the "best interests" *of the person making the decision*—"best interests" as defined by *us*. Thus, for example, some of Adolf Hitler's decisions may be viewed as rational and others are irrational, despite the fact that we may disapprove of all of them. (Dawes, 1988:7–8)

In the 1600s, René Descartes said "Cogito ergo sum," translated as "I think, therefore I am." In this chapter, two claims are made: "I think, therefore I choose," and "I think, therefore I choose what benefits me." The first reflects rational choice theory, which comes primarily from a psychological tradition. The second represents exchange theory, which is based on both psychology and economics.

Rational choice involves making a decision based on (1) one's current assets, or capability of "following through"; (2) the possible consequences of one's choice; and (3) if the consequences are uncertain, evaluation of outcomes in terms of probabilities (Dawes, 1988:8). Does my choice "make sense" or not?

It is rational to act in one's own best interest; that is, it is rational to try to maximize one's gain or profit and minimize one's loss or cost. An example from exchange theory will help:

Suppose that two men are doing paper-work jobs in an office. According to the office rules, each should do his job by himself or, if he needs help, he should consult the supervisor. One of the men, whom we shall call Person, is not skillful at the work and would get it done better and faster if he got help from time to time. In spite of the rules he is reluctant to go to the supervisor, for to confess his incompetence might hurt his chances for promotion. Instead he seeks out the other man, whom we shall call Other for short, and asks him for help. Other is more experienced at the work than is Person; he can do his work well and quickly and be left with time to spare, and he has reason to suppose that the supervisor will not go out of his way to look for a breach of the rules. Other gives Person help and in return Person gives Other thanks and expressions of approval. The two men have exchanged help and approval. (Homans, 1961:31–32)

In this example, "Person" needs help and it is rational to seek it, but it could be costly to seek it from his supervisor. "Other" sees it as rational to give the needed help, because he believes his shared expertise is appreciated and is bound to come to the attention of the supervisor. For the supervisor it is rational to ignore his own rule, because "Other" is able to give adequate help to Person, thus saving supervisor's time for other tasks. Thus, the exchange is rational; it involves help in exchange for respect and approval.

Elements of these theories can be traced back to John Stuart Mill and Jeremy Bentham in the nineteenth century, as well as several thinkers in the second half of the twentieth century. In this chapter we will begin with the work of James Coleman, who speaks to both rational choice and exchange. Then we will bring in Mancur Olson, Peter Blau, George Homans, and others under the heading of "Other Theorists."

James S. Coleman, 1926–1995

James Coleman studied with Paul Lazarsfeld and Robert K. Merton at Columbia University and received his PhD in 1955. He taught at the University of Chicago for three years and then founded the Department of Social Relations at Johns Hopkins, where he served until 1973. At that time he returned to the University of Chicago, where he spent his last 22 years as University Professor. His scholarly career, noted *Footnotes*,[1]

> was devoted to the creation and utilization of social science methodology and theory to study social phenomena and to illuminate major issues in public policy. His main contributions lay in sociological theory—including the analysis of social change, collective action, and rational choice— mathematical sociology, the sociology of education, and public policy. Exceptional ability, fertile imagination, and the courage to go against received opinion and to bear sometimes vicious attacks marked his distinguished career. ("Jim Coleman," 1995:1)

The variety of Coleman's interests is seen in his major publications: *Union Democracy* in 1956 (with S. M. Lipset and Martin Trow), *The Adolescent Society* (1961), *Introduction to Mathematical Sociology* (1964), *Power and the Structure of Society* (1974), *Individual Interests and Collective Action* (1986), and his magnum opus, *Foundations of Social Theory* (1990), which is the focus of this chapter.

---

[1]*Footnotes* is a journal of the American Sociological Association that discusses sociology meetings, issues within the discipline, and from time to time obituaries of important sociologists.

The *Foundations* book brings together many of Coleman's earlier themes in a single volume. It begins with 530 pages on rational choice and exchange theories, followed by 130 pages on modern society and social policy implications, and then closes with a 275-page application of mathematical models to the theory presented in the first 500-plus pages.

Coleman's Central Theory and Methods

Throughout his career, Coleman was interested in both theory and methods. We will begin this section with his theory, and will close with a few words on his methods.

Rational Choice and Exchange   Theory is best, maintained Coleman, when it does *not* stay at the system level, as Emile Durkheim's theory does. "An explanation based on internal analysis of system behavior in terms of actions and orientations of lower-level units is likely to be more stable and general than an explanation which remains at the system level" (Coleman, 1990:3). The "lower-level units" to which he refers are individual actors, which are Coleman's primary focus of attention. In addition, there are what he calls "corporate actors," involving multiple individuals or groups, an example being a modern corporation (Coleman, 1990:421f).

Coleman, then, begins at the individual level, focusing on purposive action based on reasons for it. "When I am asked why I did something, a possible response is 'I had my reasons.' The commonsense meaning of this is that I had an intended goal, and I perceived my behavior or action as contributing to that goal in specific and knowable ways" (Coleman, 1990:13).

A frequent criticism of such a purposive view, Coleman admits, is that it is explicitly teleological, meaning that the end is used to explain the action-based means. This view considers individuals as purposive, responsible, rational actors. A part of the criticism is that individuals often act irrationally, even self-destructively. In response, Coleman asserts that social scientists have as their purpose an

> understanding of social organization that is derivative from actions of
> individuals and since understanding an individual's actions ordinarily
> means seeing the reasons behind the action, then the theoretical aim of
> social science must be to conceive of that action in a way that makes it
> rational from the point of view of the actor. (1990:18)

In other words, a rationality assumption on the part of an actor is necessary in order to understand (explain) the behavior. While Vilfredo Pareto would argue with this assumption, viewing reasons as excuses or rationalizations, we will begin by accepting Coleman's premise in order to understand his theory.

Very early on, Coleman introduced the concept of **exchange** into his theory of rational behavior. An important aspect of rationality involves the use of resources, or those elements that actors have available to use in exchange. System is based on interdependence, and interdependence is based on these two factors—rationality and exchange. "It is this structure, together with the fact that the actors are purposive, each having the goal of maximizing the realization of his interests, that gives the interdependence, or systemic character, to their actions" (1990:29). Coleman added, "Social relations between two persons are, of course, the building blocks of social organization" (1990:43).

Coleman was cognizant of the kinds of criticisms to which he was open. His first assumption, he admitted, is a rational actor who is purely self-interested and unconstrained by societal norms or rules. This, he believed, is a necessary beginning point, so that the genesis and maintenance of norms could be introduced later, along with moral codes and identification with collectives, as problematics rather than as givens. In the same way, corporate actors would be introduced only after individual actors were clearly understood.

What, then, are the various aspects of rational action on the part of individuals? Coleman began with types of resources. These include (1) resources that affect other actors; (2) personal attributes, such as skills and looks, valued by others; (3) and resources, such as money, that can be used in direct exchange (1990:33). Thus, even though exchange theory derives from economics, resources include much more than material goods, or money and property.

Three forms of **capital** (or accumulated resources) are **physical, human**, and **social**. "Physical capital is wholly tangible, being embodied in observable material form; human capital is less tangible, being embodied in the skills and knowledge acquired by an individual; social capital is even less tangible, for it is embodied in the *relations* among persons" (Coleman, 1990:304). Social capital includes trust and trustworthiness, which enable a group to accomplish much more than if they are lacking. Trust, as we have said before, is a resource that can depreciate over time if it is not maintained and renewed.

Another aspect of the behavior of rational actors involves rights to act. These rights include control over resources and **authority**, or the granting by others of those rights. The rights due to authority may be based on delegation or permission (such as when one parent grants the other the right to instruct and discipline their children), on normative legitimation (such as traditional authority because one is in the "royal line"), and even on force (as when slavery is treated as an acceptable part of a society's structure).

Legitimation raises an important distinction between **principal** and **agent**, or controller and controlled. Though not always based on legitimate authority or the right to act, there are in society some who control the exchange process and others who are "under control." Recalling Marx's discussion, the working class under capitalism are seen as exchanging their labor for an income, but without sufficient control to keep the capitalists from extracting surplus labor value. The rationality of their behavior is based on the premise that such controlled labor is preferable to no job at all. Of course, Marx would argue that rational behavior would lead them to overthrow the system that controls and exploits them.[2]

Recalling Luhmann's and Giddens's discussions (Chapter 3), Coleman argues that another important aspect of rationality and exchange involves trust.

---

[2]Mancur Olson discusses Marx's view from a rational choice perspective; we will look at this analysis under "Other Theorists."

Trust is necessary when there is time asymmetry in an exchange. In the lower classes, notes Coleman, help is often given when another person is in need, with no expected time for "returning the favor." The giver trusts the receiver of help to reciprocate if or when the need arises; thus, this trust is based on *potential* reciprocity, not on a known condition or time of its expression. Trust, of course, can be lost as well as gained, as when an individual no longer trusts his or her spouse, because of deviant or untrustworthy behavior.

After introducing resources, rights, and trust to his rational/exchange theory, Coleman introduces **norms**—behavioral prescriptions and proscriptions. "Social norms . . . specify what actions are regarded by a set of persons as proper or correct, or improper or incorrect" (rational or irrational).

> They are purposively generated, in that those persons who initiate or help maintain a norm see themselves as benefiting from its being observed or harmed by its being violated. Norms are ordinarily enforced by sanctions which are either rewards for carrying out those actions regarded as correct or punishments for carrying out those actions regarded as incorrect. (Coleman, 1990:242)

Norms may be **conjoint** or **disjoint**. Conjoint norms are those accepted by and beneficial to everyone; disjoint norms are those that are rewarding to or practiced by some people (or groups of people) and punishing to or ignored by others. For example, the gender "double standard" is a disjoint norm that says women must restrict sexual activity while men are granted sexual freedom. Disjointness may also be seen in the old idea that a man may seek to engage in sexual behavior with a woman, while looking for a long-term relationship with a woman who has not so engaged. Furthermore, those with power or in control may have the freedom to violate a norm. During wartime, for example, money may make it possible for some to hoard scarce goods, even though there is a norm that says "Don't hoard."

Coleman readily admits that a theory grounded in rational (purposive) choice has difficulty dealing with the process whereby norms develop and become internalized. However, he maintains that this problem is no more difficult than that of the functionalist who tries to explain norms as based on societal purposes at the level of the social system (1990:292). In Coleman's theory, an important aspect of the development of norms involves coping with the limited resources of an environment (such as what is considered edible or inedible), while their internalization has to do with socialization, or the passing along of norms from one generation to the next.

Coleman summarizes his rational/exchange theory up to this point as follows:

> Actors are seen as beginning with resources over which they have some (possibly total) control and in which they have interests. Social interdependence and systemic functioning arise from the fact that actors have interests in events that are fully or partially under the control of other actors. The result of the various kinds of exchanges and unilateral transfers of control that actors engage in to achieve their interests is . . . the formation of social relationships having some persistence over time. Authority relations,

relations of trust, and consensual allocations of rights which establish norms are the principal ones that have been examined here. (1990:300)

To this point, Coleman's theory has focused on individual actors and their interrelations. However, the introduction of norms begins the transition to the supra-individual level. Norms, after all, may be enforced collectively, rather than by one individual or another. The official expression of norms Coleman calls a **constitution**—in effect, the formal expression of a society's rationality. Although this concept is not restricted to what we usually think of as a constitution, Coleman uses the common meaning to illustrate it: "The U.S., Polish, and French constitutions were perhaps the first constitutions of nation-states that had as an ideological base a social contract among equal citizens" (1990:327).[3]

So as not to be limited to individual behaviors, Coleman moves from the constitution to the **corporate actor.** A corporate actor includes more than one individual, often a principal and agent, but is more than simply multiple individuals. It is a group actor, or actors, exemplified by a corporation's owning another corporation or subsidiary. Here Coleman comes close to reifying the group level, a difficulty that he finds in Durkheim. But he tries to distinguish his view from Durkheim's by speaking of both corporate rationality and corporate authority at the level of organization—be the organization a church, corporation, or nation-state. There is, furthermore, a supra-individual control and exchange of resources, with the corporate actor mirroring the individual actor.

Coleman closes out his theoretical development with a discussion of the **self.** The self-conscious actor is able to think introspectively and decide upon rational action; such an actor may be a person or may be corporate. An important distinction is made here between subjective and objective interests. Does the self always understand what is in her or his best interest? Those in control often act as if the answer is no. After all, an outside source, such as the state, may intervene in private affairs, or on behalf of a weaker party to an interaction—the excuse being that "it is for your own good" (Coleman, 1990: 512).

This completes Coleman's rational/exchange perspective, but leaves him raising once again (as the reader might) the issue of deviations from rationality. Such deviations, he claims,

> do not substantially affect the theory developed here. To put it another way, my implicit assumption is that the theoretical predictions made here will be substantially the same whether the actors act precisely according to rationality as commonly conceived or deviate in the ways that have been observed. (1990:506)

Once again, Coleman briefly summarizes both his theory and its difficulties:

> The theory of rational action or purposive action is a theory of instrumental rationality, *given* a set of goals or ends or utilities. If a theory of internal change of actors is to be justifiable or consistent with the basic principle of

---

[3]It is perhaps noteworthy that the Code of Hammurabi is a variety of constitution that can be traced back to the Mesopotamian River basin more than four millennia ago.

action, it must do what appears to be impossible: to account for *changes* in utilities (or goals) on the basis of the principle of *maximization* of utility. (1990: 516)

Coleman later describes a perfect social system as one in which actors are rational

and in which there is no structure to impede any actor's use of resources at any point in the system. In economists' terms there are no transaction costs. Free rider problems do not exist, for actors are able to use their resources to induce others with like interests to contribute to the common good. (1990:719)

The "free rider" concept will be explained in the next section; other elements of Coleman's theory, and its relation to other theorists, will be introduced in the "Other Theories" section.

Methods In a book of readings on *Rational Choice Theory* (Abell, 1991), it is argued that this is the best theory from which to develop systematic deductive models. A number of researchers have developed testable propositions and used sophisticated statistical techniques to study relative deprivation, free ridership, collective action, the prisoner's dilemma, and so on (Kosaka, Marwell and Ames, Oliver and Marwell, Heckathorn, in Abell, 1991:291–304, 329–380).

Coleman himself, as noted earlier, devoted many pages of his book to carrying out such analyses. Although his may not be the only operationalizable theory in this volume, that is certainly one of its goals and major strengths.

Nature of Humans, Society, and Change

James Coleman was a socially active social scientist who believed the world could be changed for the better by those who understood it. He did not believe in a perfectible human nature, nor in a perfectly rational world. He was, however, a humanist in the classic sense of the term. He was engaged, as a social scientist, with the issues of his day.

Like most of the great sociologists of the nineteenth and early twentieth centuries, Coleman's commitment to his field was moral. For him, social science could not be justified merely as an intellectual exercise. Rather, it had to prove its worth by showing policy-makers how to design legislation and institutions that would be beneficial to society. ("Jim Coleman," 1995:8)

Coleman's social concern was evident in what came to be known as the "Coleman Report," which indicated that lower-class black children in the United States benefited from attending integrated schools. This finding was one of the primary bases for busing to achieve school desegregation, and was not an altogether popular conclusion.

Coleman also spoke of the social responsibility of corporate actors. He noted that major stockholders are likely to be more socially responsible, because they carry out and receive credit for civic or philanthropic activities while small stockholders do not. The small stockholder is likely to be a **"free rider,"** sharing in the benefits of corporate policies and responsibility without contributing to them in any direct way (1990:575).[4]

Change, to Coleman, is both factual and prescriptive. Much of his book speaks of changes that have already occurred in the social world. Primordial structures, such as the family and community, have given way to purposive structures, such as bureaucratic organizations. "The constructed social environment," Coleman noted, "consisting of purposive corporate actors and their agents, constitutes a large part of the social environment of most persons in modern societies" (1990:614). It is because of the dominance of such organizations, including multinational corporations, that Coleman believed a theory of rational exchange to be appropriate for today's world.

Like Max Weber, Coleman was concerned about the effect of purposive organizations on human life. Such organizations can handle those functions that can be bought and sold, but not those that cannot. The result is that relationships, even child rearing, are undermined by the organized society. But why cannot nation-state legislation simply create structures to replace the primordial or traditional ones that have been lost? Coleman argued that the multinational organization of corporate life is even beginning to make nation-states irrelevant, and their legislatures ineffectual.

What, then, were Coleman's prescriptions for change? Sounding somewhat like Immanuel Wallerstein, he argued that prescriptions must come from applied research and theory. The new social science must be dedicated to the task of replacing what has been lost, and improving what remains. Coleman believed that the beginning point is an understanding of the rational and exchange character of human relationships as they exist today (Coleman, 1990:664).

Class, Gender, and Race

Although rational choice theory can be applied to class, gender, and race, Coleman did not do so; the index at the back of his 993-page tome includes none of them. However, it is possible from some of his earlier writing to conclude that he was concerned about racial inequalities, though less about the position of women in society. Some feminist critics have argued that his theory is inadequate to handle gender issues. Later we will note how others have used the exchange perspective in family relations.

Other Theories and Theorists

Although Coleman's book has been the focus of our introduction to both rational choice and exchange, we will now back up to the 1960s and add other insights on these two theories. On rational choice theory, we will refer to Mancur

---

[4]The "free rider" idea is sometimes expressed in everyday speech as just being "along for the ride," meaning that one is going somewhere without doing anything to further the trip. See Marwell and Ames (1981).

Olson, Russell Hardin, and others; for exchange theory, we will use George Homans, Peter Blau, and others.

Rational Choice Theory   As already indicated, rational choice theory can be traced to the nineteenth century, and even earlier. However, we will begin with Mancur Olson and his work *The Logic of Collective Action*, published in 1965.

Rational behavior, according to Olson, is not necessarily selfish or unselfish. Rational simply means that "objectives, whether selfish or unselfish, should be pursued by means that are efficient and effective for achieving" them (1965:65). As an example of rationality, Olson notes that it is rational for union members to be in favor of attendance at union meetings, while not attending themselves. This is because a large turnout is helpful in achieving group goals, but attendance by any one member of a large organization has little effect on outcomes (1965:86–87).

Olson also pointed out exceptions to rational behavior. Situations in which behavior cannot be explained by rational choice include (1) acting on the basis of an emotional response or ideological commitment, as exemplified by cult members who believe in the cataclysmic end of the world,[5] and (2) working for an obviously "lost cause," which may require a psychological instead of an economic/rational explanation (1965:12, 161).

The notion of working for a lost cause brings us back to Olson's comments on whether or not Marx was a rational choice theorist. "Marx," noted Olson, "sees self-interested individuals and self-interested classes acting to achieve their interests." Many critics have attacked Marx for emphasizing self-interest and rationality too much. According to Olson, however,

> It is *not* in fact true that the absence of the kind of class conflict Marx expected shows that Marx overestimated the strength of rational behavior. On the contrary, the absence of the sort of class action Marx predicted is due in part to the predominance of rational utilitarian behavior. *For class-oriented action will not occur if the individuals that make up a class act rationally.* (1965:105)

Instead, Olson argued, it is rational for people to focus on their own individual interests, because they will benefit from any class action whether or not they participate, and it is not rational to risk life or property for a struggle in which one's individual contribution may have little effect, or even a negative personal outcome. Marx, then, is a rational choice theorist because he expects the class revolution to be successful—although those who believe it to be impossible or personally costly see him as irrational.

Russell Hardin, in his 1982 book on *Collective Action*, agrees with Coleman and Olson that not all behavior can be explained by a theory of rational choice. Extra-rational motivations may include moral sentiments, such as those governing the environmental or civil rights movements (Hardin, 1982:104, 108). A possible response to this view is that such involvements may be totally rational

---

[5]Of course, although they seem out of touch with reality, it is always possible that at some point they will be right (rational) and the rest of us will be wrong.

if we believe it is important to attempt to shape world historical events. In addition, it is rational to work for the environment if we believe that lack of such a concern will eventually lead to the irrational destruction of our world; and it is rational to be morally committed to civil rights if we believe that the world of race and ethnic relations must change or else experience some sort of cataclysm.

Hardin's book adds two more important qualifications to Coleman's version of rational choice theory. First, it is important to remember that choice is not static; it is a dynamic process. Some choices take time, and the conditions governing them change. For example, while one is deciding on the purchase of a home, an illness may occur that makes it irrational to buy at that time, or makes it rational to buy something smaller. Also, one choice often leads to another, so that rationality requires thinking ahead to multiple or serial decisions (Hardin, 1982:13).

Second, bringing exchange theory into his discussion of rational choice, Hardin notes that rational choices are often asymmetrical. The asymmetry of costs and benefits from a collective good may be such as to cause two persons to make rational but opposing choices (Hardin, 1982:67–68). For example, good schools are a collective good that is more beneficial to a family with young children than to an elderly couple. Or a good music program in school may be seen as much more beneficial by one set of parents than by another. Thus, process and asymmetry are important additions to Coleman's theory.

Exchange Theory   To add to Coleman's discussion of exchange, we must go back to the 1960s and 1970s to the insights of theorists such as George Casper Homans, John Thibaut and Harold Kelley, and Peter Blau.

For Coleman, exchange is a subprinciple of rational choice: it is rational to seek profit and avoid cost. Earlier, however, Homans (1961) laid out a more complete exchange theory intended to provide the groundwork for understanding all of social behavior. His theory "envisages social *behavior* as an exchange of activity, tangible or intangible, and more or less rewarding or costly, between at least two persons" (1961:13).

Homans's theory is stated in terms of testable propositions.[6] One such proposition is "For all actions taken by persons, the more often a particular action of a person is rewarded, the more likely the person is to perform that action" (Homans, 2d ed., 1974:16). George Ritzer calls this Homans's "success" proposition, because reward results in repetition. A second proposition states that a stimulus followed by a behavior that is rewarded will have the same result when it (the stimulus) occurs again (Homans, 1961:23). These two propositions describe the repetition effect of behavior rewarded by others, and the effect of a stimulus followed by a behavior rewarded by others.

A third proposition states that if an individual sees an action as personally rewarding (rather than rewarded by others), it will be repeated (Homans, 1974:25). However, Homans qualified this with a fourth proposition, the effect of satiation: "The more often in the recent past a person has received a particular reward, the

---

[6]George Ritzer (1983:247–250) lists and discusses Homans's propositions in his chapter on exchange theory.

less valuable any further unit of that reward becomes for him [or her]" (1961:29). In other words, behavior that is rewarding, either to oneself or to others, is repeated—but only up to a point. Finally, when behavior does not receive the expected reward, or is punished unexpectedly, the response is anger—and the aggressor will find such aggression rewarding (1961:37).

While Homans's theory of profits or benefits and losses or costs was born in economics, he did not restrict it to material exchanges. He argued that "the principles of economics are perfectly reconcilable with those of elementary social behavior, once the special conditions in which each applies are taken into account. Both deal with the exchange of rewarding goods," with goods being defined broadly (1961:68). He defined "psychic *profit* as reward less cost" and argued that "no exchange continues unless both parties are making a profit" (1961:61). Although mutual profit is important to the continuation of interaction, however, each individual is primarily concerned about his or her own profit.

Homans briefly introduced rationality to his theory of exchange. It is not a hedonistic theory, Homans claimed. "So long as men's values are altruistic, they can take a profit in altruism too. Some of the greatest profiteers we know are altruists" (1961:79). It is, after all, rational to seek profit and minimize cost, even if the profit is psychic. Homans, whose aim was explanation, left rationality to a simple assumption: "All we impute to them in the way of rationality is that they know enough to come in out of the rain unless they enjoy getting wet" (1961:82). Thus, for Coleman, rationality is the primary explanatory principle, with exchange as a subelement; for Homans, explanation is based on principles of exchange, with rationality as a simple assumption.

Two years before Homans published his *Social Behavior*, Thibaut and Kelley (1959) presented a very similar theory of social exchange. A key factor in their theoretical propositions neatly ties together rational choice and exchange. They called it the "comparison level for alternatives" and explained it thus: A choice involves more than one alternative. When it involves continuing or leaving a relationship, the question is whether there is sufficient profit to continue. It is, after all, rational to maximize benefit in the choices one makes and in the relationships one has.[7]

Unlike Coleman, neither Homans nor Thibaut and Kelley spoke of corporate actors, focusing instead on what they considered to be the elementary (or individual) level of explanation. Peter Blau (1964) came much closer to Coleman's position, recognizing the possibility of organizational as well as individual exchanges. One commentator offers the following explanation of Blau's four-stage transition leading from the individual to social structure to change:

1. Personal exchange transactions between people give rise to . . .

2. Differentiation of status and power, which leads to . . .

3. Legitimation and organization, which sow the seeds of . . .

4. Opposition and change.

---

[7]Thibaut and Kelley believed that Homans had drawn much of his argument from their work. This issue was never resolved.

However, because large groups within a social structure involve persons who may never interact with one another, their connection is by means of shared norms and shared values, rather than direct exchange (Ritzer, 1983:252, 254).

One difference between Coleman and Blau is the same as that between Coleman and Homans: Coleman's focus is on rational choice, with exchange as a secondary issue; Blau's focus is on exchange.

> Not all human behavior is guided by considerations of exchange, though much of it is, more than we usually think. Two conditions must be met for behavior to lead to social exchange. It must be oriented toward ends that can only be achieved through interaction with other persons, and it must seek to adopt means to further the achievement of these ends. . . . In brief, social exchange may reflect any behavior oriented to socially mediated goals. (Blau, 1964:5)

For Blau, exchange theory is neither a matter of equal gain (recall Hardin) nor a "zero-sum game," in which the gains of some equal the losses of others. Individuals associate with one another, according to Blau, "because they all profit from their association. But they do not necessarily all profit equally, and even if there are no direct costs to participants, there are often indirect costs borne by those excluded from the association" (1964:15), as, for example, when two members of a group pair up, to the exclusion of other potential suitors.

How does trust fit into Blau's theory of exchange? Blau used "trust" in a somewhat different way from Coleman. To Coleman, you will recall, trust is ordinarily a matter of differential timing: one person benefits now while the other trusts that she or he will (or may) benefit later. To Blau, **trust** accrues from long-term or stable obligations: "Since trust is essential for stable social relations, and since exchange obligations promote trust, special mechanisms exist to perpetuate obligations and thus strengthen bonds of indebtedness and trust" (1964:99). Trust of the sort described by Blau is, of course, crucial to family—especially marital—relationships.

Power enters into Blau's exchange theory in the following way: Suppose, he says, a person is frequently in need of services from an associate to whom he or she has nothing to offer in return. What are the alternatives?

> First, he may force the other to give him help. Second, he may obtain the help he needs from another source. Third, he may find ways to get along without such help. If he is unable or unwilling to choose any of these alternatives, however, there is only one other course of action left for him; he must subordinate himself to the other and comply with his wishes, thereby rewarding the other with power over himself as an inducement for furnishing the needed help. (1964: 22)

In other words, a result of unequal exchange is the power of one individual over another. From the standpoint of the benefactor, "overwhelming others with benefactions serves to achieve superiority over them" (1964:111). And, as Coleman stated, legitimated power is defined as authority.

One of Blau's major contributions to exchange theory was his presentation of certain dilemmas, as in the following example: What does one have to do, asked Blau, to be incorporated into a group? An individual's endeavors to impress the rest of the group with his outstanding qualities in order to prove himself attractive to them and gain their social acceptance simultaneously poses a status threat for these others that tends to antagonize them. The very outstanding qualities that make an individual differentially attractive as an associate also raise fears of dependence. (1964:318)

Another exchange dilemma noted by Blau has to do with incompatible goal states. Actions designed to attain one goal may impede the accomplishment of a second goal. Or one requirement for accomplishing a goal may interfere with another requirement for achieving the same objective or goal. An example would be a love relationship between two professionals, such as academicians, that may be extremely rewarding to them, but may make it difficult for them to pursue their individually desired professional goals of obtaining tenured positions.

Other Issues   Before we turn to critiques and conclusions, let us bring rational choice and exchange to bear on two additional issues: gender and family, and revolution.

Although Coleman did not discuss gender and family as an exchange issue, Ivan Nye and others have applied exchange theory to family relationships, showing how such resource exchanges as good looks for money or status for race occur. Such analyses have often been based on traditional gender-role stereotypes, such as the male breadwinner/female homemaker distinction.

Coleman wrote at length about revolutions, as did Blau before him. In his chapter on "Revoking Authority," Coleman began with a question: Does revolution occur when conditions are getting worse? His answer was that impoverishment leads to passivity and apathy, not revolution. Instead, revolts against nations or institutions occur when things are getting better, and when control is being relaxed. In the nineteenth century this phenomenon had been noted by Alexis de Tocqueville:

> It is not always when things are going from bad to worse that revolution breaks out. On the contrary, it more often happens that, when a people which has put up with an oppressive rule over a long period without protest suddenly finds the government releasing its pressure, it takes up arms against it. (1860:176–177)

Although this may seem irrational, Coleman maintained that it could be explained by rational choice theory. He first introduced the frustration theory of revolution (discussed briefly in Chapter 6). This theory, noted Coleman, begins with the premise that frustration results when reality falls short of expectations. But when things are in fact getting better, expectations rise even more rapidly than objective conditions. This explanation is highly individualistic, and therefore in all probability incomplete, though it is, of course, individuals who become frustrated (Coleman, 1990:473, 479).

Thus, rising expectations and accompanying frustration are, according to Coleman, inadequate for explaining revolutions. Power theories, by contrast, state that those opposed to a regime see small changes (improvements) made by an administration as an indication that they (the opposition) are winning. This gives them a sense of power, and they double their efforts. In addition, they may take this opportunity to mobilize the uncommitted, who may—if made aware—see the advantage of joining the revolution.

But what is rational about the choice to revolt? Coleman put it this way:

> If revolutionary activity and support for the revolutionary activity of others are regarded as rational actions, it becomes evident that such activity will be more likely to occur as those who have an interest in seeing the authority system replaced come to have a belief that they will succeed. (1990:480)

Thus, power theory is generally compatible with Coleman's position. Coleman noted that revolutionary activity ordinarily involves but a small portion of a population, with the majority simply being bystanders, going about their daily lives.

In developing his theory, Coleman asked what the reasons are for the revolutionary involvement of any given individual. Speaking in exchange terms, he saw three sets of benefits. First, there are the objective benefits expected if the regime changes. These, of course, may be independent of an individual's commitment; that is, there will be "free riders." The second set of benefits depends on both involvement and success. Since material benefits are in scarce supply, they will go primarily to those whose participation was important to the revolution's success. These Mancur Olson (1965) called "selective incentives." The third type of benefits results simply from participation, regardless of the revolution's success or failure. Participation benefits are of two kinds: benefits or satisfactions from being involved with one's friends, particularly in the service of an ideology to which all are committed; and the internal reward that comes from "doing the right thing," from trying to make one's society (or world) a better place (Coleman, 1990:493–494). The pursuit of such benefits was, to Coleman, rational.

Blau's chapter on "Opposition" raises some of the same issues regarding revolutions from his exchange perspective. Isolated victims of oppression are helpless, even passive in terms of action. However, as outrage and hostility are communicated to others, a social consensus emerges that legitimates the feelings and absolves the individual of guilt feelings for nonnormative attitudes. At this point a revolutionary ideology may be adopted, which turns consensual outrage into a noble cause. And pursuit of such a cause is rewarding enough that the committed are willing to pay the costs of risky action. Unlike Coleman, however, Blau emphasizes relative rather than absolute deprivation—on the part of the very poor, who feel left out of their society's benefits, and of the lower middle class, who see their superiority over the workers being threatened by labor movements (Blau, 1964:251). Thus, for Blau, revolts are a matter of— to use Thibaut and Kelley's term—the comparison level of alternatives.

Applications Coleman was greatly concerned with the application of theory to social life. The applied tradition goes back at least to Jean-Jacques Rousseau in eighteenth-century France, who believed that human understanding could be brought to bear on society's ills and inadequacies. If, wrote Coleman,

> there is no effect of social research or social theory on society's functioning, then sociologists must seriously question their purpose. If the examination

shows that there are effects, whether or not they bias functioning, then guidance is provided for optimal institutionalization of applied social research. (1990:649)

Coleman did see a danger that application conceived too narrowly might become merely a service to the powerful, which today means large corporate actors. But conceived

more broadly, this new social science becomes science that extends its knowledge to the understanding of how power comes to be distributed and accumulated in society, and to the understanding of how natural persons can best satisfy their interests in a social system populated with large corporate actors. (1990:651)

Critique and Conclusions

We must summarize and critique not only Coleman's ideas, but those of the other theorists, such as Homans and Blau, who have helped us understand rational choice and exchange.

Peter Abell, in introducing his book *Rational Choice Theory* (1991), stated his belief that this theoretical position is based on

the almost complete failure of the established theoretical traditions—be they marxist or non-marxist, functionalist or non-functionalist, interactionist or non-interactionist, structuralist or non-structuralist—to provide a framework for the systematic deductive modeling of that complex realm called "social reality." (Abell, 1991:ix)

Like Abell, Coleman and Blau are "true believers." However, Coleman and Blau pointed out the limitations of rational choice and exchange theory as well—rather than waiting for their critics to do so. Coleman stated that for "a number of reasons, this approach is not completely satisfactory. It does not deal well with socialization, internalization," or changes in the springs of action. And it does not explain deviations from rationality that result from being out of touch with reality, weakness of will, preference reversals, force, or fear. In addition, he admitted that his attempts to deal with corporate actors fell short of success.

From one perspective a corporate actor is a system of action containing actors, resources, and events, and leading to outcomes. But considered as an actor with a utility function, this same system is . . . an unanalyzed entity. Although the actions of a corporate actor would seem to correspond to outcomes of indivisible events in a system of action, these two perspectives have not been made consistent. In other words, there has not been made explicit any means of mapping between event outcomes in a system of action and utility functions . . . for that system of action considered as a corporate actor. (Coleman, 1990:932)

Thus, Coleman admitted that it was difficult to speak of a corporate actor without reifying the system level, which he saw as a problem with Durkheim, and which he sought to avoid doing in his own theory.

Blau also discussed these limitations, or aspects of social life that exchange theory had difficulty explaining. In addition, he noted the opposite problem. If all behavior, whether economic, interpersonal, altruistic, or anonymous, can be explained post hoc in terms of individual profit or gain, has anything actually been explained? As Blau put it, it is "tempting to consider all social conduct in terms of exchange, but this would deprive the concept of its distinctive meaning. People do things for fear of other men or for fear of God or for fear of their conscience, and nothing is gained by trying to force such action into a conceptual framework of exchange" (1964:89).

While Coleman and Blau both admitted the problems with rational choice and exchange theories, a most interesting debate between Talcott Parsons and Homans also contributes to this discussion.

Parsons versus Homans   The functionalist Parsons and the exchange theorist Homans had an ongoing debate when they were colleagues at Harvard. Parsons maintained that "Homans is under obligation to show how his principles can account for the principal structural features of large scale social systems" (1964:216). According to Ritzer (1983:251), Parsons "concluded that even if Homans were to try to do this, he would inevitably fail, because social facts are variables capable of explaining, and being explained, without reference to Homans's psychological principles."

Homans, on the other hand, argued that Parsons-type social facts are not explanatory. To theorists such as Durkheim and Parsons, Homans issued the following challenge:

> Let them therefore specify what properties of social behavior they consider to be emergent and show, by constructing the appropriate deductive systems, how they propose to explain them without making use of psychological propositions. I guarantee to show either that the explanations fail to explain or that they in fact use psychological propositions, in however disguised a form. (Homans, 1971:376)

In short, then, Homans would say that Parsons does not explain structure at the societal level, and Parsons would say that Homans does not explain structure at the psychological (or economic) level (Ritzer, 1983:252). Or, we might say, Homans believes that Parsons has explained nothing, and Parsons would say that Homans explains little of sociological importance.

Blau According to Ritzer   What of Blau and Coleman, who seek to use rational choice and exchange to explain not only individual behaviors, but corporate or group actors as well? Ritzer offers the following criticism of Blau:

> Although Blau argued that he was simply extending exchange theory to the societal level, in so doing he twisted exchange theory beyond recognition. He was even forced to admit that processes at the societal level are fundamentally different from those at the individual level. In his effort to extend exchange theory, Blau managed only to transform it into another theory congruent with the social facts paradigm. Blau seemed to recognize that exchange theory is primarily concerned with face-to-face relations. (Ritzer, 1983:256)

Although Blau may have recognized this limitation, he continued to apply exchange theory to the group level.

Coleman According to Neil Smelser   Neil Smelser is a functionalist in the mold of Parsons. His review of Coleman's book, therefore, parallels Parsons's response to Homans. Smelser states at the outset that Coleman's magnum opus "is the most ambitious effort ever to build a general sociology on the basis of the individualistic, utilitarian, rational-actor, voluntarist assumptions enunciated in classical economics and democratic theory" (Smelser, 1990:778). Coleman, notes Smelser, moved between the micro and macro levels, never simply treating the latter by aggregating individuals. Coleman himself, Smelser reminds us, made very explicit which theories he did *not* prefer: (1) those based on external forces, such as technology; (2) those explaining change by means of cultural values; (3) functionalism; (4) normative, or oversocialized, explanations; and (5) structural explanations, such as Weber's treatment of bureaucracy.

Coleman, says Smelser, recognized that irrational behaviors occur, but did little of theoretical value with that recognition. Coleman explained away much irrationality: "Much of what is ordinarily described as nonrational or irrational is merely so because the observers have not discovered the point of view of the actor, from which the action *is* rational" (Coleman, 1990:18). According to Smelser, once we enter Coleman's realm of individual self-interpretation, we have opened the door to the problem of unique self-understanding and non-generalizability (Smelser, 1990:780). To this we might add that we also enter Pareto's trap, wherein the individual is assumed to rationalize and justify her or his motives and behaviors.

Smelser then speaks as a functionalist (like Parsons): Perhaps the most important problem with rational choice theories is that they tend to forget "that the free economic agent and the free citizen are themselves in, and products of, a specific complex of cultural values and institutions" (1990:781). Smelser does admit that ours is in fact the kind of quasi-rationalized society about which Coleman is theorizing. While Smelser also criticizes many of Coleman's historical references and his applied concerns, it is the theory itself with which we are concerned.

Final Thoughts

As we saw in Chapter 3, Stepjan Mestrovic criticized Anthony Giddens for over-emphasizing human agency. Many humans do not see themselves as effective agents, because they are not; they are more likely to feel powerless. Here we are left with the same sort of dilemma. Just how rational are humans? And how much of modern life do Coleman's rational choice and exchange perspectives actually explain? Harrison Whyte, in the same symposium where Smelser's review is found, concludes with a most important point: Rational choice, in

> economics or political science or in Coleman's work, is a sensible and
> rational basis for model building, but only where the intervening constructs
> of preference and goal can be known and are stable—which is to say, where
> little change and turbulence is going on, little institutional change or shift
> in style. In short, rational choice will serve well where there is not much to

predict, and even then only perhaps in a society where goal-directed activity is part of socialization. (Whyte, 1990:788)

Coleman's final response to all these criticisms is easy to predict. Goal-directed activity *is* a large part of socialization today, as we are taught how to live purposefully in a rationally organized world. Besides, Coleman would say, Whyte is wrong to think that rational choice and exchange theory cannot handle change and turbulence. My book, Coleman might say, shows how to explain revolutions, collective behavior (mobs, panics, rumors, and the like), and other apparent turbulence and change. Rationality, agency, beneficial choices or not—this is one of the theoretical positions whose advocates and critics are extremely clear-cut in their opposing presuppositions and arguments.

References

Abell, Peter. 1991. *Rational Choice Theory*. Aldershot, England: Edward Elgar.

Blau, Peter. 1964. *Exchange and Power in Social Life*. New York: John Wiley.

Coleman, James S. 1961. *The Adolescent Society: The Social Life of the Teenager and Its Impact on Education*. Westport, CT: Greenwood Press.

———. 1964. *Introduction to Mathematical Sociology*. New York: Free Press of Glencoe.

———. 1974. *Power and the Structure of Society*. New York: Norton.

———. 1986. *Individual Interests and Collective Action: Selected Essays*. Cambridge: Cambridge University Press.

———. 1990. *Foundations of Social Theory*. Cambridge, MA: Belknap Press.

Dawes, Robyn M. 1988. *Rational Choice in an Uncertain World*. San Diego: Harcourt Brace Jovanovich.

Hardin, Russell. 1982. *Collective Action*. Baltimore: Johns Hopkins University Press.

Homans, George Casper. 1961/1974. *Social Behavior: Its Elementary Forms*. New York: Harcourt, Brace & World.

———. 1971. "Commentary." In Herman Turk and Richard Simpson (Eds.), *Institutions and Social Exchange* (pp. 363–376). Indianapolis: Bobbs-Merrill.

"Jim Coleman Leaves Legacy of Excellence." 1995, May/June. *Footnotes*, pp. 1, 8.

Lipset, Seymour Martin, Martin A. Trow, and James S. Coleman. 1956. *Union Democracy: The Internal Politics of the International Typographical Union*. Glencoe, IL: Free Press.

Marwell, Gerald, and Ruth Ames. 1981. "Economists Free Ride, Does Anyone Else?" *Journal of Public Economics, 15*, 295–310.

Olson, Mancur. 1965. *The Logic of Collective Action: Public Goods and the Theory of Goods*. Cambridge, MA: Harvard University Press.

Parsons, Talcott. 1964. "Levels of Organization and the Mediation of Social Interaction." *Sociological Inquiry, 34*, 207–220.

Ritzer, George. 1983. *Contemporary Sociological Theory*. New York: Alfred A. Knopf.

Smelser, Neil J. 1990. "Can Individualism Yield a Sociology?" [Review of Coleman, *Foundations of Social Theory*]. *Contemporary Sociology, 19*, 778–783.

Thibaut, John W., and Harold H. Kelley. 1959. *The Social Psychology of Groups*. New York: John Wiley and Sons.

Tocqueville, Alexis de. 1860/1955. *The Old Regime and the French Revolution* (S. Gilbert, Trans.). Garden City, NY: Doubleday.

Whyte, Harrison C. 1990. "Control to Deny Chance, But Thereby Muffling Identity" [Review of Coleman, *Foundations of Social Theory*]. *Contemporary Sociology, 19*, 783–788.

Chapter 10

Feminist Sociological Theory
Smith and Collins

Sark Women Gain the Right to Inherit Property

After more than 400 years, women finally have gained the right to inherit property in this tiny island. After a year of meetings to allow the island's inhabitants to have their say, the 52 mainly unelected rulers of Sark . . . voted . . . to change the law governing the transfer of land. Sark, between Britain and France, is the smallest independent state in the Commonwealth, and has been described as the last bastion of feudalism in the modern world. A committee is being formed to review the whole constitution, which allows wife-beating if the husband uses a stick no thicker than his finger and does not draw blood. (*Edmonton Journal*, November 26, 1999)

The above report comes as a surprise at the end of the twentieth century in Western society. It certainly gives pause to any feminist celebration that women have "come a long way" and achieved equality, at least in the West, during the twentieth century. It is a sobering note to the optimism of the feminist movements of the 1960s.

Sociology and Feminism

In Chapter 7 we discussed the social context in which the contemporary women's movements arose. Feminist theory was a concomitant development of the movement, because both were predicated on the assumption that theory and practice must go hand in hand: "The personal is political."

For many young female sociologists, the impact of the movement was emancipating. Lillian Rubin (1994:241) recalled the impact it had on her life and work, shattering "the paradigms that until then had dominated our personal, social, and intellectual worlds." For Alice Rossi (1988:45), an awareness of gender inequity came after a "jolting experience of sex discrimination" in 1962. Rossi was fired by the principal investigator of a study that Rossi had "designed, supervised the field-work for, and was happily analyzing." She had drafted a proposal for funds from the National Science Foundation to continue the project, and when it was approved, the principal investigator "decided the study was a good thing he wished to keep to himself" (1988:45). Sheila Rowbotham (1973:24) recalled the development of her feminist consciousness resulting from her realization, in the revolutionary ferment of 1968, that the "culture which was presented as 'revolutionary' was so blatantly phallic."

A part of the excitement for many women was the realization that their contemporary issues and concerns had been central to those of the women's movements of the nineteenth and early twentieth centuries. Many young feminists found to their "astonishment" that some of the pioneers of the earlier movements, such as Dora Russell and Rebecca West, were still alive (Spender, 1983:6). Spender noted that ignoring these women and not profiting from their experiences meant that post-sixties feminists "contributed to their invisibility" and "played a role in the denial of women's existence and strength" (1983:6).

Most of the young feminist sociologists were part of a relatively privileged group of women who had access to higher education, but, as Juliet Mitchell (1971:21) remarked, it is never "extreme deprivation that produces the revolutionary." Revolutionaries (as we saw in Chapter 9) come from groups who, although not absolutely deprived, nevertheless feel deprived in the light of what they have been promised or assume that they should obtain. The 1960s and 1970s were eye-opening decades for young women activists who found that, despite their contributions to civil rights and the antiwar movement, they were still "victims of male sexism" (Bernard, 1989:24). Women found that in "groups dedicated to human liberation, they were second-class members—useful at the typewriter, in the kitchen, and in bed, but expected to leave policy making to the men" (Deckard, 1983:326).

Academic women formed a significant proportion of the 1960s feminist movements' membership in its early stages, and invariably their feminist consciousness affected their academic work and interests. At the same time, their critical approach to traditional academic theories was also intended to inform movement practice. As Eichler (1992:134) pointed out, "Women's studies courses would not have come into existence without the women's movement." The movement was also a "clear recipient of benefits" of knowledge and data compiled by academics that allowed "activists to carry on the struggle."

Feminism in the academy mounted critiques of the masculine theoretical canon in what Bernard has called the "Feminist Enlightenment" (1989:25). This "Enlightenment" revealed sexism as an "invisible paradigm" that colored all aspects of women's lives. The attempt to transform, in revolutionary ways, traditional academic theory and practice met with mixed success. In sociology, feminism has had little impact on the core theoretical perspectives (Stacy and Thorne, 1985). The reason for the "missing feminist revolution in sociology," Stacy and Thorne argued, had to do with the continuing dominance of functionalist theoretical conceptions and positivist methodology, the social organization of the discipline, and the "ghettoization of feminist insights" (1985:306). Feminism seems to have had more impact in anthropology, history, and literature because these fields have strong interpretive traditions, in contrast to the positivist epistemology of sociology, political science, economics, and psychology (1985).

The relationship between sociology and feminism continues to be a fractious one.[1] The interdisciplinary character of feminist theory challenges traditional academic boundaries and their foundational assumptions, most especially the modernist dichotomies that distinguish masculine/feminine and maintain that these differences are "natural" and unchangeable. These dichotomies and assumptions have been particularly significant in nineteenth- and early-twentieth-century sociological theory.

Criticism of gender dichotomies as "natural" has always informed feminist writings; it was central to Simone de Beauvoir's *The Second Sex,* one of the influential texts for the contemporary women's movement. De Beauvoir insisted that there was no "natural" or fixed human essence. What is assumed to be male or female is a social construction. Furthermore, the social construction of the female is in reference to the male: She is the second sex to his first place, "He is the Subject, he is Absolute—she is the Other" (1974:xix). Women generally did not contest their subordinate position because it was assumed to be "natural" and unchangeable. But de Beauvoir maintained that although biology is important, it did not "establish for her a fixed and inevitable destiny." As she put it, "One is not born, but rather becomes, woman" (1974:36).

In examining gender inequality, de Beauvoir rejected explanations from biology, psychoanalysis, and Marx. She maintained that in all of these theoretical traditions, women were not presented as subjects in themselves but simply as objects for men, and most especially as sexual objects: "she is sex—absolute sex, no less" for men (1974:xix). More generally, the male was the political and economic subject of modernity whose rationality and objectivity were "natural facts" that justified the maintenance of the separate gendered spheres of home and work. Epstein (1988:233) pointed out that dichotomous thinking still prevails, especially in daily life, but also among "great scientific minds," and when comparisons are made, the characteristics assigned to men are always ranked higher.

Marxism and Feminism

One of the central debates among feminists in the 1970s revolved around the relationship between feminism and Marxism. Marxist analysis assumed that women's subordination to men was a result of their absence from the productive process. Consequently, women did not control property but were themselves property. Only when women entered paid labor did they enter into productive class relations. It was assumed that the entry of women into paid labor would contribute to the eventual triumph of the proletariat revolution, so that after the revolution women's subordination to men would be eliminated. This solution was problematic from the outset because the basis for social organiza-

---

[1]In a fairly recent sociology text, Alan Swingwood's *A Short History of Sociological Thought* (1991), there is no mention of feminism, and "gender" and "sex" do not appear in the index.

tion was supposedly found, according to Marx, in the "production and *reproduction* of immediate life" (Marx and Engels, 1845–1846:17).

Feminists had long maintained that any changes in productive relations must be matched by changes in reproductive relations if there was to be any equality between the sexes. These changes were unlikely when Marxism found the origin of class divisions in the family, "where the wife and children are the slaves of the husband" from the moment that monogamous sexual relations were established (Marx and Engels, 1845–1846:21). This view of family relationships, especially the ambiguous status of domestic labor as having only use value rather than the exchange value of "productive" paid labor, was contested by many feminists. For example, Dalla Costa and Jones (1973:7) maintained that domestic labor was productive labor because it produced and reared the next generation of workers. Consequently, domestic labor represented the "hidden source of surplus labor."

Many feminists maintained that the "woman question" for Marxists had never been a "feminist question." The feminist question is directed at "male dominance over women," whereas Marxist analysis looks at "the relationship of women to the economic system, rather than that of women to men" (Hartmann, 1981:3–4). Because patriarchy combined with, and reinforced, capitalist exploitation and oppression, it made more sense to talk about capitalist patriarchy than simply a capitalist system (Eisenstein, 1979:22).

The key to patriarchal oppression, according to Eisenstein, is the control men assert over women's sexuality and reproduction. Men have "chosen to interpret and politically use" the idea that sex differences are "natural," biologically determined differences to subordinate women (1979:25). Marxist analysis has been as guilty as any other analysis of social relations in using the idea of "natural" differences to ignore or sideline women's position and concerns. As a result, women "should not trust men to liberate them after the revolution, in part, because there is no reason to think they would know how; in part, because there is no necessity for them to do so" (Hartmann, 1981:32). Harding (1981:159) concluded that "women are now the revolutionary group in history" and that it was women who must now address the "man question" and surmount the resistance of men to feminist theory and practice.[2]

Not all feminists rejected Marxist analysis in toto, but most agreed that, like other emancipatory theoretical analyses, it was deeply flawed when it came to the analysis of sex and gender relations. Like any knowledge system, including sociology, it was understood as "particularistically biased in the direction of the male experience of the world." Therefore, all "accepted social science knowledge should be reevaluated to take account of all the actors and relations involved in the multidimensional production of social life" (Lengermann and Niebrugge-Brantley, 1990:318). For example, the idea of the "actor" has been central to sociological theorizing but, as Wallace (1989) pointed out, prior to a

---

[2]Not all feminist social theory was radical in focus; liberal feminism that continued the nineteenth-century traditions was also another important theoretical stance. For a discussion of the distinctions, see Jaggar (1983).

feminist sociology, few sociologists ever "picture the 'actor' mentioned by so many theorists as anything but male." Indeed, Homans's 1964 ASA presidential address, "Bringing Men Back In," was an "affirmation of the actor as male" (Wallace, 1989:7).

Theory and Practice

Feminist theory did retain the critical Marxist stance that stressed theoretical knowledge must be generated and used for emancipatory practice. Feminist sociology is understood as a critical enterprise on three counts:

- It takes a woman-centered perspective.
- It interrogates the core concepts and assumptions of sociology from this perspective.
- It asks how social change can be effected to produce a more humane social world.

Feminist sociological theory strengthens the "critical emphasis in sociology" by its insistence that "sociological work be critical and change-oriented, not only towards society . . . but also towards sociology itself" (Lengermann and Niebrugge-Brantley, 1990:318).

This emancipatory thrust of a feminist sociology seemed to be a more coherent project in the early years. The assumption was that a *cause* of women's oppression could be found and that, whatever the particular cause, it could be found "at the level of the *social structure*." In addition, "the idea of *oppression* . . . seemed to have self-evident application" (Barrett and Phillips, 1992:2). With some consensus on these points, feminist debates revolved around where to place the "explanatory weight." Was women's oppression "located in the sphere of work or the sphere of the family? In the realm of production or the realm of reproduction?" What weight should be given to "structures of patriarchy (or sometimes the sex/gender system) versus capitalism; and to either of these structural accounts versus social roles, or psychologies of power" (Barrett and Phillips, 1992:4)?

By the decade of the 1990s, it was clear that any feminist sociological consensus had fractured. This was a consequence of the "impact of black women's critique of the racist and ethnocentric assumptions of white feminists"; more nuanced analyses of the earlier simplistic sex/gender distinction, with more attention to psychoanalysis, the mothering experience, and the variety of sexual desire and practice; and the "appropriation and development of post-structuralist and post-modernist ideas" (Barrett and Phillips, 1992:4–5). All of these more recent developments are characterized by interdisciplinary perspectives and a critical rejection of the "master" narratives and discourses of modernity.

Master Narratives

Two important master narratives that were subjected to feminist sociological critique were structural functionalism, especially as exemplified in the work of Talcott Parsons, and positivism.

As you have seen in Chapter 2, Parsons distinguished between instrumental and expressive roles and tied them to gender roles in the occupational and family realms. Parsons claimed that women's primary focus on the expressive roles of domesticity and child care, and men's primary focus on occupational roles, were "functional" adaptations. Women's family roles suited women's nature and were functional because they eliminated "any competition for status . . . between husband and wife which might be disruptive of the solidarity of marriage" (Parsons, 1954:192). Indeed, the "broadly humanistic values such as 'good taste' in personal appearance, house furnishings, cultural things like literature and music" were functionally equivalent in Parsons's view to the husband's "competitive occupational achievement" (1954:192).

Feminist reactions to Parsons pointed to the negative aspects of this idea of separate spheres and to the fact that this family pattern was historically and culturally specific. Rossi (1964:615) pointed out that motherhood, as a full-time occupation for adult women in a nuclear family, appeared for the first time in human history among middle-class women in the 1940s and 1950s, primarily in North America. In addition, the dichotomized roles do not apply in practice. Domestic and child-care work, for example, involves instrumental as well as expressive components. Generally, structural-functional theory was critiqued as conservative, especially in Parsons's stress on the importance to social system stability of dichotomized sex-role compliance.[3]

The instrumentality that Parsons attributed primarily to men was a part of the feminist critique of positivism. Feminists suggested that positivist research methods that stressed the objectivity of the researcher reflected a particularly masculine view of the world. Positivism's idea of the "god-like" position of the researcher was rejected (Stanley and Wise, 1983:113). The idea that social reality can be "objectively constituted" and that there was "one true 'real' reality" that the emotionally uninvolved researcher can objectively find was debunked (Stanley and Wise, 1983:113). Similarly, the subject/object dichotomy, in which what is studied becomes an "object," is rejected along with the assumption that scientists are "experts in other people's lives" (1983:114).

Feminists insist that "*women* should define and interpret our experiences, and that women need to *re-define* and *re-name* what other people—experts, men—have previously defined and named for us," thus breaking the positivist "power relationship which exists between the researcher and the researched" (Stanley and Wise, 1983:144). The two theorists examined in this chapter—Dorothy Smith and Patricia Hill Collins—specifically address these methodological issues in their suggestions for sociological practice.

All of the issues discussed above remain important in current feminist sociology. What emerged from the contemporary women's movement and the work of feminist scholars were more critical and comprehensive analyses of social life, because gender became a pivotal concept in feminist research. In

---

[3]It should be noted that not all feminist sociologists rejected Parsons's work entirely. Miriam Johnson (1989:116) suggested that Parsons's "evolutionary framework and his early analyses of the family can serve as a useful framework to understand feminist thinking and the changes associated with it."

addition, feminist criticisms of traditional, positivist methodology that privi-leged the researcher as an uninvolved, objective observer have produced inno-vative and more inclusive research practices that emphasize a process of mu-tual discovery for all the participants. In this regard, feminist sociology attempts to honor the goal of empowering research subjects.

These methodological and theoretical innovations are still not universally welcomed or acknowledged in the profession. In 1990, Turner predicted that the future of sociology would be a positivist future because positivist sociology was "on the verge of developing laws and models that are the equivalent of those in the natural sciences." Turner believes that in the near future, "when the bankruptcy of much current 'theory' is recognized," positivist sociologists will finally realize "Comte's original vision for a 'social physics'" (Turner, 1990:388–389).

Turner's prediction represents a narrowly focused view of the sociological enterprise and in no way applies to the much broader social theoretical focus of feminist theory. Feminist theory is not confined by traditional academic bound-aries, including the boundaries between arts and sciences. Feminist method-ological and theoretical critiques of knowledge construction apply equally to the physical, biological, and social sciences, as well as to the whole range of special-izations under the rubric of philosophy, arts, and languages.

The work and lives of the two sociologists that we consider in this chapter il-lustrate the cross-disciplinary nature of feminist theory. Obviously, they have been selected from a very large pool of feminist social theorists. Consequently, the perspectives they advance do not represent all of the perspectives that ani-mate feminist social theory in general or feminist sociological theory in particu-lar, but their work has been pivotal to many of the theoretical and methodologi-cal debates among feminist sociologists.

Dorothy Smith and Patricia Hill Collins both focus on the "situated knowl-edge" of women in their theoretical and methodological approaches. They are both concerned with the actual activities and knowledge of subjects in relation to, or as a result of, social and ideological structural constraints. They are also linked in another way. In 1993, the American Sociological Association con-ferred the Jessie Bernard Award on Dorothy E. Smith and Patricia Hill Collins. The Association stated that both scholars had transformed sociology by extend-ing the "boundaries . . . to include the standpoint, experiences, and concerns of women; together they have extended the boundaries of gender scholarship to include the intersection of race, class, and gender"; and both scholars "seek to empower women through a dialectic of theory and practice" (American Socio-logical Association, 1993:13).

Dorothy E. Smith (1926–)

Dorothy Smith obtained her BA degree in sociology in 1955 from the London School of Economics (LSE). At LSE she met her husband, who was there on the GI bill; after she got her degree, they married and went to Berkeley. She records that as an undergraduate she had been an "independent and autonomous person" and had delighted in her "discovery of the life of the intellect," but that the "combination of Berkeley and marriage took that delight and autonomy away" (1994:46).

Her years as a graduate student, wife, and mother in Berkeley, although often unhappy, did provide her with the foundation for feminist sociology. In Berkeley she came to realize that she occupied two realms. The realm of academia was a "world organized textually . . . and organized to create a world of activity independent of the local and particular," but when she went home, she "entered a different mode of being," the mode of a mother with two small children that was a local and particular world (1987:6).

Erving Goffman supervised her 1963 PhD at Berkeley. She remained at Berkeley as a lecturer between 1964 and 1966, after which she went to the University of Essex (1966–1968), the University of British Columbia (1968–1976), and finally to the Ontario Institute for Studies in Education in Toronto, where she is currently a Professor Emeritus.

In her biographical essay, Smith records the beginnings of a feminist consciousness resulting from her experiences as a graduate student and, later, lecturer at Berkeley. She recalled deciding, when she was a lecturer, to tell women graduate students about some of the realities she had come to know of women's situation at Berkeley. "I thought they shouldn't be as naïve as I had been. That meeting was my first political move in this still-hidden women's movement that I didn't know I was a part of" (1994:48). When Smith was at Berkeley, there were more than 40 male faculty members in the sociology department and "one or two transitory women" on "temporary appointments" (1987:7).

> It was a male world in its assumptions, its language, its patterns of relating. The intellectual world spread out before me appeared, indeed I experienced it, as genderless. But its apparent lack of center was indeed centered. It was structured by its gender subtext. . . . Within the discourses embedded in the relations of ruling, women were the Other. (1987:7)

Like other women sociologists, Smith recognized that the discourse of sociology in which she had been trained was a discourse that expressed, described, and provided the working concepts and vocabulary for "a landscape in which women are strangers" (1987:52).

It was this "rupture in consciousness—the line of fault" that generated her feminist sociology. Her feminist focus was combined with Marxism in "trying to discover and trying to understand, the objective social, economic, and political relations which shape and determine women's oppression in this kind of society" (1977a:12). It was from these varied experiences that Smith began to formulate her intention to make a "sociology from the standpoint of women" that would treat the taken-for-granted everyday world as problematic (1987:8).

Smith's Central Theories and Methods

Smith's concern was to develop a sociology *for*, rather than *about* women. In this enterprise, she indicated, certain thinkers were influential in the development of her theoretical perspective—most notably, George Herbert Mead, Maurice

Merleau-Ponty, Karl Marx, and Harold Garfinkel (1987:8–9). But although the work of these theorists can be seen as influential in the development of her ideas, Smith has stated that she is not a "symbolic interactionist, nor a phenomenological sociologist, nor a Marxist sociologist, nor an ethnomethodologist" (1987:9).

Her sociology, Smith asserts, is designed to be "capable of explicating for members of the society the social organization of their experienced world, including in that experience the ways in which it passes beyond what is immediately and directly known, including also, therefore, the structure of a bifurcated consciousness" (1987:89). Smith's key focus on the "actual activities of actual people" is a "method developed from a conjunction of the materialist method developed by Marx and Engels . . . and Garfinkel's ethnomethodology. Both of these ground inquiry into the actual ongoing activities of actual individuals" (Smith, 1989:38, fn. 6).

A **bifurcated consciousness** refers to two different ways of "knowing, experiencing, and acting—the one located in the body and in the space that it occupies and moves into, the other passing beyond it" (1987:82). From the standpoint of women, the subject is located in a "material and local world," a world "directly experienced from oneself as centered (in the body). This is in contrast to a world "organized in the abstracted conceptual mode, external to the local and particular places of one's bodily existence" (1987:84). The abstract, conceptual mode is a masculine mode that sociology, conceived of as a scientific discipline, participates in. The "ethic of objectivity and the methods used in its practice" separate the knower from the known, especially from the "knower's interests, 'biases,' . . . that are not authorized by the discipline" (1990a:16).

However, to develop a sociology from the **standpoint of women** (or subjects in general) who are "located materially and in a particular place does not involve simply the transfer from one conceptual frame to another." Nor does it mean "renunciation of the rational, conceptual, scientifically rigorous method or procedure" in favor of locating a "distinctive 'female' in the subjective, emotional side, so that the alienative intellectual practices of sociology are eliminated rather than transformed." This is because the two sides of the bifurcated consciousness are not equal. The only way to enter the "abstracted conceptual mode of working" is to pass through, and make use of, the "concretely and immediately experienced"—a fact that "official" sociology obscures and ignores (1987:86).[4]

Once it is recognized that knowledge starts from the materiality of the everyday world, then sociology has a basis that begins not in "discourse but in the actual daily social relations between individuals" (1987:98). Methodologically, a sociology that begins from "where people are in the world" reverses the usual procedure of starting with a "conceptual apparatus or theory drawn from the discipline" (1987:89). Smith contends that the sociological assumption that the

---

[4]Smith takes her theoretical cue here from Merleau-Ponty, who pointed out that all human beings try to make sense of their world. Consequently, theorizing must start with the ordinary, everyday experiences of those worlds.

everyday world is "unformed and unorganized" until the sociologist's conceptual framework selects, assembles, and orders it, is the way in which sociology
obscures its complicity with the forces of domination (1987:89–90).

Reversing the methodological approach is critical because the "everyday
world is neither transparent nor obvious"; social relations are organized from
"elsewhere" (1987:91–92). A sociology for women is concerned with exposing
the way "our own situations are organized and determined by social processes
that extend outside the scope of the everyday world and are not discoverable
within it" (1987:152). Consequently, beginning with the standpoint of women
does not mean a "sociology concerned exclusively with the world of women's
experience or with the subjectivity of the sociologist herself." It means a "search
for a sociology that does not transpose knowing into objective forms in which
the situated subject and her actual experience and location are discarded," and
it gives subjects the ability to grasp "the social relations organizing the worlds of
their experience" (1987:153). That is, it produces a sociology that empowers
those who are the subjects of sociological interest by revealing the real relations
governing their everyday world.

A sociology from the standpoint of women is an "investigation and explication of how 'it' actually is, of how 'it' actually works," whatever the methods
used—"observation, interviewing, recollection of work experience, use of archives, textual analysis, or other" (1990b:160). The key questions to ask are
"How does it happen to us as it does?" and "How is the world in which we act
and suffer put together?" (1987:154).

But investigating the "problematic of the everyday world does not involve
substituting the analysis, the perspectives and views of subjects, for the investigation by the sociologist." Women, or any subjects, may be "expert practitioners
of their everyday worlds," but the "extralocal determinants" of experience do
not "lie within the scope of everyday practices." It is the discovery of these
"extralocal determinants"—the structures underlying what appears to be
"real"—that is the "sociologist's special business" (1987:161). Sociology from the
standpoint of women explores and explicates what the subject does not know—
"the social relations and organization pervading her world but invisible in it"
(1992:91).

Smith points out that taking the standpoint of women always involves a sociology in the making, "unlike sociologies that seek to generate a totalizing system"
(1992:91). It aims to produce sociological accounts that can tell subjects "how it
works" rather than producing "unitary, absolute, or final truth" (1992:94).
Smith's sociology is thus a "*method of inquiry*, always ongoing, opening things up,
discovering," having relevance for the "politics and practice of progressive
struggle, whether of women or of other oppressed groups" (1992:88). A feminist
method of sociological inquiry must, in Smith's view, "go beyond . . . interviewing practices and . . . research relationships to explore methods of thinking" in
order to produce sociological texts that "preserve the presence of actual subjects
while exploring and explicating the relations in which our everyday worlds are
embedded" (1987:111). Consequently, texts and discourse are particularly important to Smith's sociology. She sees them as the primary means in modern

societies of structuring everyday worlds and maintaining, as well as concealing, relations of domination.

Smith's examination of the contours of modernity and capitalism in terms of texts, discourse, and objectivity started with a Marxist framework. Smith initially considered Marxism the only method that addressed the particularities of the everyday/everynight in terms of social and economic processes. However, she found the engagement with Marxism a "painful and difficult experience" because of the rejection of feminism by many Marxists (1977a:12). Smith recognized that initial feminist confrontations with political Marxists in the 1970s produced important insights into gendered class and race relations, but women's standpoint was not explicitly taken into account.

Smith's conception of women's standpoint as a critique of ruling ideological practices reformulates Marx's use of the standpoint of labor as the means to critique capitalism. She points out that it is women's work that underpins the "abstracted conceptual mode of ruling" done by men (1987:81). Whether in the home or in paid labor, women mediate the abstract, conceptual actions of men and the "actual, concrete forms on which it depends," especially in the corporate capitalist world (1987:83). The mundane home work of maintaining healthy bodies and minds and the workplace activities of ensuring space, time, and resources for the production of abstract conceptualizations in the form of reports, memos, strategic plans, and the like are all largely the work of women *for* men. Women are corporate capitalism's housekeepers at home and in paid labor.

Women have been drawn into paid labor in large numbers under corporate capitalism, but this has not produced gender equality as Marx and Engels expected. Smith suggested that the "bifurcation of the world into public and private spheres" has not diminished; on the contrary, it has taken on new dimensions unforeseen by Marx or Engels (1977b:19). The increasingly abstract, objectified reality produced by texts and communicative modes are what govern, regulate, produce, and reproduce social relations. These texts and communications— whether books, television, plays, soap operas, art, or the Internet—produce the "images, vocabularies, concepts, knowledge of and methods of knowing the world" that are "integral to the practices of power" (1975:354). These abstractions embody the relations of ruling in modern society (1990b:122). By **relations of ruling**, Smith refers not simply to political organizations but to all of the various institutions that rule, manage, and administer society. And these institutional locations are largely the work of men supported by the invisible, but necessary, work of women.

Nature of Society, Humans, and Change

Society Smith has no formal definition of "society." In her work, the social is always the actual practices of human beings who are understood as "expert practitioners of their everyday worlds" (1987:161). The social practices of actual people in their everyday/everynight worlds comprise society.

The practices that produce and reproduce social relations are not "fixed relations between statuses but . . . an organization of actual sequences of action *in time.*" If social processes are seen as "ongoing activities of actual people," then attention must be paid to what has formally been regarded as "subjective or as cultural phenomena," such as discourse, texts, and ideology (1990b:160). It is these forms that produce the "internally coordinated complex of administrative, managerial, professional and discursive organization that regulates, organizes, governs, or otherwise controls our societies" (1989:38).

These organizations are not "monolithic," Smith argues, but they are "pervasively interconnected" because they are characteristically and essentially "textually mediated" (1999:49). From birth, we are all subjected to a textual record that multiplies throughout our lives—licenses, registrations, medical files, school reports, tax records, and so on—and that is presumed to be an "objective" record of our self, our life. Sociology participates in the relations of ruling by producing some of the records that other organizations use to control and manipulate individuals (1990a:14). Concepts used by sociologists such as "mental illness, crimes, riots, violence, work satisfaction, neighbors and neighborhoods, motivation, and so on—these are the constructs of the practice of government" (1990a:15).

Texts are critical, in Smith's view, to the ruling apparatus's way of organizing, regulating, and directing contemporary society. In texts, power relationships are "abstracted from local and particular settings and relationships" in order to be reproduced in those very settings. Sociology has been an important part of the textual mediation of social reality that reproduces gender, class, and racial power relationships. The "texts of the relations of ruling—newspapers; television; census and economic reports; policy documents; the reports of commissions, tasks forces, ad hoc committees, and so forth—bring a virtual reality into the presence of the sociological reader" (1990a:54). The "social facts" the sociologist works with are thus already separated from the everyday, from the "subjective presence of individuals," and they are presented in a mode that fits the bureaucratic administrative hierarchy of the relations of ruling. Consequently, the world sociologists often "encounter and rely on is *already ideologically structured*" (1990a:57).

Smith illustrates the way in which sociological methods are ideological by the use of three "tricks":

Trick 1. Separate what people say they think from the actual circumstances in which it is said, from the actual empirical conditions of their lives, and from the actual individuals who said it.

Trick 2. Having detached the ideas, arrange them to demonstrate an order among them that accounts for what is observed.

Trick 3. Then change the ideas into a "person"; that is, set them up as distinct entities (for example, a value pattern, norm, belief system, and so forth) to which agency (or possibly causal efficacy) may be attributed, and redistribute them to "reality" by attributing them to actors who can now be treated as representing the ideas. (1990a:43–44)

At the conclusion of the three tricks, the original subject and her actions have disappeared, only to reappear as an abstract, "objective" sociological account of the "actor." For example, in asking the interview question "Are single mothers a social problem?" the tricks might work in the following manner:

1. If the answer is recorded as "yes," despite any qualifications the respondent may have introduced in answering "yes," the response will be coded collectively and reported as a percentage.

2. The percentage of "yes" to "no" responses can then be tied to current social, or sociological, theories about ideal mothering.

3. The idea of the ideal mother can then be compared to the single mother—in the process constructing, in most cases, a negative picture of the individual single mother.

It is because the relations of ruling in society are obscured and mystified by the predominance of textual forms, Smith maintains, that an alternative sociology is so important—especially a sociology from the standpoint of women.

Humans   Throughout her work, Smith emphasizes the primacy of the subject who is "active in the same world as we are situated in as bodies" (1987:141). The problem she deals with in some detail is the difference between women and men in their ability to claim authority over their actions and over the explanations for those actions. The key to her focus here is Alfred Schutz's idea of **multiple realities**.

Schutz identified four realms of social reality: the realm of **directly experienced** social reality (*umwelt*); the realm of **indirectly experienced** reality (*mitwelt*); the realm of the **future** (*folgewelt*); and the realm of the **past** (*vorwelt*). All of these realms can be present at the same time in any particular activity for any individual. Smith is particularly concerned with the realms of direct and indirect experience in relation to gender differences.

The realm of direct experience of reality is the world of everyday, face-to-face encounters. The world of indirect experiences is the world of abstraction, in which personal life is suspended. The suspension of the personal, of the particular subject, is accomplished by organized theoretical practices that produce the move from "*knowing to knowledge*" (1990a:66).

Knowing is the subjective activity of a subject, but **knowledge** "discards the presence of the knowing subject" (1990a:66). This "objectification of knowledge is a general feature of contemporary relations of ruling," the organization of which is based on the work women do that enables the theorist to "forget" his bodily existence and needs. Just as the housewife takes care of the mundane realities of existence, the secretary does the same job at work.

In the gender relations of a corporate capitalist world, argues Smith, the indirect realm of knowledge, especially scientific knowledge—including sociological knowledge—is how the everyday world of women's knowing and practices is erased. Objective knowledge is a form of power that "breaks knowledge from the active experiencing of subjects and from the dialogic of activity or talk that brings before us a known-in-common object." It "subdues, discounts, and disqualifies our various interests, perspectives, angles, and experience, and what we might have to say speaking from them" (1990a:80).

According to Smith, understanding the nature and effect of "objective" knowledge is important to how human beings can be conceptualized as creative actors. For example, in the production of femininity in our society, Smith points out that it is important to look at a range of sources such as the "textual discourse vested in women's magazines and television, advertisements, the appearance of cosmetic counters, fashion displays and to a lesser extent books" (1990b:163). The "discourse" found in these diverse locations structures women's aspiration to perfection in the face of the always imperfect body. These discourses obliterate women as "autonomous subjects" at the same time as they require women's work in producing the required and desired appearance. Consequently, women are obliterated and then reintroduced as agents or subjects in the process of constructing the normative ideal of femininity (1990b:193). The "subject-in-discourse is deprived of agency," but the "subject-at-work behind her is active and skilled"—albeit active and skilled in reproducing her subordination to the ideological ideal of femininity (1990b:206).

As this example illustrates, attention to the actual activities of people reveals the ways in which they are participants in multiple realities and how, as participants, they may "give power to the relations that 'overpower' them" (1990b:161). Consequently, for Smith, a sociology that reveals the "organization and relations that are invisible but *active* in the everyday/everynight sites where people take up resistance and struggle" is a sociology that provides knowledge that "expands their and our grasp of how things are put together and hence their and our ability to organize and act effectively" (1992:96). It is a sociology that honors the knowledgeable human being and is relevant to the "politics and practices of progressive struggle, whether of women or of other oppressed groups" (1992:88). It is a sociology that deals with and contributes to progressive social change.

Social Change   The possibility of class and gender emancipatory transformations runs through all of Smith's work. It is through "doing sociology" in new ways that Smith sees the possibility of effecting change. What she wishes to establish is a sociology where "knowledge does not become a body of knowledge, where issues are not crystallized, where the conventions and relevances of discourse do not assume an independent authority over against its speakers and readers" (1987:22). However, Smith points out that she has "never seen resistance or opposition as beginning in theory, much less in sociology" (1992:96).

Smith points out that resistance and revolution need a "division of labor in which the production of knowledge plays an essential, though not a leading, part." Knowledge as "reflexive critique" has the power "to disclose just how our practices contribute to and we articulate with the relations that overpower our lives" (1990a:204). These disclosures provide a basis for reorganizing and transforming social relations.

As you saw above, Smith insists that the transformation of oppressive social relations in present-day society requires attention to the relations of ruling. It is in explicating the relations of ruling and the relations of capital, from the standpoints of the dispossessed, that sociologists can participate in "transforming oppressive relations" (1992:96).

Class, Gender, and Race

Class   Although gender is central to all Smith's work, initially her focus emerged out of a reformulated Marxist perspective. Smith points out that she is not concerned with being "faithful to Marx or to a Marxist tradition, but only to seize upon what it offers us as a means of exploring the dynamic relations in which our lives are caught up and which are continually at work in transforming the bases and contexts of our existence and our struggles" (1987:142). Just as the standpoint of labor reveals class relations, so the standpoint of women reveals gender relations. The standpoint of labor reveals that social class should not be "understood as a secret power behind our backs, determining how we think, how we understand the world, and how we act"; it should be understood as a "complex of social relations coordinating the activities of our everyday worlds with those of others with whom we are not directly connected" (1987: 135). Similarly, gender is not an innate, natural phenomenon but a complex of social relations that, like class, can be discovered in "routine, daily accomplishment" (1987:140).

In describing the contours of contemporary class and gender relations, Smith contrasts the nature of twentieth-century corporate capitalism with the more locally organized capitalism of the nineteenth century. In the nineteenth century, the market still seemed to be an external, impersonal force organizing social relations, "independent of the choices and wishes of individual capitalists," but control and administration of the enterprise were local and class relations were locally based (1987:75–76). By the end of the nineteenth century, these locally organized, individually owned enterprises began to give way to corporate enterprises controlled from some external center (1987:75).

The move from the local to the national, or even the global, enterprise involved a more "abstracted conceptual mode of organization" (1987:75). This mode includes the following characteristics:

- Differentiation of the distinct functions—whether administration, management, or professional organization.
- System functions are primarily communicative and informational.
- Communication and information functions are increasingly dependent on "secondhand knowledge organized conceptually as 'facts.'"
- Organizing functions are dependent on "generalized systems of planning" in the same communicative, textual mode. (1987:75)

Contemporary corporate capitalism is thus very different from the nineteenth-century version. The ambiguity of ownership, the conceptual abstractions that administer the productive processes, and the interconnections of economic and political power make it a more difficult entity to challenge and transform, especially from the standpoint of women.

Smith points out that contemporary conceptions of class cannot be "identical to that of Marx and Engels, for the analytic capacity of such concepts is firmly articulated to the social relations of their time." However, a concept of class is still essential to understanding the nature of struggles for liberation and equality, especially the struggles of women. What is needed is a "political economy that will explore and display the properties and movement of the complex of powers, forces, and relations that are at work in our everyday/ everynight worlds" (1999:44).

Gender   Smith explored the political economy of class in relation to gender in her 1977 article "Women, the Family and Corporate Capitalism." She looked at the alienation of the middle-class corporate manager and the way in which all the activities of his wife reinforced his alienation. The key distinction, according to Smith, is that the middle-class manager plays a **role** in contrast to the **job** of the working-class man. Although the working-class man is alienated from his labor and his wife's household labor is a personal service for the husband because he "owns the means of production on which she depends," nevertheless, when there is security of income and employment, then "making a home . . . becomes a common enterprise which is shared by husband and wife to which each contribute in different ways" (1977b:32). The relationship changes when the husband is unemployed and his position as "master in the home" is undermined. Thus, the working-class wife's dependence on her husband is a dependence on external economic arrangements over which neither the husband nor the wife has any control (1977b:30–31).

The alienation of the middle-class corporate manager is different because what is alienated is not "an object—not his product, but his activity" (1977b:25). Both worker and manager are alienated by the corporate enterprise, but for the manager it is "his ethical being, his motives, his strategies of thought and communication" that are appropriated, so that it is the "alienation of the person, not of the product" (1977b:26).

> The corporate structure requires of a manager that he subordinate himself and his private interests to the goals and objectives of the daily practices, and the "ethic" of the corporation. His *person* becomes relevant—the kind of person he is. Therefore non-functionally specific criteria—off-the-job criteria and information—become relevant. (1977b:32)

These off-the-job criteria involve the family, especially the wife, who must produce a home and family relationships that support his occupational status. Consequently, the middle-class family "becomes an enactment of the moral order legislated by the corporation" (1977b:33).

The image of the ideal family and the ideal family home is one that is produced by corporate enterprises—Martha Stewart, *Ideal Home, Homes and Gardens*, and the like. And the production of the appropriate home and family "image" is the work of the wife. Most especially, it is the wife who must provide emotional support and a "no-tension home" to ease the "injuries done to him in his occupational world." But this work produces "two double-binds" for the wife. First, supporting her husband in his role means in fact supporting the corporation that "violates him"; second, "insofar as the wife plays her own corporately-bestowed role of 'good homemaker,' she must maintain the image of the external order in the home." But the "imagined order" can make both her husband's success *and* his failure visible. Therefore, in order to be "a 'good wife' she must side with the external moral order against her husband" (1977b:39).

The public/private, work/family distinction affects both the working-class and middle-class wife, but whereas a working-class woman shares "in many ways the position of working-class men" to the relations of production, a middle-class woman's family and household labor is oriented to an external moral order of productive relations that alienate her husband and alienate her from her husband as well as from herself. Smith concludes that "monopoly or corporate capitalism" alienates both men and women of the middle classes, at the same time eliminating any "socio-economic basis for an autonomous selfhood" for women (1977b:46). The middle-class family is "subcontractual" and is "*for* the realization of the ruling-class moral order," in contrast to the working-class family which is "*for* its members" (1977b:33).

Race   Although Smith's work continues to explore the interrelationship of class and gender, she indicates that on the issue of race "I have not yet understood fully the intersection of racial oppression with the gender organization of the relations of ruling." Consequently, the "contradictions of class and racial oppression are still unsatisfied" in her work. She noted in *The Everyday World as Problematic* that such contradictions were "insistent presences speaking from beyond the text but not yet in it" (1987:8). Smith does point out that as women's issues are taken up and "accommodated to legal, administrative, and professional niches," if only in the margins, the "discourse of women" has tended to be the discourse of white women, excluding native and black women (1987:221).

Smith suggests that these exclusions can be seen in the "on-going actual activities of actual people" (1989:38), which reveal how "local and particular moments are entered into extended, generalized, and generalizing social relations." This understanding, in turn, exposes the "ideological practices" that are the "constituents of the relations of ruling" (1990a:204–205). In these ideological practices, the notion of "other" includes women, Native Americans, Asian, Hispanic, and African Americans and, at the same time, divides white women from the undifferentiated "others."

Other Theories and Theorists

Smith has always been concerned with the position of women in knowledge production, especially women in sociology. She points out that the emancipatory intentions of feminist sociology are at odds with the traditional complicity of sociology in the academy with ruling powers. "Social scientific knowledge represents the world from a standpoint in ruling relations, not from the standpoint of those who are ruled." Ruling relations are not monolithic, but generally there is enough control to ensure that the knowledge produced in the academy is "not oriented to the needs and interests of the mass of people, but to the needs and interests of ruling." Consequently, when leaks occur and loopholes appear, as they did in the 1960s and early 1970s, and those privileged with access to knowledge and knowledge production desert and "go over to the other side, their access is cut off" (1999:16).

Feminist critiques by the women's movements have been a particular challenge to the ruling hegemony of academic patriarchy. These challenges have not simply been a "matter of theory, but a matter of political practice" emerging out of activism on many fronts (1999:18). The initial reactions from within the academy were varied. In some cases, access to the academy was cut off; in other, more insidious ways, the critiques were marginalized and ignored as irrelevant or the work of the psychologically disturbed. Sociology was no more receptive than other disciplinary specialties. Laslett and Thorne (1992:60) have pointed out that a "wall of silence" still remains between "sociological theory and feminist theory," despite the fact that "feminists have more than kept their side of a potential conversation with sociological theorists." Nonetheless, "sociological theorists of virtually every school of thought have largely ignored the writings of feminists" (Laslett and Thorne, 1992:60).

Over time, the outright rejection of feminist critiques changed, and "women's studies" or even "gender studies" were incorporated into the academy. The result, notes Smith (1999), has been some success in "breaking down the radically one-sided character of the male-dominated discourses of the disciplines and sciences" and the creation of a "richness of critique and alternatives that is astonishing given the relatively brief period of our 'renaissance.'" But entry into the academy has also involved some cost, most notably the detachment from former linkages with "activism and organization outside the academy" (1999:20).

Smith is concerned that once feminists become "detached from independent sources of resistance and from the profoundly different take on the world they represent," then "feminism becomes professionalized" (1999:21). The "implicit political organization of the ivory tower university is still effective," and it is "not easy to go against it," although the recent agitation over "political correctness" suggests to Smith that feminists have been more successful than they realized (1999:26). The problem Smith points to for the future is how to "create active linkages with women working in sites outside the academy and to establish dialogue between the intra- and extra-academic" (1999:27). This is a critical task because "we know that there's desperation in society, and our social sciences don't know how to know this new and frightening world" (1999:27). But women know they have the "power and capacity to change," and this, in conjunction with the "hidden radicalism of the Enlightenment" still lurking in universities, provides Smith with hope for the future.

Critique and Conclusions

Dorothy Smith's work has generated a dialogue with various mainstream sociological theories. Smith has attempted to create an "insider's sociology, that is, a systematically developed consciousness of society from within, renouncing the artifice that stands us outside what we can never stand outside of" (1989:53). Such a sociology does not discard the "actual experience and location" of its subjects, but provides those subjects with "the means of grasping the social relations organizing the worlds of their experience" (1989:53). Smith's notion of "standpoint" does not "privilege a knower," but "shifts the ground of knowing, the place where inquiry begins." A sociology from the standpoint of women starts with the woman in her body who is "active; she is at work; she is connected with particular other people in various ways; she thinks, laughs, desires, sorrows, sings, curses, loves just here; she reads here; she watches television." The "subject/knower of inquiry is not a transcendent subject but is situated in the actualities of her own living, in relation with others." The sociological inquiry Smith proposes is concerned with the social as "people's ongoing concerting and coordinating of activities" (1992:92).

Smith's sociology is not "a feminism and nothing but a feminism" (Lemert, 1992:68). Her method of inquiry can work as a place to begin an inquiry into anyone's experience —and that anyone could be "Afro- or Chinese or Caucasian Canadian, an individual from one of the First nations, an old woman or man, a lesbian or a gay man, a member of the ruling class, or any other man" (Smith, 1992:90). Indeed, one criticism of Smith's work is, How can we know whose experience is to count as important? And why is the knowledge of women, or any minority group, better than the sociologist's knowledge (Hekman, 1997)? Smith would respond that situated knowledge is better because it offers an explanation of the actual world the subjects inhabit. As to how to evaluate whose experience is to count, Smith points out that she makes "no claim to a unitary, absolute, or final truth" as the endpoint of her sociological work (1992:94). As she remarks, "Established sociology has powerful ways of writing the social into the text, which produce society as seen from an Archimedean point," but a sociology for women says, "You can't have that wish" (1992:94).

There is no "outside"; everyone, including the sociologist, is a participant. It is in this way that Smith responds to the criticism of her work by Patricia Hill Collins. Collins (1992:79) points out that the bifurcated consciousness, which allowed Smith to produce a "new angles of vision" on women and sociology, "demonstrates the power of knowledge created by one who stands outside the dominant discourse and who possesses local knowledge, namely knowledge growing from women's experiences" (1992:79). But Collins goes on the claim that Smith came to realize that "remaining on the line of fault leaves the inner circle unchanged because the rules of what constitutes sociology remain intact." Consequently, Collins suggests that Smith "chose to adhere to the rules" and do "theoretical sociology in a way that makes sense to members of the inner circle," as demonstrated in Smith's concern with text-mediated forms of power (1992:91).

Smith (1992:97) responds that her concern with text-mediated forms of power does not mean that "this is all there is to be done or indeed all that this method of inquiry makes possible," but only that it is a method that is "powerfully relevant to making change in our kind of society." Furthermore, Smith stresses that the so-called "outside positions" of "marginality, exclusion, suppressed and oppositional cultures and positions" are, in fact, "inside." There are "no modes of investigation other than those beginning from within" (1992:94).

It is from the inside that Collins begins in her explication of black feminist thought. Collins is particularly concerned with the silencing of women, especially African American women, who have been "silenced by not being allowed to speak the language they possess, at least in most public arenas" (1992:78). The alternative traditions women speak remain "invisible and unintelligible to existing sociological approaches," which can only be rectified by recognizing "diversity" and "the varied ways in which people create local knowledge to counteract objectifying knowledge" (1992:78).

We now turn to a brief examination of the work of Patricia Hill Collins. Collins has been centrally concerned with developing an "epistemological framework that can be used both to assess existing Black feminist thought and to clarify some of the underlying assumptions that impede the development of Black feminist thought" (Collins, 1990:202).

Patricia Hill Collins (1948–)

Patricia Hill Collins is currently a Professor of African American Studies and Sociology at the University of Cincinnati. She earned her BA from Brandeis in 1969, her MA from Harvard in 1970, and her PhD from Brandeis in 1984.

Collins's central sociological concerns reflect her own experiences as a black female African American. This concern is expressed in her concept of the **outsider-within.** The outsider-within refers to the experience of being part of a society, or community or group, but at the same time set apart because of some personal attribute. Collins (1990:xi) illustrates the outsider-within position in her reflections on her own formative experiences. She recalls being "the 'first,' or 'one of the few,' or the 'only' African American and/or woman and/or working-class person in my schools, communities, and work settings." Although Collins felt that there was nothing wrong with being who she was, she came to the realization that others did not share this opinion. As a result, she reports that she "tried to disappear into myself in order to deflect the painful, daily assaults designed to teach me that being an African-American, working-class woman made me lesser than those who were not." In time she "became quieter and eventually was virtually silenced" (1990:xi).

In her book *Black Feminist Thought* (1990), Collins regains her voice with her own "self-defined standpoint." That voice is both "individual and collective, personal and political, one reflecting the intersection of my unique biography with the larger meaning of my historical times" (1990:xii). African American women in general have a "self-defined standpoint on their own oppression" that shows they have been "neither passive victims of nor willing accomplices to their own oppression." Collins's work explores the dimensions of this standpoint from the perspective of an outsider within the theoretical discourse of sociology (1989:747).

Collins's Central Theories and Methods

In *Black Feminist Thought*, Collins indicates that she draws on diverse theoretical traditions, "such as Afrocentric philosophy, feminist theory, Marxist social thought, the sociology of knowledge, critical theory, and postmodernism." However, she acknowledges that the "standard vocabulary of these traditions, citations of their major works and key proponents, and these terms themselves rarely appear in the text" because she regards the ideas, not the labels, as most important and, furthermore, she is concerned with placing "Black women's experiences and ideas at the center of analysis" (1990:xii). Instead of the usual transformation of an oppressed group's ideas and experiences into the language and conceptual framework of dominant groups, also discussed by Dorothy Smith, she seeks to present the multiple voices of those who are often silenced.

Like Smith, Collins maintains that "theory and intellectual creativity are not the province of a select few but instead emanate from a range of people" (1990:xiii). Black women's standpoint emerges from, first, their "political and economic status," which gives them a "distinctive set of experiences that offers a different view of material reality than that available to other groups"; and second, the "distinctive Black feminist consciousness concerning that material reality" that emerges out of those experiences (1989:747–748). Collins therefore uses a variety of sources, or "voices," in developing her argument. Musicians, poets, and writers, as well as political activists and scholars, are all represented in her work.

In Collins's view, the relationship between black women's standpoint and black feminist thought is a **dialectical** one in which the "everyday, taken-for-granted knowledge shared by members of a given group" is taken up by those "experts" who are part of that group who are able to articulate the taken-for-granted. By making the taken-for-granted clear, "experts" offer "Black women a different view of themselves and their world than that offered by the established social order" (1989:750). In this way, "Black feminist thought rearticulates a consciousness that already exists" and, in doing so, "gives African-American women another tool of resistance to all forms of their subordination" (1989:750). Collins points to a long history of black women intellectuals who merged intellectual work and activism—women such as Anna J. Cooper, Frances Ellen Watkins Harper, Ida B. Wells, and Mary Church Terrell, all of whom produced "analyses of Black women's oppression and worked to eliminate that oppression" (1992:29).

> Placing the ideas of ordinary African-American women as well as those of better-known Black women intellectuals at the center of analysis produces a new angle of vision on feminist and African-American concerns, one infused with an Afrocentric feminist sensibility. (1990:16)

Collins's major objective is to develop an epistemology that can "assess existing Black feminist thought and . . . clarify some of the underlying assumptions that impede the development of Black feminist thought." She believes this is necessary because "traditional epistemological assumptions concerning how we arrive at 'truth' simply are insufficient to the task of furthering Black feminist thought." Consequently, in the "same way that concepts such as women and intellectual must be deconstructed, the process by which we arrive at truth merits comparable scrutiny" (1990:17).

A definition of what constitutes black women's standpoint is complicated, notes Collins, by the complex relationships between "biological classification, the social construction of race and gender as categories of analysis, the material conditions accompanying these changing social constructions, and Black women's consciousness about these themes." She suggests that black feminist thought "consists of specialized knowledge created by African-American women which clarifies a standpoint of and for Black women." It therefore consists of "theoretical interpretations of Black women's reality by those who live it" (1990:22).

Collins stresses, however, that "ethnicity, region of the country, urbanization, and age combine to produce a web of experiences" that produce diversity among African American women. Consequently, it is "more accurate to discuss a Black *women's* standpoint than a Black *woman's* standpoint" (1990:24). In this respect, Collins sees her work as somewhat different from that of Smith. She claims that the "everyday" Smith examines is "individual, a situation reflecting in part the isolation of white, middle-class women," whereas her "everyday" is "collective as well as individual" because it reflects the "collective values in Afrocentric communities" and the "working-class experiences of the majority of Black women" (1990:40, fn. 5).

Methodologically, Collins rejects **positivist** epistemology, which she characterizes as "Eurocentric masculinist." In her view, distancing the researcher from the "object" of study, the elimination of emotions and ethics and values from the research process, and an adversarial approach to the establishment of truth claims cannot produce adequate knowledge of the black experience. Such an approach asks "African-American women to objectify themselves, devalue their emotional life, displace their motivations for furthering knowledge about Black women, and confront, in an adversarial relationship, those who have more social, economic, and professional power than they do" (1989:754).

Knowledge must include feelings, values, and interests, whether it is black female knowledge or knowledge generated by any other constituency. Collins's approach is to examine the "situated, subjected standpoint of African-American women in order to understand Black feminist thought as a partial perspective on domination." In this way, black women's standpoint can be related to "larger epistemological dialogues concerning the nature of the matrix of domination" (1990:236).

Nature of Society, Humans, and Change

Collins's views on society recognize the hierarchal relations of race, class, and gender. She identifies the core theme in black feminist thought as that of oppression. The legacy of struggle against oppression is central to black feminist understanding of society and self. In Western society, and in U.S. society especially, black women are, as Zora Neale Hurston pointed out, the "mules uh de world" (Collins, 1990:43).

Society   Collins's work concentrates on the "society" of black experience that is different from but related to the "society" of Western whites. Collins points to an **Afrocentric** worldview that is distinct from and opposed to a Eurocentric worldview (1990:26). Although black people have been forced to adapt Afrocentric belief systems to the "institutional arrangements of white domination," nonetheless the persistence of this worldview has been "fundamental to African-American resistance to racial oppression" (1990:27).

The Afrocentric viewpoint is a collective, as opposed to an individualistic, orientation to social relations. For example, African American "community norms traditionally were such that neighbors cared for one another's children"

(1990:120). When African Americans continue this tradition, they challenge "one fundamental assumption underlying the capitalist system itself: that children are 'private property' and can be disposed of as such" (1990:122). African Americans exist within multiple levels of domination, but an Afrocentric viewpoint, Collins believes, can be the basis for the empowerment of African Americans in general, and black women in particular.

Humans Collins suggests that human beings may "experience and resist oppression on three levels: the level of personal biography; the group or community level of the cultural context created by race, class, and gender; and the systemic level of social institutions" (1990:227). All three levels are sites of domination and possible resistance. Most important, however, is the personal level of consciousness.

Each person has a "unique personal biography," notes Collins, and as "no two individuals occupy the same social space, . . . no two biographies are the same." In addition, "human ties can be freeing and empowering" or "confining and oppressive." Thus, the "same situation can look quite different depending on the consciousness one brings to it." It is at the level of "individual consciousness" that "new knowledge can generate change." Collins rejects the idea that domination only "operates from the top down by forcing and controlling unwilling victims to bend to the will of the more powerful superiors." The idea of top-down domination makes the "willingness of a victim to collude in her or his own victimization," or the persistent resistance of victims "even when chances for victory seem remote," difficult to explain. Black feminist thought, Collins maintains, challenges domination by emphasizing the "power of self-definition and the necessity of a free mind." That is, consciousness is understood "as a sphere of freedom" (1990:227).

The framework for African American women's power of self-definition is connected to their historical cultural context. Four critical aspects of Black women's experience provide the basis for their "difference" as well as for their resistance: concrete experience as a criterion of meaning; the use of dialogue in assessing knowledge claims; the ethic of caring; and the ethic of personal accountability.

In her discussion of the use of **concrete experience as a criterion of meaning**, Collins distinguishes between two types of knowing: knowledge and wisdom. Black women's survival depends upon knowledge of the "dynamics of race, gender, and class subordination" and "wisdom in assessing" that knowledge (1989:758). The distinction is "essential" because "knowledge without wisdom is adequate for the powerful, but wisdom is essential to the survival of the subordinate" (1989:759). Credibility is therefore tied to concrete experience rather than to knowledge gained from books or abstract speculations. In attaching value to the concrete, African American women invoke "not only an Afrocentric tradition, but a women's tradition as well" (1989:761).

Support for valuation of the concrete is centered in two institutions: black extended families and black churches. In these two institutions, "Black women experts with concrete knowledge of what it takes to be self-defined Black women share their knowledge with their younger, less experienced sisters"

(1989:762). Sisterhood is a "model for a whole series of relationships" among African American women that black men, although "supported by Afrocentric institutions," cannot share (1989:762–763).

The valuing and evaluation of concrete experience is developed in dialogue. The **use of dialogue in assessing knowledge claims** is rooted in "an African-based oral tradition" and in the "knowledge-validation process of enslaved African-Americans." The importance of dialogue is exemplified in the interactive "call and response discourse mode" and the stress on the "active participation of all individuals" in the testing and validation of ideas in black communication (1989:763). Again, the use of dialogue in the assessment of knowledge claims is a central dimension of black feminist epistemology as well as being, more generally, a "female way of knowing" (1989:765).

The **ethic of caring** is also central to the validation of knowledge. The ethic of caring "is rooted in a tradition of African humanism" that sees each individual as a "unique expression of a common spirit, power, or energy expressed by all life" (1989:766). This emphasis on individual uniqueness involves valuing **personal expressiveness**. Two other components are also important to the ethic of caring: **emotions** and **empathy** (1989:766). Emotion is a sign that the "speaker believes in the validity of an argument," and the capacity for empathy is important to making connection with the "other." Collins points to the convergence of "Afrocentric and feminist values in the ethic-of-care dimension of an alternative epistemology" but claims that, for white women, few institutions other than the family "validate this way of knowing," whereas for African American women, both family and church validate such knowledge (1989:768).

The **ethic of personal accountability** is also an Afrocentric as well as a feminist value. The ethic insists that individuals "develop their knowledge claims through dialogue and present those knowledge claims in a style proving concern for their ideas" and that they be accountable for such knowledge claims (1989:768). Thus, the assessment of any individual's knowledge claims is also an evaluation of the individual's "character, values, and ethics." In this way, the "Eurocentric masculinist belief that probing into an individual's personal viewpoint is outside the boundaries of discussion" is rejected. In sum, in Afrocentric feminist epistemology, "values lie at the heart of the knowledge-validation process such that inquiry always has an ethical aim." Central to such an aim, for Collins, are resistance and struggle (1989:769).

Social Change   According to Collins, the development of black feminist thought is a continuation of the African American tradition that emphasized the value of education as education for the entire race in order to "assist in the economic, political, and social improvement of the enslaved and later emancipated African-Americans" (1990:148). More specifically, educated black women saw their education as "something gained not just for their own development but for the purpose of race uplift" (1990:149).

Education has been particularly important to black women as a means of empowerment and political activism because of their traditional exclusion from, or suppression within, "organizations devoted to institutional transformation"

(1990:154). As a result, black women have attempted to create a "female sphere of influence" that "indirectly resists oppressive structures by undermining them" (1990:141). For example, a style of activism favored by black women in the pursuit of social change reflects a "belief that teaching people how to be self-reliant fosters more empowerment than teaching them how to follow" (1990:157).

Black women may not have been the leaders, but they have been active in institutional transformation in "civil rights organizations, labor unions, feminist groups, boycotts, and revolts" (1990:142). Generally, however, black women's activism has encompassed both spheres of influence and institutional transformation. Collins sees the dual nature of black women's activism as both "conservative and radical," especially in their maintenance of an Afrocentric culture (1990:144). She believes that African American women are more likely to use "strategic affiliation and reject ideology as the overarching framework structuring . . . political activism." This does not mean that black women "lack ideology but, rather, that our experiences as othermothers, centerwomen, and community othermothers foster a distinctive form of political activism based on negotiation and a higher degree of attention to context" (1990:160).[5]

The key to practical, emancipatory action is the idea articulated by Angela Davis of "lift as we climb"—that is, try to "guarantee that all our sisters, regardless of social class, and indeed all of our brothers climb with us" (quoted in Collins, 1990:158). However, Collins sees the "changing social class structure of African-American families and communities" as possibly changing the "shape and effectiveness of this long-standing Black women's activist tradition." For example, she suggests that many black college students, especially those attending white institutions, often fail to see the significance of their education for black "group survival" and institutional transformation (1990:160).

Class, Gender, and Race

As the previous discussion illustrates, issues of class, gender, and race are all interrelated in Collins's work.

Class   Collins points out that the primary sociological models of social class—status attainment and the conflict model—do not adequately explain black social class relations, especially black women's social class relations and experiences. **Status attainment** relies on identification of the occupational status of traditional male jobs, from which women's class position was supposed to derive. But black male unemployment rates, racial discrimination that provides only a narrow set of occupations for African Americans, and the "existence of household arrangements other than the two-parent nuclear families" make this model unsuitable to explain "Black social class dynamics" (1990:45).

Similarly, for the **conflict model,** the focus on paid labor, and especially on a particular type of paid labor—industrial factory jobs that many blacks, irrespective of gender, do not have access to—makes this model equally inadequate

---

[5] The references to othermothers and centerwomen relate to Collins's point about the collective, communal nature of mothering in African American communities.

as an explanation of black social class. Only "placing women's work and family experiences at the center of the analysis" can provide a view of African American social class locations. Understanding the "intersection of work and family in Black women's lives is key to clarifying the overarching political economy of domination" (1990:45). Black feminist theory must therefore be concerned with the "changed consciousness of individuals" as well as the "social transformation of political and economic institutions" (1990:221).

Although all African American women "encounter the common theme of having our work and family experiences shaped by the interlocking nature of race, gender, and class oppression," the commonality and "racial solidarity" that these experiences generated in the past is increasingly strained as a significant black middle class appears in stark contrast to the poor, working-class women of the inner-city neighborhoods (1990:65). For Collins, reforging the traditional relationship of sisterhood is one of the important ways in which African American women can overcome the changing dynamics of class to involve all black women in political activism (1990:211).

Gender and Race   Gender and race cannot be separated in Collins's work. Only by seeing the everyday world through the "both/and conceptual lens of the simultaneity of race, class, and gender oppression and of the need for a humanist vision of community," argues Collins, can a "fundamental paradigmatic shift in how we think about oppression" be achieved (1990:221–222). Black feminist thought "reconceptualizes the social relations of domination and oppression" by replacing "additive models of oppression with interlocking ones" (1990:222, 225).

An interlocking model involves recognizing that although race, class, and gender have been the fundamental systems of oppression for African American women, other oppressions such as "age, sexual orientation, religion, and ethnicity" affect other groups. The key is to place the excluded group in the "center of analysis" and, in doing so, open up "possibilities for a both/and conceptual stance, one in which all groups possess varying amounts of penalty and privilege in one historically created system." Collins sees a "matrix of domination" so that, depending on the context, "an individual may be an oppressor, a member of an oppressed group, or simultaneously oppressor and oppressed" (1990:225).

The **matrix of domination** "contains few pure victims or oppressors" because each individual "derives varying amounts of penalty and privilege from the multiple systems of oppression which frame everyone's lives" (1990:229). It is by recognizing these multiple standpoints, and engaging in dialogue, that domination can be resisted. Because each group knows its knowledge is partial and thus "unfinished," each group is "able to consider other groups' standpoints without relinquishing the uniqueness of its own standpoint or suppressing other groups' partial perspectives" (1990:236).

Dialogue is a necessity to transcend difference and transform relations of domination. In Collins's view, black women's contributions to any dialogue are particularly important because being treated as an "invisible Other" gives black women their "peculiar angle of vision" and their "outsider-within status"

(1990:94). Black feminist scholars, as outsiders-within academic discourse, also have an important part to play in challenging the "content of what currently passes as truth" and simultaneously challenging the "process of arriving at that truth" (1989:773).

Other Theories and Theorists

Collins criticizes the white academic depiction of black women as strong matriarchs who "allegedly emasculate their lovers and husbands" (1990:74). In this interpretation, the "absence of Black patriarchy is used as evidence for Black cultural inferiority" and for black men's underachievement. But W. E. B. Du Bois had earlier pointed out that "Black women's centrality in Black Families" was not a *"cause* of African-American social class status" but an *"outcome* of racial oppression and poverty" (1990:73). The notion of black matriarchy, Collins points out, diverts attention from the "political and economic inequality affecting Black mothers and children and suggests that anyone can rise from poverty if he or she only received good values at home" (1990:74).

The notion of the black matriarchal family is constructed in terms of the "mythical norm of the financially independent, white middle-class family organized around a monogamous heterosexual couple" (1990:165). Moreover, argues Collins, the presumed "deviance" of the black family is related to assumptions about unrestrained, animalistic black sexuality. By "labeling Blacks as sexually animalistic," Collins maintains, "whites in actuality aim to repress these dimensions of their own inner being" (1990:196). Collins is equally critical of the sexism of black men, but recognizes that it is often fueled by black men's acceptance of the white notion of a domineering black matriarchy.[6] What has to be recognized, she insists, is that sexuality and power on both the personal and the structural level reinforce the sex/gender hierarchy, which ensures the "smooth operation of race, gender, and class oppression" (1990:196).

Critique and Conclusions

Both Collins and Smith are centrally concerned with developing a theoretical stance that will be inclusive of groups previously excluded from abstract knowledge and knowledge production. In this aim, Collins is more successful than Smith. One of the major criticisms of Smith's work is that it is difficult for women outside the academy to comprehend because it remains situated in the language and form of sociological disciplinary specialization. bell hooks (hooks and West, 1991:72) points out that professionalization in the academy "limits those of us who want to speak to broader audiences," especially because editorial practices make all writing appear alike.

One further critique is related to the emphasis on experience. Grant (1993: 100) maintains that experience cannot "in and of itself, be the ground for an

---

[6]For a discussion of the "myths" developed by black men, with the collaboration of some black women, that divest black women of power and freedom, see Barbara Smith (1983).

epistemology." There is "simply too much left unexplained," such as whose experience is to count as most important. For both Collins and Smith, the response to this criticism is essentially that the analysis of women's oppression provides a key to the "development of integrated analysis and practice based upon the fact that the major systems of oppression are interlocking" (Barbara Smith, 1983:xxxii). Furthermore, although the experiences of particular groups give rise to a plurality of knowledges, black women and white women share "a history of sexism and certain core experiences relating to female biology, sexuality, motherhood, and roles in the household and workplace" (Seidman, 1994:259).

Final Thoughts

Collins (1990:73) points out that "race, class, gender, and heterosexism" present major challenges to sociology, but despite "significant changes, the inner circle of sociological theory—its membership, epistemology, and theoretical frameworks—remains strangely untouched by the changes." The work of both Smith and Collins, and the multidisciplinarity of much feminist work in general, represent challenges to the "sanctity" of the theoretical inner circle. While both of them draw on a variety of theoretical traditions and are representative of the interdisciplinarity of feminist studies, both of them deal centrally with the issues that have concerned all sociological theorists. Both theorists are radical in their politics and their sociological focus.

The focus on these two sociologists in this chapter should not obscure the contributions to feminist social theory made in the past three decades by historians, political scientists, psychoanalysts, and anthropologists, as well as those in feminist literary studies and cultural studies, all of whom have presented important challenges to the theoretical hegemony that the classical, and in some cases the current, sociological tradition embodies. Some of the current feminist social theory from French feminists, from feminists influenced by Habermas and Foucault, and from new psychoanalytic perspectives will be touched on in Chapter 11.

References

American Sociological Association. 1993. "ASA Award Winners Reflect Broad Spectrum of Sociology." *Footnotes, 212*(7), 13.

Barrett, Michele, and Anne Phillips. 1992. "Introduction." In Michele Barrett and Ann Phillips (Eds.), *Destabilizing Theory* (pp. 1–9). Stanford, CA: Stanford University Press.

Bernard, Jessie. 1989. "The Dissemination of Feminist Thought: 1960 to 1988." In Ruth A. Wallace (Ed.), *Feminist Sociological Theory* (pp. 23–33). Newbury Park, CA: Sage.

Collins, Patricia Hill. 1989. "The Social Construction of Black Feminist Thought." *Signs, 14*, 745–773.

———. 1990. *Black Feminist Thought*. Cambridge: Unwin Hyman.

————. 1992. "Transforming the Inner Circle: Dorothy Smith's Challenge to Socio-logical Theory." *Sociological Theory, 10,* 73–80.

Dalla Costa, Mariarosa, and Selma Jones. 1973. *The Power of Women and the Subversion of Community.* Bristol, England: Falling Wall Press.

de Beauvoir, Simone. 1974. *The Second Sex.* New York: Alfred A. Knopf.

Deckard, Barbara Sinclair. 1983. *The Women's Movement.* New York: Harper and Row.

Eichler, Margrit. 1992. "Not Always an Easy Alliance: The Relationship between Women's Studies and the Women's Movement in Canada." In Constance Backhouse and David H. Flaherty (Eds.), *The Women's Movement in Canada and the United States* (pp. 120–135). Montreal and Kingston: McGill–Queen's University Press.

Eisenstein, Zillah. 1979. "Developing a Theory of Capitalist Patriarchy and Socialist Feminism." In Zillah Eisenstein (Ed.), *Capitalist Patriarchy and the Case for Socialist Feminism* (pp. 5–40). New York: Monthly Review Press.

Engels, Frederick. 1972. *The Origin of the Family, Private Property and the State.* New York: Pathfinder Press.

Epstein, Cynthia Fuchs. 1988. *Deceptive Distinctions: Sex, Gender, and the Social Order.* New Haven, CT: Yale University Press.

Friedan, Betty. 1963. *The Feminine Mystique.* New York: Dell.

Grant, Judith. 1993. *Fundamental Feminism: Contesting the Core Concepts of Feminist Theory.* New York: Routledge.

Harding, Sandra. 1981. "What Is the Real Material Base of Patriarchy and Capital?" In Lydia Sargent (Ed.), *Women and Revolution* (pp. 135–163). Montreal: Black Rose Books.

Hartmann, Heidi. 1981. "The Unhappy Marriage of Marxism and Feminism: Towards a More Progressive Union." In Lydia Sargent (Ed.), *Women and Revolution* (pp. 1–41). Montreal: Black Rose Books.

Hekman, Susan. 1997. "Truth and Method: Feminist Standpoint Theory Revisited," *Signs, 22,* 341–365.

hooks, bell, and Cornell West. 1991. *Breaking Bread.* Toronto: Between the Lines.

Jaggar, Alison M. 1983. *Feminist Politics and Human Nature.* Sussex, England: Harvester Press.

Johnson, Miriam. 1989. "Feminism and the Theories of Talcott Parsons." In Ruth A. Wallace (Ed.), *Feminism and Sociological Theory* (pp. 101–118). Newbury Park, CA: Sage.

Laslett, Barbara, and Barrie Thorne. 1992. "Considering Dorothy Smith's Social Theory: Introduction." *Sociological Theory, 10,* 60–62.

Lemert, Charles. 1992. "Subjectivity's Limit: The Unsolved Riddle of the Standpoint," *Sociological Theory, 10*(1), 63–72.

Lengermann, Patricia, and Jill Niebrugge-Brantley. 1990. "Feminist Sociological Theory: The Near-Future Prospects." In George Ritzer (Ed.), *Frontiers of Social Theory* (pp. 316–344). New York: Columbia University Press.

Marx, Karl, and Frederick Engels. 1845–1846/1947. *The German Ideology.* New York: International Publishers.

McClure, Kirstie. 1992. "The Issue of Foundations: Scientized Politics, Politicized Science, and Feminist Critical Practice." In Judith Butler and Joan W. Scott (Eds.), *Feminists Theorize the Political* (pp. 341–368). New York: Routledge.

Mitchell, Juliet. 1971. *Women's Estate.* Harmondsworth, England: Penguin.

Parsons, Talcott. 1954. *Essays in Sociological Theory.* Glencoe, IL: Free Press.

Rossi, Alice S. 1964. "Equality Between the Sexes: An Immodest Proposal." *Daedalus, 93,* 607–652.

———. 1988. "Growing Up and Older in Sociology: 1940–1990." In Matilda White Riley (Ed.), *Sociological Lives* (pp. 43–64). Newbury Park, CA: Sage.

Rowbotham, Sheila. 1973. *Woman's Consciousness, Man's World*. Harmondsworth, England: Penguin.

Rubin, Lillian B. 1994. "An Unanticipated Life." In Katheryn P. Meadows Orlans and Ruth A. Wallace (Eds.), *Gender and the Academic Experience*. Lincoln: University of Nebraska Press.

Schutz, Alfred. 1932/1967. *The Phenomenology of the Social World*. Evanston, IL: Northwestern University Press.

Seidman, Steven. 1994. *Contested Knowledge*. Oxford: Blackwell.

Smith, Barbara (Ed.). 1983. *Home Girls: A Black Feminist Anthology*. New York: Kitchen Table, Women of Color Press.

Smith, Dorothy E. 1975. "Ideological Structures and How Women Are Excluded." *The Canadian Review of Sociology and Anthropology, 12*, 353–369.

———. 1977a. *Feminism and Marxism: A Place to Begin, A Way to Go*. Vancouver: New Star Books.

———. 1977b. "Women, the Family and Corporate Capitalism." In Marylee Stephenson (Ed.), *Women in Canada* (pp. 17–48). Don Mills, Ontario: General Publishing.

———. 1987. *The Everyday World as Problematic: A Feminist Sociology*. Toronto: University of Toronto Press.

———. 1989. "Sociological Theory: Methods of Writing Patriarchy." In Ruth A. Wallace (Ed.), *Feminism and Sociological Theory* (pp. 34–64). Newbury Park, CA: Sage.

———. 1990a. *The Conceptual Practices of Power*. Toronto: University of Toronto Press.

———. 1990b. *Texts, Facts and Femininity*. London: Routledge.

———. 1992. "Sociology from Women's Experience: A Reaffirmation." *Sociological Theory, 10*, 88–98.

———. 1994. "A Berkeley Education." In Kathryn P. Meadows Orlans and Ruth A. Wallace (Eds.), *Gender and the Academic Experience*. Lincoln: University of Nebraska Press.

———. 1999. *Writing the Social*. Toronto: University of Toronto Press.

Spender, Dale. 1983. *There's Always Been a Women's Movement This Century*. London: Pandora Press.

Stacy, J., and B. Thorne. 1985. "The Missing Feminist Revolution in Sociology." *Social Problems, 32*, 301–316.

Stanley, Liz, and Sue Wise. 1983. *Breaking Out: Feminist Consciousness and Feminist Research*. London: Routledge and Kegan Paul.

Swingwood, Alan. 1991. *A Short History of Sociological Thought*. London: Macmillan.

Sydie, R. A. 1987. *Natural Women, Cultured Men*. Toronto: Methuen.

Turner, Jonathan. 1990. "The Past, Present, and Future of Theory in American Sociology." In George Ritzer (Ed.), *Frontiers of Social Theory* (pp. 371–391). New York: Columbia University Press.

Wallace, Ruth A. 1989. "Introduction." In Ruth A. Wallace (Ed.), *Feminism and Sociological Theory* (pp. 7–19). Newbury Park, CA: Sage.

Chapter 11

Knowledge, Truth, and Power
Foucault and Feminist Responses

Human knowledge and human power come to the same thing, because ignorance of cause frustrates effect. (Francis Bacon, *Novum Organum*)

Knowledge has always been linked to power, in the sense of having the power to have an effect on individuals or, more generally, on society. The fear of the village gossip, for example, was a fear of the gossip's presumed knowledge. The power of knowledge is even more important today with the proliferation of electronic systems that can store enormous amounts of data, recording the most intimate aspects of any individual's life. These data are stored in places that are accessible to governments and to those individuals, corporations, and institutions whose requests for such knowledge are deemed "legitimate," but the same data are often not accessible, or easily accessible, to the subjects who have contributed the information. This electronic capacity makes supposedly autonomous individuals into bureaucratic cases without control over the dispersal of knowledge about their lives and their intimate, inner being. Furthermore, there is often the suspicion that the "knowledge" stored in these sophisticated ways may be no more informed than the knowledge of the village gossip.

Michel Foucault's central concern was how knowledge related to power. He was especially concerned with charting how different regimes of knowledge shaped modern society. Foucault did not regard knowledge *as* power but as contributing in different ways, in different contexts, to the exercise of power. Foucault thus qualified Bacon's assertion that knowledge and power are like cause and effect. Knowledge itself does not provide any inevitable, predictable effects. Furthermore, power itself can produce knowledge. Foucault's concern is particularly timely given the way in which information about individuals is monitored, evaluated, and stored in modern society, effectively abolishing the classic Enlightenment distinction between a public and a private realm.

Michel Foucault (1926–1984)

Michel Foucault was born in Poitiers, France, to a prosperous bourgeois family. His father was a surgeon and obstetrician; his mother, who was independently wealthy, managed the household and her husband's medical practice. Foucault's adolescence was marked by the experience of World War II. He later recalled the fear he had felt about whether he would live through the bombing and, if he did, whether he would be German or French at the end of the war (Macey, 1993). Foucault, like many postwar intellectuals, felt it "intolerable to have a 'bourgeois' professional future as a professor, journalist, writer, or whatever," given the "urgency of creating a society radically different" from the one before the war (Trombadori, 1991:47). Foucault resisted his own bourgeois origins by rejecting the idea of following in his father's footsteps and becoming a doctor, despite a family tradition dictating that the eldest son study medicine. Foucault's defiance of his father's wishes resulted in a career that in fact encompassed the roles of professor, journalist, and writer.

Foucault attended the École Normale Supérieure, the training ground for the French cultural elite, and graduated with a philosophy degree in 1948. While there, he studied with Jean Hippolite, who taught Hegel, and with the Marxist Louis Althusser. In 1950 Foucault joined the Communist party, supposedly at the urging of Althusser (Macey, 1993:37). However, it would seem that Foucault was not a very enthusiastic party member—no one recalled his attendance at any meetings—and by 1953 he had left the party (Macey, 1993:38).

In 1952 Foucault completed a diploma course in psychopathology at the Institut de Psychologie, and he was then hired at the University of Lille in the philosophy department to teach psychology to philosophy students. His teaching duties were light, and because "pastoral duties in a French university are traditionally so light as to be almost nonexistent, and staff–student relations tend to be formal, if not distant," Foucault had considerable time for other research and teaching (Macey, 1993:49). Foucault taught part-time at the École Normale Supérieure, and he was an unofficial intern at the major psychiatric hospital, Hôpital Sainte-Anne. In 1955 he went to the French Institute in Uppsala, Sweden, to teach French language and literature. Some years later, Foucault stated that he went to Sweden because it was "supposed to be a much freer country," but once there, he found that a "certain kind of freedom may have, not exactly the same effects, but as many effects as a directly restrictive society" (Kritzman, 1988:5). He left Sweden for Warsaw in 1958 to take charge of the University's Centre Français. Foucault was transferred to Hamburg as a cultural attaché in 1959 and returned to France in 1960 to become a professor at the University of Clermont-Ferrand in the Department of Philosophy.

In 1961 Foucault successfully defended his doctoral thesis, which was published as *Historie de la folie (History of Madness)*. Foucault remained at Clermont until 1966, when he went to Tunisia to teach philosophy at the University of Tunis. He returned to Paris in 1968 to teach philosophy at the new University of Vincennes. In 1970 Foucault was elected to the Chair in the History of

Systems of Thought at the most prestigious institution in France, the Collège de France.[1]

Foucault was often invited to lecture in North America, which he liked, especially California, finding the "intellectual life freer and more open than in France" as well as providing more opportunity to explore the "uses of pleasure," especially in the bathhouses of San Francisco (Macey, 1993:430). Foucault confessed that he preferred American to French food and declared a "good club sandwich with a coke. That's my pleasure. It's true" (Kritzman, 1988:12). Foucault visited San Francisco for the last time in 1983 and, according to Miller (1993:34), frequented the bathhouses despite the growing knowledge about, and fear of, AIDS. Foucault died in 1984. In his reflection on Foucault's death, Miller quoted from Foucault's *History of Sexuality*: "Sex is worth dying for" (1976:156).

Foucault's Central Theories and Methods

Foucault's work was not sociological in the North American sense of disciplinary specialization. His work ranged over a number of disciplines, including sociology, but also history, criminology, psychiatry, and philosophy. At the École Normale, his training was largely philosophical. Foucault recalled that when he was at the École, the philosophical currents were Hegel and phenomenology but that he had also become enthused about Nietzsche's work. Marx, Freud, and structuralism also figured in his training, but Foucault claimed that "I have never been a Freudian, I have never been a Marxist and I have never been a structuralist" (Kritzman, 1988:22). He described his intellectual training as based on a "pantheon of authors read 'against' Sartre and Hegel" (Macey, 1993:34). Foucault noted that prior to the 1960s, "France knew absolutely nothing . . . about the current Weberian thought" and critical theory, and the Frankfurt School was "practically unheard of" (Kritzman, 1988:26).

Foucault claimed that it was his reading of Nietzsche, along with other authors such as George Bataille, Maurice Blanchot, and Pierre Klossowki, that enabled him to "move away from [his] original university education" (1991:30). What interested him about these authors was that they did not construct systems but wrote from "direct, personal experience" (1991:30). By 1951, Foucault's intellectual interests were in the history of science, philosophy—especially Nietzschean philosophy—and psychology (Macey, 1993:35).

Foucault's interest in science had been stimulated by the work of George Canguilhem in biology and medicine. Canguilhem's work was predicated on the notion that "it is the abnormal which arouses theoretical interest in the normal" (quoted in Miller, 1993:60). Foucault's examinations of madness, prisons, and sexuality exemplify Canguilhem's view. Foucault was also influenced by the French philosophers of science, who stressed the idea that scientific "progress"

---

[1]The Collège is unique. It does not give degrees, and the 50 chairholders are elected by the other professors to "reward the most distinguished French practitioners in arts and sciences, from music to mathematics" (Miller, 1993:183). The only requirement is that the chairholders give an annual course of lectures, open to the public, in which they discuss their work in progress.

was not some smooth accumulation of "truths" but resulted from conceptual revolutions in how the world was understood. These conceptual revolutions produced demonstrable breaks or fault lines that transformed scientific disciplines (Miller, 1993:61).[2]

Foucault concluded that instead of "asking science to what extent its history has approached the truth (or impeded access to it)," science and scientific claims should be examined in the light of the idea that "the truth consists of a certain relationship that discourse and knowledge has with itself" (1991:62). That is, science and the scientist are historically situated, and there is no single "truth" but a "series of collective rational experiences" that construct the "knowing subject." Consequently, the scientist, as well as the research she or he produces, are part of the knowledge produced; they are both the "object" that is "known" (1991:63–64).[3]

Each historical age is characterized by particular forms of knowledge. Foucault called these particular knowledge forms an **episteme**, meaning sets of presuppositions that organize what counts as knowledge, truth, and reality and indicate how these matters can be discussed. For example, while the historian of science was busy determining "the constitution of scientific objects," Foucault would ask another question: "How does it happen that the human subject makes himself into an object of possible knowledge, through which forms of rationality, through what historic necessities, and at what price?" (Foucault, quoted in Lotringer, 1989:245).

Since the eighteenth century, the modern episteme has focused on the idea of the autonomous, rational subject—"Man"—as the subject *and* object of discourses about life and labor (Foucault, 1966:312). The "price" paid in making the human subject an object is control over that subject-become-object. This control is effected through the formulation of new kinds of knowledge about subjects as a result of the interrelated practices of documentation, surveillance, and confession. For example, in *Discipline and Punish* (1977), Foucault described how new kinds of scientific knowledge about the human body had given rise to new ways of controlling bodies.

> The human body was entering a machinery of power that explores it, breaks it down and rearranges it. . . . It defined how one may have a hold over other's bodies, not only so that they may do what one wishes, but so that they may operate as one wishes, with the techniques, the speed and the efficiency that one determines. Thus discipline produces subjected and practiced bodies, "docile" bodies. (1977:138)

Foucault's concern with knowledge was thus related to his concern with **power** and how it connects with **truth**. The background to Foucault's position is found in Nietzsche's analysis of good and evil in the *Genealogy of Morals*.

---

[2]This perspective is very similar to that of Thomas Kuhn in his *The Structure of Scientific Revolutions* (1962), which, according to Miller (1993:61), is not surprising as Kuhn knew and admired the French historians of science.

[3]Foucault indicated that he came to this conclusion as a result of reading Nietzsche in conjunction with the philosophers of science.

Nietzsche argued that there was no essential, or original, definition of truth. Truth was an interpretation tied to the operation of power and domination. Truth is therefore produced by power, and the consequences of the exercise of power are formulated as "truth."

> Power and knowledge directly imply one another . . . there is no power relation with the correlative constitution of a field of knowledge, nor any knowledge that does not presuppose and constitute at the same time power relations. (Foucault, 1977:27)

For example, government administrators "render phenomena (such as an expanding number of people) into objects (such as population) amenable to scientific study" at the same time that "scientific methodologies provide knowledge of these objects that render them amenable to government" (Simons, 1995:27–28).

"Truth," based on scientific discourse and the institutions producing such discourse, has the following traits, according to Foucault:

- "Truth" is centred on the form of scientific discourse and the institutions which produce it.
- It is subject to constant economic and political incitement (the demand for truth, as much for economic production as for political power).
- It is the object, under diverse forms, of immense diffusion and consumption (circulating through apparatuses of education and information whose extent is relatively broad in the social body).
- It is produced and transmitted under the control of a few great political and economic apparatuses (university, army, writing, media).
- It is the issue of a whole political debate and social confrontation ("ideological" struggles). (Foucault, 1980:131–132)

Power is also refigured in Foucault's discussions. The traditional understanding of power is that it is possessed by someone or something. Foucault suggests a different perspective on power. First, power is **exercised** rather than possessed. Second, power is not simply or inevitably **repressive** or **coercive** but can be **productive.** For example, in modern society power is exercised through the various practices and discourses that produce mad as opposed to sane people, or healthy as opposed to sick people, or "normal" as opposed to deviant people. Third, power does not flow from a **centralized source** but also flows from the **bottom up—** that is, from the multitude of interactions at the micro level of society.

Power is diffused throughout society. It is something that circulates: It is "never localised here or there, never in anybody's hands, never appropriated as a commodity or piece of wealth. . . . And not only do individuals circulate between its threads; they are also in the position of simultaneously undergoing and exercising power" (Foucault, 1980:98).

Central to the operation of power/knowledge/truth connections are discourses and texts. Foucault's emphasis on discourses and texts in the examination of epistemes, together with his conception of history as a series of ruptures and breaks rather than a unified, progressive totality, provides the basis of his methodology. He called his methodological procedures archaeology and genealogy.

Archaeology involves the study of discourses that set the conditions for what counts as knowledge in particular historical periods. It involves "comparison of one discursive practice with another and a discursive practice with the non-discursive practices (institutions, political events, economic and social processes) that surround it" (Sheridan, 1980:105). These practices determine, for example, what is "moral" or "scientific" and how the moral or scientific status of the object or event is to be described. The focus is on the type of knowledge produced in certain periods that generate a particular "object" that becomes the focus for disciplines—for example, sociology, biology, or medicine—and then becomes the knowledge of that discipline.[4] For example, in the nineteenth century "society" became an object of study in its own right and then became the linchpin of the new discipline of sociology.

Genealogy means tracing descent, and Foucault uses it to describe a different approach to historical research. Instead of assuming a discoverable causality for historical events, Foucault examines the contingency of historical objects. The focus is on the ruptures, transitions, and discontinuities that produce historical concepts and definitions. This involves tracing not only the historical "winners" but also the "losers" in the interplay of events. Contrary to Marx, Foucault sees no inevitable historical necessity for any particular events. Instead, he argues, the historian has to examine the possibility that what transpired could have been otherwise.

Archaeology is the "intellectual subconscious" of disciplines (Gutting, 1994:9). Genealogy is "**eventalization**"—that is, the investigation of history on the assumption that it need not have taken the course it did, that events were not "as necessary as all that." For example, it involves the recognition that it was not a "matter of course that mad people came to be regarded as mentally ill; it wasn't self-evident that the only thing to be done with a criminal was to lock him up" (Foucault, 1991:76). Eventalization means "rediscovering the connection, encounters, supports, blockages, plays of forces, strategies and so on which at a given moment establish what subsequently counts as being self-evident, universal and necessary" (1991:76).

Genealogy has three "domains" in Foucault's work:

- First, a historical ontology of ourselves in relation to truth through which we constitute ourselves as subjects of knowledge;

- Second, a historical ontology of ourselves in relation to a field of power through which we constitute ourselves as subjects acting on others;

- Third, a historical ontology in relation to ethics through which we constitute ourselves as moral agents. (Foucault, 1984a:354)

---

[4]Using the word *knowledge* to refer to the two procedures is somewhat confusing because of a translation problem. Foucault used *savior* and *connaissance*, both of which translate into English as knowledge. Foucault explained the difference this way: By *connaissance* I mean the relation of the subject to the object and the formal rules that govern it. *Savior* refers to the conditions that are necessary in a particular period for that type of object to be given to *connaissance* and for this or that enunciation to be formulated (Translator's note, Foucault, 1972:15, fn. 2).

According to Foucault, all three domains were present in his first work, *Madness and Civilization*, "although in a somewhat confused fashion." Truth was studied in *The Birth of the Clinic* and *The Order of Things*, power in *Discipline and Punish*, and ethics in *The History of Sexuality* (Foucault, 1984a:352).

Foucault was not interested in proposing a "global principle for analyzing society" as other historians and sociologists had done. He was interested in the history of "the way things become a problem" and how the problem was constructed in discourse. As he put it, "my problem is to see how men govern (themselves and others) by the production of truth (I repeat . . . that by the production of truth I mean not the production of true utterances, but the establishment of domains in which the practice of true and false can be made at once ordered and pertinent)" (Foucault, 1991:79). This means that the certainties that sociologists have taken for granted, such as society as a sui generis entity, must be rejected as immutable truths, along with the idea of rationality as a natural human quality. This makes it somewhat difficult to use here the subheads "Society" and "Humans" that we have used in each chapter—a difficulty that Foucault would have found both amusing and obvious. Nonetheless, the following section is organized by those subheads, even if they are only contradicted by Foucault's work.

Nature of Society, Humans, and Change

Foucault does not have any conception of society as a definable structure or system. "Society" is the product of discourses and practices, especially those discourses and practices of the human or social sciences. Similarly, he rejects any timeless notion of the nature of human beings. According to Foucault, before the "end of the eighteenth century, *man* did not exist" (Foucault, 1966:308). That is, the idea of "Man" as both subject and object—as an individual who produces knowledge as well as that entity about which knowledge is produced—was not part of the discourses of truth prior to the eighteenth century.

The recent social constructions of "society" and "man" in the Western world have developed from a complex web of interconnections and conflicts in the social arena. To Foucault, the social arena is an historically situated and variable arena of power/knowledge, and the key to understanding society, humans, and social change lies in uncovering the power/knowledge grid. We will examine Foucault's *Discipline and Punish* first to illustrate how a variety of ideas and institutions gave rise to the notion of modern society as, ideally, a collection of disciplined, docile bodies.

Society   Foucault introduces *Discipline and Punish* with a description of a public execution in 1757 and a timetable of rules drawn up in 1837 for Parisian prisoners. The two descriptions represent two different forms of punishment and two different understandings of what constitutes a crime.

The description of the execution seems particularly horrific today, but at the time it was observed by many and calmly reported in its details by several observers. For example, the last part of the execution involved quartering, but "because the horses were not accustomed to drawing . . . instead of four, six were needed; and when that did not suffice, they were forced, in order to cut off the wretch's thighs, to sever the sinews and hack at the joints." But the spectators were "edified by the solicitude of the parish priest of St. Paul's who . . . did not spare himself in offering consolation to the patient" (Foucault, 1975:3). Foucault claims that this form of punishment was "normal" until the eighteenth century, when torture and mutilation of the body, along with public executions, disappeared.

Public executions, and lesser forms of assault on the body such as amputation or branding, were both juridical and political acts. Prior to the eighteenth century, the law represented the sovereign's will. A crime was thus a personal attack on the sovereign and had to be publicly avenged in order to reassert/restore the power of the sovereign. A public execution demonstrated the power asymmetry between "the subject who has dared to violate the law and the all-powerful sovereign who displays his strength." Punishment had to be an exercise in terror in order to reinforce the belief, among the rest of the population, in the awe-inspiring power of the sovereign (Foucault, 1975:49).

By the nineteenth century, public punishment had virtually disappeared in Western societies. In fact, Foucault states, punishment became the "most hidden part of the penal process" (1977:9). Punishment became more "gentle" but more thorough, the object being to "punish less, but to punish more deeply in the social body" (Foucault, 1975:82). It was the prison that marked the transformation in the power and practice of punishment. The target of punishment became the body and soul of the prisoner, in an effort to remake the prisoner into an obedient subject. The prisoner is therefore subjected to the **discipline** of "habits, rules, order, and authority that is exercised continually around him and upon him, and which he must allow to function automatically in him" (1977:129). Discipline is reinforced by techniques of surveillance that constantly "see" and monitor behavior.

> The perfect disciplinary apparatus would make it possible for a single gaze to see everything constantly. A central point would be both the source of light illuminating everything, and a locus of convergence for everything that must be known: a perfect eye that nothing would escape and a center toward which all gazes would be turned. (1977:173)

The perfect model of such a disciplinary apparatus was Jeremy Bentham's plan for a Panopticon. The architecture of the Panopticon would enable a single observer, standing at the center of the cylindrical tower, to see each individual inmate in the cells ranged around the walls of the tower. The guard can see all, and all prisoners are conscious of their "permanent visibility," which in turn assures the "automatic functioning of power" (Foucault, 1977:201). The prisoners know they can be seen, but they do not know when they are being seen. As a result, prisoners will monitor or discipline themselves in case they are being observed. The "gaze" eliminates the need for "arms, physical violence, material constraints" because, under the gaze, each individual becomes his own "overseer . . . thus exercising this surveillance over, and against, himself" (1977:155). Although the Panopticon was never built, the panoptic principle was important in defining new power relations in everyday life. In fact, we live under the gaze of the remote, all-seeing eye of video cameras. We are captured on film in retail outlets, banks, and other public places in an ostensible effort to control crime.

Foucault argued that the panoptic principle of generalized surveillance had been gradually extended throughout society to form the **disciplinary society** (1977:209). From the eighteenth century on, the organization of prisons was complemented by the organization of workhouses for the poor, asylums for the mad, factories for the workers, and hospitals for the diseased, all devoted to disciplining the unruly bodies of the poor, the mad, the sick, and the underclasses. The modern disciplinary society was an historically constructed entity involving "economic, juridico-political, and . . . scientific" efforts (Foucault, 1977:218).

The disciplinary society was, in Foucault's view, a critical part of the transition of Western societies to modernity.

> If the economic take-off of the west began with the techniques that made possible the accumulation of capital, it might perhaps be said that the methods for administrating the accumulation of men made possible the political take-off in relation to . . . subjection. In fact the two processes—the accumulation of men and the accumulation of capital—cannot be separated. (1977:221)

The accumulation of men required a productive process capable of sustaining and using them, and "techniques that made the cumulative multiplicity of men useful accelerated the accumulation of capital" (1977:221). The conjunction of these processes required "docile bodies" who generally disciplined themselves as good citizens and diligent workers. The operation of power that produces docile bodies is obscured, however, by the "enlightened" modern assumption of the agency of the rational, autonomous individual (recall Giddens).

A key aspect of the disciplinary society, Foucault observes, is the "reversal of the political axis of individualization" (1977:192). In feudal society, the more power and privilege a person possessed, the more the person was regarded as an individual. In modern disciplinary regimes, however, "as power becomes more anonymous and more functional, those on whom it is exercised tend to be more strongly individualized." For example, "the child is more individualized than the adult, the patient more than the healthy man, the madman and the delinquent more than the normal and the non-delinquent," and when one individualizes the "healthy, normal and law-abiding adult, it is always by asking him how much of the child he has in him, what secret madness lies within him, what fundamental crime he has dreamt of committing." All the "sciences, analyses, or practices employing the root 'psycho'—have their origin in this historical reversal of individuality." It is when the "sciences of man became possible" that the "new technology of power and a new political anatomy of the body were implemented" (Foucault, 1977:193).

Humans   Foucault's recognition of the fragmentation of the "individual" through the specialized disciplinary practices of the human and medical sciences, and the manner in which the autonomy of the individual has been compromised, is a critique of the Enlightenment concept of the rational, autonomous subject. When Foucault said "the concept of Man is a fraud," he did not mean that "you and I are nothing" (Hacking, 1986:39). What he meant was that the humanist celebration of the abstraction "Man" obscured the multitude of ways in which the subject is constructed. For Foucault, there is "no sovereign, founding subject, a universal form of subject to be found everywhere"; on the contrary, the subject is "constituted through the practices of subjection, or, in a more autonomous way, through practices of liberation . . . on the basis . . . of a number of rules, styles, inventions to be found in the cultural environment" (Foucault, 1988a:50–51).

The concept of Man, however, is necessary to the operation of a disciplinary society, as it provides the yardstick by which unruly minds and bodies can be controlled. The transformation of the "mad" illustrates this point.

In *Madness and Civilization,* Foucault points out that the construction of modern mental illness is quite different from earlier conceptions. Madness is thus historically contingent and not, as you might imagine, a universally recognized condition of unreason in contrast to reason. Furthermore, reason *as well as* madness is a social construction.

In medieval society, the madman, the fool, or the simpleton was regarded as the "guardian of truth" because "his simpleton's language which makes for no show of reason" was in fact "the words of reason" that revealed the truth (Foucault, 1961:14). It was in the seventeenth century that the understanding of madness began to change. Madness became identified with "poverty, . . . incapacity for work, . . . inability to integrate with the group." The transformation was linked to the new importance given to the "obligation to work, and all the ethical values that are linked to labor," as illustrated in Weber's *The Protestant Ethic and the Spirit of Capitalism.* Madness, which before had "floundered about in broad daylight: in *King Lear,* in *Don Quixote,*" was now set apart and confined, "bound to reason, to the rules of morality and to their monotonous nights" (1964:64).

In the eighteenth century, madness as unreason resulted in the confinement of the mad: "Madness . . . became the paradoxical manifestation of non-being," and confinement was not to suppress but to "eliminate from the social order a figure which did not find its place within it" (Foucault, 1961:115). Confinement cements unreason as the "empty negativity of reason"; by confinement, "madness is acknowledged to be *nothing*" (1961:116). The confined were not simply the demonstrably disturbed but also disruptive people, such as beggars, vagrants, and prostitutes, whose behavior deviated from the bourgeois model of the moral, industrious citizen.

It was Freud who restored to medicine the "possibility of a dialogue with unreason" (Foucault, 1961:198). The psychiatric discipline was different from the medical discussion of "'diseases of the head' or 'nervous diseases' found in eighteenth-century medical treatises" (1961:179). Psychiatry emerged out of a "whole set of relations between hospitalization, internment, the conditions and procedures of social exclusion, the rule of jurisprudence, the norms of industrial labor and the norms of bourgeois morality, in short a whole group of relations that characterized for this discursive practice the formation of its statements. Psychiatry is another disciplinary practice" (Foucault, 1972:179).

According to Foucault, however, psychiatry retains the Enlightenment stamp, with its notion of a true, unified, and fixed self that can be uncovered by the confessional practices of psychoanalysis. Freud's analysis of the Oedipal complex was, in Foucault's view, another part of the power regime of modern society, reinforcing a normative conception of family and, more specifically, sexual identification and practice. In modern society, the key to a person's true self is believed to be sex: "We demand that sex speak the truth . . . and we demand that it tell us our truth, or rather, the deeply buried truth of that truth about ourselves which we think we possess in our immediate consciousness" (Foucault, 1976:69).

Sex as the Truth of Self   In the first volume of his *History of Sexuality*, Foucault traces the historical conjunction of sexuality, subjectivity, and truth. By the end of the eighteenth century, a "new technology of sex" had emerged. Sex became a state concern—a "matter that required the social body as a whole, and virtually all of its individuals, to place themselves under surveillance" (Foucault, 1976:116). Contrary to the assumption that the Victorians confined and repressed sexuality, Foucault states that sex was spoken of "*ad infinitum,* while exploiting it as *the* secret" (1976:35). Sex was not confined to a "shadow existence" in the Victorian age only to emerge in the free-spirited 1960s; on the contrary, sex was a central preoccupation of the age.

The idea that the nineteenth-century advent of "modern industrial societies ushered in an age of increased sexual repression" must be abandoned. The evidence Foucault uncovers indicates that there was an "explosion of unorthodox sexualities," a "proliferation of specific pleasures and a multiplication of disparate sexualities" under modernity (1976:49). Even the term "sexuality" did not appear before the beginning of the nineteenth century (Foucault, 1984c:3).

The new discourses and technologies of sex involved four strategies of "knowledge and power" that provided the means for a disciplinary control over sexual desire and practice (1976:103):

- The *"hysterization of women's bodies"* (1976:104). Women's bodies were understood to be "saturated with sexuality"; as a result, they were unstable bodies subject to hysteria.

- The *"pedagogization of children's sex"* (1976:104). All children indulged in sexual activity, but that it was seen as an activity "contra to nature." To protect children from the physical and moral dangers of sexual exploration, parents—and, more important, experts such as "educators, doctors, and eventually psychologists"—had to take charge of this "dangerous and endangered sexual potential." It is from this discourse that the myths about the dangers of masturbation arose.

- The *"socialization of procreative behavior"* (1976:104–105). Procreation became linked to the regulation of populations. State and medical experts encouraged the limitation or, alternatively, the proliferation of births in relation to their estimates of the "needs" of the society. Thus, the various financial inducements offered for procreation that societies have used, and continue to use, developed, as well as the provision of contraception for the limitation of births according to the "needs" of the social body. The "needs" were, and are, determined politically, using medical and demographic specialist information.

- The *"psychiatrization of perverse pleasure"* (1976:105). Sexuality became a "separate biological and psychical instinct," prone to anomalies that psychiatry normalized or pathologized, at the same time devising corrective technologies for the anomalies.

The four strategies produced four privileged objects of knowledge that were targets and anchor points for social control: the "hysterical woman, the masturbating child, the Malthusian couple, and the perverse adult" (1976:105).

With the modern transformation of sexuality, the individual became aware of the self as the subject of sexuality. For the "first time in history . . . biological existence was reflected in political existence," and power was exercised not simply over "legal subjects over whom the ultimate dominion was death, but with living beings" (1976:142–143). The four strategies produced what Foucault called **bio-power**—that is, "life and its mechanisms" were brought into the "realm of explicit calculations," and this knowledge/power conjunction produced an ability to transform human life (1976:143). At the "juncture of the 'body' and the 'population,' sex became a crucial target of power organized around the management of life rather than the menace of death" (1976:147). Prisons controlled individuals from the outside; the internalization of sexual norms and practices controlled individuals from the inside.

Foucault indicated that after completing the first volume of *The History of Sexuality* he had intended to trace the historical evolution of this knowledge/power connection up to the nineteenth century, but he realized that an important question remained: "Why had we made sexuality into a moral experience?" (1988a: 252). He turned to the investigation of how "for centuries, Western man had been brought to recognize himself as a subject of desire" (1984b:6). The second volume, *The Use of Pleasure*, investigates the way in which sexual practice was understood as an ethical practice in classical Greece (1984b:91).

Desire and the Ethical Subject   In classical Greece, the ethical domain demanded self-control, especially "dominion of self over self," in the face of acts "intended by nature," such as sex, and "associated by nature with an intense pleasure, and naturally motivated by a force that was always liable to excess and rebellion" (1984b:91). The ethical strictures in classical Greece emphasized austerity with respect to the body, marriage, and the love of boys (1984b:92). These strictures produced three techniques for self-control designed to produce the ethical subject: "dietetics, economics, and erotics" (1984b:251). **Dietetics** focused on the "right time" for sexual pleasure, taking into account the "variable states of the body and the changing properties of the seasons" (1984b:251). **Economics** involved conduct in marriage and family, including the "masculine art of governing a household—wife, servants, estate" (1984b:163). The "faithful" husband was not someone who renounced all sexual pleasure with others but one who "maintained the privileges to which the wife was entitled by marriage" (1984b:164).

Erotics referred to the moderation that should be exercised in relationships with boys. The love of boys generally involved an older man and a young boy, and was only condoned when it involved free citizens. What the relationship

required was a delicate balance in which the older man was "master of his pleasure" but still made "allowance for the other's freedom." That is, love for the
younger man must be balanced by the respect for the younger man's "future
status as a free citizen." At the same time, the younger man must not respond to
sexual urges of the older man because in doing so he made himself a passive sex
object and thus unworthy of being a free citizen. Sex, as a test of self-control,
did not mean "pure and simple abstention," but it did tend to stress the "ideal of
a renunciation of all physical relations with boys" (1984b:252).

In the third volume, *The Care of the Self*, Foucault moves his investigation of
the connection between sexuality and morality to the early Roman Empire. Foucault records a shift in emphasis from classical Greek ideas to a "greater importance accorded to marriage and its demands, and less value given to the love of
boys" (1984c:36). The significance attributed to marriage began in the age of em-
perors, starting with Augustus. The change was connected to various economic
and political transformations in the Empire, most notably a decline in the political significance of alliances among family groups in favor of the importance of
close ties to the emperor. Marriage arrangements became "freer"—"free in choice
of wife; free, too, in the decision to marry and in the reasons for doing so"
(1984c:74). Marriage became more a "voluntary union between two partners,"
and a woman's "inequality diminished to a certain extent but did not cease to
exist" (1984c:74). Foucault claims that the wife became more of a "companion to
whom one opens one's soul" and marriage was more of a symmetrical relationship of "love, affection and mutual sympathy" (1984c:179, 148).

The change in marital relations was connected with the development of a
"culture of the self" that involved all aspects of daily life (1984c:59). A variety of
practices, procedures, and recipes was "developed, perfected and taught," and
included in these management practices was sexuality (1984c:59). Sexuality
was both a pleasure and a danger. It was a danger because of the strength of uncontrolled passions and therefore must only be indulged in at appropriate times
and with appropriate partners. It was an austere regime that played on the
"haunting fear of the individual misfortunes and the collective ills that can result from disorderly sexual behavior" (1984c:64). There was a necessity, therefore, for a "rigorous mastery of desires . . . and the annulment of pleasure as the
goal of sexual relations" (1984c:64).

Foucault's investigation of classical Greece and imperial Rome are contrasted
with his analysis of Christian views on sex. Chastity and restraint were worthy
virtues in the pre-Christian era, but it was in the Christian era that the idea of
sin became connected to sexuality. This connection meant that individuals had
to interrogate themselves as to their inner worth and constantly confess their
transgressions. Christianity "prescribed as a fundamental duty the task of passing everything to do with sex through an endless mill of speech" (1976:21).

Foucault sees this policing of the sexual self in the confessional mode as
eventually spreading to include all social relations: "one confesses one's crimes,
one's sins, one's thoughts and desires, one's illnesses and troubles. . . . One admits to oneself, in pleasure and in pain, things it would be impossible to tell
anyone else, the things people write about in books." The result is, "Western
man has become a confessing animal" (1976:59). Sexuality as the truth of the

person provides an avenue for the exercise of power. The sciences of medicine, psychology, demography, and sociology seize on the confessional body as an object of concern and manipulation (Merquior, 1985:121).

The last two volumes in the sexuality series are about the aesthetics of the self and body and mark a change in Foucault's perspective on the question of the subject. In these two works, the subject has agency, makes choices, and sets out goals (Shumway, 1989:154). But no *general* theory of the subject emerges. Foucault still maintained that human beings are different in different historical periods. "My objective . . . has been to create a history of different modes by which, in our culture, human beings are made subjects" (quoted in Drefus and Rabinow, 1983:20). This is why Foucault, following Nietzsche, saw the humanist concept of "Man" as a recent Western invention. He also indicated that ideas of autonomy, individual dignity, and self-determination were tied to the development of Western industrial capitalism and the development of a disciplinary society. These ideas are the means through which individuals become subjects *and* objects of knowledge and power.

A key question in the light of Foucault's rejection of any essentialist idea of the subject and the power/knowledge connection is how social change occurs. What is, or who is, the "motor" of social change?

Social Change Foucault rejected any abstract, generalizing theory of social change. Ideas about causality, development, evolution, and the "spirit of the age" are rejected. What Foucault was interested in was an "analysis of *different types of transformation*" (1991:55). He examined **discontinuities** that demonstrated how the past was different from the present and that the present was not a product of some historical necessity. He rejected the Enlightenment idea of progress resulting from an inherent human rationality, just as he rejected the Marxian notion that progress can be achieved when human beings realize their basic material needs and capacities. In fact, Foucault maintained that "it is a bad method to pose the problem as: 'How is it that we have progressed?' The problem is: how do things happen?" keeping in mind that "what happens now is not necessarily better or more advanced, or better understood, than what happened in the past" (1980:50).

Central to how things happen, and thus how things change, is the operation of power. Power has a "capillary form of existence." It reaches "into the grain of individuals, touches their bodies and inserts itself into their actions and attitudes, their discourses, learning processes and everyday lives" (Foucault, 1980:39). Power is seductive. It is not simply a "force that says no, . . . it traverses and produces things, it induces pleasure, forms of knowledge, produces discourse" (1980:119). Power should therefore be thought of as a "productive network which runs through the whole social body" (1980:119). Thus, it is not social classes, the state, or other institutional sites of power that are the prime movers in social change.

For Foucault, the question "Who exercises power?" cannot be answered apart from the question "How does it happen?" (1988b:103). Sociology can "show us who the bosses of industry are at present, how politicians are formed and where they come from," but even knowing who the decision makers are, "we will still not really know why and how the decision was made, how it came to be accepted by everybody, and how it hurts a particular category of person" (1988b:103–104). As Foucault pointed out, there is no "*one* knowledge or *one* power, or worse, *knowledge* or *power* which would operate in and of themselves. Knowledge and power are only an analytical grid" historically situated (1997:52).

Understanding power requires understanding the **strategies of power**— that is, all the ways in which decisions are made, accepted, and enforced (1988a:104). Power is never established for all time, because **resistance** is always possible. There are "no relations of power without resistances; the latter are all the more real and effective because they are formed right at the point where the relations of power are exercised" (1980:142). Among the important points of resistance are the "subjected knowledges"—that is, the "naïve" knowledge of the housewife, the mental patient, the poor, and the dispossessed that is disqualified by specialist, scientific knowledge regimes (1978:82). Counter discourses, such as feminism, are therefore ways in which power is resisted.

The key issue for Foucault was not to pinpoint some specific social/historical moment or event as pivotal in changing society, but to understand how the present has been constituted from a past of various, disparate events and ideas. In his essay "What Is Enlightenment?" Foucault indicated that the search for some principal cause of social change was replaced in his work by a genealogy that reassesses taken-for-granted notions of truth and looks for the "multiple determining elements" that eventually give rise not to a product as such but to an effect (1997:57). For example, in thinking about modernity, the question is not how does modernity come about, but how do individuals come to understand themselves as modern? Modernity is "an attitude rather than a period of history" (1997:113).

The question of modernity is tied to the Enlightenment linkage of reason and progress that remains, for Foucault, an important linkage and promise. The emancipatory promise can be sustained, in his view, by understanding "what we think, say, and do as so many historical events," thereby generating the possibility of "no longer being, doing and thinking what we are, do, or think" (1997:125–126). It was the task of specific intellectuals to provide the bases for these forms of understanding.

Foucault contrasts the **specific intellectual** with the **universal intellectual**, such as the Marxist vanguard intellectual, who claims to represent the enlightened consciousness of the dispossessed. Foucault remarked that the "role of the intellectual was not to tell others what they have to do"; rather, it is to "question over and over again what is postulated as self-evident, to disturb people's mental habits, the way they do and think things, to dissipate what is familiar and accepted, to reexamine rules and institutions and on the basis of this re-problematization (in which he carries out his specific task as an intellectual) to participate in the formation of a political will (in which he has his role as citizen to play)" (1988b:265). Foucault insists that the specific intellectual provides the tools of analysis, but "as for saying, 'Here is what you must do!,' certainly not" (1980:62).

The stakes are high, according to Foucault, because the growth of knowledge has always been accompanied by the growth of power. The key question is, "How can the growth of capabilities be disconnected from the intensification of power relations?" (1977:126).[5] Foucault does not have a precise answer to this question, but contrary to Habermas (see Chapter 4), Foucault did not believe that there could be a society without relations of power. The problem was "not of trying to dissolve them in the utopia of a perfectly transparent communication, but to give one's self the rules of law, the techniques of management, and also the ethics, the *ethos*, the practice of self, which would allow these games of power to be played with a minimum of domination" (1988b:18). The self-management that Foucault advocates, however, is somewhat problematic in the case of gender and race relations.

Class, Gender, and Race

Foucault's discussions of class, gender, and race are framed by his concern with the question of power.

Class   For Foucault, power relations could not be adequately understood in terms of the dominance of the state, the nature of the class struggle, or the idea of capitalist exploitation. Foucault remarked that Marxist analyses of class struggle actually paid little attention to "struggle." Marxists, although not Marx himself, when speaking of class struggle as the "mainspring of history, . . . focus mainly on defining class, its boundaries, its membership, but never concretely on the nature of struggle" (1988b:123).

It was not the analysis of class power but the possibilities of resistance and struggle that interested Foucault. As he stated, his general theme was the "discourse of true and false" and the "formation of domains and objects and of the verifiable, falsifiable discourses that bear on them; and it is not just their formation that interests me, but the effects in the real to which they are linked" (Foucault, quoted in Burchell, Gordon, and Miller, 1991:85). For Foucault, then, the issue was not one of identifying class relations in the regime of power but of analyzing how those relations were formulated through discourses and practices. Foucault constantly questioned the idea of a universal subject—whether proletariat, abstract humanity, or Man—and the idea of a society free from power relations, asking instead how these ideas arose and what were their effects.

Foucault was skeptical about Marxism as a political blueprint for change that many French intellectuals endorsed in the postwar period. He regarded Marxism as a "dogmatic framework" that declined after the French student uprising of May 1968. One of the disillusioning features of the 1968 student rebellion was the lack of support from the proletariat. In fact, in Foucault's view, the French Communist party seemed to act as merely another repressive force. He maintained that the lesson learned from the events of 1968 was that "oppression associated with power could not be located within a single socio-political

---

[5] Throughout his career, Foucault acted as a specific intellectual. He was involved in prison reform, gay rights, and support for Poland's Solidarity movement. He initially supported the Iranian revolution against the repressive regime of the Shah, until the evidence of human rights abuses by the new Islamic regime was revealed.

apparatus; it was dispersed in complex networks of social control that encompassed the bureaucracy of an ossified revolutionary party" (Kritzman, 1988:x–xi). The "new political, new cultural interests concerning personal life" that appeared in the aftermath of these events, Foucault believed, made his own work more appealing (Foucault, 1988a:8).

In the context of Foucault's analysis of discourses and practices, his discussion of bio-power—that is, the regimes of discipline and population control—addresses most directly the question of class, gender, and race. According to Foucault, for example, the development of capitalism would not have been possible "without the controlled insertion of bodies into the machinery of production and the adjustment of the phenomenon of population to economic processes" (1976:141). Part of this process involved the gradual "moralization of the poorer classes" that took the form of "juridical and medical control of perversions, for the sake of a general protection of society and the race" (1976:16).

The moralization of the poor was connected with a form of bourgeois class consciousness in the eighteenth century that stressed the "affirmation of the body" (1976:16). The bourgeois "mechanisms of power are addressed to the body, to life, to what causes it to proliferate, to what reinforces its species, its stamina, its ability to dominate, or its capacity for being used" (1976:147). The cultivation of the ideal body was not simply "a matter of economy or ideology, it was a 'physical' matter as well" (1976:125). Important to the deployment of power over the physical body were the regimes of sexuality that defined the "normal" as opposed to the "perverse"; these were particularly important for the control of women and racial "others."

Gender   As Morris has remarked, "Foucault's work is not the work of a ladies' man" (1988:26). Although Foucault provided no distinctive discussion of gender, his work has nonetheless been useful to feminist social theory.

Foucault's work is particularly important for feminist theory in its repudiation of biological accounts of gender difference. As you have seen, his analysis in the first volume of *The History of Sexuality* pays attention to the way in which women's bodies were subjected to control and discipline in modern society. The modern link between expert, scientific knowledge and sexuality is based on the family as the "chief agents of the deployment of sexuality," supported by an array of medical, psychiatric, and educational specialists (1976:110). This regime gives rise to "new personages, . . . the nervous woman, the frigid wife, the indifferent mother—or worse, the mother beset by murderous obsessions—the impotent, sadistic, perverse husband, the hysterical and neurasthenic girls, the precocious and already exhausted child, and the young homosexual who rejects marriage or neglects his wife" (1976:111). But Foucault's interest in the sexualized subject was an abstract interest in the "human subject" and not focused on issues of gender inequities in modern society.

Foucault did make a brief comment on the women's movement in an interview. He stated that the "real strength of the women's liberation movement was not of having laid claim to the specificity of their sexuality and the rights pertaining to it, but that they have actually departed from the discourse conducted within the apparatuses of sexuality." He believed this departure resulted in a "displacement effected in relation to the sexual centering of the problem, formulating the demand for forms of culture, discourse, language and so on, which are no longer part of that rigid assignation and pinning-down to their sex which they had initially in some sense been politically obliged to accept in order to make themselves heard" (Foucault, in Gordon, 1980:219–220).

Race   Bio-power is again important in Foucault's discussions of modern racism. Foucault pointed out that modern racism has a background in the aristocratic understanding of "blood." It was the "antiquity of its ancestry and the value of its alliances" that made blood the marker of caste distinction (1976: 124). Power "spoke *through* blood: the honor of war, the fear of famine, the triumph of death, the sovereign with his sword, executioners, and tortures; blood was *a reality with a symbolic function*" (1976:147). This aristocratic preoccupation with descent became a preoccupation with hereditary that found expression in the proliferation of "biological, medical, or eugenic precepts" (1976:124).

The dream of perfecting the species through the control of sex is the basis of modern racism's emphasis on the purity of blood to ensure the triumph of a race. The resulting "eugenic ordering of society, with all that implied in the way of extension and intensification of micro-powers, in the guise of unrestricted state control . . . was accompanied by the oneiric exaltation of superior blood" (1976:149). This exaltation implied the "systematic genocide of others" (1976:150). The expression of the symbolic importance of blood in eugenic programs justified the elimination of inferior traits and races; in this respect, "Nazism was doubtless the most cunning and the most naïve . . . combination of the fantasies of blood and the paroxysms of a disciplinary power" (1976:149). Ironically, Foucault maintains that the new forces of anti-Semitism began in socialist milieus with a "theory of degeneracy" that claimed the Jews were degenerate "firstly because they are rich, secondly because they intermarry" (1976:224). This theory is encountered in French "socialist literature down to the Dreyfus affair" and later in the "nationalist antisemitism of the Right," which adopted these themes pre-Hitler (1976:224).

Eugenics was a foundation for racist politics in many Western countries, but it was also an important part of the deployment of sexuality in respect to women and their bodies. It was mainly women who were, and still are, subject to control through sterilization, forced abortions, and detention in the interest of preventing the reproduction of the unfit and the degenerate. Again, Foucault does not discuss these specific gender consequences of the deployment of discipline and power over blood and bodies, but despite this omission, or perhaps because of it, many feminist theorists have appropriated his work. The appropriation has always been a critical one.

Other Theories and Theorists

Foucault edited two memoirs, one by Herculine Barbin (1978) and the other by Pierre Rivière (1975). The memoirs of Herculine Barbin were an example of the way in which bio-power becomes an "agent of transformation of human life" (1976: 143).

Herculine Barbin was a nineteenth-century hermaphrodite who lived as a girl for the first 20 years of her life. When it was discovered that she was a hermaphrodite, the doctors advised a sex change operation. It was the emphasis on precise categorization of "true" sexual identity that resulted in Herculine's being declared a man and forced to change. Despite the sympathy for her plight in the community, Barbin committed suicide. In Foucault's view, she was a victim of the new scientific medical passion for pinning down an exact, "true" sexual identity; in the past, "it was simply agreed that hermaphrodites had two" sexes (1978:vii).

The memoirs of Pierre Rivière concern his confession of the murder of his mother, sister, and brother. Rivière, a peasant, planned the murders carefully. He put on his Sunday clothes for the occasion and, after the act, wandered around the countryside and readily confessed when he was caught. He wrote his memoir in prison while awaiting trial, thus providing evidence against himself. At the trial, half of the experts—six lawyers and six doctors—considered Rivière insane, and the other half considered him sane. With a hung jury, Rivière was imprisoned rather than executed. He committed suicide some years later. The point that interested Foucault about this account was its demonstration of the confusion that attended the conjunction of medical and legal knowledge in the interest of social control in modern society. For Foucault, the case illustrated the ways in which unscientific beliefs constructed scientific knowledge of what was to be judged as "normal," which was then acted upon.

What is interesting about the two memoirs is that they are both confessional documents. In Foucault's view, psychoanalysis is the modern variant on the Christian injunction to confess, especially to confess the "truth" of sex. Two ideas—"that we must not deceive ourselves concerning our sex, and that our sex harbors what is most true in ourselves"—are central to the definition of what constitutes normality in modern society (1978:x). For feminists, however, the injunction to speak the truth of sex is a troubling issue when it is tied to the patriarchal idea of a "natural" sexual order.

Critique and Conclusions: Foucault and Feminist Social Theory [6]

Foucault stated that "man is an invention of recent date. And one perhaps nearing its end" (1966:328). Ricci asks, "With the disappearance of man, what happens to women?" (1987:11). This is an important question because the rejection of the Enlightenment subject seems to have arrived most opportunistically. Hartsock asks, "Why is it that just at the moment when so many of us who have been silenced begin to demand the right to name ourselves, to act as subjects rather than objects of history, that just then the concept of subjecthood becomes problematic?" (1990:163).

Foucault's rejection of modernity and his critique of humanism at first glance seem an attractive position for feminists concerned with critiquing the androcentric Enlightenment ideas of "rational man" and "natural woman." Western humanism has, in fact, been "built on the backs of women and people of color" (Diamond and Quinby, 1988:xv). Diamond and Quinby (1988:x) suggest four points of convergence between Foucault and feminist theory:

---

[6]Although the focus in this section is on feminist critiques, philosophers, historians, political analysts, and psychiatrists have all mounted critiques of Foucault's work. See, for example, Dean (1994), Simons (1995), Gane and Johnson (1993), Goldstein (1994), and Davidson (1997).

- "Both point to the local and intimate operations of power rather than focusing exclusively on the supreme power of the state."
- "Both identify the body as a site of power, that is, as the locus of domination through which docility is accomplished and subjectivity constituted."
- "Both bring to the fore the crucial role of discourse in its capacity to produce and sustain hegemonic power and emphasize the challenges contained within marginalized and/or unrecognized discourses."
- "And both criticize the ways in which Western humanism has privileged the experience of the Western masculine elite as it proclaims universals about truth, freedom, and human nature."

But Foucault was not specifically concerned with the different effects of a power/knowledge regime on the dominated, such as women or racial and ethnic minorities. And although Foucault clarified the ways in which discourse was implicated in power relations, he did not take account of the "relations between masculinist authority and language, discourse, and reason," which means that language is never gender-free (Diamond and Quinby, 1988:xv).

Foucault's "neutral" analysis of discourses of power, truth, and sexuality is a masculine analysis. Seeing power, as he does, "everywhere and, at some level, as available to all, it can encourage us to overlook women's systematic subordination of other women, as well as systematic domination by men" (Ramazanoglu, 1993:10). Furthermore, if power is the "principle of *all* human relationships, then power cannot be seen *in itself* as a bad thing" (Grimshaw, 1993:55). Hartsock (1990:169) points out that if power is not a "single individual dominating others or . . . one group or class dominating others," because power is everywhere, then it would seem that "dominated groups participate in their own domination"—in other words, "blame the victim." But feminists need to distinguish between "malign and benign forms of power," and a critique of power requires some "independent critical stance or perspective" (Grimshaw, 1993:55). Foucault's work may contribute to "the feminist 'deconstructive' project" but "in the end offers nothing to the projects of articulating a vision of the future, a critical feminist ethics, or a coherent feminist politics" (Grimshaw, 1993:55).

Yeatman (1990:293) is even more critical of Foucault, contending that his "postmodern relativism reveals itself as the last-ditch stand of modern patriarchy." Ricci (1987:23) points out that "society did not wait for the invention of man" to repress or oppress woman. Foucault's jettisoning of an autonomous subject and his pluralities of power call into question feminist identity politics. Martin (1988:17) points out that Foucault's ideas, if taken to "their 'logical' conclusion, if made into imperatives rather than left as hypotheses and/or methodological provocations, could make the question of women's oppression obsolete." According to Martin, feminists must refuse a political stance "which pins us to our sex" and must "refuse to be content with fixed identities or to universalize ourselves as revolutionary subjects" (1988:16).

Not all feminists have seen Foucault's position on the issue of subjectivity and identity as problematic for feminist politics. Judith Butler suggests that the idea of the constructed subject does not preclude the possibility that the subject has agency. On the contrary, she believes construction is the "necessary scene of agency" (1990:147). The subject is a discursive production, and identities are unstable "fictions," which makes for a "subversion of identity." Butler maintains this instability allows for "new possibilities for gender that contest the rigid codes of hierarchical binarisms," especially as the insistence on an either/or gender identification invariably produces "failures"—the effeminate male, the assertive female, the lipstick lesbian (1990:145).

Butler does not suggest that the "political necessity to speak as and for *women*" should be abandoned, but that the term "women" should be understood as a "field of differences" that cannot be reduced to a single identity (1992:15). In fact, the very "rifts among women over the content of the term" represent the "ungrounded ground of feminist theory." Women's agency becomes possible when the term "women" is released from the "normalized, immobilized, paralyzed" position of subordination and becomes the basis for an ongoing "radical, democratic impetus of feminist politics" (1992:16).

Butler notes the importance to feminist politics of the way in which the dualities of bodies and sex maintain "reproductive sexuality as a compulsory order" (1992:17). The control over bodies and minds of individuals that is the mark of modern power/knowledge regimes is particularly invasive for women. In this context, Bartky (1988) uses Foucault's insights on modern power/knowledge regimes to illustrate how women's bodies are subject to disciplinary practices that produce the culturally approved face and figure. A range of practices are designed to produce a "body of a certain size and general configuration"; practices that elicit from the body a "specific repertoire of gestures, postures, and movements"; and practices that are "directed toward the display of the body as an ornamental surface" (1988:64). Diets, exercise, modest deportment, and attention to makeup and clothes mark the production of the feminine, but inferior, body. But the "disciplinary project of femininity is a 'setup'; it requires such radical and extensive measures of bodily transformation that virtually every woman who gives herself to it is destined in some degree to fail" (1988:71).

Despite persistent failure, women continue to seek perfect femininity because the work is undertaken for the male. A "panoptical male connoisseur resides within the consciousness of most women: they stand perpetually before his gaze and under his judgment" (Bartky, 1988:72). Consequently, the "top sergeant in this disciplinary regime of femininity" is not simply, or only, the law, parents, teachers, the media, or so-called "beauty experts," but "everyone and yet no one in particular" (1988:74). Resistance is, however, possible. As more women realize that their increasing "political, economic, and sexual self-determination" brings them "more completely under the dominating gaze of patriarchy," they are likely to resist (1988:82). For example, "dress for success" is an injunction that has a particular and restricting meaning for women. As women learn the consequences of these cultural messages, they develop "oppositional discourses and practices"—for example, women "pumping iron" who have little concern for the "limits of body development imposed by the current canons of femininity" (1988:83).

Despite the usefulness of Foucault's insights to many feminist theorists, others have had some grave reservations about his work. Foucault's observation that power is productive as well as prohibitive, that it is everywhere, that it is not the possession of any specific group or individual, and that it is capillary and constituted in the practices of the subjected has been seen as limiting for a feminist politics. If power is all-pervasive, how is resistance possible, and if it is possible, on what grounds can the resistance be mounted? As Fraser (1989:53) asks, "Why should we oppose a fully panopticized, autonomous society?" Relations of power/knowledge may change in ways charted by Foucault, but these changes seem merely to reaffirm "women's marginal status" (Ricci, 1987:24).

The problem with Foucault's analysis, contends Fraser (1989:32), is that "he calls too many different sorts of things power." She grants that cultural practices involve constraints, but the constraints are of a "variety of different kinds and thus demand a variety of different responses. Granted, there can be no social practices without power—but it does not follow that all forms of power are normatively equivalent nor that any social practices are as good as any other." Foucault seems oblivious to the "existence of a whole body of Weberian social theory with its careful distinction between such notions as authority, force, violence, domination, and legitimation," and his lumping them all under the label "power" results in "a certain normative one-dimensionality" (1989:32). Unlike Habermas, who was concerned with continuing the emancipatory promise of the Enlightenment, Foucault (whom Habermas called a "young conservative" because he was opposed to the project of modernity) elaborated a critique of humanism as inhumanism in practice. Foucault's critique has no obvious normative basis, which it needs if it is to be an effective critique.

Fraser maintains that Foucault "adopts a concept of power that permits him no condemnation of any objectionable features of modern society"; at the same time, his "rhetoric betrays the conviction that modern societies are utterly without redeeming features" (1989:33). For example, the regime of discipline and bio-power strikes the reader as objectionable, but why is this so? The objection, answers Fraser (1989:63–64), rests on the grounds that "(1) it objectifies people and negates the autonomy one usually prefers to accord them, and that (2) it is premised upon hierarchical and asymmetrical relations and negates the reciprocity and mutuality usually valued in human relations." These objections suggest that there may still be some emancipatory potential surviving in the humanism that Foucault has rejected (1989:64). Despite her criticisms of Foucault, Fraser does concede that he has "done more, perhaps, than anyone since Marx to expose and warn against the enormous variety of ways in which humanist rhetoric has been and is liable to misuse and co-option" (1989:65).

Foucault's work has been useful precisely because he articulated and documented the problems generated by the grand narratives of social theory that celebrated the "rational man" and placed a "natural," and inferior, woman (as well as racial and ethnic others) as the opposite, or object, to this Enlightenment subject. Sociology is both "a product of and active contributor to this categorical, dualistic, gender-permeated culture," as the dualistic concepts of "organic and mechanical solidarity, gemeinschaft and gesellschaft, . . . primary and secondary groups, capitalist and proletarian, achievement and ascription, universalistic and particularistic, micro and macro . . . hard and soft methodology" illustrate (Lengermann and Niebrugge-Brantley, 1990:333).

Using Foucault to address feminist issues, however, is not a simple matter. Ramazanoglu (1993:9–10) points out that Foucault's "deconstruction of power releases feminism from rigid conceptions of, for example, universal patriarchy, racism or heterosexism" and acknowledges the "multiplicity of difference" and "the end of 'woman' as a universal category." But Foucault's work carries the danger of reverting to "speaking in abstracted terms of deconstructed 'women,' because of the absence of . . . class, racism or gender as categories of power" (Ramazanoglu, 1993:10). The challenge for feminist social theory is to be constantly aware of the different, cross-cutting standpoints and interests, at the same time recognizing where common threads persist in the exercise of power. Foucault's work on discipline, docile bodies, bio-power, and the "gaze" are important contributions to this effort.

Soper (1993:29) suggests that Foucault has been "fortunate to have attracted the attention he has from feminists, since it is not clear that he has done much to deserve it." In fact, Soper reverses the connection, suggesting that the "deepest and most persistent impact on the *zeitgeist*" has been feminism and that the "Foucault–feminism connection" must be adjusted to reflect "not only what Foucault has to offer feminism, but also the interest Foucault has himself acquired in virtue of the feminist climate of his times" (1993:30). It is interesting that Foucault was writing at the same time that the second wave of feminism surfaced. His seeming indifference to the movement is all the more curious given the importance of the work of several French feminists such as Luce Irigaray, Julia Kristeva, and Helene Cixous. In fact, Cixous was a colleague of Foucault's during his tenure at the University of Vincennes and became a close friend (Macey, 1993:221).

In many ways, Foucault's work confirms and consolidates previous feminist critiques. Thus, Soper suggests, it is unwise to approach his work with too much deference. In fact, feminists need to retain considerable skepticism about notions of the "end of man" and Foucault's later emphasis on an aesthetics of self as a means of resistance. Foucault offers feminist social theory a critical method and the recognition that "dogmatic adherence to categories and assumptions as well as the elision of differences to which such dogmatism can lead" is what feminists must be ever alert to and try to avoid (Sawicki, 1991:29).

Final Thoughts

Foucault claimed that his work was a "history of the present" and the object of his studies was to "learn to what extent the effort to think one's own history can free thought from what it silently thinks, and so enable it to think differently" (1984c:9). The goal was a "history of truth" (1984c:11). What Foucault's work means for sociology is that the certainties of classical, and much contemporary, sociological theory are called into question—certainties that have proved, in practice as well as in theory, less than emancipatory for the majority of human beings, whatever the rhetoric addressed to post-Enlightenment "Man." Foucault's work has not been greeted with overwhelming interest in North American sociology, in contrast to other disciplines such as literary and cultural studies. This is not surprising, given his critique of concepts dear to the sociological tradition such as agency, social structure, evolutionary progress, and objectivity.

Foucault stated that "Truth is a thing of this world: it is produced only by virtue of multiple forms of constraint. And it induces regular effects of power. Each society has its regime of truth, its 'general politics' of truth; that is, the types of discourse which it accepts and makes function as true" (1980:131). Sociology has been part of the "general politics" of truth since the Enlightenment. To break out of the straitjacket of contingent "truths," sociology needs to practice "problematizing theory"; that is, sociology must analyze the "trajectory of the historical forms of truth and knowledge." When sociologists do this, they will disturb the "narratives of progress and reconciliation, finding questions where others have located answers" (Dean, 1994:4). In fact, Dean maintains, "After Foucault, no longer must sociological knowledge ground itself in truth" (1994:125). Whether or not Foucault's approach is as fruitful as Dean suggests for sociology, it is clear that the cross-disciplinary nature of his work and his unsettling of modernist "truths" have to be confronted by any sociological theory concerned, as it should be, with having practical and ethical relevance for the public, political sphere.

References

Bartky, Sandra Lee. 1988. "Foucault, Femininity, and the Modernization of Patriarchal Power." In Irene Diamond and Lee Quinby (Eds.), *Feminism and Foucault* (pp. 61–86). Boston: Northeastern University Press.

Burchell, Graham, Colin Gordon, and Peter Miller (Eds.). 1991. *The Foucault Effect: Studies in Governmentality*. Chicago: University of Chicago Press.

Butler, Judith. 1990. *Gender Trouble: Feminism and the Subversion of Identity*. New York: Routledge.

———. 1992. "Contingent Foundations: Feminism and the Question of Postmodernism." In Judith Butler and Joan W. Scott (Eds.), *Feminists Theorize the Political* (pp. 3–21). New York: Routledge.

Davidson, Arnold (Ed.). 1997. *Foucault and His Interlocutors*. Chicago: University of Chicago Press.

Dean, Mitchell. 1994. *Critical and Effective Histories: Foucault's Methods and Historical Sociology*. London: Routledge.

Diamond, Irene, and Lee Quinby (Eds.). 1988. *Feminism and Foucault: Reflections of Resistance*. Boston: Northeastern University Press.

Drefus, Hubert L., and Paul Rabinow (Eds.). 1983. *Michel Foucault: Beyond Structuralism and Hermeneutics* (2nd ed.). Chicago: University of Chicago Press.

Foucault, Michel. 1961/1965. *Madness and Civilization* (Richard Howard, Trans.). New York: Pantheon.

———. 1966/1970. *The Order of Things* (A. Sheridan, Trans.). New York: Random House.

———. 1972. *The Archaeology of Knowledge* (A. Sheridan, Trans.). London: Tavistock Publications.

———. 1973. *The Birth of the Clinic* (A. Sheridan, Trans.). New York: Vintage Books.

———. 1975. *I, Pierre Rivière, Having Slaughtered My Mother, My Sister, and My Brother: A Case of Parricide in the 19th Century* (Frank Jellinek, Trans.). New York: Random House.

———. 1976. *The History of Sexuality: Vol. 1. An Introduction* (Robert Hurley, Trans.). New York: Vintage Books.

———. 1977. *Discipline and Punish* (A. Sheridan, Trans.). New York: Pantheon Books.

———. 1978/1980. *Herculine Barbin* (Richard McDougall, Trans.). New York: Random House.

———. 1980. *Power/Knowledge, Selected Interviews and Other Writings, 1972–1977* (Colin Gordon, Ed.). Brighton, England: Harvester.

———. 1984a. *The Foucault Reader* (Paul Rabinow, Ed.). New York: Pantheon.

———. 1984b/1985. *The History of Sexuality: Vol. 2. The Use of Pleasure* (Robert Hurley, Trans.). New York: Vintage Books.

———. 1984c/1986. *The History of Sexuality: Vol. 3. The Care of the Self* (Robert Hurley, Trans.). New York: Pantheon.

———. 1988a. *Michel Foucault: Interviews and Other Writings* (A. Sheridan and others, Trans.). New York: Routledge.

———. 1988b. "'The Minimalist Self': Interview with Stephen Riggins." In Lawrence D. Kritzman (Ed.), *Michel Foucault: Politics, Philosophy, Culture* (pp. 3–16). New York: Routledge.

———. 1991. *Remarks on Marx, Conversations with Duccio Trombadori* (R. James Goldstein and James Cascaito, Trans.). New York: Semiotext(e).

———. 1997. *The Politics of Truth* (Sylvere Lotringer and Lysa Hochroth, Eds.). New York: Semiotext(e).

Fraser, Nancy. 1989. *Unruly Practices: Power, Discourse and Gender in Contemporary Social Theory*. Minneapolis: University of Minnesota Press.

Gane, Mike, and Terry Johnson (Eds.). 1993. *Foucault's New Domains*. London: Routledge.

Goldstein, Jan (Ed.). 1994. *Foucault and the Writing of History*. Oxford: Basil Blackwell.

Gordon, Colin (Ed.). 1980. *Power/Knowledge: Selected Interviews and Other Writings, 1872–1977*. Brighton, England: Harvester.

Grimshaw, Jean. 1993. "Practices of Freedom." In Caroline Ramazanoglu (Ed.), *Up Against Foucault* (pp. 51–71). London: Routledge.

Gutting, Gary (Ed.). 1994. *The Cambridge Companion to Foucault*. Cambridge: Cambridge University Press.

Hacking, Ian. 1986. "The Archaeology of Foucault." In David Couzens Hoy (Ed.), *Foucault: A Critical Reader*. Oxford: Basil Blackwell.

Hartsock, Nancy. 1990. "Foucault on Power: A Theory for Women?" In Linda J. Nicholson (Ed.), *Feminism/Postmodernism* (pp. 157–175). New York: Routledge.

Kritzman, Lawrence D. (Ed.). 1988. *Michel Foucault: Politics, Philosophy, Culture*. New York: Routledge.

Kuhn, Thomas. 1962. *The Structure of Scientific Revolutions*. Chicago: University of Chicago Press.

Lengermann, Patricia, and Jill Niebrugge-Brantley. 1990. "Feminist Sociological Theory: The Near-Future Prospects." In George Ritzer (Ed.), *Frontiers of Social Theory* (pp. 316–344). New York: Columbia University Press.

Lotringer, Sylvere. 1989. *Foucault Live*. New York: Semiotext(e).

Macey, David. 1993. *The Lives of Michel Foucault*. London: Vintage Books.

Martin, Biddy. 1988. "Feminism, Criticism, and Foucault." In Irene Diamond and Lee Quinby (Eds.), *Feminism and Foucault* (pp. 3–19). Boston: Northeastern University Press.

Merquior, J. G. 1985. *Foucault*. London: Fontana.

Miller, James. 1993. *The Passion of Michel Foucault*. New York: Simon and Schuster.

Morris, Meaghan. 1988. "The Pirate's Fiancée: Feminists and Philosophers, or Maybe Tonight It'll Happen." In Irene Diamond and Lee Quinby (Eds.), *Feminism and Foucault*. Boston: Northeastern University Press.

Poster, Mark. 1989. *Critical Theory and Poststructuralism*. Ithaca, NY: Cornell University Press.

Ramazanoglu, Caroline (Ed.). 1993. *Up Against Foucault*. London: Routledge.

Ricci, N. P. 1987. "The End/s of Woman." *Canadian Journal of Political and Social Theory*, *11*(3), 11–27.

Rouse, Joseph. 1994. "Power/Knowledge." In Gary Gutting (Ed.), *The Cambridge Companion to Foucault* (pp. 92–114). Cambridge: Cambridge University Press.

Sawicki, Jana. 1991. *Disciplining Foucault*. New York: Routledge.

Sheridan, Alan. 1980. *Michel Foucault: The Will to Truth*. London: Tavistock.

Shumway, David. 1989. *Michel Foucault*. Boston: Twayne Publications.

Simons, Jon. 1995. *Foucault and the Political*. London: Routledge.

Soper, Kate. 1993. "Productive Contradictions." In Caroline Ramazanoglu (Ed.), *Up Against Foucault* (pp. 29–50). London: Routledge.

Trombadori, Duccio. 1991. *Michel Foucault: Remarks on Marx* (R. James, Trans.). New York: Semiotext(e).

Wuthnow, Robert, James Davison Hunter, Albert Bergesen, and Edith Kurzweil (Eds.). 1984. *Cultural Analysis*. London: Routledge and Kegan Paul.

Yeatman, Anna. 1990. "A Feminist Theory of Social Differentiation." In Linda J. Nicholson, (Ed.), *Feminism/Postmodernism* (pp. 281–299). New York: Routledge.

Chapter 12

Final Thoughts on Contemporary Sociological Theory

Ilya Prigogine in 1997 reminded us that humanity has gone through three major hurts to its pride: First, Copernicus demonstrated that the earth is not the center of the universe; second, Darwin argued that humans are an evolutionary species of animal; and third, Freud explained human behavior as being governed by biological drives and the unconscious, rather than strictly by reason (Prigogine, 1997; Wallerstein, 1999). These "hurts," along with dramatic social and technological changes, have left humanity and its analysts with a high level of uncertainty.

We are not only uncertain about the present; we are also uncertain about the past. We live in the era of cable television, e-mail, and the Internet. It is difficult for any of us—including those of us who are older—to project ourselves back to the 1930s. In the early- to mid-twentieth century, we had no computers, and many families listened to the radio in the evenings. Not only was communication not instantaneous, it was slow; what is now called "snail mail" was all there was, and it was considered fast. There had been no so-called "world wars."

Sociological Theory Since 1930

Despite some uncertainty about the past, the timeline at the back of the book gives a sense of the important political and technological events both before and after 1930. The years since 1930 have seen the Great Depression; World War II and many smaller wars; the successful struggle for independence of many colonies, especially in Africa and Asia; increasing feminist and racial movements for equality, and their theoretical justification; and the rise and decline of ideologically Marxist societies. Let us look briefly at sociological theories responding to these developments.

Functionalism

Most observers have stated that the dominance of functional thinking in sociology, led by Parsons and Merton, peaked in the middle third of the twentieth century. The functionalist approach sees society as a differentiated organism, based on consensus and on structures developed to meet human needs and centered in politics, economics, or both. Kingsley Davis went so far as to claim that the view that societies are integrated makes every sociologist a functionalist, and modernization theorists asserted that the world's societies are striving to be like those of Europe and the United States. At the turn of the twenty-first century, however, there are few true-believing functionalists. Instead, former disciples of Parsons, such as Niklas Luhmann, have explained modern society as consisting of semi-independent subsystems, with no institution—political or economic—dominant or in control. And although there is clearly a division of labor, this does not necessarily increase society's efficiency in accomplishing its tasks.

Marxism

The other major theoretical position regarding modern society is that it is held together by ruling-class exploitation and oppression. For much of the twentieth century, the Soviet Union was held up as the vanguard of a worldwide overthrow of capitalism. By the latter third of the century, Eastern Europe and a scattering of societies around the world had adopted a Marxist ideology, though to a much lesser extent the structural characteristics that Marxists believed were necessary. By mid-century, however, the Marxist Dunayevskaya had asserted that the Soviet Union was not an example of true socialism, but was in fact state capitalism. And by the end of the century, the Soviet bloc of nations had renounced its Marxist ideology. In the 1990s, many capitalist theoreticians and ideologues stated that Marxism is dead and there is now a capitalist world order. At the beginning of the twenty-first century, few remaining Western Marxists are willing to argue that the revolutionary overthrow of capitalism is inevitable—despite their continuing negative assessment of the nature of capitalism.

Power

Not all the important theories of society are covered either by the chapter subheadings (such as class and gender) or by the major themes of this book (such as capitalist industrialization). Many of the theories we have studied have as an important element the explanation of power.

Marxism began by treating control of the means of production as the basis for power, and later Marxists have used false consciousness and hegemonic ideology to explain why the oppressed have accepted inequities as inevitable or even good. Feminist theorists and writers on race show how the power of white males has been structured into society and then justified by ideology ("what is, should be"). Foucault, for example, notes how notions of racial "blood" and genetic inequalities have been built into both colonialism and racial oppression in Western societies. He and his feminist critics also explain the way power is expressed through sex and violence—two very popular topics in contemporary culture.

Luhmann, following Weber, explains power as both a system and a personal characteristic. To this, Luhmann, Habermas, and Foucault add that power requires communication. Luhmann also argues that the semi-independence of society's subsystems makes it difficult to be "all-powerful," or to have society-wide—much less worldwide—power. Finally, one point on which Luhmann departs from his mentor Parsons is in emphasizing the potential misuse of power. Power, then, is explained by economic structures and propaganda-based hegemony and authority, and includes the factors of violence, communication, and misuse.

Views of Change

What do you believe is changing in your world, and why is it changing? Let us bring together some of the views of change encountered in this book.

A few theorists still believe that change is evolutionary and progressive. Even fewer believe that change will be brought about by a mass revolution that will result in economic and social equality. Non-Marxist theorists of revolution, such as Skocpol, suggest that structural strains and early signs of change, rather than total oppression, lead to revolution. Others, such as Wallerstein, believe that changes such as increased crowding and speed are negative, making the world a worse and more difficult place in which to live, with mass destruction a real possibility and danger. Many others, following Durkheim and Giddens, adopt the liberal view that change is incremental and takes place by means of society's established or administrative mechanisms. Finally, there are still those who claim, with Pareto, that except for technology, nothing important ever changes. Human motives and selfish desires are the same as they have always been, and humans are no more and no less rational than ever.

Theory and Ideology

Throughout the book we have tried to make clear the way theory or explanation and ideology or justification are intertwined. Those who theorize that capitalist society is a self-corrective organism that meets people's needs are usually overtly status quo conservatives, or supportive of the capitalist status quo. Even the positivists, who claim understanding as the goal, may be covert conservatives, since they are willing to accept what is, in the process of studying it. Those who explain society as based on exploitation and oppression are at the same time likely to be ideological radicals who see capitalist society as bad and its revolutionary overthrow as desirable.

As for human nature, some see it as good but corrupted by society, whereas others view it as aggressive and requiring control by civilization. Many theorists, however—from micro-theorists of the self to feminists to critical theorists—believe that humans are eminently malleable, adaptable to what the environment contains, what society expects, and what technology provides.

The Future of Society

One thing is clear: The future will include many more technological changes. Some may be as simple as the video-telephone, through which we can both see and hear another person; others may involve biotechnology, such as cloning.

Other, far less certain but nonetheless interesting predictions can be made, based on what we believe we already know and understand. One such prediction involves surveillance. Ever since George Orwell wrote *1984*, the notion of "Big Brother" in complete control has been of concern. The risk of almost total lack of privacy comes from both satellite surveillance and business and government knowledge based on tax and credit card information. This risk is seen as both likely and dangerous.

A column in the *Washington Post* by Neal Peirce (2000) raises two other future possibilities, each a change from the dominance of the nation-state in the year 2000. The first, the "citistate," refers to a prediction by Robert Kaplan and others. Urban corridors, such as that from Boston to Washington, DC, will become dominant worldwide, each controlling the surrounding territory—a development already occurring in various parts of the world. Coupled with Luhmann's theory that claims no dominant politico-economic system, but semi-independent subsystems, this can be seen as portending the decline of the nation-state.

In the same article, Peirce refers to Daniel Kemmis's argument that global economy and global ecology will simply flow around and over existing structures of governmental sovereignty. When such globalism is combined with either the multinational corporation's quasi-state character or the notion of regional and then world government, it gives a global politico-economic spin to the "new world order." Thus, Peirce's article looks in both directions from the nation-state: citistates and supranational—even global—politico-economic units.

Finally, Wallerstein's 1999 book, *The End of the World As We Know It*, in effect predicts, as Prigogine (1997) put it, "the end of certainty." But Wallerstein declares uncertainty in very strong terms: We are, he says, headed toward some sort of cataclysm—not the Marxist revolution, which in his early days he had favored, but something unpredictable and terrifying. Such a prediction, while hardly of great help, is simply a way of saying that "things are out of hand," and perhaps headed toward chaos.

The Future of Sociological Theory

All intellectual disciplines and institutions take for granted that not everything has been said, written, or recorded; that words already heard or pronounced are not the last words. (Lyotard, 1984:37)

We live in an imperfect world, one that will always be imperfect and therefore always harbor injustice. But we are far from helpless before this reality. We can make the world less unjust; we can make it more beautiful; we can increase our cognition of it. (Wallerstein, 1999:250)

In *Classical Sociological Theory,* we discuss the eighteenth- and nineteenth-century background to the development of sociology.[1] An important part of that beginning, whatever the theorist's ideology, was the idea that sociology could contribute to a more perfect social world. For Enlightenment philosophers, and later for sociologists, the way to a more perfect social world lay in the use of critical reason and science. Many theorists believed that a new era was at hand, a "modern" era that would produce the "emancipation of humanity from poverty, ignorance, prejudice, and the absence of enjoyment" (Lyotard, 1988:302). Modernity would bring the "victorious struggle of Reason against emotions or animal instincts, science against religion and magic, truth against prejudice, correct knowledge against superstition, reflection against uncritical existence" (Bauman, 1987:111).

From Comte on, many sociologists were confident in promising the truth about society. However, as you have seen, agreement about the specifics of that truth and its explanation has been sadly lacking. In fact, sociology has been a contentious exercise in theoretical and methodological multidimensionality (Ritzer, 1992).

The most recent critiques of sociological theorizing have focused on the categorizations that have characterized much of this volume: traditional/modern, male/female, conservative/radical, public/private, objective/subjective, and class divisions. Lyotard, in *The Postmodern Condition* (1984), claimed that transformations both in society and in the production of knowledge make such postmodern rethinking both inevitable and necessary.

But what do postmodernists claim, and what do they criticize? According to Bentz and Kenny (1997:83), they claim that the

> "order" theories of Spencer, Comte, Durkheim, Merton, Parsons, and Sumner have lulled us into belief that we are part of a "real" social order which protects, balances, and regulates our activities. "Conflict" theories from Marx, Simmel, and Mills to Marcuse and Habermas, while revealing that all was not right with this ordered world, have reaffirmed the possibility of a reordered and right world. Marxist and neo-Marxist theorists present the hope that some new group—the workers, the students, or the new professional class—may bring about a more just social order. And finally, symbolic interactionists have filled in the cracks of the social world with "selves" who are created and reproduce social order.

Postmodernism seeks not only to deconstruct the accepted social categories, but to depict a world produced by and producing multiple discourses. Its critical position points to the Eurocentric character of the "grand narratives," both in

---

[1]Our book *Classical Sociological Theory,* published by Pine Forge Press in 2002, describes the beginnings of sociology and social theorizing from the early 1800s to the 1930s. It covers 25 important thinkers, including Auguste Comte, Harriet Martineau, Herbert Spencer, Emile Durkheim, Karl Marx, Rosa Luxemburg, Max and Marianne Weber, Georg Simmel, Vilfredo Pareto, Thorstein Veblen, Joseph Schumpeter, Charlotte Gilman, Beatrice Webb, W. E. B. Du Bois, Charles H. Cooley, George H. Mead, and Sigmund Freud.

their meaning and in the way they support global power relations. As Seidman (1991a:139) puts it, the grand narratives of modernity,

> industrialization, bureaucratization, urbanization, secularization, democratization, those sweeping stories that presume to uncover a uniform social process in a multitude of different societies . . . repress important differences between (and within) societies; they perpetuate Western-world hegemonic aspirations and national chauvinistic wishes: they are, in short, little more than myths that aim to authorize certain social patterns.

Certainly in our sections on class, gender, and race, these male Eurocentric tendencies and thought patterns have been apparent.

In 1941, Pitirim Sorokin predicted that by 2000 a period of nihilism would occur and any genuine, authoritative, and binding public opinion would disappear to be replaced by the "pseudo consciences" of pressure groups so that the "magnificent contractual sociocultural house built by Western man during the preceding centuries will collapse" (1941, 4:776). This pessimistic prediction is echoed in the criticisms of postmodernists. The new subjects—feminists, gays and lesbians, a rainbow of ethnic and racial identities—and the resulting approaches to the sociological enterprise question the sociologist's ability to be objective or to stand apart from the data in order to reveal the truths about the social. Their question is "Whose truth?"

The end of the universal "Man" and the recognition of basic differences raise important issues for sociological theory. Seidman points out that Marxists, feminists, gay liberationists, and others continue to appeal to the agency (to use Giddens's term) or effective action of the working class, women, blacks, and homosexuals. Yet these categories are no more fixed or uniform in their meaning than the concept of "Man." Seidman's point is that "categories of identity are always multiple and intersect in highly idiosyncratic and diverse ways."

> There is no reason to believe that a middle-class southern heterosexual Methodist woman will share a common experience or even common gender interests with a northern working-class Jewish lesbian, [and it is] equally naive to assume that whatever gender commonalities they do share will override their divergent interests. (Seidman, 1991a:141–142)

Critics of postmodern discourse claim that postmodernism goes too far in the direction of giving up all attempts at practical generalization and assuming that statements about social reality tell the reader only about the writer. The idea that today's conditions and diversity efface all differences between truth and falsehood, reality and illusion, serious and nonserious dialogue may simply be a reflection of current times.

One critic of postmodernism argues that the postmodern "willingness to jettison every last notion of truth, justice, or critical understanding" and to reduce "all philosophy to an undifferentiated 'kind of writing'" becomes simply an "escape-route from pressing political questions and a pretext for avoiding any serious engagement with real-world historical events" (Norris, 1990:44). It is too easy, critics of postmodernism say, in a society giving itself increasingly to amoral acquisition, to give up the search for truth and justice.

So, should we abandon all the theoretical arguments and insights summarized in the first part of this chapter? Must the student of sociology now throw out both the "modern" categories of Durkheim, Parsons, Giddens, and Goffman and the claim that their particular expertise can help us both understand and benefit society? Must sociology, in other words, give itself up to ever-changing subjectivity, discourse, and de-categorization? To us, the answer is no. Though a sociological gospel of order and system is certainly overstated, if not misguided, sociology can still offer cultural resistance, critique, and understanding.

As Lyotard puts it, the task of sociology for the twenty-first century is still to uncover and expose—to further the questioning that thinking and writing offer "to established thought, to what has already been done, to what everybody thinks, to what is well known, to what is widely recognized, to what is 'readable,' to everything which can change its form and make itself acceptable to opinion in general" (Lyotard, 1988:302). Sociological theory itself "must challenge the authority of all theories of the world" (Lemert, 1992:245). Seidman (1991b:190) adds that sociology's legitimacy in the future rests on its encouragement of "an open, reflexive, elaborated culture of public debate on the meaning and moral character of our social arrangements." Sociological theory remains an important resource as long as it continues to seek, as Merton puts it, finer distinctions and the insights not available to the untrained eye. The difference

> between what we know without sociology and what we know after we have heard its comments is not the difference between error and truth (though, let us admit, sociology may happen to correct our opinions here and there); it is, rather, the difference between believing that what we experience can be described and explained in one way and in one way only, and knowing that possible—and plausible—interpretations are plentiful. Sociology . . . is not the end of our search for understanding, but an inducement to go on searching. (Bauman, 1990:215)

Sociological theory is always an exciting but unfinished business as long as it encourages a fascination with and skepticism about the complexity and messiness of the social world, as well as about the efforts to clear up, order, and control that messiness. It is an enterprise that, if it is true to its heritage, must be concerned with the promotion of ways and means to transform that world in order to offer dignity, health, and security to all human beings.

References

Bauman, Zygmont. 1987. *Legislators and Interpreters: On Modernity, Post-Modernity, and Intellectuals.* Ithaca, NY: Cornell University Press.

———. 1990. *Thinking Sociologically.* Cambridge, MA: Blackwell Press.

Bentz, Valerie Malhotra, and Wade Kenny. 1997. "Body as World: Kenneth Burke's Answer to the Postmodernist Charges Against Sociology." *Sociological Theory, 15,* 81–96.

Lemert, Charles. 1992. "Sez Who?" *Sociological Theory, 10*(2), 244–246.

Lyotard, Jean-François. 1984. *The Postmodern Condition: A Report on Knowledge.* Manchester, England: Manchester University Press.

———. 1988. *The Differend: Phrases in Dispute*. Minneapolis: University of Minnesota Press.

Norris, Christopher. 1990. *What's Wrong with Postmodernism: Critical Theory and the Ends of Philosophy*. Baltimore: Johns Hopkins University Press.

Orwell, George. 1961. *1984*. New York: New American Library.

Peirce, Neal. 2000, January 9. "Citistates: Their Time Ripens." *Washington Post*.

Prigogine, Ilya. 1997. *The End of Certainty*. New York: Free Press.

Ritzer, George (Ed.). 1992. *Metatheorizing*. Newbury Park, CA: Sage.

Seidman, Steven. 1991a. "The End of Sociological Theory: The Postmodern Hope." *Sociological Theory, 9*, 131–146.

———. 1991b. "Postmodern Anxiety: The Politics of Epistemology." *Sociological Theory, 9*, 180–190.

Sorokin, Pitirim A. 1941/1962. *Social and Cultural Dynamics* (Vol. 4). New York: Bedminster Press.

Wallerstein, Immanuel. 1999. *The End of the World As We Know It*. Minneapolis: University of Minnesota Press.

Credits

———•———

Chapter 3

Luhmann, Niklas, *The Differentiation of Society*, translated by Stephen Holmes and Charles Larmore. New York: Columbia University Press. Copyright © 1982.

Chapter 4

Habermas, Jurgen, *The Theory of Communicative Action*, 2 volumes, translated by Thomas McCarthy. Boston: Beacon Press. Copyright © 1984.

Horkheimer, Max, *The Eclipse of Reason.* New York: Oxford University Press. Copyright © 1947 by Oxford University Press. New material copyright © 1974 by The Seabury Press. Reprinted by permission of The Continuum Publishing Group.

Jay, Martin, *The Dialectical Imagination: A History of the Frankfurt School and the Institute of Social Research 1923–1950.* Boston: Little, Brown and Company. Copyright © 1973. Reprinted with permission of the publisher.

Chapter 8

Goffman, Erving, "The Arrangement Between the Sexes," in Charles Lemert and Ann Branaman (Eds.), *The Goffman Reader.* Oxford: Blackwell Publishers. Copyright © 1997.

Chapter 9

Coleman, James S., *Foundations of Social Theory.* Cambridge, MA: The Belknap Press of Harvard University Press. Copyright © 1990 by the President and Fellows of Harvard College. Reprinted by permission of the publisher.

Chapter 10

Collins, Patricia Hill, *Black Feminist Thought.* Cambridge: Unwin Hyman Publishers. Copyright © 1990.

Smith, Dorothy E., *The Everyday World as Problematic: A Feminist Sociology.* Boston: Northeastern University Press. Copyright © 1987 by Dorothy E. Smith. Reprinted by permission of Northeastern University Press.

Chapter 11

Foucault, Michel, *The History of Sexuality.* New York: Vintage Books. Originally published in French as *La Volonté de Savoir.* Copyright © 1976 by Editions Gallimard. Reprinted by permission of Georges Borchardt, Inc., for the author.

Foucault, Michel, *Power/Knowledge*, edited by Colin Gordon, translated by Colin Gordon, Leo Marshall, John Mepham, and Kate Soper. Brighton, Sussex: Harvester Press. Copyright © 1980.

Index

CPSIA information can be obtained
at www.ICGtesting.com
Printed in the USA
BVHW041328121120
592907BV00009B/4